"This excellent book is an inspiring reminder of the vital importance of a free press in any society that is struggling with difficult social and political problems. Throughout 2019, international observers relied on the *South China Morning Post* to reveal the full complexity of the Hong Kong situation. This book provides a chance for readers to reflect on what happened, and draw lessons for the future."

Kurt Tong, former United States Consul General to
Hong Kong and Partner at The Asia Group

"One of the British Prime Ministers once complained of bias in the media and he was asked in which direction, and he said it's biased in every direction." – Chris Patten. The events in 2019 shocked and polarized Hong Kong. A fearless and vibrant press is indispensable in such times. It is the price to pay for a free and pluralistic society that the press provokes disagreement, irritates, or even occasionally gets it wrong. The pieces in this volume will not – and are not designed to – please everybody. This is in the best traditions of the *Post* – long may it continue. I congratulate the *Post* for a job well done."

Paul Shieh SC, former Chairman,
Hong Kong Bar Association

"As mentioned in this book, the protests in Hong Kong against the extradition bill of 2019 were 'among the world's most visible political events in history'. Like the 2003 protest against the national security bill and the 'umbrella movement' of 2014, the 2019 movement was a watershed moment that raised fundamental questions about the future of 'one country, two systems'. This book, written by *South China Morning Post* journalists who eyewitnessed the turmoil is an indispensable guide for anyone who wants to know what happened and to understand why."

Albert H.Y. Chen, Cheng Chan Lan Yue
Professor of Constitutional Law, University of Hong Kong,
and member of the Basic Law Committee

"2019 was a turbulent and tumultuous year for Hong Kong. Events followed fast upon each other. This collection of stories, interviews and analysis by seasoned reporters from the *South China Morning Post* performs the crucial service of recording what happened, asking why it happened, and, most important of all, not rushing to any quick conclusions. A powerful, and at times moving, account of a city under siege, but trying to find its way."

Kerry Brown, Director, Lau China Institute,
King's College London

REBEL

HONG KONG'S YEAR OF WATER AND FIRE

CITY

SCMP Team

Editors: Zuraidah Ibrahim, Jeffie Lam

Writers: Raquel Carvalho, Gary Cheung, Kimmy Chung, Owen Churchill, Robert Delaney, Nectar Gan, Kristin Huang, Zuraidah Ibrahim, Jeffie Lam, Chris Lau, Mimi Lau, Danny Lee, Christy Leung, Linda Lew, Clifford Lo, Kinling Lo, Alvin Lum, Danny Mok, Andrew Raine, Dewey Sim, Jasmine Siu, Phila Siu, Sum Lok-kei, Fiona Sun, Crystal Tai, Victor Ting, Meaghan Tobin, Denise Tsang, Emily Tsang, Wang Xiangwei, Natalie Wong, Cannix Yau

Commentaries: Cliff Buddle, Chow Chung-yan, Cary Huang, Yonden Lhatoo, Tammy Tam, Wang Xiangwei

Designer: Huy Truong

Copyeditors: Alan John, James Legge, Andrew Raine, Tan Yi Hui

Photo editor: Robert Ng

WSPC Team

Desk editors: Jiang Yulin, Nicole Ong, Katie Tsoi

Page layout: Jimmy Low

REBEL

HONG KONG'S YEAR OF WATER AND FIRE

CITY

EDITED BY

ZURAIDAH IBRAHIM & JEFFIE LAM

Published by

World Scientific Publishing Co. Pte. Ltd.
5 Toh Tuck Link, Singapore 596224
USA office: 27 Warren Street, Suite 401-402, Hackensack, NJ 07601
UK office: 57 Shelton Street, Covent Garden, London WC2H 9HE

and

South China Morning Post Publishers Limited
19/F, Tower One, Times Square, 1 Matheson Street
Causeway Bay, Hong Kong

National Library Board, Singapore Cataloguing in Publication Data
Name(s): Zuraidah Ibrahim, editor. | Lam, Jeffie, editor.
Title: Rebel city : Hong Kong's year of water and fire / edited by
    Zuraidah Ibrahim & Jeffie Lam.
Description: Singapore : World Scientific Publishing Co Pte Ltd ; Hong Kong : South China
    Morning Post Publishers Limited, [2020] | Includes index.
Identifier(s): OCN 1140723502 | ISBN 978-981-121-859-0 (hardback) |
    ISBN 978-981-121-860-6 (paperback) | ISBN 978-981-121-861-3
    (electronicbook for institutions) | ISBN 978-981-121-862-0 (electronic book)
Subject(s): LCSH: Hong Kong Protests, Hong Kong, China, 2019– | Protest movements--
    China--Hong Kong. | Civil disobedience--China--Hong Kong. | Hong Kong (China)--
    Politics and government--1997–
Classification: DDC 322.44095125--dc23

British Library Cataloguing-in-Publication Data
A catalogue record for this book is available from the British Library.

For any available supplementary material, please visit
https://www.worldscientific.com/worldscibooks/10.1142/11777#t=suppl

Printed in Singapore

CONTENTS

FOREWORD

I am proud of this book and yet humbled by it.

It is a chronicle of the greatest social and political upheaval that Hong Kong has undergone in our times, a non-partisan account of the events of 2019 encapsulating the blood, sweat and tears of a world city at a crossroads.

It's also a fact-based attempt to explain all the contradictions, nuances and complexities of the story of the anti-government protest movement that was triggered by the ill-fated extradition bill, and continues to impact this city and the lives of its 7.4 million people.

And it's a labor of love by a team of outstanding journalists at the *South China Morning Post*, supported by a wider network of dedicated colleagues, who deserve a separate book someday to tell the story of their passion for the job and their professionalism against formidable odds.

I am talking about the grueling hours, the relentless pressure, and the immense personal risks at the front lines of often-violent protests, all to tell the story of their times.

Reporters, photographers, videographers and artists, along with editors, made many sacrifices, regularly working marathon hours and toiling late into the night for weeks on end, to cover the chaos sweeping the city, all too often at great risk to their own safety and health.

The physical and emotional stress on the people who produced the articles collected in this book has been tremendous.

At the worst moments, some have been tear-gassed, pepper-sprayed and hit with projectiles during chaotic confrontations between police and protesters, while others have been intimidated and threatened for doing their job.

And it wasn't only our journalists – take, for instance, one of our key administrative staff members having her car petrol-bombed while on her way to work.

But we stayed the course, kept calm and remained focused, doing what it took to tell the world the real story of what happened to our city, warts and all, without taking sides, and without fear or favor.

Our coverage has been as comprehensive as it has been objective and professional throughout. It has sifted through sharply conflicting narratives and bitterly divided opinions to bring out every shade of color in between the ubiquitous blue and yellow that lit up much of what was dubbed "the revolution of our times" by activists but condemned as "rioting" and "illegal" behavior by both the local and central governments.

This book brings out the grave implications all this will have on Hong Kong's relations with mainland China, which have been thrown into extreme uncertainty by the social unrest and political chaos. It digs deep into the many cross-border problems that were swept under the carpet for more than two decades after the city's handover to Chinese sovereignty, festering and eventually snowballing into a crisis that made global headlines.

Consider this book but a sampling of some of the best work that the award-winning journalists of the *South China Morning Post* have been putting out and continue to produce.

We present it to you, dear readers, with pride and humility.

Tammy Tam,
Editor-in-Chief, South China Morning Post

ACKNOWLEDGMENTS

This book is the embodiment of teamwork. The *South China Morning Post* newsroom mobilized resources across desks to stay on top of a story that had a new twist every day and made headlines on every continent.

For colleagues in the thick of covering the action, there was barely time to catch a breath. Yet, nobody bemoaned the arduous workload. Many had to be forced to take days off, and when they did they still contributed to our coverage.

Some were pepper-sprayed, tear-gassed and injured by flying objects – and, in the case of one colleague, by a rubber bullet. Everyone knew that history was being made before our eyes. Nobody wanted to blink.

From our exhaustive and exhausting reportage, we have compiled this anthology of essays and a brief selection of commentary. We thank those who helped update and augment their articles for this book, despite being caught up in the coverage of another life-changing story: the coronavirus pandemic.

We are also so grateful to our newsmakers and sources on all sides of this complex story. Everyone, we can safely say, has been traumatized at some level by what happened in 2019. No one has emerged from it unscathed. This book would not have been possible if they were not willing to share their perspectives so generously.

We would like to thank our editor-in-chief Tammy Tam for being as excited about this book as we were when we proposed it to her. We appreciate the guidance and support she provided together with executive editor Chow Chung-yan and chief news editor Yonden Lhatoo throughout the months of coverage.

We are indebted to copyeditors Yi Hui, Alan, Andrew and James, designer Huy and photo editor Robert. All put in many, many extra hours on top of the daily grind. We would also like to acknowledge colleagues at the Hong Kong and Asia desks who covered for us while we dove into this project.

Finally, on behalf of the SCMP team that covered the protests in 2019 and 2020, we would like to thank those dear to us whom we were forced to neglect for long periods. We would not have survived these months without your love and support.

Zuraidah Ibrahim and Jeffie Lam

INTRODUCTION

Zuraidah Ibrahim

Through the first half of 2020, Hongkongers struggled to read one another's mood. Surgical masks hid their faces and muffled their normally expressive Cantonese. These accessories were deemed so essential in the fight against the novel coronavirus that millions of Hongkongers ritually put them on whenever they stepped out of their homes, to protect themselves and others.

The irony was not lost on residents of the city. During the previous six months, face masks had been commonplace too. Worn by protesters to protect against pepper spray, tear gas, and surveillance cameras, masks were so associated with dissent that the government banned them – not that the injunction affected their status as *de rigueur* street fashion items for the autumn and winter seasons of 2019.

Just as they would during the Covid-19 pandemic, the masks made Hong Kong more inscrutable. Despite being togged in the same black attire to express solidarity with their cause, the protesters were diverse in their backgrounds, attitudes and emotions.

Most tried to show courage; many were fearful. Beyond the "yellow" camp of mask-wearing protesters too, Hong Kong as a whole became harder to recognize and decipher. It was more sullen and divided, and gripped by unfamiliar sights, sounds, and smells – brick-strewn roads, screaming matches, and acrid tear gas.

Reporting on the tumult of 2019, the adjective "unprecedented" kept turning up in our copy. Protesters' methods grew in audacity. Their targets widened and their means became more extreme. Police escalated their use of force, from water cannons to physical beatings and live rounds. Yesterday's shocking development became today's new normal.

Hong Kong, which had thought of itself as vibrant and entrepreneurial but also orderly and safe, suddenly found itself on guard.

The protest movement had to develop communication networks to keep one step ahead of the police force's feared shock troops, the Raptors. The MTR system, fully expecting that their repairs would only last until the next attack, replaced shattered glass walls with cold sheet metal. Residents wanting to enjoy city life downloaded apps to tell them which parts of town were no-go areas.

A year has passed since the demonstrations were triggered by the government's much derided extradition bill. There is no closure to the social unrest in sight. The protests are in a suspended state, held in abeyance by a health crisis that, far from uniting the population, has further exposed its deep polarization between the pro-Beijing "blue" camp and the anti-government "yellow" – with the latter seeing the pandemic as further proof that mainland China will be the death of Hong Kong.

Conversations with protesters suggest they are at a crossroads, contemplating their next course of action. Some admit to feeling lost and lacking leadership. The criminal charges brought against hundreds have also dampened spirits. But the despair that drove the protests has not been assuaged.

With the situation in limbo, the final word on Hong Kong's protest movement cannot be written. This book does not attempt that. What it can do is gather some of the best reporting on the crisis so far, from the perspectives of dozens of journalists who call this city home.

Through a series of detailed snapshots, we hope to give readers a fuller sense of not only the headline events of an extraordinary year, but also their behind-the-scenes dynamics, and the feelings behind the masks.

At one level, the 2019 protests were among the world's most visible political events in history. The action could be viewed on multiple live streams. At the front lines, dozens of local and international reporters recorded the confrontations between protesters and police. Never have so many had access to what they would consider incontrovertible evidence of what exactly happened on a given day and time.

Yet, debates about who the villains and the victims were raged on. This was the Rashomon effect in the age of Facebook Live and Twitter. As in the fabled Akira Kurosawa movie, eyewitnesses came to conflicting conclusions. To many Hongkongers, police were to blame for the escalation of violence. To others, they were the thin blue line protecting the city from anarchy.

While many observers had the luxury of being both expert witness and judge, the *South China Morning Post* had to be more modest in our approach. First, because we have more feet on the ground and greater access to all sides than most news organizations do, we are unable to see things in simple black-and-white – or yellow-versus-blue – terms.

Second, this is our city. For most of the world's media, the Hong Kong unrest was newsworthy largely because it was an apparent proxy war between China and the United States. For the *Post*, this was a local story. Most of the journalists covering the city's affairs grew up here, fell in love, married, and are raising children here. We live among the people we report for and about, making it harder to rush to judgment.

Our journalists have strong feelings about recent events and close ties with the community. The city's pain is our pain, its scars our own. But, collectively, the *Post* has tried to stick to the basics of fact-based journalism, respecting our community enough to inform it without being swayed by any ideological bias.

Of course, the *Post* has a firm editorial position on the larger questions facing Hong Kong. It operates within and defends Hong Kong's press freedoms, and the special status the territory enjoys within the People's Republic of China. In our editorials, the *Post* commented on the extradition law's shortcomings, especially the need for stronger safeguards against abuse. Witnessing widespread opposition to the bill, we called for its withdrawal. We also appealed for an inquiry into police conduct, to assuage concerns on the ground; and we condemned violence by all sides. We accepted that universal suffrage, while a worthy goal, would be difficult to accomplish in the current environment.

Our primary function, though, has been to keep our readers informed. From March to December 2019, the *Post* published more than 4,515 articles containing the term "extradition," plus more than 400 videos, 11 multimedia infographics and 55 live blogs. Our archive contains tens of thousands of photos and art.

This book is an edited anthology of that coverage. In some of these stories, we have left the narrative untouched. But in many others, we have gone back to the key newsmakers to have them reflect on the year that went by. Some essays go over similar ground but from different vantage points. The book does not pretend to break new ground. And there are still questions that we are unable to fully answer, like the extent of external interference in the course of events.

But the following pages do go some way in unmasking the fractured yet fluid spirit of a city going through historic change. It captures the landmark events, key debates, and the diverse cast of characters that made this an unforgettable year for all who experienced it.

PATH TO A FIRESTORM

"THE GOVERNMENT WAS COMPLETELY INEFFECTIVE, AND LOST CONTROL OF THE NARRATIVE."

Regina Ip, Executive Council member

Top girl Carrie Lam takes a city to the brink

Jeffie Lam and Gary Cheung

Throughout her 13 years at St Francis' Canossian School and its sister college, Carrie Lam Cheng Yuet-ngor was always a top girl – except once, when she came fourth in a mid-year class examination. She went home in tears that day, fearful of how her teachers and family would regard her, she revealed in a 2016 interview, just before taking office as Hong Kong's chief executive.

Asked what she did next, Lam replied: "I took the No 1 place back."

She shared that anecdote when recalling unforgettable low points in her life before her rise to become the city's first woman leader. It is safe to assume that nothing in Lam's life could have been worse than the political storm that engulfed her through the second half of 2019, when she sank to the bottom of the public's estimation.

What began as public anger at a controversial extradition bill, which critics said could effectively remove the legal firewall between Hong Kong and mainland China, morphed into expressions of hatred toward Lam not only as author of the legislation but also as an arrogant leader who insisted on pressing ahead with it despite opposition from all quarters. It sent Hong Kong hurtling into its most serious political crisis since the former British colony returned to Chinese rule in 1997.

The combative Lam doubled down even after an estimated 1 million Hongkongers marched on June 9 to protest against the bill and demand her resignation. That turnout was double the size of a historic 2003 procession that forced the government to shelve a controversial national security bill.

Defending the legislation, Lam said a day after the march: "We were doing it and we are still doing it out of our clear conscience and our commitment to Hong Kong." It took another protest on June 12 – which resulted in violent clashes between protesters and police, with tear gas and rubber bullets deployed and more than 80 people injured – before she said the bill would be suspended.

But the legislation was not scrapped. Angry protesters, mostly in their 20s, demanded the withdrawal of the bill and went on to stage more demonstrations, blocking major roads and besieging government offices. As the protests degenerated into violence, vandalism and intense confrontations between masked radicals and police officers, all the rules of engagement for Hong Kong's long-standing culture of peaceful demonstrations were rewritten.

The protracted battle became an embarrassment to Beijing as the protesters made emotional appeals to Western countries, in particular the United States, against the backdrop of the US-China trade war and at the G20 summit in Osaka that June. They waved the American flag in the city, urging Washington to back a proposed Hong Kong Human Rights and Democracy Act to give the US discretion to sanction those deemed responsible for acts that undermine Hong Kong's autonomy from mainland China. It was approved with bipartisan support and signed into law in November 2019.

Lam faced the wrath of even loyal allies in the Legislative Council, who feared she would drag them down. Their concerns were not unfounded. In November, the pro-establishment bloc suffered a humiliating rout in the district council elections. From controlling all 18 district councils, they were left in charge of only one, retaining merely 60 out of 452 seats at stake.

What went so wrong for the top girl who became chief executive? By the end of 2019, she was viewed as a lame duck and a likely one-term city leader. Interviews with members of her cabinet, pro-establishment lawmakers and Beijing insiders suggest it was a potent combination of policy failure caused by an overconfident leader trapped in groupthink, inadequate preparation of the ground and a lack of political experience on the world stage. There was no doubt by December that heads would roll once calm returned, but whose and when remained unclear.

Rushing headlong into disaster

Lam's journey to the brink of disaster and beyond began at 10am on January 29, 2019. Members of the Executive Council, Hong Kong's top decision-making body, were given a policy paper outlining proposed amendments to the city's extradition law. It was their last meeting before the Lunar New Year holiday.

Lam was moved to change the extradition rules in late 2018 after receiving emotional letters from the parents of a young woman who was found dead in Taipei, her body stuffed in a suitcase. The pregnant woman had gone there on holiday with her boyfriend, but he returned to Hong Kong alone. He was suspected of being the killer, but could not be sent to Taiwan to help with investigations because Hong Kong has no extradition arrangement with the island, which China regards as a renegade province.

Aides said Lam took the pleas of the dead woman's family to heart and decided to act after discussing the matter with Secretary for

Security John Lee Ka-chiu, the city's first security chief promoted from the police force.

But their extradition bill went considerably further than making it possible to send a wanted man to Taiwan. It also sought to allow the transfer of fugitives on a case-by-case basis to other jurisdictions with which Hong Kong had no extradition arrangement, including mainland China.

Plugging that loophole would have fulfilled a long-standing wish of Beijing. For years, Hong Kong had been a refuge for corrupt officials and businessmen fleeing the mainland, as well as a transit stopover for political dissidents. Sources said Lam saw in the Taiwan case a unique opportunity to cross off an item on Beijing's wishlist for Hong Kong.

Even though political crimes were not among extraditable offenses under the bill, the very idea that people in Hong Kong could be sent across the border to face possibly unfair trials in a less than robust legal system made many jittery. The pan-democratic camp sensed the anxious mood on the ground and went to work to capitalize on it even as Lam dismissed such concerns as irrational. Pro-establishment camp insiders said her confidence that the bill would be passed, coupled with Lee's security background, resulted in an exercise that was hasty and rushed.

The government also shrugged off the need for a full consultation, giving the public only 20 days to submit views. They argued that time was of the essence for the Taiwan murder case, and believed – mistakenly, as it turned out – public sympathy for the dead woman's family was on their side.

"Lee, with his police force background, only sees things from one perspective, to bring suspects to justice," said a Beijing-friendly lawmaker. "Even some mainland officials we talked to said they had foreseen the political implications and possible backlash, but he and Lam failed to do so."

Lee's officials apparently saw no problems with the bill either. Every discussion paper on major policy initiatives submitted to Exco usually included an assessment of the possible impact on the Basic Law, Hong Kong's mini-constitution, as well as "mainland implications" and anticipated "public reaction." A former minister said these comments sometimes required a full page.

However, the first paper on the extradition bill, prepared by the Security Bureau, included no hint of possible controversy or trouble ahead. "No red flag was raised in the 'public reactions' paragraph," a source close to the government said. "The paragraph was quite short. It was obvious that the top echelons of the administration did not expect massive opposition."

Some senior officials were also kept in the dark during the early stages of the drafting of the legislation. It was not sent to the high-level policy committee, comprising all ministers and chaired by Chief Secretary Matthew Cheung Kin-chung, before the Security Bureau revealed on February 12, that it intended to amend the law. "The Security Bureau, which took the lead in drafting and promoting the amendment bill, should be held accountable for not sounding out its plan at the policy committee meeting before announcing it," a source said.

Another high-ranking government source said Security Bureau officials showed that they lacked political savvy on two counts. First, they did not anticipate opposition from Taiwan, which was deep in the throes of politicking ahead of elections. Second, they underestimated the depth of Hongkongers' distrust of the mainland's legal system. "Their lack of sensitivity may stem from the fact that all three political appointees in the Security Bureau are former police officers," the source said, referring to Lee, undersecretary Sonny Au Chi-kwong and Lee's political assistant Cassius Lau Fu-sang.

Although the government's 20-day consultation exercise was brief, it might have served to bolster Lam's resolve, as two-thirds of the 4,500 submissions supported amending the extradition law. But there were murmurings early on, and even Lam's advisers in Exco had wind of them. The Exco members included those from Hong Kong's finance and business elite, but they failed to convey the concerns of the sector.

"When I first heard Tommy Cheung Yu-yan mention the existence of this bill, I immediately sensed something was wrong," recalled pro-establishment Liberal Party leader Felix Chung Kwok-pan, whose colleague Cheung is an Exco member. Chung, who has been running a textile factory on the mainland since 1993, said: "Those who have not done business on the mainland would not be aware of our fears."

Many businesspeople were worried they might inadvertently break the law on the mainland. Some pointed to the complicated tax system and the fact that "gifts" – which could be deemed bribes in some contexts – were an inevitable part of striking deals. They feared that the extradition bill, once passed, might be used to bring them to book there. Chung said these concerns would have been flagged to the administration early, if only Lam had fully engaged the pro-establishment bloc.

Instead, the lack of consultation meant that the city's two leading pro-business parties – the Liberals and the Business and Professionals Alliance – were unusually vocal in opposing the bill, despite being Beijing-friendly. They urged the government to exempt white-collar crimes from the list of extraditable offenses. In 2019, Hong Kong's 70-member legislature had 43 pro-establishment lawmakers who formed the majority and usually backed the government, even on critical issues. So, when they spoke up, trouble was clearly brewing.

The fears of the business sector resonated with the wider community. In March, the American Chamber of Commerce (AmCham) became the first group of foreign investors to voice objections to the bill, warning that it could deal a blow to the city's reputation as a business hub.

When AmCham took a stand, the international ramifications were laid bare. Several Exco members told the *South China Morning Post* they had asked top security officials if the bill needed to be explained better, but their views were waved aside. "The government was confident the bill would be passed because the pro-establishment camp had an overwhelming majority in Legco," a person familiar with the issue said.

Too few changes, too late

In late March, the government gave in to the business sector. It amended the bill to exempt nine white-collar crimes from the proposed list of 46 extraditable crimes and raised the threshold for extradition to offenses punishable by three years in prison, instead of one year. However, that failed to assuage the business community, including AmCham.

Despite discontent swirling in the pro-establishment camp, there were no indications at that point of Beijing's views on the bill, a source from the Business and Professionals Alliance said. Hong Kong delegates to the annual parliamentary "Two Sessions" meetings in Beijing in March received no "instructions" or "reminders" to support the amendment. The delegates realized then that the bill was not being introduced at Beijing's behest.

In mid-March, the head of China's Ministry of Foreign Affairs in Hong Kong issued a mildly worded statement reminding other countries to respect the city's rule of law and its normal legislative process. Even key mainland experts on Hong Kong affairs, including those specializing in the city's Basic Law, did not know much about the bill or its rationale, according to groups in contact with them.

However, Beijing did reach a turning point, according to Tam Yiu-chung, the city's sole representative on China's top legislative body, the National People's Congress Standing Committee. This was after a group of Hong Kong pan-democrats went to the US in March to rally support against the bill. The delegation, led by former chief secretary Anson

Chan Fang On-sang, and which included lawmakers Dennis Kwok and Charles Mok, met congressmen and Vice-President Mike Pence, and urged Washington to oppose the bill. A domestic Hong Kong issue was suddenly becoming a potential new front in the geopolitical rivalry between the US and China, already in the middle of a trade war.

In April, Beijing's liaison office in Hong Kong invited a group of government supporters to set up a pro-bill alliance. This outfit then set up street booths and collected hundreds of thousands of signatures from Hongkongers supporting the legislation. In May, Zhang Xiaoming, head of Beijing's Hong Kong and Macau Affairs Office and its top man in charge of the city's affairs then, broke his silence. He said the legislation was necessary, but he also asked Lam's government to address people's fears.

In Legco, outnumbered pan-democrat lawmakers were unsure they could block the bill. Remembering all too well that the 79-day Occupy protests of 2014 had failed to get Beijing to budge on political reforms, the camp was splintered, listless and uncertain of its prospects. "We weren't optimistic," Democratic Party leader Wu Chi-wai recalled. "We knew our hands would be tied once the bill was put to a vote."

He and others decided instead to do their utmost to drag out the bill's passage. The usually calm Wu got into a scuffle in May as pro-establishment and pro-democracy lawmakers fought for control of a committee scrutinizing the bill. Punches were thrown, with one lawmaker landing in hospital and at least three others injured.

Their efforts to stoke opposition to the bill began to produce results. The first protest march they organized in April attracted an estimated 12,000 people. A second drew an estimated 130,000 – the largest turnout since Occupy.

Pro-establishment lawmakers began sensing that the ground was fast souring. One said it dawned on her in early April that the government had lost the propaganda war. "I urged security officials to produce 'pamphlets for dummies' about the bill," she said. Officials rebuffed her, confident that they could get the bill passed. She felt the pro-establishment camp had a blind spot in that many believed the pan-democrats were spreading lies about the bill's negative effects, and these would be exposed once it was passed.

On the pan-democrat side, Wu recalled: "By around May, we could feel the escalating momentum. Ordinary citizens had started to care." Some were unhappy with the government's dismissive attitude toward the Bar Association, which had repeatedly criticized the bill and had urged officials to find other ways to deal with the Taiwan murder case, he said.

Pro-business lawmaker Chung said: "It isn't surprising for the administration to ignore the pan-democrats, but it should not have turned a deaf ear to the Bar Association, which is a well-respected body." When concerns were also raised by the more conservative Law Society, representing the city's solicitors, it was clear that the bill was in dire straits.

A funeral for Hong Kong

By now the anti-bill movement was beginning to look more like a grass-roots effort, with plenty happening online. Young, active members of the online forum LIHKG began dishing out anti-bill statements. Hundreds of petitions criticizing the bill mushroomed online, drawing support from students and alumni of more than half of the city's 506 secondary schools, Christians, Hongkongers living abroad and housewives.

When the Civil Human Rights Front planned a third protest march for June 9, even pro-establishment politicians expected a large turnout. An estimated 1 million people showed up. Many wore white, as if attending a funeral for the death of Hong Kong.

Such was the gap of understanding between Lam's government and the people that a source said: "Until the June 9 march, most Exco members were not aware of the existence of massive opposition to the bill." It exposed the administration's inability to gauge public sentiment.

A government source said officials did not expect that people unlikely to be affected by the bill would believe that changing the law could put their personal freedoms at risk. "We were outdone by the opposition camp's public relations campaign. We couldn't get our messages across effectively, particularly to young people," the source said.

Regina Ip Lau Suk-yee, leader of the pro-establishment New People's Party and an Exco member, said it was also plain that the government lacked an effective publicity machine. "Opponents of the bill made many videos and distributed a lot of fliers on public housing estates. A lot of lies were spread, telling new arrivals from the mainland that if the bill was passed, they would be grabbed by mainland law enforcers overnight without seeing their lawyer," she said. "The government was completely ineffective, and lost control of the narrative."

She was particularly annoyed that senior officials had failed to respond to criticism of the bill in the international media. Instead, Exco members like herself and others had to step up. Ip asked: "What kind of government declines to speak to the foreign media, given the magnitude of the international attention the bill provoked?"

In hindsight, Ip agreed that the government should have allowed a longer public consultation period and narrowed the scope of the bill to cover murder cases only. "We were persuaded by the chief executive that we wanted to deal with the Taiwan case," she said, adding that she did not believe she had done anything wrong in giving her support to the bill then. "How to control the narrative, how to mount counter-publicity and whether to put the brakes on the bill were for the chief executive to decide. We did our part by giving advice."

Ahead of the June 9 march, the government made a second round of amendments to the bill. It further tightened the scope of extraditable crimes and introduced human rights safeguards for ad hoc agreements with jurisdictions that request extradition. Major business groups and political parties welcomed these changes, but critics wanted the safeguards written into the law to make them legally binding.

Business and Professionals Alliance lawmaker Priscilla Leung Mei-fun, a member of the Basic Law Committee, said: "I called an official and asked the administration to make a further concession by writing the human rights safeguards into the law, but I got cold-shouldered."

On June 9, the third extradition bill march was a massive procession that went on until late at night. At 11.09pm, before the protest organizers wrapped up, the government issued a statement making it clear that nothing was about to change. It said Legco would resume debating the bill on June 12 as scheduled.

A senior civil servant said he and his peers were taken aback, because that statement just made matters worse. "What the government did went against our common sense. We are not trained that way." The pro-establishment camp was shocked too. A Beijing-friendly lawmaker said: "I supported the bill, but after reading the statement, I seriously considered not casting my vote. The government's attitude truly crossed the line."

Lam's change of heart came only after protesters besieged the Legco complex on June 12 to prevent lawmakers from entering to begin scrutinizing the bill. Violent clashes broke out, and social media was soon awash with images of bloodied protesters and police officers.

On June 15, a grim-faced Lam announced that the bill would be suspended. She admitted shortcomings in her government, expressed sorrow and regret for causing inconvenience and disputes in society, and promised to be humble, but made no apology.

The next day, an estimated 2 million people thronged the streets, condemning Lam and demanding more than the withdrawal of the extradition bill. Now they also wanted an inquiry into alleged police brutality, an end to referring to the June 12 protest as a riot, amnesty for those arrested during the protest, and universal suffrage. The turnout was a new record for Hong Kong.

Lam issued a written apology on the same day. On June 18, she made a formal apology in person, but rejected all the other demands. Lam then retreated from public view until June 27. She canceled the weekly Exco meeting two weeks in a row, and called off a public forum related to district council elections in November.

Ronny Tong Ka-wah, another of Lam's advisers, recalled that she teared up during urgent Exco meetings after the two massive protests. "I didn't take it as a sign of weakness. That showed she had feelings," he said.

But the old impassive Lam returned after July 1, the day hundreds of black-clad protesters stormed and vandalized the Legco complex. At a 4am press conference, Lam said she was outraged and called on the community to condemn the violence and vandalism. That day marked her second anniversary as city leader.

Too much for a bureaucrat to handle

A source close to the administration said Lam missed the opportunity to stem the crisis when she dismissed advice to withdraw the bill after the second mass protest, and to ask the police chief to stop referring to the June 12 protest as a riot.

It took almost three months more before Lam finally announced on September 4 that the bill would be withdrawn, a move which sources said required the approval of President Xi Jinping.

Behind the scenes, Lam appeared to distance herself from Beijing, hinting that she had limited power and that her hands were tied. In a leaked transcript of a private gathering held in August, Lam said she had little choice, given that the massive backlash against the bill had elevated the issue to a national level problem, and "a sort of sovereignty and security level" matter. Once that happened, the "political room for maneuvering is very, very, very limited," she was recorded as saying to a group of business leaders.

Lam rejected speculation that she herself, or someone from the administration, had deliberately leaked the recording in order to shift the blame to Beijing. She was also reported to have said at the same gathering that she would have quit if she had the choice. But again Lam denied saying so. "I have not given myself the choice of taking an easier path, and that is, to leave," she said in a statement after the leaked recording emerged.

Lawmaker Ip revealed that, at one point, she and other Exco members had considered resigning en masse, but Lam had stopped them. "The chief executive said we were on the periphery, merely giving advice, meaning if anyone had to be held accountable, Exco members would not be the first," Ip said. Political scientist Ma Ngok, of Chinese University, said: "In other countries, the leader and officials would have stepped down if such a large number marched on the streets."

Two sources close to the government said Lam's troubled tenure exposed the weakness of a leader lacking global political exposure and the experience of elections. "During most of her career, Lam was a bureaucrat tackling domestic issues," said one. "If she could have understood the political headwinds of the US-China tensions and seen how the bill could get entangled in that, she would have thought twice from day one." The other said: "Lam and the absolute majority of ministers are former civil servants who lack experience in elections. That's why they underestimate negative public sentiments."

New year, and a pandemic takes over

The new year brought Lam unexpected respite from the protests, only because of the arrival of the deadly coronavirus pandemic. She now led the administration's efforts in combating the biggest public health crisis in years. Health professionals went on strike when Lam refused to seal Hong Kong's border with the mainland, but she introduced a series of bolder-than-expected measures to deal with the outbreak.

To slow the spread of the coronavirus, Hongkongers had to get used to social-distancing measures that include a ban on public gatherings of more than four people and the temporary closure of places of worship, pubs, cinemas, spas and massage parlors. Restaurants were told to operate at half capacity and employers were asked to let staff work from home. The government announced a total relief package of HK$287.5 billion (US$37.1 billion) in cash handouts, tax breaks and a raft of subsidies aimed at easing the financial burden on residents and businesses.

While the Covid-19 outbreak ravaged countries worldwide, including in the US and Europe, by late April Hong Kong managed to keep the coronavirus under control. New infections were in single-digits and as of April 24, it recorded 1,035 cases and four deaths. For Lam, however, a sense of alienation from those closest to her lingered. In a letter sent to Beijing in March and leaked to the media, she allegedly complained about the "disappointing" pro-establishment bloc, accusing them of joining in criticizing the government's response to the pandemic instead of being supportive. She called her Exco members "unsatisfactory" and claimed she was "facing enemies on all sides." Her allies were angered, but Lam did not deny saying those words.

Lau Siu-kai, vice-chairman of the Chinese Association of Hong Kong and Macau Studies, a semi-official think tank, said the pandemic had upset the momentum of the protests and provided Lam an opportunity to recover some lost ground with the public. "Hong Kong's fiscal reserves and medical system gave the government more leeway than many other countries in tackling the coronavirus," he said, adding that Hongkongers could see how people elsewhere were worse off.

Despite all that had happened in 2019, he did not think Beijing wanted to remove Lam. "Replacing the chief executive would be equivalent to surrendering to the opposition and that would only bring endless troubles," he said.

Alvin Yeung Ngok-kiu, leader of the Civic Party, said Lam would be mistaken to believe she could breathe a sigh of relief because Covid-19 had stopped the protests. "There will be more people joining because of the poor [coronavirus-related] policies," he said.

The extradition bill saga cost Lam heavily in terms of her public approval ratings. Her popularity plummeted by more than 60 per cent from 47.4 out of 100 points in February 2019 to 18.1 points in February 2020, according to Hong Kong Public Opinion Research Institute surveys. Her handling of the Covid-19 crisis helped her claw her way up to 25.5 points in April.

At a closed-door meeting in the midst of the protests, Lam was quoted as saying: "Many people thought I died, but I won't die."

That was the top girl speaking.

— *With reporting by Kimmy Chung*

The murder behind Hong Kong's worst political crisis

Jasmine Siu and Chris Lau

A love story gone badly wrong in Taiwan sparked Hong Kong's biggest political storm. The search for justice has not ended.

I t was a Valentine's Day vacation that went horribly wrong. When Chan Tong-kai and Poon Hiu-wing boarded their flight to Taiwan on February 8, 2018, they were a picture of happiness, two young adults celebrating a pregnancy and the prospect of a long, loving future together. Yet by their return flight just nine days later, that picture would be shattered. Only one of them would make the journey back to Hong Kong; the other would be dead, the corpse abandoned and left to rot in an unfamiliar land.

When Poon's badly decomposing body was found in thick bushes on the outskirts of Taipei a month later, all the evidence pointed to Chan. He had not only explained in detail to police where to find the body, but had also admitted to the killing, saying he had attacked Poon after hearing the baby was not his and viewing a video of his lover having sex with another man.

To a stunned city, the details of the case were shocking and tragic enough. Yet this was a tragedy in two acts. And what nobody could have foreseen was that, like a butterfly causing a far off tsunami with the flapping of its wings, the ripples of a single crime of passion in Taiwan would one day become a tidal wave bearing down on 7 million Hongkongers.

Nobody could have known then that the city was about to be swept into one of its worst periods of civil unrest; that Poon's murder would expose a loophole in its justice system; or that attempts to close that loophole would spark widespread violence and the arrests of thousands.

A love story gone wrong

Long before the couple's story sparked a political cataclysm, it was a personal one.

Poon and Chan had met in July 2017 at a company where both were working part time and the former students clicked immediately.

Within a month they were lovers and by December of the same year, 20-year-old Poon told Chan she was pregnant. Chan, 19, appeared delighted and, believing he was the father, splashed out on a romantic getaway to Taiwan to celebrate.

At this point, at least to her friends, Poon had given every sign of being happy with how the relationship was progressing, sharing in her last Facebook post before leaving for Taiwan that Chan had said she was his "first and last girlfriend."

To her homemaker mother she had been more guarded, waiting until the day of her flight to mention that she was going on holiday with a friend, and even then not sharing the identity of her traveling companion.

She did, however, send a WhatsApp message to her mother in the early hours of February 17 to say she would be returning to Hong Kong that night.

But Poon never returned.

As the days went by her parents became increasingly distraught, eventually deciding to search their daughter's flat. They found copies of Chan's arrival and departure cards from the trip and these revealed the name of the hotel in Taipei's Datong district where the couple had stayed.

On March 5, Poon's mother filed a missing persons report. Then her husband headed for Taipei to search for his daughter and help Taiwanese police in their investigations.

It was not long before they found a smoking gun. Surveillance footage showed Poon and Chan entering the Purple Garden Hotel on February 16, the night before their flight, but there was no footage of Poon ever leaving. There were only images of Chan checking out the next day, dragging a heavy, pink suitcase.

Confession time

Tipped off by investigators in Taipei, Hong Kong police questioned Chan on March 13. Under caution, the teenager said that on their last night in Taipei, he and Poon had quarreled over how to pack the new pink suitcase they had bought at a night market earlier that evening.

They made up and made love, he said, but began arguing again in the early hours of the next morning when Poon blurted out that the father of her baby was her ex-boyfriend. Chan said Poon had then shown him a video of her having sex with another man, and he flew into a jealous rage.

He smashed Poon's head against the wall and, when she fell to the floor, strangled her with both hands, struggling with her writhing body for several minutes until she fell still. He then stuffed her corpse into the suitcase they had bought together and went to bed.

At 7am, he got rid of Poon's belongings by leaving them at various rubbish collection points near the hotel. He then wheeled her body out of the hotel in the suitcase and caught a train, traveling 15 stations before dumping the corpse in a thicket at a park near Zhuwei station.

He threw away the empty suitcase but kept Poon's iPhone 6, her Casio digital camera and HSBC cash card. He then used the card to withdraw NT$20,000 (HK$5,160) and went shopping for clothes before catching the 11.22pm flight back to Hong Kong. Over the next two days, he used Poon's ATM card to withdraw a further HK$19,200 (US$2,470) to pay his credit card bills.

The details of the case seemed clear and, with Chan having confessed, Hong Kong police formally arrested him. Taiwanese police found Poon's decomposing body later that day, exactly where Chan said it would be.

A crisis unfolds

When news first spread of the young woman's gruesome death, nobody could have imagined the case would spark the biggest political crisis to have faced Hong Kong since the city returned to Chinese sovereignty in 1997.

The problem was that while Chan had admitted killing Poon, he could not be tried in Hong Kong for an offense committed in another jurisdiction. Nor could he be sent against his will to Taipei as the two cities lacked an extradition agreement.

Instead, the best Hong Kong could do was charge Chan on theft and money-laundering offenses related to the use of Poon's credit card, an outcome that would be hard to disguise as anything but a travesty of justice. In Hong Kong, murder carries a mandatory life sentence, while the maximum punishment for money laundering is 14 years in prison and a HK$5 million fine. What's more, given the relatively small sums involved, it was likely that even if he was found guilty, Chan would receive a substantially lighter sentence and could be freed within just a year.

It was against this backdrop, with Poon's parents repeatedly appealing for their daughter's killer to be brought to justice and the Taiwanese authorities eager to pursue him, that Chief Executive Carrie Lam Cheng Yuet-ngor proposed changing the law so that Hong Kong could extradite fugitives on a case-by-case basis to those jurisdictions it did not have agreements with.

It had been a year since Poon's death when Lam introduced her extradition bill in February 2019 and Chan was in remand, still awaiting trial. Lam said the bill had been inspired by Chan's case and the need to close the loophole that was preventing him facing trial for murder.

Immediately, there were backers for the bill, with the pro-Beijing political party, the Democratic Alliance for the Betterment and Progress of Hong Kong, holding a press conference on the day of its introduction to give its seal of approval. Poon's mother was among those who spoke at the event. She said she and her husband could still not accept the fact that her daughter was gone or that, one year on, her killer had not been brought to justice.

"The cruel scenes of how the murderer had carried her body around in a suitcase, dumped it in bushes and allowed the stray dogs to eat it keep creeping into my mind. It breaks my heart," she said, weeping. "The only thing we can do for our daughter is to make sure justice is served."

Given the grief-stricken backdrop, Lam might have thought passing such a bill would be relatively straightforward. It needed to be done before Chan was out of prison and could in theory flee the city.

But from the beginning there were persistent criticisms from a public that would not be easily silenced. Opponents said the bill, supposedly created to fix a legal loophole, would create even bigger loopholes of its own. Not only would it pave the way for extraditions to Taiwan, it would also – far more controversially – open the floodgates to extraditions to mainland China, something many people suggested had been Lam's real motivation all along as an attempt to ingratiate herself with her political masters in Beijing.

Even more damaging was that many critics – some of the top legal minds in the land among them – felt that the bill represented an erosion of the "one country, two systems" arrangement under which Hong

Kong was governed and which provided the foundation of its independent judiciary.

Whether the criticism was fair or not, an increasing number of Hongkongers believed the bill threatened their way of life and they were not willing to go down without a fight.

With Lam sticking to her guns, the ranks of the dissenters began to swell, their anger gathering steam and finally erupting into large-scale marches and demonstrations from June 2019. Eventually, Lam relented and formally withdrew the bill in September, but by then it was too late.

The protests had already morphed into an increasingly violent anti-government, anti-Beijing movement, with demands for greater democracy and police accountability. Masked radicals blocked roads, started fires and hurled petrol bombs at police. They smashed up MTR stations and any businesses they deemed as linked to Beijing. Thousands were arrested, with hundreds facing the charge of rioting, which carries a jail term of 10 years.

Freedom for some

While Hongkongers were growing increasingly concerned about losing their freedoms, Chan was about to regain his. As the opposition to Lam was mounting, he pleaded guilty to the money-laundering charges and on April 29, 2019, was jailed for 29 months. The sentence was backdated to the time of his arrest, and with good behavior, he would be eligible for release that year.

On October 23, 2019, Chan emerged from the maximum-security Pik Uk Correctional Institution in Clear Water Bay to face a Hong Kong in turmoil.

It had been a month since Lam had withdrawn the bill supposedly inspired by his crime, yet the chaos it had unleashed was still in full swing.

REBEL CITY: Hong Kong's Year of Water and Fire

Chan bowed before the media crowd waiting for him. He apologized to Poon's family and the people of Hong Kong, saying: "I am willing, for my impulsive act and the things I did wrong, to surrender myself to Taiwan to face sentencing."

He said he hoped this would give Poon's family some relief and that her soul could rest in peace. He also thanked his own parents: "Even though I've made the worst mistake, they still care for me, support me and won't give up on me."

Then he begged Hongkongers for forgiveness, bowed a second time and left in a white seven-seater vehicle, without taking questions from the dozens of reporters present.

Watching Chan's release on television, Poon's father told friends the scenes deeply saddened the family and reminded them all over again of the senseless killing of their only daughter. A family friend said Poon's father just wanted "things to be over as soon as possible" – and for justice to be served.

A fugitive, frozen in time

Chan's pledge to surrender gave a sliver of hope that the family might yet get the closure they had so desperately longed for. At his side that day was Reverend Canon Peter Koon Ho-ming, a senior Anglican priest who had been visiting him in prison every week and had helped persuade Chan to surrender to the Taiwanese authorities. The priest's presence made Chan's willingness to repent seem genuine, but in a development that piled only more pain onto Poon's parents, the worlds of politics and justice were once more about to collide.

At the time of Chan's release, Taiwan's presidential election was looming and the incumbent Tsai Ing-wen had made the issue a staple on her campaign trail. Her Democratic Progressive Party, which leans toward favoring independence from mainland China, had played up the

Hong Kong protests as an example of how Beijing was encroaching upon and curtailing the city's freedoms. It was a cautionary tale, she warned, of what might happen were Taiwan to reunify with the mainland.

Meanwhile, Taiwan and Hong Kong officials were also bickering over how to send Chan back to the self-ruled island, and the argument became increasingly bitter. At one point, Tsai's government had even suggested Chan's offer to surrender might be an elaborate plot, hatched by Beijing, aimed at circumventing the need for formal negotiations between Hong Kong and Taipei (something that they alleged could be seen as implying recognition of Taiwan's claims to self-rule).

Given the political sensitivities, Koon said Chan felt he would not get a fair trial in Taiwan until after the election in January 2020. So Chan would hold back on handing himself in, at least for the time being.

Tsai won the election handsomely with 57.1 per cent of the vote, the highest winning margin ever achieved by her party. Most analysts saw her stance on the Hong Kong protests as the main reason.

Yet even with the election over, the time for justice had not arrived. The next month, the outbreak of the coronavirus prompted Taiwan to restrict incoming travel from Hong Kong. The chances of Chan's surrender seemed suddenly more complicated than ever.

By now two years had passed since Poon's death, during which time the political landscapes of both Taiwan and Hong Kong had been transformed, yet somehow the prime suspect in her killing still appeared no closer to facing a murder charge.

At the time of publication, Chan remained in Hong Kong as if his case were frozen in time, an inconvenient reminder of a period some would prefer to forget.

As Reverend Koon put it, life for Chan was "at a standstill." For Poon's parents, so too was their search for justice.

Kill bill: The law that tore a city apart

Jeffie Lam

The birth of Carrie Lam's extradition bill was how the protests began but even its death could not bring them to an end.

There were two schools of thought as to the motivation behind Carrie Lam Cheng Yuet-ngor's unpopular extradition bill and why she so doggedly stuck to it even in the face of unprecedented opposition.

One explanation, the one offered by Lam herself, was that she had been moved by the plight of two Hongkongers seeking justice for their murdered daughter, Poon Hiu-wing, who was killed in February 2018 while holidaying in Taipei with her boyfriend Chan Tong-kai.

Chan, the prime suspect in the killing, had managed to return to Hong Kong and was effectively thumbing his nose at the justice system, having admitted killing Poon to Hong Kong police, safe in the knowledge there was little they could do about it.

Authorities could not extradite him to Taiwan to face a murder charge as the two jurisdictions lacked a treaty. Instead he could be charged only with more minor offenses committed on local soil – theft and money laundering – and could be freed before 2019 was out. Empathizing with Poon's parents, Lam stepped in to prevent a travesty of justice.

That's one explanation. But there was another, less charitable view. It held that the ambitious Lam saw in the case a perfect opportunity to please her political masters in Beijing by delivering something they had

26

wanted ever since the handover from British rule in 1997: a rethink of colonial-era laws that had expressly ruled out extraditions between Hong Kong and mainland China.

As things stood, Hong Kong had extradition agreements with just 20 jurisdictions, covering 46 crimes from murder to tax evasion and 15 corporate violations, and neither Taiwan nor mainland China were among them. A canny politician might be able to kill two birds with one stone.

Why the rush?

On February 12, 2019, almost a year to the day since Poon's death, the extradition bill was unveiled. It proposed changing the relevant laws so that fugitives could be transferred to jurisdictions outside the 20 places Hong Kong had agreements with.

These transfers would be decided on a case-by-case basis and would follow a set process once a request was received. First, the chief executive would decide whether to seek an arrest warrant. Then, if she did so, the Hong Kong courts would decide whether to grant that warrant.

There were a couple of other provisos: only crimes that carried a sentence of at least one year's imprisonment would be considered and the subjects of extradition requests would have the right to challenge them before the courts.

The government was in a hurry to get the bill passed. So it skipped the lengthy consultation period that would normally have involved months' worth of public discussion and instead gave the city's residents just 20 days to give their feedback.

Why the rush? Well, again there were two schools of thought.

One explanation, the one offered by Lam, was that the Taiwan murder case meant time was of the essence. She was backed on this by pro-establishment and pro-Beijing political parties that seemed confident that public sympathy for Poon's grieving parents would mean that the bill would sail through the legislative process smoothly.

But there was another, more cynical view. This was that Lam was trying to rush the bill through before anyone had time to digest the profound implications it would have for Hong Kong's relationship with mainland China.

Time to act?

Supporters of the bill said there were yawning gaps in the justice system, which it could plug. If Hong Kong had extradition agreements with just 20 jurisdictions, they pointed out, that meant the city was rolling out the welcome mat for fugitives from more than 170 others. And many such fugitives already lived in the city, among them convicted criminals from Taiwan and 300 people on the run from mainland China. The loophole needed to be closed if the city was to uphold its own criminal justice system, they said.

And the mainland had turned over about 200 criminal suspects to Hong Kong since 1997, so why could the city not return the courtesy? After all, Beijing had signed extradition treaties with 50 countries, 37 of which had been ratified, and they didn't seem to have a problem. As senior counsel and former director of public prosecutions Grenville Cross put it, the bill was needed to prevent Hong Kong from becoming "China's criminal sanctuary."

Mistrust of the mainland

Others were more skeptical – both of Lam's motivations and Beijing's record on the rule of law.

Concerns over Hong Kong's status as a separate jurisdiction had lingered since 2015, when five men linked to Causeway Bay Books –

which sold salacious publications on the private lives of China's top leadership – went missing in various places, only to emerge in mainland custody. The saga climaxed when the shop's owner was taken from Hong Kong to the mainland, without any official record of his departure, sparking fears that he had been abducted by government agents.

Then, in 2017, billionaire Xiao Jianhua mysteriously vanished from a luxury hotel in the city, with many, including local government sources, believing he had been spirited across the border by mainland agents.

So when the extradition bill was introduced in February 2019, many saw it as an attempt to fully remove the firewall between Hong Kong and the mainland. Pan-democratic lawmakers warned that Beijing could use the law to pursue political dissidents, white-collar criminal suspects and even visitors passing through the city, perhaps by trumping up charges so that its extradition requests were granted.

They said that once Hong Kong surrendered a fugitive to the mainland – or indeed any other jurisdiction with a dubious human rights record – it would no longer be able to ensure that individuals received a fair trial or adequate legal representation.

At the core of these objections lay a deep mistrust of the legal process on the mainland, where many cases take years to come to trial and even then the conviction rate is unnervingly high – reportedly 99.9 per cent in 2014.

"Are we really confident of handing over an accused person to be tried on the mainland?" asked legal sector lawmaker Dennis Kwok. "The law there stipulates that cases have to be heard within six months, but many defendants have been held incommunicado for three, five or even seven years."

Judges judge

Lam and her officials dismissed such criticisms, insisting that the courts would play a gatekeeping role in scrutinizing extradition requests and that there were robust safeguards. But many among the legal community – including 12 current and former chairs of the Bar Association – felt this "often repeated claim" about gatekeeping was misleading.

They said extradition hearings were too limited in scope to allow them to probe whether requests were justified, and that even if they did so they could come under political pressure from Beijing.

What was more, they argued, the law preventing extraditions to mainland China was not a gap that needed filling, but a necessary safeguard because the two legal systems were fundamentally different and there were concerns over Beijing's track record on human rights.

As Professor Albert Chen Hung-yee, a member of the Basic Law Committee, put it, Hong Kong courts would be left in the "difficult and invidious" position of deciding whether the mainland's legal system complied with human rights standards.

Essentially, the lingering doubt was whether Hong Kong would be able to say no to Beijing. And if it could not, what did that mean for the "one country, two systems" model under which the city has been governed since the handover from British rule? Could it still claim to have a high degree of autonomy?

"The one country, two systems model stems from our lack of trust in the mainland's judicial model," said Democratic Party chairman Wu Chi-wai. "Once the firewall is gone, there will only be one country, one system."

Down to business

While Lam and company seemed to weather the criticism from lawmakers and legal eagles, they found it harder to ignore another section of society.

Business leaders wanted the bill changed to exempt people suspected of white-collar crimes and they made clear that their concerns centered on the possibility of extradition to mainland China.

The American Chamber of Commerce, Hong Kong's most influential US network, warned that the bill would damage the city's reputation as a haven for international business. The problem was the mainland's flawed justice system, said the chamber. There was no independent judiciary, detention was arbitrary and trials were often neither public nor fair.

James Tien Pei-chun, honorary chairman of the business-friendly Liberal Party, said the bill threatened Hong Kong's competitiveness. "Do you think investment banks like JP Morgan and Citibank, or AIA, would still set up their headquarters in Hong Kong if anyone could easily be extradited to the mainland?" he asked.

Significantly, there was opposition even among pro-Beijing business figures attending China's biggest annual political event, the "Two Sessions" of the National People's Congress and the Chinese People's Political Consultative Conference. One of them, Hong Kong's former No 2 official Henry Tang Ying-yen said that while Hongkongers supported plugging legal loopholes that allowed fugitives to shelter in the city, only those accused of the most serious crimes should be extradited.

Meanwhile, two Hong Kong business groups backed a suggestion to allow transfers for the most serious crimes, but to exempt 15 white-collar crimes, including those relating to taxes, fraud and money laundering.

Even the European Union weighed in, criticizing Lam's government for not conducting a more in-depth public consultation on such a sensitive issue – and for not consulting the 20 jurisdictions with which it already had extradition agreements.

Lam stews

On March 19, Lam hinted that the government's stance was softening. A week later, she agreed to exempt nine economic crimes included in the original proposal. Her cabinet then endorsed a revised bill that would allow extraditions only for offenses punishable by at least three years' imprisonment, rather than one as originally proposed.

The revised bill also excluded white-collar crimes related to taxes, securities and futures trading, intellectual property, company offenses and the unlawful use of computers, but retained those related to bribery, fraud and money laundering. Thirty-seven crimes remained on the list, down from the original 46.

Announcing the changes, Lam maintained that the death of Poon in Taiwan had been her government's only motivation in wanting the law changed. "All this huge amount of work done by my colleagues is driven only by empathy and sympathy," she said.

Was that enough to cut the mustard with critics? Well, the answer depended on whom you asked.

The business sector generally welcomed the changes. Others remained unconvinced if not mistrustful, criticizing Lam for heeding the concerns of a small, privileged sector of the community while refusing to address broader issues, such as the lack of a guarantee of fair trials on the mainland.

Even Cross, the former director of public prosecutions who supported the bill in its original form, was concerned about the amendment. "It is clearly illogical that some people suspected of serious crime should be liable to surrender if apprehended in Hong Kong, whereas others can enjoy safe haven," he said. "After all, criminal justice is all about equality of treatment."

For Lam, there were bigger problems ahead. Opposition to the bill was snowballing, leading to protests that would continue for the rest of 2019.

Even after she amended the bill again in May, then suspended it in June, declared it dead in July and withdrawn in September, and formally removed it from the legislative agenda in October, the protests continued.

Coincidentally, later that month, Chan – the convicted money launderer and murder suspect whose case the bill had been meant address – completed his jail sentence and walked out a free man. As he left the prison gates, Chan apologized to the Hong Kong public for all the fuss he had caused and vowed to turn himself in voluntarily to the Taiwanese authorities.

But still the protests did not skip a beat. After all, things were no longer about Chan, Poon and her grieving parents. Ironically, they were no longer about the killed bill either.

Chaos in Legco: The pan-democrats' campaign

Jeffie Lam

Adrift and struggling for relevance, the pro-democracy camp suddenly found itself galvanized by an urgent political fight.

D emocratic Party chairman Wu Chi-wai has a reputation for being mild-mannered. But in May 2019, he lost his cool as Hong Kong lawmakers clashed repeatedly in the Legislative Council over the government's extradition bill. The draft legislation was introduced in February and required scrutiny, but for several weeks there was no progress as members bickered and disagreed over fears the proposed law would lead to fugitives being sent to mainland China. At the heart of their increasingly bitter exchanges lay the pan-democratic bloc's mistrust of Chief Executive Carrie Lam Cheng Yuet-ngor's motives for proposing extraditions, on a case-by-case basis, to jurisdictions with which Hong Kong had no exchange arrangement. They feared the change would leave anyone in the city at the mercy of party-controlled courts north of the border, where a fair trial is not guaranteed.

On May 9, Wu was among six lawmakers ejected from the chamber for hurling insults and yelling profanities at Lam, calling her a liar after she issued a strongly worded defense of the extradition bill. An enraged Wu accused Lam of toeing the Communist Party line in pushing forward the bill, saying: "How many people do we need to take to the street, pull their business and move elsewhere, to force you to stop?" As he was being escorted from the chamber, he shouted at Lam: "You are useless dead or alive, b***h!"

✿

34

Two days later, on May 11, Legco was the scene of unprecedented chaos as rival groups of lawmakers pushed, shoved and shouted at each other as they fought to take control of the bills committee scrutinizing the legislation. This happened after 42 pro-establishment lawmakers demanded that Democratic Party member James To Kun-sun be removed from presiding over the committee, as he had delayed the election of a chairman for weeks, thus preventing the panel from getting down to real work. As the longest-serving Legco member, To presided automatically over the body until a chairman was installed. The pro-establishment bloc replaced him with veteran lawmaker Abraham Razack, even though this violated Legco convention.

The pan-democratic bloc was not having any of it. Both camps called separate meetings of the bills committee, each claiming the other's was illegitimate. When Razack arrived, scores of pan-democrats tried to prevent him from entering the meeting room, as pro-establishment lawmakers formed a cordon around the 73-year-old. As they brawled, Wu shouted: "Abraham, please don't be remembered as a sinner!" Both camps later filed police reports about the clash, which forced the meeting to be adjourned. One lawmaker was taken to hospital and three others said they had been injured. Razack said afterward: "I have never seen such a hostile situation in my 19 years here as a member of Legco."

Looking back in January 2020, Wu said his uncharacteristic outbursts had been unplanned, though he would not apologize for anything he said or did. He said his conduct, as well as the tactics of his colleagues in the pan-democratic camp, helped raise public awareness of the reasons they opposed the extradition bill so strongly, and sowed the seeds of the anti-bill sentiment. "Some people told me they decided to look into what was going on after seeing that even the Democratic Party, considered a moderate faction of the camp, had adopted such an attitude toward the bill," he recalled.

Publicity on the pan-democrats' actions in Legco also began to give the camp a much needed boost after a season in the doldrums. Hong Kong's social movement lost steam after the pro-democracy Occupy protests, which shut down parts of the city for 79 days in 2014, fizzled out and failed to move Beijing. As a blame game played out, the camp found itself splintered and weakened by infighting, leaving supporters frustrated and disenchanted by the ineffectiveness of street protests. Young people walked away, drawn instead to new "localist" parties that had sprung up. Following the Legco elections in 2016, four pan-democrats and two pro-independence lawmakers lost their seats for their improper oath-taking. The nadir for the camp came in 2018, when its candidates lost two Legco by-elections to pro-establishment candidates.

Pan-democrat lawmakers also failed in 2017 to stop their pro-establishment opponents from amending the Legco rule book to curb filibustering, despite warning that the change would allow the administration to bulldoze controversial legislation into law. Only around 100 protesters – mostly middle-aged and older – gathered outside Legco on the day the amendments passed.

The following year, pan-democrats failed to block a contentious bill to set up a mainland customs and border checkpoint at the new West Kowloon terminus of the high-speed cross-border railway. The change would allow, for the first time, mainland laws to be enforced in a part of Hong Kong. This time, about 300 protesters showed up on the day the bill was passed. A source from the pan-democrat camp said: "What hurt us most was that citizens did not seem to care at all." Wu recalled: "The series of blows seemed to suggest that the legislature was impotent and useless. Even some of our supporters thought that was an accurate description."

When Lam unveiled the extradition bill in February 2019, pan-democrat lawmakers knew they had to give their all to block it. As well as opposing it ideologically, they saw an opportunity to remind the city of their relevance: to be a check on the government. Although opposition to the bill was initially mild, fears that the proposed law might expose Hongkongers to the mainland's legal system eventually gave the camp a chance to turn their fortunes around. They realized early on they needed to seize the narrative decisively. In May 2019, lawmakers previously criticized for being too moderate or ineffective made headlines by paralyzing the bill's passage through Legco and participating in scenes of unprecedented chaos.

They lobbied the international community, attended protests and stood between hard-core masked radicals and riot police in the midst of tear gas and even gunfire. The sight of Democratic Party lawmaker Roy Kwong Chun-yu outside Legco on June 12, perched precariously on metal railings and supported by hard-core protesters in helmets, masks and goggles, was previously unimaginable. Kwong, a 37-year-old romance novelist, used to be mocked by some protesters, who felt the pan-democrats had achieved nothing. Now he was recognizable as a lawmaker who appeared regularly on the front lines. That day he dissuaded the crowd from clashing with police at Legco, urging them to take care and avoid being arrested. Several other pan-democrats were seen at the front lines, although their mediating efforts were sometimes in vain and came in for criticism by the police. Democratic Party lawmaker Ted Hui Chi-fung was arrested during clashes in North Point in September. Kwong said: "I think it is a new role for lawmakers, to be the buffer between protesters and the police. I want to be with the protesters and I think my presence helps put them at ease."

As anti-government protests gathered steam, the camp presented a rare picture of unity, leading eventually to its landslide victory in the district council elections of November 2019. Pro-democracy candidates swept almost 90 per cent of 452 seats, taking control of 17 of the city's 18 district councils. The bloc also appeared to have reconnected with the youth. "The Communist Party has exhausted every means to divide the camp since the city's handover and the infighting reached its peak in 2018 when we lost two Legco by-elections," Wu said. "Our unity now is a slap in the party's face."

From the start, pan-democrat lawmakers viewed the extradition bill with suspicion, regarding it as one of the biggest threats to the former British colony since its return to Chinese rule in 1997. They feared that, if passed, it would fundamentally alter the "one country, two systems" principle under which Hong Kong has been governed since the handover. They immediately set about dividing the work that needed to be done to warn the public of the potential danger. The lawyers among them focused on marshaling legal arguments. Others began meeting foreign diplomats, overseas media and chambers of commerce.

At first, not many foreigners saw a problem with the bill. After all, it appeared sensible to extradite criminals to jurisdictions where they could face justice. Civic Party leader Alvin Yeung Ngok-kiu recalled: "Everyone in Hong Kong understood we had a separate legal system from that of mainland China, but they could not see why it would be harmful to have an extradition agreement with China when that was something so ordinary in their countries. We had to go back to square one and stress how much damage the bill could do to Hong Kong's legal system, which turned out to be something that foreign stakeholders, including foreign governments and business chambers, treasured the most." Even then, getting the message across was not easy. A pan-democrat involved in the lobbying effort, who preferred to remain anonymous, said: "In private, many expressed fears and said they knew how bad the bill was. But they hesitated to voice their views openly because of the dollar sign. There was a lot of maneuvering." Then, in March, the American Chamber of Commerce became the first powerful foreign business network to oppose the bill, warning the Hong Kong government it would damage the city's reputation as a "secure haven for international business." The same month, former chief secretary Anson Chan Fang On-sang and two pan-democratic lawmakers, Dennis Kwok and Charles Mok, embarked on a 10-day trip to the United States at the invitation of the White House and were received by Vice-President Mike Pence. Chan, now a pro-democracy critic of the government, said they discussed Hong Kong residents' human rights and the special trading relationship between the city and the US. In a speech she delivered during the trip, she urged Americans doing business in Hong Kong to voice their concerns over the extradition bill "before it is too late."

These messages began sinking in, if early protests were anything to go by. On March 31, an estimated 12,000 people took to Hong Kong streets to oppose the bill. On April 28, a much larger crowd showed up, with the organizers claiming 130,000 and police putting the number at 22,800. Meanwhile in the legislature, pan-democrats used many methods to stall scrutiny of the bill, leading to the chaos of May 11. Democratic Party lawmaker Kwong said their efforts effectively slowed the legislative process, giving Hongkongers time to grasp the potential impact of the bill. Others said Lam should have sensed the seriousness of the crisis by May, given the lengths to which pan-democrats went to oppose the bill, risking arrest for their antics and criticism by their own moderate supporters. Eventually, seven pan-democrat lawmakers were either arrested or informed of their pending arrest for actions during the chaos of May 11.

One lawmaker from the camp said: "Of course we struggled before switching from our usual peaceful approach, but we were backed up by public support. God gave Lam all the signs, but she refused to back down."

Lam and other government officials condemned the chaos in Legco, and refused to stop championing the bill. Lam and security chief John Lee Ka-chiu said repeatedly that the bill would not undermine Hongkongers' rights, and still expected lawmakers to approve it by mid-July. On June 9, however, an estimated 1 million people took part in a march to oppose the bill, firing the starting gun on social unrest that would continue for months to come. On June 12, protesters clashed with police outside Legco, and police fired tear gas for the first time in the city since 2014. On June 15, Lam announced that the bill was being suspended, and would effectively be "dead" by July. But she still rejected demands for its complete withdrawal, prompting another record-breaking march the next day – drawing 2 million people this time, according to organizers' estimates.

Members of the pan-democrat camp said it was the very nature of the extradition bill that helped their efforts and denied that they had lied to or misled the public. People could see the dangers, they said, of allowing China to demand the return of suspects from the city. "It's something even pro-establishment people in Hong Kong are afraid of," Wu said. Unlike previous controversial legislation, the bill drew opposition from more than "the usual suspects" of opposition lawmakers, legal experts and social workers. It was significant that even the local and international business communities, traditionally close allies of the government, took the rare step of voicing their concerns. Civic Party leader Yeung said Hong Kong's legal system was probably one of the last lines of defense for the one country, two systems model. "The extradition bill goes directly to the core of the criminal justice system," he said. "For ordinary people, it is the deep fear of the fate of 'one country' over 'two systems'. They have good reason to share this fear."

A strained alliance

Gary Cheung and Kimmy Chung

The pro-Beijing camp, always supportive of the government, paid a price for backing the extradition bill.

The pro-establishment Hong Kong Federation of Trade Unions (FTU) was in an upbeat mood in early 2019 as its leaders assessed its prospects for the district council elections due near the end of the year. "We set the goal of ensuring the re-election of our 29 incumbent district councilors and winning at least another five seats," FTU president Stanley Ng Chau-pei recalled in January 2020.

There were many reasons for that optimism, not least the labor and political group's ample resources, its 420,000 members and strong grassroots network. "Under normal circumstances, the pro-establishment camp usually has an advantage in district council elections which are dominated by bread-and-butter issues," Ng said. All 18 councils were dominated by the camp, and at the start of 2019, the opposition pan-democrats were in disarray and still smarting from back-to-back defeats in two Legislative Council by-elections the previous year.

Punished at the polls

Nobody foresaw the debacle to come for the pro-establishment camp, as protests against city leader Carrie Lam Cheng Yuet-ngor's extradition bill snowballed into a wider anti-government movement through much of 2019. In the district council elections on November 24, pro-establishment candidates were trounced, winning only 60 out of 452 seats.

Sweeping to a stunning victory, the pan-democrat bloc won 392 seats and seized control of 17 out of 18 councils. As for the FTU, only five of its 62 candidates won, with three of its four Legco members failing to retain their district council seats. (District councilors are eligible to run as Legco members and vice-versa.)

In a postmortem of their pathetic performance, some in the camp conceded afterward that they had failed to read the signs early enough, and did not realize that the extradition bill controversy could end up hurting them so deeply. Most in the camp actually had seen nothing wrong with the bill rolled out by the government to allow the case-by-case extradition of fugitives to jurisdictions with which Hong Kong had no exchange arrangement, including mainland China. When they met residents, they sensed that most were indifferent to the bill.

"They thought it related only to a tiny group of fugitives and had nothing to do with them," said Tam Yiu-chung, former chairman of the Democratic Alliance for the Betterment and Progress of Hong Kong (DAB), the largest pro-establishment party. Only 21 of the DAB's 179 candidates won in November, a massive rout for a party which had 119 district council seats before the polls.

Regina Ip Lau Suk-yee, chairwoman of the pro-government New People's Party and an Executive Council member, said she rarely came across residents who were unhappy about the extradition bill. It was "something too remote" for most people, she said. Her party fielded 28 candidates in the district council elections, but all lost.

In retrospect, Ip and Tam agreed, the tide turned after a group of Hong Kong pan-democrats, led by former chief secretary Anson Chan Fang On-sang, went to the United States in March 2019. They highlighted concerns that the extradition bill could lead to fugitives being sent from Hong Kong to mainland China, and lobbied support from top US officials and members of Congress. That proved a turning point for Beijing as well. A domestic Hong Kong issue now had become a potential new front in the geopolitical rivalry between the US and China, said Tam, Hong Kong's sole representative on the National People's Congress Standing Committee, the nation's top legislative body.

The following month, Beijing's liaison office in Hong Kong invited a group of government supporters to set up an alliance to defend the extradition bill. The group then opened street booths across Hong Kong and collected hundreds of thousands of signatures from the public supporting the proposal to change the law. That seemed to be another sign that there was support on the ground for the bill.

The FTU's Ng, deputy convenor of the alliance, admitted that his labor group misread ground sentiment. "We supported the government's decision to push the bill because we agreed there was a need to plug the legal loophole in the existing law," he said. "Our judgment was based on whether the move was in line with justice, not whether it could have a negative political impact."

The pro-establishment camp remained firmly behind the bill even as its progress through Legco was delayed by pan-democrats. After the chaos and brawling in the legislature in May as members from rival sides fought for control of the bills committee which would scrutinize the legislation, the pro-establishment side supported fast-tracking the bill and bypassing the committee. City leader Lam was determined even then to press ahead with the process to have the bill passed in Legco, and the camp supported her.

What followed, however, were massive shows of opposition to the bill and the government in June, including the first violent clash between protesters and police on the 12th of that month. Three days later, Lam announced that the bill would be suspended but it was not until September that the legislation was formally withdrawn. By then, the anti-bill protests had grown into a wider anti-government movement.

Blame game

Looking back, Tam said that in mobilizing opposition to the extradition bill, the pan-democrats succeeded in exploiting the distrust that a substantial proportion of Hongkongers have toward the mainland. As for the pro-establishment camp, he said: "We also underestimated the level of Hong Kong people's distrust in mainland China. When the pan-democrats' efforts were producing results in May, we thought it was natural for pan-democrats to oppose everything the government proposed."

Tam said that in hindsight, after the first massive march on June 9 in which organizers estimated that 1 million people took part, the pro-establishment camp could have urged the government to apply the brakes on the bill. But after months of supporting the draft law, the camp had to think hard over how it would look if it switched now to opposing it. "Our supporters may have had reservations if we backtracked. We had to take into account their views," he said.

The FTU's Ng said: "There was no point in our asking the government to halt the legislative process in May or June as we didn't say as much in February." Even after the June 9 march, the FTU felt that, being a government ally, it could not stop Lam from pressing on with a bill aimed at sending criminal suspects to face justice elsewhere. "The government was worried that if it made any concessions, it would be interpreted as giving in to criminals," Ng said. "If we asked the government not to go ahead with the bill, would we be condoning criminals and fugitives?"

So even as the numbers turning up at demonstrations rose, the pro-establishment camp still hoped to get the bill passed as quickly as possible. "We believed that all fears about the extradition bill would prove unfounded once it was passed," Tam said, adding that the government thought so too. For both, that optimism was based on their experience the year before, when the strong opposition faced by the high-speed rail for allowing mainland immigration facilities to be on the Hong Kong side petered out when the network opened.

Almost a year later, Ip remained adamant that there was nothing wrong with the government wanting to push ahead with the extradition bill. What went wrong was that there was insufficient time for public consultation on the proposed legislation, and the government's handling of the controversy as it played out. "The government lost the publicity war, as the opposition succeeded in instilling fear in the public by using powerful slogans," she said. The pro-establishment camp also did not expect that Hong Kong would be dragged into the US-China trade war, Ip said, referring to American politicians making statements about the city and President Donald Trump mentioning Hong Kong a number of times during talks with China. "Hong Kong was used by the US as a pawn in the trade war," she said.

Ip, an ambitious former security minister who resigned in 2003 after 500,000 people marched in protest against a proposed national security law, insisted that it was ultimately the government and not the pro-establishment camp that was to blame for the extradition bill disaster. "The government has to bear the brunt. The chief executive has a 180,000-strong civil service but we are only a small party," she said.

Complaisance at the core

But as leaders of the pro-establishment camp criticized pan-democrats for scaremongering and encouraging interference by Western countries to intensify opposition to the bill, and pointed at Lam's bullheadedness in pressing on regardless of the growing anger, at least one veteran pro-government lawmaker was prepared to say the camp itself needed to shoulder some blame.

Sources close to the government said it had been confident right up until early June 2019 that the bill would be passed, given the pro-establishment camp's overwhelming majority in Legco. There are 43 pro-establishment lawmakers in the 70-member legislature, and they usually side with the government even on critical issues.

"The major problem with some people in the pro-establishment camp is complaisance. They too eagerly accept requests or instructions from the power bloc," said Abraham Razack, who has spent nearly two decades in Legco representing the real estate sector. He had been in the thick of the Legco chaos in May, when both sides tussled for control of the committee to scrutinize the bill.

On June 11, a day before the bill was due to go before Legco, Razack dropped a bombshell. He spearheaded mainland-funded developer Goldin Financial Holdings' decision to give up the right to buy a HK$11.1 billion (US$1.4 billion) site at the old Kai Tak airport, citing "social contradiction and economic instability." The move, which meant forfeiting a HK$25 million deposit, was viewed widely as a sign that business confidence had been shaken by the extradition bill controversy. By that time, Razack, an independent non-executive director of Goldin, had expressed his reservations about the bill as well as the government's attempt to rush it through the legislature.

Reflecting on the missteps, he said: "It disregarded legislative due process. It undercut the rule of law. It weakened human rights safeguards. It undermined the promise of 'one country, two systems'. It fueled social confrontation. It dampened investor confidence. In short, it destabilized Hong Kong." He said Lam was convinced the bill would do good, and was condescending in her determination to impose her will. "Our officials were suffering from tunnel vision. They were so focused on plugging the so-called loophole in extradition law that they lost sight of a much bigger hole that was cracking wide open in the dam," he said.

Even after the bill was withdrawn in September, the anti-government protests continued. Increasingly, the district council elections in November came to be viewed as a barometer of support for the protest movement and the government. Although district councilors handle mainly municipal matters and have no say on policy, campaigning was intense. On November 24, nearly 3 million Hongkongers – 71.2 per cent of the electorate – came out to vote, a record turnout. The message from the ballot box was strong and unambiguous across Hong Kong, with pro-democracy newcomers sweeping aside pro-government veterans with long track records in many districts.

Beijing, however, brushed off the pro-establishment camp's massive defeat, and news of the pan-democrat camp's big win was censored heavily on the mainland. State media focused instead on calls to preserve law and order, accusing Western countries of instigating unrest in Hong Kong.

The shock in the pro-government camp has been plain to see. The leaders of major parties in the bloc have been left with no reason to be optimistic about their next challenge: the Legco election in September 2020. Half of Legco's 70 seats will be contested in geographical constituencies, while the rest will come from trade-based functional constituencies. In the 2016 Legco election, pan-democrats and localists won 30 seats and pro-establishment candidates secured 40. After the district council polls outcome, analysts and key figures within the pro-establishment camp expect the bloc's Legco candidates to be punished again.

Labor movement leader Ng, who started 2019 full of optimism about his party's chances at the district council polls, began 2020 preparing for the worst in the next electoral test. "There is a real risk that the opposition camp will win more than half of the total seats in Legco," he said in January 2020. He fears that the pro-establishment camp's traditional strongholds in functional constituencies, such as engineering, catering, and sports and culture, may also fall to the opposition. On top of lingering unhappiness among voters related to the doomed extradition bill, the government started the new year by coming under fire for its slow response to the Covid-19 public health crisis caused by the coronavirus. That has added to the pessimism in the pro-government camp. "We will also suffer from the growing public discontent with the government's handling of the pandemic," Ng said.

"IT UNDERCUT THE RULE OF LAW ... IT UNDERMINED THE PROMISE OF 'ONE COUNTRY, TWO SYSTEMS'. IT FUELED SOCIAL CONFRONTATION. IN SHORT, IT DESTABILIZED HONG KONG."

Abraham Razack, pro-establishment lawmaker

——

WATER AND FIRE

"THAT IS THE HONGKONGERS' SPIRIT. WE HAVE NOT CHANGED."

Anna Chan, protester and teacher who marched in 2003 when she was 18 and marched in 2019

On one mat, no matter how perilous

Jeffie Lam

A s she dived into the sea of demonstrators, Anna Chan Wah shrugged off the scorching heat, the blaring loudspeakers and, in the pit of her stomach, a gnawing fear of failure.

"We know our street protest today is not going to change anything," the sixth former said solemnly. "But we are here to fight for democracy in Hong Kong and to show that we still have a voice."

That was back in 2003 and Chan was 18 when she joined the half a million people who poured onto the streets to oppose a piece of national security legislation the government had introduced. Chan feared the bill, which was to deal with treason and sedition against Beijing, would curb the freedoms and rights of Hongkongers guaranteed by the "one country, two systems" governing blueprint.

She was the first recruit of a new union of pupils against the legislation. She later co-founded the Hong Kong Secondary Students Union. "My mum asked me not to get involved and focus on my studies," she said. "But we need to show our concern, not just through discussion but action."

Chan kept her word. Long after the bill was aborted, she continued to attend democracy rallies, first as an undergraduate and then as a secondary school teacher.

On June 9, 2019, when an estimated 1 million people marched in protest against the extradition bill which would have allowed fugitives to be tried on the mainland, Chan was in the crowd. "Hongkongers might seem to care only about money most of the time but they would definitely stand up when their freedoms and core values are eroded," said Chan, now 34 and mother of an eight-year-old son.

"That is the Hongkongers' spirit. We have not changed."

Protesters on that day wore white to symbolize the death knell of the city with the passing of the bill. They chanted *"faan sung zung"* again and again. A Cantonese phrase which means "oppose being sent to China," it is in effect a pun that also means sending someone to their death. That double entendre summed up their fears over the bill.

Like Chan in 2003, many admitted feeling pessimistic about their chances of quashing the legislation. But they were not giving up without a fight. As Hongkongers, taking to the streets to send a message was a freedom they intended to use to the fullest, many of the marchers said, as they explained why they were spending seven to eight hours that Sunday on the streets. Protesting was what being a Hongkonger was about, commentators mused aloud in those early days of the cause. The protest instinct was in city residents' DNA, others said.

Defending Hong Kong

The way protesters understood it, the extradition bill would effectively remove the legal firewall between the city and the mainland. The move would bring Hong Kong one step closer to being a mainland city. That slogan – *faan sung zung* – induced in many an anxiety that everyone risked being sent to the mainland, not just criminals, who were the target of the legislation. But it also spoke to their fear – fanned by the opposition and activists – that the bill would rob them of their freedoms and identity as Hongkongers.

"Hongkongers have to speak up to express themselves and tell the world Hong Kong is different from China," said social worker Janus Wong, 40, on June 9. "People on the mainland might dare not to speak up regarding what their government has done, but Hongkongers will."

Retiree Lily Chan, 70, who went on her own in a motorized wheel-chair to join the march along Hennessy Road, said she was protesting for the next generation. "I am here because you can't trust the Chinese government," she declared. She feared that if the bill passed, Hong Kong would send people such as the protest organizers to the mainland. "The freedom we have in Hong Kong is being eroded," she warned.

"Withdraw! Withdraw!" The crowd chanted that day, referring to the bill. That night, they received an answer. The final sentence of a 564-word statement issued by the government at 11.09pm read: "The second reading debate on the bill will resume on June 12."

On June 12, tens of thousands besieged the Legislative Council complex to block lawmakers from scrutinizing the bill. Chaos ensued and tear gas was fired, for the first time since the Occupy protests of 2014. Police branded the day's mayhem a riot.

It took Chief Executive Carrie Lam Cheng Yuet-ngor another three days, on the eve of another mass march, to declare the bill suspended.

"No one knew whether it was the June 9 march or the June 12 clashes that triggered the backdown, but mainstream society, including the demonstrators, agreed that it was the combination of both peaceful and radical protests that forced the concession," said political scientist Edmund Cheng Wai, of City University.

But the concession proved to be too little, too late. After police fired 150 rounds of tear gas – more than double the amount during Occupy – at the June 12 melee, the target of anger widened to include not just the government, but also the officers. As pictures and videos of bloodied protesters circulated on social media, accusations of police brutality took a life of their own.

Protesters soon came up with a list of five demands: full withdrawal of the bill; a commission of inquiry into alleged police brutality; retracting the classification of the June 12 protest as a "riot"; amnesty for arrested protesters; and the resignation of Carrie Lam. The final demand was later changed to the implementation of universal suffrage as they argued that Lam's departure would not save the city from the quagmire of her own making.

A day after the bill's suspension, an estimated 2 million Hongkongers returned to the streets demanding its complete withdrawal. If June 9 was about death, June 16 was about mourning. Protesters, young and old, wore black.

Many were also mourning the death of a male protester who had fallen a day earlier from near the top of Pacific Place, a shopping mall in Admiralty, after unfurling an anti-bill banner. An impromptu shrine of white carnations, lilies and origami cranes went up at the site for the man they called the "raincoat martyr" who had been wearing a yellow waterproof jacket when he fell.

In Victoria Park that Sunday, amid chants for Lam to resign, a retiree surnamed Li urged the government to vindicate the students who clashed with police on June 12. "They were both wrong – but the students never had the gear the police had," the 70-year-old said, her voice breaking and eyes brimming with tears as she recounted a video clip of a protester with his face drenched in blood. "I am just glad no one was killed that day," she said. By that weekend, the narrative of police brutality had taken hold in the wider community.

Protesters doubled down. It was the school holidays, and many were students with time on their hands. They set up secret Telegram channels to communicate and, before long, they were touting the slogan "be water." Inspired by the late Hong Kong martial arts star Bruce Lee, to be water was to be formless, shapeless, agile and mobile in their actions. They would stage spontaneous demonstrations that ebbed and flowed without warning.

As the weeks progressed, new slogans emerged. Activists urged each other to be "strong like rice" when clashing with the police, "fluid like water" to stretch police resources, "gather like dew" for flash-mob actions and "disperse like mist" to avoid capture.

Wo lei fei and jung mou united as one

July 1, the 22nd anniversary of the city's return to Chinese rule, marked a critical juncture for the protests. Thousands of demonstrators skipped the annual peaceful procession and forced their way into the Legco complex after smashing glass entrances with a metal cart and iron poles. Inside, they vandalized the city's emblem, trashed the chamber and spray-painted graffiti on walls. A number of pan-democratic lawmakers who had previously stopped protesters from escalating their actions were outflanked and shouted down.

Among them was Leung Yiu-chung. He tried to spread his arms to prevent the protesters from charging ahead with their metal cart. A black-clad protester in goggles and helmet swooped in and tackled the grey-haired 66-year-old to the ground. "They questioned what could the legislature still achieve when even 2 million people had failed to budge the government," Leung said, recalling the anger of that day. "Sadly, I could not answer. These young people are in despair and they have no hope for the government anymore."

Violence as a means to an end was not easy to endorse but hard to abhor, supporters of the movement said repeatedly in the aftermath of July 1. Labour Party lawmaker and social worker Fernando Cheung Chiu-hung, who had tried to dissuade a group of young protesters from breaking into the Legco complex at the height of the Occupy protests in 2014, said the change in attitude was stark. The protesters of 2014 preached "peace and love." The demonstrators of 2019 had no qualms about the use of force, even if it cost them their future or, worse, their lives, he said. They were not a fringe group, he warned.

Cheung said news about three unusual deaths around then had been a trigger for the rampage on July 1. The trio had either left suicide notes or other references to the political crisis. "These protesters believed they should be held responsible for the three victims as they had failed to force the government to address their cause," Cheung said. "They were sad, angry, guilty and in despair. They have a strong desire to sacrifice themselves regardless of the consequences. This is very different from five years ago. It is very sad and a really dangerous sign."

That same evening, a hotel front-desker who goes by the initials CC sat in his office canteen transfixed by the live broadcast of protesters' attempts to smash Legco's glass doors. Police were nowhere to be seen. CC sighed and concluded that it was a trap; that law enforcers had deliberately retreated from the legislature, hoping the public would be so shocked by the protesters' actions it would withdraw its support. The 30-year-old went home with a heavy heart.

A university graduate, CC made up his mind that night to throw himself fully to the cause. He said he had to ensure the movement could carry on if frontliners were arrested after the night of July 1. A supporter who had considered himself a *wo lei fei* – a term for peaceful, rational and non-violent protesters – he decided he had to change. He would become one of the *jung mou*, or the "courageous and fierce ones," the romantic Cantonese term the radicals used for themselves.

The remarks of a French colleague played on his mind. "He said … the peaceful protests were not going to force the government to do anything," CC recalled. "So, yes, why have we been so polite and apologetic about the protests we staged?"

The next day, CC woke up to find Hongkongers leery of condemning the previous day's violence. Supporters of the protesters stuck to two key messages purveyed online that would have a talismanic effect on the movement.

First was the pledge of "no mat-cutting" – or *bat got zek* – which urged protesters to neither blame nor distance themselves from one another despite their different approaches. The second was the precept of "two brothers climbing a mountain, each making his own effort" – meaning different routes to reach the same summit were acceptable.

Almost every weekend after that, clashes between black-clad frontliners and police became the rule rather than the exception. Frontline radicals also became more sophisticated in their protective gear, trading cling film – used to repel the sting of tear gas and pepper spray – for body armor, and swimming goggles for gas masks.

Hard-core mobs at first blocked roads by digging up bricks and building barricades made of bamboo poles or metal fences and bins. They went on to trash railway stations and vandalize banks and restaurants seen as Beijing-linked, before turning to making and throwing petrol bombs and starting fires.

Often overwhelmed by the mayhem protesters caused in multiple locations with their "be water" strategy, police expanded their range of crowd-dispersal weapons from tear gas, rubber bullets and beanbag rounds to deploying water cannons which fired a blue-dyed, pepper-based solution.

On July 21, CC was among those who besieged the Beijing liaison office in the western part of Hong Kong Island, pelting it with eggs, splashing black paint on the national emblem and scrawling anti-Beijing expletives on its walls. Previously, the most daring thing he had done was to hold up umbrellas to shield the identity of his comrades when they dismantled metal railings at roadsides. But that night, he helped build barricades, pushing them all the way to the front line to fend off police.

That night too it dawned on him he was risking arrest and possibly jail time. "I was caught by surprise when a protester came over, swiftly covered the logo of my Puma sneakers with black tape and asked me to protect myself well," he recalled. CC later formed his own frontliner squad of four to six people, each with his own assigned role. One person always stayed at home to monitor live television broadcasts, while others sourced supplies or planned their next moves. CC's job was to locate exit routes.

Wo lei fei and *jung mou* demonstrated a rare unity born of the lessons gleaned from the Occupy protests. The endless infighting between the moderate and radical factions of Occupy in the end gutted the movement from inside. The strategy of occupying spaces over long stretches inconvenienced people and drained their goodwill. Remembering these missteps, protesters like CC were disciplined about adopting short, seemingly random bursts of rampaging to sustain momentum and public support and elude any police dragnet.

They also worked hard at cultivating the image of a leaderless movement, so there would be no ringleaders to arrest. The reasoning went that even if influential figures were picked up by police, others could step in. "Occupy is like a mirror – we are actually doing the opposite of what we did five years ago," CC said. "The failure of 2014 has made the 2019 protests very different, even though we have yet to succeed."

Broad support

While Hong Kong has long had a tradition of peaceful protests, the turn to violence in 2019 should not have come as a surprise, said political scientist Cheng. The Mong Kok riot three years earlier provided a preview. Pro-independence activist Edward Leung Tin-kei and his associates had gone to the shopping area on Lunar New Year to avenge what they saw as the poor treatment of unlicensed hawkers. For hours, they clashed with police, throwing bricks and setting fires, even setting police vehicles ablaze.

Activists were weary of "old and useless" peaceful tactics, Cheng said, and decided on actions that would exact a higher cost on the authorities. "They had prepared for it since 2016 and it is not something new to the frontliners today."

At the time, the scenes of chaos in Mong Kok shocked Hongkongers. In 2019, after a few clashes and with an emerging narrative of police violence, many became inured to the sight of physical fights between the two sides, the mess and mayhem and the clouds of tear gas fired. One argument protesters used to justify their violence was that police were using disproportionate force to take on ill-equipped young people. Moreover, they argued, while the protesters caused minor inconvenience, police were choking innocent people with their tear gas. Broad swathes of society – the *wo lei fei* and also middle-class bystanders across the generations – sided with the protesters, becoming the political vitamin sustaining the movement.

Engineer George Chu, 40, was among them. "Police officers, with public power, have been using stronger weapons so it is only reasonable for protesters to escalate their actions," Chu said at a Kennedy Town rally on August 4, an event that, again, ended in chaos and tear gas.

CC recalled how some middle-aged residents had cheered for him and his comrades when they were fighting on the streets. He was even rescued once by an elderly man who tipped him off to head to a nearby shelter when he was dodging riot police along Hillwood Road in Tsim Sha Tsui on November 18. "The support from these middle-aged people stemmed from their sympathy toward the youngsters who had gambled away their futures," he said. "They might not care about democracy at all."

A joint study by Cheng, Lingnan University political scientist Samson Yuen Wai-hei and Chinese University (CUHK) journalism professor Francis Lee Lap-fung confirmed that supporters had no qualms accepting the protesters' violence. An analysis of 18,000 questionnaires collected at protest sites from June 2019 to early January 2020 found that more than 90 per cent of respondents strongly agreed that "the peaceful faction and militant faction are in the same boat."

The study also found that supporters who were most tolerant of radical actions were young people born after the 1980s and those now in their 60s. "The inverted U-shape suggested older people who are in a comfortable position now had a sense of guilt toward the youngsters who sacrificed themselves," Cheng said.

A multiple-round telephone survey conducted by CUHK suggested that fewer Hongkongers insisted on peaceful methods as the protests dragged on. In mid-June, almost 83 per cent of respondents agreed the protests must stay non-violent, but that share gradually slid to 71.6 per cent in August and to 69.4 per cent a month later.

October 1 marked another turning point. As protesters declared the 70th anniversary of the founding of the People's Republic of China a day for mourning, clashes with police broke out in several places early on. Radicals embarked on a spree of violence, lighting fires, hurling bricks and petrol bombs and smashing mainland-linked businesses. Amid the chaos, hard-core frontliners cornered and assaulted outnumbered police officers with rods in Tsuen Wan. One of the radicals, who was battering an officer, was hit in the chest with a live round. The high school student survived but protesters were outraged by the shooting of a teenager and vowed that a "debt of blood" had to be paid.

Among those who became radicalized was a transport worker who used to keep away from the *jung mou* back in June. But as the clashes intensified, the 32-year-old changed his stance. He raised money online and began supplying gas masks and goggles to frontliners. At the height of some of the most violent clashes, including the siege of CUHK in

November, the transport worker was in the thick of the action, ferrying supplies. "Many people changed, myself included," he said. "I stopped caring about what the protesters did. I would have been happy to see police officers injured. I didn't care about what happened to them."

CUHK political scientist Ma Ngok said Hongkongers' anger toward police and their acceptance of road blockades and vandalism snowballed as the movement rolled on. "They no longer think it's reasonable to blindly obey the law when there is no punishment for the officers' wrongdoings," he said.

Self-restraint mechanism

Few cared to blame the protesters, whether quietly or openly. But the protesters did fret about their standing. Online data showed LIHKG, the Reddit-like site which became the protesters' virtual command center, recorded the biggest bump in traffic on weekends, followed by another spike on Mondays, according to Cheng. The chatter showed protesters critiquing their actions after each weekend.

In mid-August, they apologized and promised to reflect on their strategy, after causing massive disruption at the city's airport, leading to nearly 1,000 suspended flights and thousands of grounded travelers. "Being stranded for three days, canceled flights and forced changes of itinerary are not what you deserve, nor is this what we initially aspired to do," implored a statement by a group of anonymous protesters. "For the sake of the youngsters' pursuit of freedom, democracy and human rights, please understand our difficulties."

On October 4, hours after masked radicals went on a rampage, trashing railway stations and vandalizing a large number of shops and banks perceived to be Beijing-friendly in response to the newly introduced mask ban, several posts popped up on LIHKG questioning the wisdom of such moves. Someone soon offered new "guidelines" reminding comrades to trash only businesses run by gangsters, as well as government offices and offices of pro-Beijing politicians. Shops and restaurants owned by Beijing-friendly businessmen should only be "decorated" with graffiti.

"We are largely fighting for democracy and freedom, but what we are doing now appears to be attacking those who are not with us," a user wrote on LIHKG. Another said: "Only dictators are intolerant of dissenting views. What's the difference between the Communist Party and us, if we 'renovate' the stores just because their owners have a different point of view?"

Others called for the violence to be scaled back to retain international support, particularly from the United States, whose lawmakers were then planning to pass a bill that could impose diplomatic action and economic sanctions against Hong Kong supposedly to further democracy in the city.

Observers close to the ground said there was a dynamic collective restraint mechanism within the movement, which helped preserve the unity between radicals and peaceful supporters. "It's like a rubber band where they learn from each other. The radicals could lead the moderates to take a step further, while the moderates could also pull back the radicals each time they went too far," said Cheng.

But the self-restraint mechanism had weakened by October and November. A 57-year-old construction worker who confronted radicals vandalizing facilities at Ma On Shan MTR station on November 11 was torched. He suffered second-degree burns to his chest and arms, as well as head trauma. Protesters were out on the streets that day to paralyze the city's traffic after the death of student Chow Tsz-lok, who succumbed to his injuries days after he fell mysteriously from a car park near the site of a police dispersal operation in Tseung Kwan O.

By November, protesters had lost sight of their "be water" strategy too. In their clashes at Polytechnic University to bring Hong Kong to a standstill by blocking an important harbor crossing, 1,000 of them found themselves kettled on campus after a day of heavy violence.

Human rights activist Johnson Yeung Ching-yin, former convenor of the pro-democracy umbrella group Civil Human Rights Front, believed the weakened self-restraint mechanism was due partly to hardcore members moving their online discussions to encrypted channels to ensure secrecy.

"In the beginning of the movement, protesters tended to make decisions via platforms such as LIHKG and Telegram. The chosen options were bound to be relatively mild if 100,000 had voted following deliberation and compromises," said Yeung, 28. "But by October, protesters no longer relied on these popular platforms. They had formed their own groups for decision-making and by then no longer had to care about mainstream opinion."

Yeung's observation was corroborated by the shrinking number of posts on LIHKG from early November.

Another reason for the increasing radicalization was the change in the ranks of the frontliners, according to Cheng. "Some newcomers decided to join because their friends had been arrested or beaten. They are more emotionally driven," he said. Compared with earlier frontliners, they were less tactical and organized in their methods.

Victoria Hui Tin-bor, associate professor in the political science department of the University of Notre Dame in the US, said spontaneous violence was the "worst downside" of any movement lacking clear leadership.

"Spontaneous violence is really common everywhere. People get angry. It takes training to maintain non-violent discipline," she said, noting how the Occupy leaders had spent a year training its some 1,000 core supporters on non-violence. "But beyond the core, it is never easy to stop others from acting on impulse."

The cost of embracing violence

Even as authorities toughened their stance and meted out harsher reprisals against protesters, supporters were confident the movement would not peter out. Clinical psychologist Christian Chan, an associate professor at the University of Hong Kong's psychology department, said a combination of psychological factors was working to perpetuate the feeling of inter-group conflict on both sides.

"Young people perceive a visible common enemy and internalize a messianic mission of defending Hong Kong, their home. Fighting along with your band of brothers and sisters, in a clear and present danger, is inherently risky, but also inherently thrilling," he said. "Similarly, police officers are also determined to defend their comrades who were injured and assaulted. They also think that they possess the noble calling of defending Hong Kong, their home."

But Chan said the range of weapons the police had seized since the end of 2019 – including homemade bombs and explosives – warranted greater public concern. Hong Kong police handled nearly 190 explosives cases throughout the year – nearly two-thirds more than the year before – amid what they saw as an "almost unprecedented" bombing campaign.

In another troubling sign, in January 2020, police arrested 10 members of a radical anti-government group on suspicion of conspiracy to manufacture explosives and possession of explosives, drugs, and other instruments. They included two students, a kindergarten teacher, a barista and two unemployed men. All 10 were also arrested for illegal assembly during a protest rally on New Year's Day.

"The fact that there hasn't been wider concern is very dangerous because it suggests that the norm – or what is generally perceived as acceptable – is shifting. People are habituating to violence," Chan said.

He said some netizens might also mistake the expressions of

solidarity online as the rest of society supporting violence. "This is a form of heuristics that may not reflect reality; they do not realize that the voice expressed in the Reddit-like site is not necessarily an accurate representation of the society at large," he warned.

Even veteran activist Avery Ng Man-yuen of the League of Social Democrats, whose party is known for its street actions and antics, did not believe that violence was the solution. (The only "violence" Ng himself ever committed was hurling a tuna sandwich at former city leader Leung Chun-ying.) The increasing use of force would lead not only to more protesters paying a price, he said, but the movement could also be depleted if other supporters retreated out of fear they might be arrested next.

"And after all, the protesters and the force are in an asymmetrical position – officers are equipped with bullets but protesters only have bricks," he said. "Injuries eventually would be on our side."

Ng also warned that well-meaning donations of food coupons or battle gear were actually putting more protesters at risk of injury and arrest. "It's a dilemma," he said, as such efforts were equal to condoning the violence.

Pro-democracy lawmakers confessed to facing a similar Catch-22 situation. While psychologist Chan expressed disappointment with politicians and intellectuals who lacked the courage to speak out against violence, several democrats defended their reticence. They had no choice if they wanted to retain ties with the protesters and hope to be of some influence, they insisted.

Democratic Party lawmaker Lam Cheuk-ting alluded to their delicate relationship. "The hardcores might consider our situation when they mull over their next steps as long as we are in the same boat. We could still exchange views," he explained. "Once we part ways, they would no longer see us as their allies and would not consider our difficulties anymore. It could be even more dangerous."

Staying united was the only way forward, he argued, citing the camp's landslide victory in the district council elections in November as proof that the public endorsed the alliance. But another pan-democratic lawmaker, who spoke on condition of anonymity, admitted that such an approach could lead to more dangerous incidents in future. The situation was a ticking time bomb, he warned.

However, Cheng did not think the radicals had the organization or resources to be an underground resistance force, as feared by doomsayers who warned they were becoming like the Irish Republican Army. A more likely scenario, given their strategy of fluidity and unity, is that protesters' actions will wax and wane, depending on circumstances. He did not see any easy resolution ahead.

Student activist turned teacher Anna Chan said her heart ached each time she saw students risking their future to join the clashes. A year on, the young protesters still believed in a now-or-never chance to fight for their cause. Many believed this would be the denouement of their demand for democracy, and appeared to be prepared to risk everything. Chan, who has one student who is a hard-core radical, said: "I totally understand them. They fear they will regret it for the rest of their lives if they do not speak up now."

Chan confessed to feeling helpless at not being able to help them. For now, she said, she had made a pledge to herself not to shy away from difficult issues in her classes so that the Hong Kong spirit could endure. "The city needs more people with kind hearts and critical minds so one day they can change the world. I have only full love for Hongkongers and their spirit to stand up for their rights."

— With reporting by Phila Siu

The storming of Legco

Zuraidah Ibrahim and Jeffie Lam

On the anniversary of the handover, an angry crowd attacked the legislature, ransacking the chamber and issuing their demands.

July 1 has been a bittersweet day for Hong Kong for more than two decades. On that day in 1997, Britain returned the city to Chinese sovereignty. Less than 24 hours later, thousands of people braved intermittent rain to march on the city's streets, demanding democracy. Since then, the anniversary has been marked by both official celebrations and street processions, with the turnout surging or shrinking each year depending on the issues gripping Hongkongers.

In 2019, the handover anniversary arrived amid a build-up of protests against the government's extradition bill, with two massive street marches in June. As in previous years, there was a July 1 march from Victoria Park in Causeway Bay. It attracted about 550,000 people, by organizers' estimates, who took part in a largely peaceful march. But most of the action that day occurred at Tamar Park, in Admiralty, where thousands of demonstrators had gathered from the early morning. Mostly young and masked, they barricaded key roads in Admiralty and Wan Chai and clashed with police, pelting officers with corrosive substances, eggs and bottles.

In the evening, at about 9pm, a mob smashed its way into the Legislative Council building. Unchecked by police and ignoring the earlier appeals of lawmakers urging them to stop, dozens made their

69

way into the chamber where Hong Kong's legislators meet. Over several hours, they vandalized the premises, smashing official portraits, defacing the emblem of the city and spray-painting protest slogans on the walls. It was well past midnight before the last protesters left. July 1, 2019 marked the day the extradition bill protesters entered uncharted territory, ransacking an institution, pledging more confrontation and violence ahead.

City leader Carrie Lam Cheng Yuet-ngor's day began with a change of plans for the official flag-raising ceremony and singing of the national anthem, *March of the Volunteers*. The 8am event was moved indoors for the first time since 1997, ostensibly to avoid a drizzle, but the authorities were more worried protesters would interrupt and ruin the festivities. So, instead of gathering at Golden Bauhinia Square in Wan Chai, Hong Kong's top officials, dignitaries and guests made their way to the nearby Hong Kong Convention and Exhibition Centre for a muted celebration. Lam had announced the suspension of the unpopular extradition bill two weeks earlier, but protesters were not satisfied and insisted on its full withdrawal. In her anniversary speech, Lam promised to reform her style of government and improve communication with lawmakers and people from all walks of life, including young Hongkongers. She acknowledged the need to "grasp public sentiments accurately."

Over at Tamar Park, a stone's throw from government headquarters and Lam's office, the black-clads were already geared up for action. They started arriving from about 4am and, by daybreak, had erected metal and wooden barriers on roads in the area. Overnight, someone had removed the national flag from one of two flagpoles and replaced it with their protest ensign, a white bauhinia flower against a black background. As their numbers swelled through the morning, they blocked Harcourt Road, fronting the park, and nearby streets leading to the Legco building and government complex. By lunchtime, there were thousands in the area, with hundreds gathered around the Legco complex. As tension mounted, frontline protesters charged at police, who responded with pepper spray. Protesters hurled a corrosive liquid – believed to be drain cleaner – at the officers, sending 13 to hospital.

According to protesters present, there was no method to that day's mayhem. At earlier protests, participants discussed their plans in advance, using the encrypted messaging service Telegram. This time, however, decisions appeared to be taken on the fly and by small groups. At about 11.30am, a protester in a green mask called out to about 30 people at Harcourt Road: "Show your hands if you agree to escalate and go radical." Most raised their hands. Next, he asked: "Do you prefer to remain peaceful?" No hand went up. Their preference was conveyed at around noon to the larger group of about 200 near the Legco building.

Random protesters then tossed up ideas about what they should do, including suggestions to storm Legco as well as government headquarters. Most supported breaking into Legco, but there was no concrete plan on how exactly to do so. Some preferred to wait for more people to show up, as the July 1 march from Victoria Park was due to reach the area late in the afternoon. But others said no. "They said those who wanted to be peaceful would only try to stop the rest," said a 26-year-old protester who declined to be named. Some feared a delay would only allow the police to get prepared. University student Nick Yeung, 22, said: "We decided to occupy Legco and paralyze it to make the authorities face our demands." Several had concerns about the legal risks, but such worries were brushed aside. "We didn't discuss what would happen if we got arrested," Yeung said.

It was around then that some in the group found a caged metal cart, and protesters began throwing poles and scrap metal items into it. Then, as about 40 police officers watched, they wheeled the cart toward the Legco building and started bashing it against the glass walls. Holding up umbrellas to shield themselves from cameras, they rammed the cart repeatedly against the glass. Others used makeshift weapons, including metal bars and rods, to strike the glass walls. Some threw bricks at the doors of the building, while others heckled police officers inside. Shouts of *gar yau*, "add oil!," a common Cantonese refrain of encouragement, echoed through the area as protesters egged on those creating the chaos. Opposition lawmaker Leung Yiu-chung was seen trying to stop the protesters, but he was shoved aside and fell to the ground.

Others from the camp, including Roy Kwong Chun-yu and Lam Cheuk-ting, pleaded with the protesters to remain peaceful, but their appeals fell on deaf ears too. In one Telegram group with more than 20,000 members, some expressed disapproval. "What's the purpose of smashing the glass?" asked one user. Others called on the protesters to stay united, with one saying: "If we manage to storm Legco, it means we have the ability to overthrow the government. Carrie Lam has been ignoring us because she thinks we are harmless. This is meant to tell Carrie Lam, 'If you don't respond to our appeals, we will tear down your house.'"

Inside the building, about 1,000 police officers stood on guard in full riot gear. Their warnings to the protesters were drowned out. At about 6pm, Legco issued a red alert, telling everyone inside the building to leave. Outside, there appeared to be some confusion among the protesters, with some appearing unsure about whether to enter. Moments before those in front finally breached the main entrance at 9pm, some protesters tried to dissuade them from entering, shouting: "Come back! There are police inside and it's all locked down, there's no point in storming! It will just send you to jail!"

In one part of the building, radicals succeeded in smashing a glass panel, creating an opening. Elsewhere, the main entrance and another section were breached. Despite their initial hesitation, the mob soon stormed the legislature. As an air horn sounded amid the clanking of metal on metal, they poured in, pumping their fists in the air. The ransacking of Legco was about to begin. Inexplicably, the riot police inside the building retreated. The vandals made their way through several floors, trashing furniture, smashing security cameras and television monitors, and spray-painting slogans on walls.

Finally, the group entered the wood-paneled Legco chamber and began wreaking havoc, as surreal scenes of the devastation wrought by the masked intruders were broadcast live on television. Some began covering the walls and columns with graffiti that read, among other things: "Dog officials"; "Down down, Carrie Lam"; "Carrie Lam, step down"; "Release the protesters"; "We want genuine universal suffrage"; and "Hong Kong is not China." Many of these messages were familiar from the month of protests in Hong Kong. But there was a new line scrawled outside the chamber, as if to explain the day's violence: "You taught me that peaceful protests are useless."

The intruders were not done yet. As a canopy of umbrellas opened to shield the perpetrators from television cameras, some clambered over the Legco president's seat and daubed it with black paint. Their target was the emblem of Hong Kong, the symbol of the "one country, two systems" principle. They blackened the image of the bauhinia at the center and smeared paint over the words "of the People's Republic of China," leaving only "Hong Kong Special Administrative Region" untouched. They tried to hang a British colonial flag over the emblem but, failing to do so, draped it across the president's podium.

A mock funeral procession ensued, with a group holding black-and-white portraits of Carrie Lam, security minister John Lee Ka-chiu, justice minister Teresa Cheng Yeuk-wah and police commissioner Stephen Lo Wai-chung. They held up a banner that read: "There are no mobs, only tyrannical rule." Remaining in the chamber and the antechamber, a resting area for lawmakers, the protesters tore up documents, including copies of the Basic Law, Hong Kong's mini-constitution. Legco officials later reported that computer servers and hard disks had gone missing. The protesters said they had deliberately avoided damaging the library and left cash for drinks they had taken.

While the protesters succeeded in breaking into the Legco chamber, it soon became clear that they had no intention of remaining indefinitely, but had no exit strategy either. As the night wore on, there was uncertainty and confusion as some protesters urged those inside to leave. In the presence of journalists, they debated their next course of action. Four appeared determined to stay. Among them was 25-year-old graduate student Brian Leung Kai-ping. As an activist during the Occupy protests of 2014, which shut down parts of Hong Kong for 79 days, he had experienced firsthand the disappointment of seeing a movement fragment after failing to achieve its goals.

Now, in the Legco chamber, Brian Leung stood on the lawmakers' desks and read out a manifesto later dubbed the Admiralty Declaration. The list of 10 demands included a call for democratic elections to give Hongkongers the right to choose their lawmakers and chief executive. At one point, he dramatically removed his mask – becoming the only one to do so willingly throughout the protests – and shouted: "The more people are here, the safer we are. Let's stay and occupy the chamber, we can't lose anymore."

The storming of Legco played out on live television for nearly 12 hours. Leung and the last of his comrades in the chamber were finally carried out by other protesters. After issuing several warnings, about 3,000 riot police officers moved into the Legco compound and fired tear gas outside the building, but they made no arrests.

Leung fled the city the next day for the United States, where he is studying for a doctorate in political science. He said later: "The pursuit of freedom and democracy is fundamentally what drove hundreds of protesters into Legco that day. I volunteered to be in front of the camera to read out the key demands of protesters in the chamber. The last thing I wished was to have no clear demands put on the table." He had been impulsive in removing his mask, he admitted, but called it "a beautiful mistake." He said the protesters had to act to grab the attention of those in power as well as those in the movement, to register the accumulated frustrations of an unfair electoral system. "It is time to look past the short burst of 'violence', and read deeper into what people, particularly the younger generation, are really thinking," he said.

At 4am on July 2, a grim-faced Carrie Lam appeared at a press conference at police headquarters to condemn the day's violence, vowing to pursue those responsible to the end. Their actions had saddened and shocked a lot of people, she said, calling for their violence and vandalism to be condemned, as "nothing is more important than the rule of law in Hong Kong."

The trashed Legco had to be closed. It was repaired during the summer, re-opening only in October 2019. The bill for the damage: HK$40 million (US$5.1 million).

— With reporting by Alvin Lum

A night of terror in Yuen Long

Jeffie Lam

On July 21, 2019, a white-shirted mob went on a rampage attacking protesters and ordinary Hongkongers.

Before July 21, chef Calvin So Jee-leong had attended only one anti-government protest. He was among the record-breaking 2 million people who, according to organizers' estimates, braved the sweltering heat to march on June 16.

He had gone only because his friends were going, and admitted that at the time he had no strong feelings about the extradition bill protests. "All I wanted to do after a 10-hour shift in the kitchen was play video games," he recalled of his life at that time.

He was unprepared for what happened to him on the night of July 21. It was about 9.45pm when he finished work at a restaurant in Yoho Mall, a shopping center next to Yuen Long railway station, and as he headed out he noticed something unusual. He muttered aloud: "There are lots of people in white clothes here." Almost immediately, about 20 men armed with sticks and rattan canes began assaulting him. He tried to get away, but they continued raining blows on him. He dropped his smartphone as he fled, but the men chased after him and struck him several more times. So suffered severe injuries to his back, hands and legs and his shoulders swelled up. He spent three days in hospital, and was on medical leave for more than a month to recover.

It was only the morning after the attack that he learned he was

76

among more than 40 people assaulted during 45 minutes of terror, when about 100 men in white thrashed MTR passengers and members of the public at the station in northwestern Hong Kong. The masked men, believed to be triad gangsters from the area, descended on the station wielding sticks, rods and canes. Some waved Chinese national flags and placards that read: "Defend Yuen Long, defend our homeland."

As screams filled the air, they charged and struck at crowds taking the escalators, people on the platform – even passengers inside a train that stopped there. The thugs targeted people dressed in black – protesters on their way home after attending an anti-government demonstration elsewhere – but they also hit others in their way, women as well as men, including a handful of journalists and a pregnant woman. The assaults left several victims injured and bloodied, but police were nowhere to be seen. The mob attack was mostly over by the time officers showed up. The force came under intense criticism for taking so long to arrive at the scene, many accusing it of turning a blind eye to the attack or even colluding with the mob, a charge the force denied.

The events in Yuen Long that night came to be known as "the July 21 incident" and marked a turning point in public attitudes toward police. There had already been criticism of police handling of protests, with accusations of brutality by some frontline officers. But the apparent inaction of police during the attack shocked even moderates, with some saying the incident made them lose all confidence in the force. Chef So, for one, said: "Most people did not consider police a very serious problem before July 21. People only wanted to hold one or two officers accountable for brutality. But now we realize it is not a problem of one or two frontline officers. There is something wrong with the police force, and the government which insists on backing it."

After that night, So began watching live broadcasts of protesters clashing with police, and started attending protests in his free time. At work, his colleagues switched from listening to pop music in the kitchen to tuning in to the proceedings of Legislative Council meetings and press conferences.

Protests, clashes in the city, violence in Yuen Long

The Yuen Long incident occurred while anti-government protesters were locked in pitched battles with riot police in the heart of the business district on Hong Kong Island. That Sunday afternoon, organizers estimated that 430,000 people had gathered to march from Causeway Bay to Wan Chai. Most were dressed in black and wearing masks. The protesters made their way to Sai Ying Pun, where radicals on the front lines broke away and laid siege to Beijing's liaison office, throwing eggs and smearing the national emblem. It was to be a long night of clashes, with riot police firing rounds of tear gas and rubber bullets to disperse the crowd.

The trouble in Yuen Long was not entirely unexpected. From Sunday evening, word spread over social media that a crowd of suspicious-looking men wearing white T-shirts had gathered in the town, near Fung Yau Street East. Johnny Mak Ip-sing, a Yuen Long district councilor, said that he had filed a police report and had alerted a local sergeant to what he saw at about 8pm. In the city, protesters began receiving messages warning them not to get off at Yuen Long railway station if they were heading home to the New Territories. They were also advised not to wear black. At Central MTR station on Hong Kong Island, protesters left stacks of clothes of every color at the ticket machines, with written notes telling those going to Yuen Long to change out of their black protest gear.

In Yuen Long itself, a message had spread the day before, advising residents not to wear black. Villagers in the district said afterward that rural leaders advised them to avoid going out on Sunday. It emerged later that Li Jiyi, director of the Beijing liaison office's New Territories branch, had urged Yuen Long villagers to protect their towns and drive away any protesters, during a community banquet held 10 days before the attack.

As word of imminent trouble in the town spread on Sunday evening, Democratic Party lawmaker Lam Cheuk-ting, who was at the protest on Hong Kong Island, decided to leave for the New Territories. He made his way to Mei Foo station, a mid-point between Hong Kong and New Territories West, a short distance from Yuen Long. Not long after arriving at Mei Foo, one of his companions received a video clip showing chef So being attacked. He got on a train heading for Yuen Long. "I called a police community relations officer at 10.22pm asking him to stop the attack, and was told that plainclothes officers had already been deployed," Lam recalled afterward. "I also urged him to keep an eye on Long Ping and Yuen Long railway stations and he promised to pass the message to his seniors."

The moment the train doors opened at Yuen Long station, Lam heard a young man crying out for help. He was shocked by the scene unfolding before his eyes. The white-clad mob was beating anyone they came across with rods and rattan canes. There was blood on the floor, and broken sticks scattered everywhere. As the attackers charged into the paid area of the station, alarmed passengers yelled: "Don't come in!" People tried protecting themselves with unfurled umbrellas, and grabbed children to shelter them. Some called out to others to avoid provoking the uncontrollable mob, as a group chanted defiantly at their attackers. A few tried to fight back using a fire hose and an extinguisher from the station, but they were overwhelmed as the white shirts stormed toward the platform.

Passengers inside the train began screaming as they realized what was happening. The attackers struck the passengers for about 10 minutes. Video footage, captured by others in the carriage using smartphones, showed a man kneeling at the train door, imploring the mob to stop.

Women were seen standing on their seats, pleading for mercy.

"Please don't beat us, I beg you," one woman cried out.

"I'm only trying to head home after a day's work," said another.

"We are just civilians," cried a third woman.

Then the MTR made an announcement declaring services suspended and asking everyone to leave the train. But people refused to leave, fearing they would be attacked on the platform, where there were more men wearing white, armed and masked. It was past 11pm when the train driver, responding to passengers' pleas for help, pulled away from the platform once the doors could close. The railway operator explained later that initially the driver could not see what was happening and was only aware that the doors were blocked.

Video clips began circulating online and on television, showing the chaos as frightened passengers scrambled for cover. Lawmaker Lam, who posted live video footage over Facebook, was also attacked and needed 18 stitches for injuries to his mouth. Throughout the entire ordeal, police did not show up. Vincent Lo, a fourth-year university student, said that at about 10.30pm he saw a large crowd of armed, white-clad men outside the station and called 999. "The officer noted my request coldly and, only when I asked, said police would arrive in 10 to 15 minutes," he recalled afterward. "That, to me, seemed too long. It was totally unreasonable that they arrived only at 11.20pm."

Other witnesses, as well as the management of Yoho Mall, which is linked to the station, said they tried to call but could not get through to police. The force explained later that its New Territories North call center was overwhelmed by hundreds of emergency calls between 10pm and midnight that day. Responding to criticism of the force, then police commissioner Stephen Lo Wai-chung said two officers arrived at the station at 10.52pm, seven minutes after they received a report about the violence, but they called for reinforcements when they realized that they did not have enough protective gear. The force was mocked when a photograph showing two officers walking away from the scene of violence and chaos was shared widely.

A police source defended the officers' actions, saying several weeks of mass rallies and protest violence had put a serious strain on the force's manpower and resources. To deal with that Sunday's mass march on Hong Kong Island, he said, all five police regions had to send manpower to help. He said there was a series of emergencies happening in Yuen Long at the same time that evening, and the district police did not have the resources to deal with them all. When violence broke out at the train station, officers from the Emergency Unit, whose vehicles are equipped with anti-riot gear, were dealing with other incidents such as fights, assaults and a fire in the district. More than 500 officers from a regional response contingent, who were in the midst of clearing protesters in Sheung Wan, Hong Kong Island, had to be redeployed to Yuen Long.

When more than 30 officers finally arrived at the scene, it was 11.20pm and most of the thugs in white were gone. "I saw a lot of people in white shirts running right past police, and they did not even stop them," a witness said. An angry crowd, joined by local residents who had rushed out after finding out about the violence on the news, surrounded the officers. Some hurled profanities at the officers, while others shouted: "Where have you been? You are supposed to protect us. Why are you allowing those men to leave so easily?" Police's explanation was that the officers did not see anyone breaking the law when they arrived and could not arrest people just because of the color of their clothes.

A second round of violence occurred at about midnight, after more than 200 people confronted a group of men in white who had gathered near the entrance of Nam Pin Wai, a village next to Yuen Long station. Police officers soon arrived to investigate. Some of the men in white retaliated by throwing various objects at dozens of protesters standing on the staircases outside the station exit. The alarmed protesters were forced to retreat into the station, where they banged desperately on the window of the station's control room, urging MTR employees to shut the gate of the exit. The staff eventually did so. About two dozen of the white-clad men then appeared at the gate, forced open the shutters and rushed into the station. The trapped protesters fled toward Yoho Mall through another exit, but those who could not get away quickly enough were attacked. Once again, there were no police officers in the station when the white gang struck.

Meanwhile, some white-clad men emerged from Nam Pin Wai and chased a group of protesters down a street. A man wearing a dark shirt was seen being hit over the head with sticks, resulting in bloody injuries. Several white-clad men armed with clubs smashed several cars, whose drivers had come to pick up protesters and other train passengers stranded in the area. At 1am, a team of about 100 riot police officers went to the village, where many men in white were gathered, but again no arrests were made. Police said they did not find any weapons or come across anything suspicious.

The Yuen Long incident remained a sore point for months afterward, with angry protesters gathering at the scene on the 21st of every month to criticize the police response that day and demand an independent probe into the force's handling of events. The Independent Commission Against Corruption, the city's graft-buster, began investigating whether any police officer was guilty of misconduct.

Questions lingered over the mob in white. Pro-establishment lawmaker Junius Ho Kwan-yiu found himself in hot water when a video clip showing him shaking hands with men in white T-shirts in Yuen Long that Sunday night circulated widely online. Speaking to the media the following day, Ho enraged many when he defended the mob involved in the attack, saying they were merely "defending their home and people." As for the men he was seen shaking hands with, he said: "Some of them I know, some are village chiefs, teachers, shop owners and car mechanics." He said that it was just a coincidence that he happened to be in the neighborhood. "I live in Yuen Long, so it is normal for me to be there," he said. Ho denied that he had known about the attack in advance or that he had any role in it. Instead, he accused lawmaker Lam of "leading protesters to Yuen Long."

Over the days that followed, police arrested a total of 37 people – some with links to triads – for their alleged roles in the violence. As of January 2020, seven had been charged with rioting. Months after the event, police said they were still collecting evidence. Despite the arrests, lawmaker Lam was unsatisfied that none of those charged was believed to have organized the violence. He and seven other victims, including chef So, filed a lawsuit against the police commissioner, seeking a total of HK$2.7 million (US$350,000) in compensation. Lam said the Yuen Long attack proved a watershed for the protest movement. Accusing the police of colluding with the gangsters that day, he said: "They have lost their credibility." The distrust fueled a worrying trend of vigilantism, he noted, as protesters involved in clashes with rival groups began preferring to "resolve matters privately." "They used to ask lawmakers to mediate and reported to police only if disputes could not be solved, but not after July 21," he claimed.

Police chief Lo categorically denied the suggestion of collusion between his officers and the Yuen Long attackers, but the force was put on the defensive. Senior Superintendent Kelvin Kong Wing-cheung said in January 2020 that the trouble that night was caused by "a group of people who led some protesters to Yuen Long." But who were they, what did they want, and who was behind them? Those questions remained unanswered, continuing to provide protesters and opposition lawmakers alike political grist for criticism of the police force.

The white-shirt attack also affected residents in the area for months afterward, with people preferring not to stay out late at night and businesses reporting that they were hit too. A popular beef brisket restaurant in the area claimed that its monthly revenues were halved in the wake of the incident. "We used to target diners who return late from work, but now many choose not to eat out and head home as early as they can," its owner, surnamed Hui, said. "Who is to blame for the fear?"

— With reporting by Clifford Lo and Natalie Wong

The takeover of Hong Kong's airport

Victor Ting

For five days in August, the city's international airport, which has won the best airport title over 75 times, was crippled by a protest sit-in that ended in fisticuffs, tear gas and arrests.

I n August 2019, Jack Lo sat for three days with thousands of others on the floor of the arrivals hall at Hong Kong International Airport, one of the world's busiest aviation hubs.

The self-professed radical protester, 17, was exhausted from waving anti-government placards, handing out fliers and trying to explain to foreign visitors what Hong Kong's anti-government demonstrations were about. He was also frustrated that despite the inconvenience, most travelers came and went, seemingly unaffected and indifferent. The government also appeared unmoved. And now there were rumors swirling that riot police were preparing to swoop in on the airport and clear out the protesters. On Monday, August 12, his fourth day there, Lo was impatient for real action that would make people around the world sit up and take notice. The way to do that, he was convinced, was for the protesters to move to the departure area and stop travelers from leaving. Lo thought to himself: "It's now or never."

He shared his views with the group of about 20 protesters around him, saying: "The clock is ticking. There is not a moment to waste." Not everyone agreed that drastic action would work. Some asked, what if they only ended up alienating the international community? Lo held his ground, saying: "To have an effect, protests need to be disruptive and cause discomfort to some people and the status quo. We must up the ante and strike now, or we might as well pack up and go home."

In his corner of the airport terminal, Lo succeeded in persuading his group. At 3pm that day, he led his squad to join thousands of other black-clad demonstrators who swarmed across the departure area, blocking distressed passengers and airline crew alike. The Airport Authority canceled all outgoing flights after 4.30pm. News of the chaos at Hong Kong's airport, which generally handled 800 flights daily, swept across the world.

The airport first featured in Hong Kong's protests on July 26, when hundreds of flight attendants and airport staff staged a sit-in at the arrivals hall. They wanted visitors to know what happened at the Yuen Long MTR station on July 21, when scores of white-clad men believed to have triad connections attacked train passengers and black-clad protesters wantonly, with police nowhere in sight. That protest passed peacefully.

On August 5, more than 200 flights were canceled when a record number of pilots, airport ground staff and other aviation industry workers called in sick and joined a citywide strike to press for the movement's five demands, which included an independent probe into allegations of police brutality, as well as universal suffrage for Hongkongers. On Friday, August 9, Lo and thousands of others showed up at the airport for what was meant to be a three-day sit-in.

Hong Kong's anti-government protests were in their third month, and elsewhere in the city, the weekend of August 10 and 11 witnessed some of the most violent clashes between hard-core radicals and police. As mobs rampaged across parts of Tsim Sha Tsui, Sham Shui Po, Wan Chai and Kwai Chung on Sunday, August 11, police responded with tougher tactics. That day, a young woman in the crowd at Tsim Sha Tsui was injured in the right eye, and protesters said she was hit by a beanbag round fired by officers. Police refused to take the blame before investigations were carried out, suggesting that she might have been hit by a projectile from a protester's catapult. A photograph of the woman, with a bloodied patch over her right eye, rapidly became a symbol of alleged police brutality.

The airport sit-in should have ended that Sunday, but news of the woman's injury sparked anger against police and moved tens of thousands of protesters to head for the airport on Monday and Tuesday, August 12 and 13. Many arrived on foot, bringing traffic along nearby roads to a standstill. Several wore eye patches, showing their solidarity with the injured woman. The worst of the airport chaos followed, especially after protesters occupied the departure areas. On Monday alone, more than 180 departures were canceled after 4pm with the airport hoping to resume flights from 6am on Tuesday.

But more disruption followed, effectively shutting down the airport for a second day. The impact was severe, with 421 flights axed. The airport unrest led to the cancelation of a total of 979 flights. Tens of thousands of travelers were stranded, and many were furious at having to scramble for accommodation or make alternative travel arrangements.

Some angry travelers accused demonstrators of acting "like the mafia." Pavol Cacara, 51, from Slovakia, tried reasoning with some of those blocking travelers, but they shrugged him off. "They are turning public opinion against them," he said. "Is it right to take away the freedom of someone else, when they are trying to fight for their freedom?"

Australian Helina Marshall burst into tears when her group of five could not leave. She said: "We have an old lady here, 84 years old, and she has heart problems. They can't let her through, to go back home?" Her elderly companion, Barbara Hill, in a wheelchair, said: "I was sympathetic to their cause, but I think they are harming it by stopping passengers from getting through." A Thai woman, comforting her son, ticked off protesters, saying: "You can fight with your government, but not me, understand? I just want to go home! We pay money to come to your country but you do this to us. We will never come here again!"

A few travelers made it through the blockade, including pregnant women and an official Hong Kong team of swimmers heading to Singapore for the FINA World Cup competition. Swimmer Leo Fung pleaded with protesters, saying: "We understand and support what you are doing, but we have qualified and hope to represent Hong Kong at the World Cup. There aren't that many competition opportunities like this, and I hope you will let us through."

Looking back on all that happened at the airport, protester Lo said in February 2020 that he had no regrets. "We were trying to get travelers around the world on our side, and at that point we needed a more radical course of action to grab international headlines, and we succeeded in doing that," he said. Far from being apologetic for the inconvenience and damage done to Hong Kong's international reputation, he said: "The airport occupation was a logical and natural progression from road blockades and rail disruption at MTR stations. They were all disruptive, but made a point."

Mainland officials watching the increased violence on Hong Kong streets and the shutdown of the airport said it bordered on terrorism. Up until then, Hong Kong's social movement had received scant coverage in mainland media. But two incidents of violence at the airport on August 13 – when two men wrongly suspected of being undercover state agents were assaulted – unleashed a storm of anger on the mainland against Hong Kong protesters.

The first man, Xu Jinyang, was surrounded and attacked twice, at 7pm and again at 9pm, after a group of protesters found wooden sticks on him and claimed that the name on his travel documents matched that of an officer from the Futian police station in Shenzhen. The young man told reporters he was from Shenzhen and was at the airport to see off friends who were traveling. He denied he was a public security officer. Protesters surrounded him, secured his hands with cable ties, and would not let paramedics move him after he lost consciousness at about 10pm. It was another hour before he was taken to hospital by ambulance, but there was more trouble outside the terminal as protesters turned on police who had come to help the ambulance leave. Police vehicles were attacked, their windows smashed.

After Xu was taken away, hundreds of protesters surrounded another mainlander inside the terminal, cable-tying his hands to a luggage trolley. They had found a light blue T-shirt in his backpack emblazoned with the slogan "I love HK police." Only the previous week, on August 5, a mob wearing T-shirts bearing the same message had attacked protesters with sticks. Despite being detained, the man, later identified as Fu Guohao, smiled and calmly told the mob in English and Cantonese: "I support Hong Kong police. You can beat me now." Enraged, one protester poured fluid from a bottle over his head, while others punched, kicked and hit him with umbrellas. Fu turned out to be a journalist for the Chinese nationalist tabloid *Global Times*.

At the scene was lawmaker Fernando Cheung Chiu-hung, from the pan-democratic Labour Party. He had shown up to try and mediate between the protesters and police. As Fu was being attacked, Cheung urged the angry crowd to stop the violence, but they ignored him. Fu's ordeal lasted about an hour before he was rescued by dozens of riot police and taken away by ambulance at about 12.30am with scratches on his face.

Recalling that day's chaos, Cheung said in February 2020 that he thought the airport occupation was a good tactic to force the government's hand. "And if the government took a wrong step, it would be a global humiliation and blunt their legitimacy to govern. I went there expecting to prevent aggressive police action," he said. "When I got there ... tempers were frayed and the air was thick with tension ... Of course, as a believer in peaceful protests, I don't agree with violence. But I can understand why the protesters were angry and did what they did."

The events at the airport that night brought police into the terminal building. Officers were seen rushing in and subduing some protesters, with injuries reported on both sides. In a late-night chase that lasted about 15 minutes, protesters threw bins and water bottles at police from behind barricades fortified by baggage trolleys, while officers used batons and pepper spray on them. At one point, some protesters grabbed an officer's baton and began striking him with it. He responded by drawing his gun and pointing it at them, an act criticized by protesters as being disproportionate and dangerous, but defended vigorously by police as an appropriate act of self-defense.

On the mainland, it was the attack on journalist Fu that drew the biggest response. Chinese social media was awash with vitriol against Hong Kong's protesters and praise for Fu, who was hailed as a hero for standing up to his attackers. The hashtags "Fu Guohao is a real man" and "I also support Hong Kong police" spread like wildfire on Weibo, China's largest social media network. "The injuries on his face reflect the injuries in the hearts of all Chinese people," read one of the most popular comments. Another asked: "How many Chinese will have sleepless nights? Our state power should take action now!" Fu's provocative challenge to the protesters – "You can beat me now" – was even immortalized on a T-shirt, which sold for 98 yuan on online shopping platform Taobao.

The Hong Kong protests, which had been off-limits and a heavily censored topic on Chinese social media, suddenly burst into the open, amplified further by the mainland's mainstream media. *People's Daily*, the Communist Party's mouthpiece, praised Fu's "manliness" and said in a Weibo post shared widely: "Let's remember Fu Guohao and his awe-inspiring righteousness while being held. This is what a dignified and upright Chinese should be like." The two mainland men attacked at the airport were discharged from hospital the day after. Fu told supporters as he left the hospital: "In Hong Kong, I complied with everything a citizen should do. I didn't do anything unlawful or behave in a way that would stir controversy. I think I should not be treated violently."

Reflecting on the outpouring of emotion on the mainland, lawmaker Cheung said: "I read some of those comments online and thought there was palpable anger in some unfamiliar quarters, not just the usual nationalist types. The effect was certainly to turn or silence those originally sympathetic to the protests. The Fu incident definitely showed that the propaganda machine went into overdrive to whip up nationalist fervor."

As protesters and police clashed at the terminal building on August 13, the Airport Authority went to the High Court and obtained an interim injunction to ban unlawful and wilful obstruction of the proper use of the airport as well as the roads and passageways nearby. It prohibited people from "inciting, aiding and/or abetting" such acts, and confined any demonstrations to two designated areas at either end of the arrivals hall. Flouting the injunction would amount to the criminal offense of contempt of court, with a penalty of a jail term and fine. The injunction was the first in the ongoing anti-government protests, and drew some criticism as an abuse of the legal process.

But Victor Dawes, the Airport Authority's lead counsel, who had the order extended indefinitely a week later, said: "An injunction, unlike the by-laws of the Airport Authority, carries with it the express authority of the courts, and therefore may command higher respect and compliance among the general public." He rejected the suggestion that this was an abuse of the law, saying protesters or other relevant groups could argue their case in court. No legal challenge was filed.

Others, including businesses, welcomed the move. The Hong Kong General Chamber of Commerce, the city's largest business group, supported the airport's injunction application to boot out protesters.

"Left unaddressed, the closure of the airport would have seriously tarnished Hong Kong's reputation and role as an air transport hub for the region," it said.

The five days of the airport occupation ended on Tuesday, August 13. The next day, hundreds of protesters were back, this time to say sorry for causing the flight cancellations and inconvenience to travelers. A hand-written sign, one of many with similar messages, said: "Dear tourists, we are deeply sorry about what happened yesterday. We were desperate and made imperfect decisions. Please accept our apology."

There were no references to the two mainlanders who were attacked, but a statement issued by "a group of fellow Hongkongers longing for freedom and democracy" said the overreaction of some protesters left them feeling heartbroken and helpless.

The administration team of the Telegram encrypted messaging group for the airport sit-in, which had close to 40,000 members, posted a message too, saying: "What happened on Tuesday is not perfect, but it does not mean that the sit-in is officially terminated. What we need to do now is to look forward, to maintain confidence in ourselves and our peers, to reflect on our deeds, and to believe that we will perform better next time." Internet users had fierce debates on the LIHKG online forum – the de facto virtual command center of the protest movement – with some saying they should reflect on their strategies to win back public support. At the airport, protester Spencer Ho, 39, a salesman, distributed food to passengers. A placard on his trolley read: "We were desperate. Please accept our apology."

Looking back at the airport protests, lawmaker Cheung said: "It was definitely a watershed moment because radical protesters felt more able to push the envelope afterward and see how much they could get away with." He said the protesters' motto to stay united with the more extreme elements within the movement also sowed the seeds for more violence to come.

After Wednesday, August 14, few protesters continued to stay at the airport while others moved their battlefield to nearby towns like Tung Chung over the next few weekends. Over the weekends that followed, they tried to block access routes to the airport, including throwing rods and metal objects at the railway tracks of its express train line. On September 1, travelers were stranded for hours at the airport or forced to lug their suitcases and walk at least 15km on a highway to find transport into the city. Protesters tried the same tactics again in subsequent weeks, but with little success.

To date, the airport remains a tightly controlled facility with passengers required to present their boarding pass at barricaded entrances, their family and friends generally barred from entering the building.

But while the protests there came to an end, Lo dismissed the suggestion that occupying the terminal building was a failure. "Victory comes in many ways, shapes and forms," he said, adding that the episode taught the movement to harness its firepower and hone its mobilization skills for other action, including the occupation of the Polytechnic University campus in November 2019. "We can lose one battle to win the war. We are in this for the long haul," he said.

October 1: Celebrations in the capital, clashes in the city

Jeffie Lam

A red-letter day in the nation sparked a violent chain of protests culminating in a shooting of a radical teenager.

From his rostrum at Beijing's Gate of Heavenly Peace, President Xi Jinping stood ready for the ceremonies to mark the 70th anniversary of communist rule. Hundreds of millions watched on television or online what was described as the grandest military parade in the history of the People's Republic of China, at the very spot where Mao Zedong stood when he declared the founding of the republic on October 1, 1949. Xi was flanked by his predecessors, Jiang Zemin and Hu Jintao, as he delivered a short speech praising the accomplishments of the Chinese people over seven decades and pledging to achieve his "Chinese dream" of national rejuvenation and global prominence. "No force can shake the status of our great country, no force can stop the Chinese people and the Chinese nation from marching forward," he declared.

Among the guests was a smiling Carrie Lam Cheng Yuet-ngor, Hong Kong's embattled chief executive, leading a delegation of more than 240 government advisers, professionals, pro-establishment lawmakers and businessmen. In his message, Xi said that China must uphold the principle of "one country, two systems" that promises a high degree of autonomy to Hong Kong while preserving its freedoms and unique way of life following its return to Chinese rule. Also present was Fanny Law Fan Chiu-fan, one of Lam's advisers in the Executive

Council. She was impressed by the patriotism of young Chinese at the military parade. "So many young people in the parade are wearing big smiles and chanting 'Long live our country'," she gushed. "I look forward to the day when young people in Hong Kong join the National Day Celebration with the same pride, joy and optimism."

Around the same time in Hong Kong, however, the scene could not have been more different, as defiant young people had other ideas for October 1, 2019. On social media, the hashtag #NotMyNationalDay caught fire among Hongkongers who branded it a day of mourning. The national flag flew on government buildings and at Beijing-friendly conglomerates and associations, but there were signs of impending trouble from the morning. The official flag-raising proceeded at Golden Bauhinia Square in Wan Chai, but government officials and hundreds of guests moved indoors to watch the ceremony on screens at the nearby Hong Kong Convention and Exhibition Centre. The streets near popular tourist spots were empty, shopping malls stayed closed and eight major MTR stations were shut by 11am.

Crowds defied a police ban of a "national grief" march planned by the Civil Human Rights Front and began gathering in Causeway Bay just before noon. Many shouted one of the popular slogans: "Fight for freedom, stand with Hong Kong!" Tens of thousands of black-clad protesters waged guerilla-style battles across the city, with masked mobs attacking police with bricks, petrol bombs, acid bombs and sticks. They set fire to the national flag and burned portraits of Xi and Lam, while spray-painting the gates of state-owned banks with slogans such as "Happy crack-up of 'Chee-na'" – a derogatory name for China.

Police responded with tear gas and rubber bullets. At Wong Tai Sin in Kowloon, officers fired volleys of tear gas after 2pm to disperse protesters who tried to blockade a main road. There were pitched battles at Tuen Mun, in the New Territories, as protesters hurled umbrellas and various projectiles at police, who chased after the crowd with their batons. The force later condemned their actions, noting how officers had been surrounded by "a large group of rioters" who attacked them with bricks and other hard objects. "The rioters later threw corrosive fluid onto the people at scene, causing burn injuries to the officers and reporters," the police said.

The fighting was more vicious and intense than in previous days, with the most serious clashes breaking out at about 4pm near Tai Ho Road in Tsuen Wan, in the western part of the New Territories. For the first time in more than four months of anti-government demonstrations, a protester was shot after a police officer was attacked by a mob.

Video footage showed a group of black-clad protesters ambushing and chasing after the officer, who was alone after being separated from his colleagues. The officer fled, holding on to his protective shield, but he fell. The mob began raining blows on him immediately, with at least one protester seen wielding a hammer, while another waved a wrench.

A second officer then ran over to rescue his stricken colleague, but he was stopped by two protesters armed with rods. The officer pointed his service revolver and shouted a warning at the group attacking the man on the ground. When a protester swung at him with a rod, the officer opened fire, hitting his assailant in the chest. Another masked radical lunged forward, but was immediately tackled to the ground and subdued.

Bleeding from the chest, the protester who had been shot called out his Hong Kong identity card number and name. He was Tsang Chi-kin, an 18-year-old Form Five student. "My chest hurts a lot, I need to go to the hospital," he said.

By evening, clashes had erupted in at least 12 districts across Hong Kong. Protesters hurled petrol bombs, which started fires on roads, trashed shops and banks linked to the mainland and vandalized government buildings and the offices of pro-establishment politicians. In Mong Kok, police fired warning shots in the air twice after a mob assaulted an officer who had fallen to the ground.

Apart from the shooting of Tsang, police also fired five live rounds as warning shots that day, as well as 1,400 rounds of tear gas, 900 rubber bullets, 190 beanbag rounds and 230 sponge grenades. The force said that 30 officers had been injured, and about 100 petrol bombs had been hurled. A total of 269 people aged between 12 and 71 were arrested that day.

Instead of concern over the mounting violence on all sides, Tsang's shooting unleashed and concentrated anger at police, sparking a new wave of fiery protests. Critics demanded to know why the officer had shot the teenager in the chest instead of firing a warning shot in the air or aiming at his limbs instead. Students and alumni from the teenager's school, the Tsuen Wan Public Ho Chuen Yiu Memorial College, staged a sit-in outside the campus the next day, accusing the officer who shot him of "attempted murder," and demanding an explanation for what happened.

Elsewhere, among office workers at a lunchtime protest in Central was Kathy Chau, 26, an employee of a multinational financial firm who backed the movement. "Doing the right thing is more important than worrying about what my boss or colleagues think of me," she said at the time. Chau felt that she had to support the protest because the bullet had hit Tsang just centimeters from his heart. "We have been seeing an escalation in police abuse of power over the past few months," she said.

Civil Rights Observer member Icarus Wong Ho-yin wanted police to explain why the officer who came to the aid of his colleague under attack did not use rubber bullets or beanbag rounds instead. The officer had a rifle in his left hand, presumably loaded with non-lethal ammunition, but arrived pointing his service revolver at the mob. "When an officer deliberately skips the step of using rubber bullets or beanbag rounds, there ought to be a comprehensive review to see if excessive force was used or if his action was not aligned with police guidelines," Wong said. He also said police commanders were responsible for ensuring that their officers did not end up being isolated during such confrontations.

In a joint statement, 24 opposition lawmakers condemned police for unnecessarily escalating the use of force and using deadly live ammunition. It said: "The policeman's close-range shooting seems to be an attack rather than an act of self-defence."

Defending the officer involved, then police commissioner Stephen Lo Wai-chung said the shooting was a "reasonable and lawful" use of lethal force under extreme circumstances. Lo, who retired in November 2019, reminded critics that officers at the scene did not start the confrontation and were the ones attacked by radicals armed with hammers, rods and petrol bombs. The National Day protest was "one of Hong Kong's most violent and chaotic days," he said.

Chief Superintendent John Tse Chun-chung questioned whether the force's critics were qualified to comment when they had not been trained in the use of firearms. "They are letting their emotions override logic," the force's chief spokesman said, pointing out that critics chose to ignore the fact that one officer was under fierce attack when the second fired his revolver. He urged people to stop smearing the force.

China's state media defended the police action in the shooting incident, with a Xinhua commentary calling it "totally legal, legitimate and appropriate." Tsang underwent surgery to remove the bullet from his chest. He was still in hospital when he was charged with one count of rioting – which carries a maximum sentence of 10 years in jail – and two counts of assaulting a police officer, an offense punishable by up to six months' jail and a HK$5,000 (US$645) fine. At the time of publication, Tsang was still awaiting trial.

The violent National Day protests led city leader Lam to invoke draconian emergency powers over the following days to ban the use of face masks. She said the ban was necessary because almost all of the protesters who were involved in vandalism and violence covered their faces and became more daring when they concealed their identity. The ban on masks took effect on October 5, but protesters ignored it. In November, it was struck down by a Hong Kong court. After much legal wrangling, in April 2020, the Court of Appeal ruled that the government had a right to ban the wearing of masks at unauthorized or illegal assemblies but not for approved demonstrations. Ironically for the government, by then, the Covid-19 pandemic had made masks ubiquitous in the city, with some medical professionals even calling for them to be mandatory.

Hong Kong now awaits whether future October 1 celebrations will spark similar attempts by protesters to spoil the party.

Campus battlegrounds: Five days that changed Chinese University

Sum Lok-kei and Andrew Raine

A protester's mysterious fall from a building unleashed a wave of violence that turned university campuses into fiery warzones.

Nobody could be sure of the events that led to the death of Chow Tsz-lok. The only certainty was that afterward things would never be the same.

The 22-year-old was a quiet, unassuming computer science undergraduate, whose main preoccupations in life were solving math problems, playing basketball and planning a holiday to Japan, according to his friends.

On the morning of Sunday, November 4, 2019, few could have guessed he would soon be dead under murky, unexplained circumstances – and fewer still that his death would be the spark that set a city on fire.

It is unclear what Chow, a student at the Hong Kong University of Science and Technology (HKUST), had been doing that Sunday evening when he fell from the third floor of a car park in Tseung Kwan O. Surveillance cameras recorded him wandering alone, but did not capture his fall. And since he fell into a coma from which he never recovered, his account of what happened will never be known.

Still, rumors provided an incendiary narrative the cameras could not disprove. They linked Chow's fall to a clash between anti-government protesters and police at the nearby Crowne Plaza hotel, where demonstrators had gatecrashed a police officer's wedding to disrupt the celebrations before being chased through the streets – and some into the car park – by riot squads firing tear gas.

To this day, no evidence has emerged to place Chow among the group. But in the cauldron that was Hong Kong as the city entered its sixth month of civil unrest, even the suggestion was enough to bring matters to a boil. Over the following week, as rumors spread that the comatose student had been pushed by police, or that officers had blocked paramedics from treating him, the mention of his name was enough to bring protesters to the streets.

And by the time on Friday that a teary HKUST president Wei Shyy announced Chow's death to students at a graduation ceremony, the news left students reeling in shock, grief and anger.

Venting their rage, protesters in the student community rampaged through the campus, leaving chaos in their wake. They trashed cafeterias, a Starbucks outlet and a Bank of China branch and vandalized the president's residence.

Then the violence spread to the city, as confrontations with police broke out across districts. Both sides were up for the fight. In Tuen Mun, a riot officer taunted an angry horde: "Come and take revenge on us, cockroaches! We are opening a bottle of champagne to celebrate tonight!"

It was a gauntlet the radicals readily accepted. At first light on Monday they launched "Operation Dawn," one of their most audacious plans yet to wreak havoc. The two-pronged action was an attempt to paralyze the city through widespread traffic disruption and a general strike, but it soon spiraled out of control.

In the morning, a traffic police officer shot a live round into a 21-year-old student's torso; in the afternoon, a protester splashed flammable liquid on a man he had been arguing with and set him alight.

Hong Kong was catching fire, and the world could only watch in disbelief.

Day 1: A new arena, 'rioters' university'

While much of the media's attention was focused on the chaos unfolding on the streets, a profound shift was taking place in the protesters' tactics.

Until now, demonstrations had taken place mostly in the public arena; places like streets, parks, shopping malls and MTR stations – locations that were good for getting their voices heard, but hard to thwart one of Asia's best-trained police forces. But what if protesters were to redraw the front lines and occupy property they could claim as their own?

Protesters descended en masse upon university campuses across the city and dug themselves in, blocking nearby roads and train services, starting fires and vandalizing property. It was as if they had turned the words of the Tuen Mun riot officer on their head. Celebration time for the "popo" – their name for the police – was their moment for mourning and revenge, they seemed to be saying.

As Ma Ngok, a political scientist at Chinese University (CUHK), one of the campuses the students had occupied, explained: "In the past [the protests] were all about making your voice heard on the streets, but now protesters were trying to defend against physical intrusion. Such militancy had never before been seen in Hong Kong's history."

With protesters vowing never to give in, many feared Hong Kong was hurtling toward a modern-day Tiananmen moment of a violent confrontation between students and the powers-that-be. And nowhere were those fears greater than at CUHK.

Set in lush green hills and woodlands covering 137 hectares of Hong Kong's bucolic New Territories, CUHK's campus might not have looked like a plausible setting for an end-of-days-style showdown, but the university has a history of being a hotbed of student activism that stretches back to its founding in 1963.

And that history is a matter of some pride to many of its 20,000 students; when someone maliciously renamed it "rioters' university" on a Google map in June, many of them took it as a compliment.

Apparently eager to burnish that reputation, at about the same time that the traffic officer was discharging his gun at a student 20km away in Sai Wan Ho, black-clad radicals at CUHK began to cross the campus's No 2 Bridge. They did not know it at the time, but it would be there, over the next five days, that some of their heaviest fights would occur.

A bridge too far?

The bridge was important to protesters because it spans the Tolo Highway, a public road, and the tracks of the East Rail line train service. By throwing debris down from above they could force the closure of two major transport routes.

The bridge also held symbolic value because, even though it is above public arteries, it was the property of the university. Police could not take it from them without entering the campus – a move that would represent an escalation that no one was certain the force would be willing to make.

It soon became crystal clear that it was. Police swept into the campus shortly after 8am when they saw radicals throwing debris onto the rail tracks. They occupied the bridge and set up a defensive perimeter around it, facing off with the mobs who responded by creating their own defensive line out of scrap metal, bricks and hurdles from the sports hall. Each side demanded that the other leave.

Meanwhile, at the other end of the university at the Tai Po Road entrance, another group of officers engaged protesters armed with bricks and petrol bombs. For the first time ever, shortly before noon, they fired tear gas onto the campus of a Hong Kong university. The radicals responded by fanning out to guard the entrance, shielding themselves with umbrellas.

With battle lines now established on two fronts, the fighting intensified, as black-clads hurled petrol bombs and bricks while police fired back with more than 100 rounds of tear gas, sponge grenades, rubber bullets and beanbag rounds.

By nightfall, five protesters had been arrested and there was a pause in hostilities as both sides regrouped. But nobody thought it would be the end of the matter. In the minds of many protesters, students and alumni among them, a Rubicon had been crossed.

"This is our campus," said Kajal, 20, an Indian-born full-time student who had helped to supply frontline protesters with water, food and pliers. "Police entered without permission or a warrant. It is unjust."

The force insisted that its actions were legal, questioning how many of the protesters were actually students. "Are they CUHK students? I hope not," said Chief Superintendent Kelvin Kong Wing-cheung. "They threw petrol bombs and objects at officers. No university campuses should be havens for criminals."

Day 2: The Hunger Games begin

Shocking though the scenes from day 1 were, it was on day 2 that the campus truly descended from a seat of higher learning into a hellish, smoking battleground.

While police maintained their presence on Bridge No 2 overnight, the protesters camped out on the university's sports field, where they began building a makeshift arsenal that was likened by many observers to the dystopian scenes of the movie *The Hunger Games*.

Chainsaws and javelins, as well as bows and arrows were repurposed as weapons and a sports field was converted into a firing range where the radicals could practise hurling petrol bombs, fine-tuning their aim and honing their techniques using dummy bottles filled with water. Soccer posts were ripped out and turned into roadblocks. Everything was now either a weapon or a tool of resistance.

News bulletin images of the previous day's clashes acted as a recruitment message, helping to swell the radicals' ranks with a steady stream of volunteers arriving throughout the morning.

Realizing that they needed to feed their growing army, the black-clads took over an unstaffed canteen and began to prepare meals. Out went the school dinner-style menu of white rice, sausages and eggs and in came an improvised, expanded repertoire based on fresh food donated by supporters, many of whom stuck around to cook, wash up and do the laundry.

Amid such surreal scenes, increasingly horrified university staff made the first of two ill-fated attempts to broker a truce. Vice-president Dennis Ng Kee-pui succeeded in getting police to retreat slightly at about 3pm, but hopes of a breakthrough were soon dashed.

The mobs seized the moment, lobbing petrol bombs and bricks as they charged toward the retreating force. They ran straight into a hail of rubber bullets and tear gas that stopped them in their tracks, injuring many and eventually forcing them to retreat deep into the campus to regroup and tend to the wounded.

Again, news images of the clash only swelled their ranks further. Businessman Ricky Wong Wai-kay, an alumnus of the university, was among those calling for reinforcements. "CUHK people, return to safeguard CUHK and fight against police brutality," he urged online.

Hundreds answered the call, arriving with food, medical supplies and materials to make petrol bombs. Among them was Ray, a postgraduate student in his 30s, one of many who felt an urge to protect his alma mater. "The people you despise have entered a place you love, it was that simple," he said.

Aunties' army

Ray said many of his fellow volunteers had played walk-on parts at protests before, but now they were hungry for more. "There were aunties making petrol bombs despite not knowing how to do it," he said, using a colloquial Hong Kong term for mature women.

He said people knew they could be hurt or arrested, but "couldn't care less" – the sounds of gunshots had driven them there, determined as they were to protect their friends and loved ones on the front lines.

Graduate Apple Chan, in her 30s, joined hundreds of others on a "production line" making petrol bombs. At first she had to be shown how to insert the towel and which type of bottle worked best. Soon she was a pro.

"I never imagined I would be making these," she said. "But I was so angry when police walked into CUHK that I could not even work, so I left early and came here." As more supporters arrived, the gymnasium was converted into a field hospital manned by volunteer medical professionals.

After dusk, university president Rocky Tuan Sung-chi made a second attempt at mediation, as protesters demanded that he call for the unconditional release of all who had been arrested so far. Again, this failed to ease tensions.

As Tuan approached the police cordon flanked by a group of students, the force fired volleys of tear gas at them. An officer on a loudspeaker warned that now was "not the time to negotiate" and the battle exploded once more. Frontliners pelted police with petrol bomb after petrol bomb, scorching the earth, lighting up the night and even forcing police to retreat, just a little.

But the skirmishes were taking a heavy toll on the radicals, dozens of whom were injured and forced to return to the gym for treatment. Amid such desperate scenes, the protesters had one last trick up their sleeve: comrades across the city who began to set fires to divert police's attention.

In Kowloon, a mall's Christmas tree went up in flames; in Causeway Bay, it was a China Mobile shop. In Sheung Shui, a train was firebombed; in Tin Shui Wai, a police station began to burn. At 10pm the tactic appeared to be working as police posted on Facebook that they were retreating to seek a "peaceful solution."

But not before they unleashed another action. Within minutes, water cannons were at the scene, mounted on a police anti-riot vehicle and spraying the CUHK protesters with a pepper-based blue dye that burned their eyes and skin. More tear gas was fired and there was no choice for the protesters but to retreat behind their defensive lines.

Who won the "Battle of CUHK" was a matter of dispute. Ten minutes after firing the water cannons, police withdrew. Whether it was because they felt their objective had been reached – or whether it was because they found themselves fighting fires on too many fronts – may never be known.

What was not in doubt was that the ferocity of the battle would go down in folklore. By the night's end, police had fired 1,576 rounds of tear gas, 1,312 rubber bullets, 380 beanbag rounds and 126 sponge-tipped rounds. At least 70 protesters had been injured.

On average, about a round of tear gas was fired every minute on that day. Police spokesman Kong defended the extraordinary use of force, saying officers had faced students armed with bows and arrows and that at one point extremist protesters had been lobbing more than one petrol bomb a minute. Officials would later describe the university campuses in Hong Kong as weapons factories.

"I can certainly tell you we do not intend to charge into the campuses," Kong said. "We are just trying to disperse and arrest alleged criminals – unless you're telling me it is not criminal to throw objects onto highways."

But police did not shut down the radicals. With officers gone, the occupiers trickled back to Bridge No 2, slowly at first, but their numbers soon became a torrent. They ignored, then heckled the university's former vice chancellor Joseph Sung Jao-yiu when he beseeched them to leave peacefully. "You cannot believe police," they said.

Days 3-5: A siege mentality

On the third day, the protesters' tactics changed again. Now their attention turned to siege warfare. Expecting police to return, the hard-core radicals at CUHK and other universities fortified their strongholds with roadblocks and barricades.

At CUHK they set up a makeshift checkpoint of bamboo sticks, umbrellas and the door of a trashed car. They searched all visitors to the campus, often roughly, and demanded that they explain their reasons for visiting.

While supporters continued to send medical and food supplies, the mood among some people on campus was starting to turn. University staff began to resent the checks and the behavior of the black-clad radicals, many of whom were obviously not CUHK students.

The black-clads took over coaches and vans and continued to camp out near Bridge No 2. All around, the campus was charred and littered with the remains of petrol bombs and ammunition shells.

Jacky So Tsun-fung, the student union president at the time, said the protesters' prolonged stay had led to conflicts between demonstrators who were from CUHK and those who were from elsewhere.

"CUHK students felt it was unnecessary to break into certain facilities, whereas those from outside treated the campus as just another government location."

General lawlessness then prevailed. Protesters would smoke cigarettes near flammable liquids, said So, while others drove on campus despite not having licences. One protester had to go to hospital after he rammed a car into a metal barrier.

So said this was where the protesters began to go wrong. They had abandoned the principle of "being water," which had sustained them for so long, and this was losing them support.

Recalling the battle for the campus, a CUHK alumnus in her late 20s, who only gave her surname Wong, said she could not bear to return to her alma mater after such distressing scenes at a place she had loved. "I don't want to face it," she said in March 2020. "It seems the CUHK I remember is no longer there."

It would remain a painful experience for all students, staff and alumni, she said. There was no winner.

This sense of disillusionment was pervasive. Wilson Wong Wai-ho, associate professor of CUHK's department of government and public administration, said many alumni had returned to the campus to defend it, but had since felt conflicted. "Unfortunately, our campus had been hijacked by radical protesters," Wong said.

With the violent marauders still massed on campus and the surrounding roads still blocked, CUHK announced on November 13 that the school term would be terminated due to security concerns. Police provided a boat so that students from the Chinese mainland, who were facing growing hostility, could leave.

Zhou, 28, a CUHK doctoral student from the mainland, stayed on. Nevertheless, he felt that something had been lost. "The protests have seriously affected our use of libraries and other resources," he said. "It has hurt the spirit of the universities."

A farewell to alma mater

On November 15, vice chancellor Tuan condemned the continued blocking of roads as "irresponsible acts" and asked both protesters and staff to leave the campus, saying: "The university is a place of learning, not a weapons factory, battlefield for violent acts, or political arena." The university also clarified that at no point had it asked police to enter the campus.

The occupation of CUHK was over by that night. Many of the protesters headed to Polytechnic University in Hung Hom, where another even more ferocious battle was to happen. On their way out, some could not resist one last blow out, setting fire to a car at Bridge No 2, causing multiple explosions.

They left behind a trail of destruction. Campus chiefs estimated the damage at HK$70 million (US$9 million), about HK$30 million of which was for repairing or replacing 75 damaged school buses and other vehicles.

There was also a huge mess: discarded food, water bottles, and clothes. There was something more dangerous too. On Monday, November 18, when police returned to search the campus, they found more than 3,900 petrol bombs, and a similar amount the following day. All had presumably been destined for the streets of Hong Kong. Hazardous chemicals had also been stolen from the laboratories.

The city's leader, Chief Executive Carrie Lam Cheng Yuet-ngor, would later obliquely refer to CUHK as a "weapons factory."

Five days of violence that had started with a mystery also ended with one. The sheer numbers of people involved in the protests suggested only a fraction could have been bona fide CUHK students. Who were the rest of the radicals hiding behind the masks? Were they really from other universities, as many claimed? Or from secondary schools, as others speculated? While it was impossible to know for sure, it was apparent that many had no real link to the university at all. Some might not even have been students.

"We think most of them were not our students," said Professor Wong Kam-fai, associate dean of the university's engineering faculty. "That makes me feel a little uncomfortable."

Still, some chose to focus on the good that came out of the traumatic five days that scarred their campus. So, who stepped down as student union president a few months after the siege ended, found solace in the fellowship of the university community.

"Those were difficult times, but I saw that the students, staff and alumni were united," said the third-year student of government and public administration. "It made me love this place even more."

The siege of Polytechnic University

Phila Siu and Victor Ting

A campus occupation, after a day of mob violence across the city, became a turning point for the movement.

Polytechnic University (PolyU) student Jonathan Wong, 20, was almost in tears when he returned to the campus in January 2020, nine weeks after it was the scene of the worst clashes between black-clad radicals and police in more than five months of anti-government protests in Hong Kong. "I became emotional when I saw the blackened walls and burn marks on the footbridge to Hung Hom MTR station. I thought to myself, these walks will never be the same again," said Jonathan*.

In November 2019, more than 1,100 hardcore protesters and their supporters occupied the compact campus in Hung Hom, a densely built-up area in Kowloon just minutes from the malls and tourist attractions of Tsim Sha Tsui. Hundreds of police officers were mobilized as the campus was locked down in a siege that lasted 13 days and turned the place into a war zone. Masked radicals threw petrol bombs repeatedly at toll booths for the nearby Cross-Harbour Tunnel, and shut it down. At the height of violent clashes on November 17, they also set fire to footbridges and the campus entrance. A police armored vehicle was set ablaze and pelted with petrol bombs. An arrow shot by a protester pierced a police officer's calf.

As the siege dragged on, police did not storm the campus, as many had expected them to, but ordered protesters to leave. Many did so but others, like Wong, chose to escape without being arrested. He spent five days on campus before he and five others fled via a sewer, wading for almost half an hour in knee-deep water before reaching a quiet street outside, where waiting supporters helped them get away. After the siege ended, police found nearly 4,000 unused petrol bombs on the premises, along with explosives, corrosive liquid, hammers, air guns, bows and arrows and catapults large enough to launch bricks. There was extensive damage to university facilities, reducing PolyU to a filthy, stinking state. The grounds were strewn with petrol bombs, broken gas masks and helmets. The gymnasium and canteen reeked from mounds of rotting trash, and the library was flooded, apparently from broken fire hoses.

Surveying the wrecked campus, a subdued-looking PolyU president, Teng Jin-guang, said: "We are the biggest victim in this political incident. This has had a devastating effect on the teaching and research of our universities." Repairs would need at least six months. Teng revealed that only 46 of the more than 1,000 people arrested leaving the campus were registered students of the university.

From quiet campus to disaster zone

PolyU started as a trade school in 1937 before being upgraded to a technical college and polytechnic and then becoming a full-fledged university in 1994. It has more than 27,000 students and a 9.4-hectare campus dominated by red brick buildings. On November 11, 2019, masked protesters started moving onto the campus, heeding calls for a citywide strike to pressure the Hong Kong government into satisfying the key demands of the protest movement. There were unmistakable signs of the trouble to come after masked radicals and their supporters began preparing for battle. They manned the campus entrance and frisked everyone who arrived, searching bags. Two days later, on November 13, they caused severe damage to the nearby Cross-Harbour

Tunnel, setting up barricades and torching toll booths. Their wanton violence forced a two-week closure of the tunnel, a vital link used by 110,000 private and public vehicles daily between Hung Hom and Causeway Bay, over on Hong Kong Island. Over the days that followed, radicals used the university's 50-meter swimming pool as a practice area for hurling petrol bombs, turning the pristine water into a blackened pit that stank of motor oil. Elsewhere, others practiced shooting bows and arrows. Protesters broke into labs and removed flammable chemicals. The windows of several buildings were smashed. Graffiti was sprayed across the wall of a building displaying: "Some people moved on. But not us."

The situation escalated swiftly from the morning of Sunday, November 17, when about 100 mostly middle-aged people arrived at the campus and began clearing the barricades put up by protesters on the roads. Black-clad mobs attacked the group, sending bricks raining down on them. Riot police arrived soon afterward, bringing two armored vehicles and two water cannons. Undeterred, the radicals attacked police with bows and arrows, and catapults firing projectiles from the campus rooftop. A sergeant handling media liaison was injured when an arrow pierced his left calf. In the ensuing clashes, police responded with water cannons, 1,448 rounds of tear gas, 1,391 rubber bullets, 325 beanbag rounds and 265 sponge grenades. That night, police sealed all PolyU exits, effectively confining the radicals and their supporters within the campus. The force declared that day's events a riot, and said that anyone who entered or remained on campus risked arrest for taking part in a riot, an offense carrying a maximum penalty of 10 years in jail.

Masked protester Tsang, a 20-year-old salon worker, said on a campus footbridge, as tear gas canisters flew past him that night: "Of course I am worried about my safety. But we have sacrificed a lot already, we cannot just stop. I know the risk, but I am not leaving."

Life in lockdown

Police urged everyone inside PolyU to leave peacefully, making clear that everyone would have their personal details recorded. Those aged 18 and above would be taken to police stations, while anyone younger would be allowed to go home. However, the force also said that all who emerged, regardless of age, could still be charged. For the next 11 days, police waited outside the campus while those inside decided their next move. Many protesters and their supporters chose to leave, and were arrested or had their particulars recorded. Others escaped, in groups or alone, leaving an unknown number holed up.

From the time the first protesters moved onto the campus, the gymnasium had been used as a common sleeping area, and was strewn with hundreds of mats. Once the siege began, however, hardly anyone slept there as the holdouts split up to sleep in classrooms or secret nooks. The gymnasium was left littered with food scraps, drinks and other rubbish. In the early days of the occupation, a volunteer crew manned the "resistance canteen" and dished up meals of eggs, macaroni and noodles for everyone.

After the siege began, the communal preparation of meals ended and people had to fend for themselves or their groups. Supplies of food, water and first aid items began running out. The campus convenience store was completely looted, but nearby ATMs were left untouched. By the end of the siege, the canteen area was a filthy mess with piles of rubbish and maggots crawling over putrefying food.

A 24-year-old construction worker who called himself K said that, during his six days there, his four-member squad was constantly searching for food and bottled water. They survived mostly on biscuits. "PolyU was like a prison with a high degree of freedom. Your movements were not restricted inside, but you could not leave," he said. As the siege continued, he noticed that some of the protesters still on campus appeared disorientated. "They were glassy-eyed, with messy hair, and looked very frustrated. They gave irrelevant answers when you talked to them and would not look you in the eye," he said. His squad tried to find ways to escape. They picked up numerous tips for possible escape routes posted on the Telegram messaging app, but none worked. "Every time we arrived at an escape point, there were already about 30 people ahead of us. It was frustrating," he said. Getting by on barely two hours' sleep each day, K said that he had been so exhausted that he fell off a chair while napping one day and broke two teeth. He finally called for an ambulance to get out. Police recorded his details, but did not arrest him.

Edward, a 22-year-old Chinese University student, also recalled having trouble sleeping, and said that he was plagued by nightmares of being arrested at home or on the street. He said while he was at PolyU, he had only helped to run the communal canteen, and what he had done could hardly be described as rioting.

As the days went by, newly appointed police commissioner Chris Tang Ping-keung said he hoped the saga would end peacefully. "There are many explosives and petrol bombs inside. The conditions are deteriorating. To the people who remain inside, I think you do not want your friends and family to be worried," he said.

A dash to freedom

With no end to the siege in sight, and no clear indication of the number of protesters still inside PolyU, educators, politicians, pastors and counselors got police permission to enter the campus and speak to the holdouts. Some managed to persuade protesters to leave, and even accompanied them out. Others failed to move protesters who insisted on remaining, come what may. A week after the siege began, it appeared that only dozens of protesters remained on campus, refusing to get out.

University of Hong Kong (HKU) vice chancellor Zhang Xiang arrived one night, hoping to meet any of his students among the protesters. Before entering PolyU, he sent a voice message which later circulated on WhatsApp, saying: "I am worried about you. Please stay safe. I want to see you again. As your vice chancellor, I promise I will do my best to help you. Trust me. I need you to rebuild the future with me." After 1½ hours inside the campus, however, he emerged saying that he had not found any HKU students.

There were various accounts of the holdouts on campus, with some protesters said to be hiding by themselves while others huddled together in small groups. To avoid arrest, many chose to make their own way out. One night, several protesters were spotted using ropes to let themselves down from a campus footbridge to a highway below, where waiting supporters helped them get away on motorbikes. Riot police arrived, fired tear gas and arrested several of them. Ah Sei, 24, was waiting for his turn to go down the ropes when police showed up, forcing him to abandon his escape bid. He tried fleeing through the sewers three times, but failed each time. "Even though we were wearing masks, the smell inside the sewers was so strong and my head kept hitting the sewer's ceiling," he said. He eventually left the campus by ambulance.

Among those who succeeded in escaping was James Wong*, a 22-year-old community college student. Like Ah Sei, he had tried to flee through the sewers, but gave up when he found it unbearably stifling, smelly and filthy. His chance came one morning when he realized there were no police guarding the roads near a campus building. He made his dash for freedom. "I ran across two highways and through some bushes," he said. "I just kept sprinting. There was no turning back. I kept thinking that I wanted to get home, get bathed, lie on my bed and put an end to this." He got home and scrubbed himself like never before. Still, he said, he had no regrets about participating in the occupation of PolyU.

On Monday, November 25, there was a flurry of activity from PolyU's leadership, which said the destruction and chaos on campus was no longer bearable and called for the end of the police blockade. Police said they were ready to enter the campus, but the university preferred to check the premises itself. It assembled teams that conducted two days of searches, going room by room, floor by floor in all the buildings. They found only one young woman, who wandered off after speaking to the team that came across her. Police moved into the campus that Thursday, and the siege of PolyU ended on Friday, November 29.

In all, 1,380 people were arrested during that episode of Hong Kong's anti-government protests. By the end of January 2020, almost 300 of them had been charged with offenses such as rioting, unauthorized assembly and arson. None of those who left the campus after the siege began had been charged yet.

The PolyU siege, which began with brazen attacks and culminated in extreme scenes of violence by protesters, remains a surreal episode for the movement. Many protesters said they were left with conflicting feelings of being traumatized, defeated and yet defiant all at once, while others recognized that they had broken one of their own early pledges, to "be water" and elude capture. Hui Lai-ming, director of the Social Workers' General Union, who was on campus for several days to offer support to the protesters, said she and others suffered various degrees of post-traumatic stress disorder after they left. "For a period of time after I came out of the campus, I was in very bad spirits. I would cry when I saw things that reminded me of my time inside PolyU," she said. She left the campus through the police checkpoints, and had not been charged. She continued to appear at different protests afterward, saying that she felt the urge to do so because Hong Kong was going through a "humanitarian crisis." She had no regrets about staying inside the campus during the siege.

Months after the siege, Jonathan Wong* still remembers the many cockroaches he saw while crawling out of the sewer to leave the campus. But he shrugs off such flashbacks as a small price to pay. He took part in that week's protests to defend the "dignity" of his university against "police invasion," he said, certain that it had put maximum pressure on the government. It also solidified support for the pro-democracy activists, leading to their landslide victory in that month's district council elections, he believes.

One other undeniable outcome, however, was lower turnouts for protests in the following weeks and the remaining months of 2019. But Wong insists it is a respite to regroup. "People can take stock and think long and hard about the way forward," he said. "They may even come up with a new model for the movement that can carry us through to the long term."

Names have been changed to protect identities.

— *With reporting by Alvin Lum and Chris Lau*

THE MOBILIZED AND THE MARGINALIZED

"THERE IS NO 'MAIN STAGE' ... THERE ARE IN FACT MANY 'SMALL STAGES' IN THIS MOVEMENT. EVERYONE COULD BE A LEADER."

Ventus Lau Wing-hong, activist

———

Everyone could be a leader

Jeffie Lam

Their faces masked, eyes shielded by goggles and arms bound in cling wrap, the hordes stood at the junction of Harcourt Road and Tim Wa Avenue, waiting, still and silent except for the odd waft of a whisper.

"Advance now!" shouted a young man standing on top of the metal barricades, which separated them from police. The protesters pushed forward, counting "one, two; one, two" almost in lockstep.

That scorching summer afternoon of June 12, 2019, was the day of reckoning as protesters tried to surround the Legislative Council complex to block lawmakers from advancing work on the extradition bill. In the lead-up to the protests, they had swapped ideas on the Reddit-like site LIHKG and several channels on encrypted messaging app Telegram. On the day itself, many in the crowd checked their phones incessantly, looking for the latest updates published on "612 Reminder," a Telegram channel they had set up the day before, giving a checklist on strategies and safety tips for the siege.

Earlier, traffic on Harcourt Road and Lung Wo Road near the complex came to a halt at about 8am, as protesters surfaced in waves without warning. At almost the same time, at least six private cars driven by protesters blocked Queensway by stopping in their lanes on different routes into the area, executing a plan they had hatched on the encrypted platform. Just as swiftly, other black-clad protesters hoisted barricades improvised from metal railings they had pulled out from road dividers, rendering the roads impenetrable to traffic. Protesters seemed to know their different tasks intuitively, like they had rehearsed everything.

At any given time, at least one protester could be spotted standing on a barricade at each junction, for a view of the latest police movements. Others manned supply booths and first aid stations. Mobile first aid trolleys popped up, towels were whipped out and volunteers were ready with saline solution for anyone who might have their eyes stung by tear gas or pepper spray.

"Scrap it! Scrap it!" the protesters shouted, chanting such slogans on and off, and clapping in rhythm to keep the atmosphere upbeat. "No retreat if it's not scrapped!" they cried out, referring to the extradition bill they wanted crushed. The camaraderie was palpable, even though many insisted they did not know other protesters beyond their immediate circle of friends. Someone yelled: "Anyone has asthma medication?" and the request was repeated and echoed throughout their ranks. Aid came within minutes, to cheers and applause.

The scenes were reminiscent of the Occupy protests of 2014, but with one difference: the near absence of obvious leaders in the crowd. The Civil Human Rights Front – the city's biggest activist platform, which organized a march that drew an estimated 1 million people the previous weekend – remained studiously low-profile to avoid stealing the limelight or taking the lead this time. It was bent on sending the message that there was only one convenor of this movement: Carrie Lam Cheng Yuet-ngor, the city's leader, who insisted on pressing ahead with the bill despite the public outrage.

"In the absence of a leader, we all hope to go the extra mile and be more devoted in our protest. There were some hiccups at the beginning but we soon knew how to play our own roles," said Bevis Lo, 23, an event industry worker who was at Lung Wo Road that morning. "Everyone somehow wants a leader, but there are just so many different opinions, stances and approaches among ourselves."

It also appeared to be a lesson they had learned from Occupy; a new tolerance toward different views and camps, various protesters repeatedly said. The city's pro-democracy bloc splintered soon after the Occupy protests, which opposed Beijing's plan for electoral reform. Leadership tussles and blame games ensued as some pointed fingers at the *daai toi* or the "main stage," the label given to the student leaders and groups that coordinated actions then, for being too moderate, if not incompetent. "During Occupy, we mostly listened to the 'main stage' and cooperated with them, as we were young and inexperienced with mass resistance," said Adam Yip Yat-san, a 32-year-old trading firm worker who took part then and was on the streets again in 2019. This time, Yip and many others turned to online platforms for information and made their own decisions on how to participate.

The scenes on June 12 showcased the early features of the faceless and seemingly leaderless protests. Demonstrators had adopted the "be water" philosophy – named after a saying of the late martial arts star Bruce Lee – as they opted for spontaneous road blockades that could appear and disappear at a rapid pace, to elude police but also to sustain momentum and retain public support. During Occupy, prolonged, stationary sit-ins caused inconvenience and tested ordinary Hongkongers' patience.

On the morning of June 12, protesters also devised their own way of communicating in a crowd after attempts with a loudhailer failed. Those further back could barely hear and were left confused. So, they came up with hand signals to indicate requests from the front or the back. It became a smooth operation. Hundreds of them formed a human

REBEL CITY: Hong Kong's Year of Water and Fire

chain to pass supplies, using the hand signals. The moving of hands up and down above their heads meant more helmets were needed; showing both index fingers pulling away horizontally was a request for cable ties; making an X sign with the forearms indicated sufficient supplies. Runners could also be seen bringing the requested materials to the front along the human chain. The hand signals were put into a guide shared on social media that afternoon and were on full display at major protests, such as during the July 1 storming of Legco.

In the months that followed, protesters who had appeared underdressed for battle upgraded their gear, wearing helmets, ballistic goggles and gas masks, not just simple surgical masks or home-made balaclavas improvised from T-shirts. They also began forming squads of four or five when at the front lines, calling each other *sau zuk*, or brothers- or sisters-in-arms, even though many were strangers to each other. The teams would then divide the work. Some organized roadblocks while others dug out bricks or placed them on the roads to halt traffic. "Once the first roadblock was set up, people would come together and discuss its effectiveness and where else we would need another to bar the officers from advancing," said a 25-year-old protester, a graphic and web designer who only gave his name as Kelvin.

Protesters would join whichever team needed help. As the months wore on, ordinary protesters were even drafted in to help with *fo mo faat* or "fire magic," their euphemism for making petrol bombs, which some had learned from tutorials online. "There is no designated squad responsible for making them," Kelvin said. "Someone in the crowd would ask if there were any materials nearby, such as turpentine, then all sorts of people would just join the production line once they were sourced."

For a movement hostile to the influence of a communist government, Hong Kong's protesters were embracing Karl Marx's maxim of "from each according to his ability," as the wider community pitched in during the summer months.

Some crowdfunded millions of dollars to place advertisements in 19 newspapers across 13 countries to raise international awareness of the movement ahead of the G20 summit, while others helped to source protest equipment, provided logistical support or gave medical or legal assistance. Volunteers also launched an online platform to document arrests in real time by sharing the picture and name of the arrestees, along with the license plate number of the police vehicle that took them away, to make sure their family and friends could arrange lawyers for them.

"Rather than saying there is no 'main stage', a more accurate description would be there are in fact many 'small stages' in this movement," said Ventus Lau Wing-hong, an activist who organized several actions and rallies after the movement erupted in June. "Everyone could be a leader."

Decentralized leadership

On June 26, Lau addressed hundreds of participants at Chater Garden in Central, who had heeded his calls to petition one foreign consulate after another in a marathon march, two days ahead of the G20 summit in Osaka, which President Xi Jinping would attend. "We have already obtained the police approval for our actions so you do not have to worry," the 26-year-old assured the crowd using a loudspeaker. "Our mission today is to call on the participating countries to exert pressure on Chinese President Xi Jinping during the summit and raise concerns on the human rights situation in Hong Kong." The protest, deemed a success by protesters because of the international media coverage, was the result of rounds of online discussions Lau held with many others he had never met in real life. "We floated the idea on Telegram, people echoed and offered help," Lau recalled. "We once thought it would be a tough task to translate our petition letter into different languages, but we ended up spending only two days on it. People kept telling us they knew the various languages, even Russian."

Lau, a former student leader at Chinese University (CUHK), co-founded the Civil Assembly Team with his new comrades, to organize protests. The decentralized leadership of the movement had made it more creative, resilient and sustainable, Lau said. Instead of counting only on the Civil Human Rights Front, Lau said anyone could now help share the burden by taking turns to hold marches with different themes. Indeed, from July, marches and rallies became a weekend routine in Hong Kong, with messages as diverse as decrying police brutality, railing against cross-border traders, and even highlighting the plight of animals injured by tear gas. On LIHKG, protesters debated endlessly the effectiveness of different tactics and explored new possibilities.

They uploaded a detailed manual online, complete with protest strategies, post-mortems of key battles, a list of dos and don'ts for protesters and even user ratings for protective gear. To avoid potential culpability, the Google document was written as a guide to a video game called "Heung Shing Online." Heung Shing was a fictional city used in the city's public examinations, a thinly veiled pseudonym for Hong Kong. The specific duties of different characters in the game, as well as the gear they should bring along, were illustrated in the introductory chapter of the guide. The "dragon egg catcher," for instance, refers to those responsible for extinguishing tear gas canisters. The guide advises them to place the burning canisters in bottles filled with salt or wet towels, or cover them with metal plates, to snuff them out.

On August 23, an estimated 210,000 people joined hands across the city. Standing on pavements in snaking rows that stretched along three railway lines – and even along the slopes of the famous landmark Lion Rock, which at 495 meters high is deemed a high-risk hiking spot – they formed a human chain they dubbed the Hong Kong Way. Inspired by the Baltic Way protests against Soviet domination of Estonia, Latvia and Lithuania exactly 30 years previously, the idea took just under 10 days to execute from the time it was floated online on August 14. Volunteers then planned routes, created district-based Telegram channels to connect participants, and publicized the events. They also offered assistance to tell people where to go and how to keep in line. As one LIHKG user put it, Hongkongers were so energized back then that they were ready to try anything, no matter how absurd and unthinkable it might have sounded when first pitched online.

In the meantime, more than 100 Telegram channels mushroomed to provide all sorts of aid to protesters, including job-matching services and secret medical treatment for people reluctant to visit public hospitals with protest-related injuries. Steve Cheung, 30, was one of the channel operators. He had arrived just two weeks earlier with two friends after closing down his catering business in Vancouver and returning to his childhood home to support the cause. After seeing protesters scrambling to buy single-journey train tickets at the end of a demonstration – to avoid any trace of their movements on their Octopus cards – Cheung and his friends decided to pitch in. The trio would go to train stations near protest sites and buy stacks of single-trip tickets for various destinations, which they later gave out to comrades fleeing the scene to escape police. At first they used their own money, but then other supporters started to make donations as they walked past them. "The donations – albeit just coins – were so plentiful that I once personally bought tickets worth HK$7,000 (US$898) a night," Cheung recalled.

He then decided he ought to do more. After seeing piles of donated materials – including protective gear, first aid kits and second-hand clothing – left behind after each demonstration for lack of coordination, he rented a storage unit and began running a protest equipment supply booth. At first, Cheung and his team just packed them in boxes or nylon travel bags and took them home via public transport. As the boxes became bigger, they found volunteer drivers to help them. Cheung's team also began sourcing protective gear, buying them first on eBay and Amazon, and then directly from manufacturers 3M, for a lower warehouse price.

In August, following online appeals that the mostly young demonstrators had little money left for meals after buying protective gear, Cheung's group started collecting and giving out food coupons and even cash to those in dire straits. At its peak, his Telegram channel – named "Let me pay for your meal" – had more than 4,000 subscribers and received about 100 requests for assistance daily. Most recipients had either been fired for their participation in protests or left home after family quarrels.

As summer ended, his two friends returned to Canada, but Cheung remained in Hong Kong. He now has more than 50 volunteers who run the platform, whose functions evolve depending on need. "This movement has motivated many Hongkongers to contribute in their own way," he said. "It's like having many departments where everyone divides work and does different things."

If Cheung's department was supplies, then 37-year-old business owner Chan ran the transport division. Calling himself a peaceful protester with family and business obligations preventing him from doing more, Chan, who would only give his surname, joined the team of "Uber ambulances" – which was not actually affiliated with the ride-hailing firm – in July to help ferry protesters home after clashes. He decided the service was needed after the Yuen Long railway station attack, which left protesters at the mercy of an armed mob. But demonstrators, he soon found, waved off his offers of help, fearing the volunteers were actually plainclothes police officers trying to trap them. "They are very careful as they do not know who you are," Chan said. "I have to ask them to look for me again in future after sending them home. I feel like I am a taxi driver looking for customers." After gradually building a "protester base," Chan co-built a closed group on Telegram with about 100 trusted allies, including drivers, first-aiders, protesters and their "contact persons." (At least one secondary school teacher is among the contact persons in the group to help her students look for free rides after protesting.)

The rides could be dangerous, Chan said, not just because the volunteers often had to drive through tear gas and scattered bricks – strewn ironically by the radicals they were saving – but also because of the risk of arrest. They would definitely be picked up if the police found "stationery" – an insider term for protest gear – in their vehicles. By October, the private group Chan co-founded had become like a sophisticated taxi call center. While drivers were usually too busy to dive into hundreds of messages, about seven volunteers, dubbed "admins," would take shifts to run the channel round the clock. They matched drivers with protesters, and monitored news coverage and maps to plot routes and pick-up points away from police. Wong, a 32-year-old marketing officer who asked to be identified only by her surname, was a volunteer who had her eyes glued to multiple screens monitoring the road situation for the drivers during protest days. "The movement hit me very hard. It made me want to be more involved," she said. "I think we are all doing what we can to help each other achieve the same goal."

Chan and Wong and the others never met one another, until they had a gathering at a pro-protester pub near Polytechnic University (PolyU) in December. They did it to support the pub, whose business dried up after the campus siege, and also to swap stories of their actions. Over drinks, they revealed to each other what they did. One was a motorcyclist who rescued escapees from the campus; another was a first-aider trapped inside. The stories went on until 3am, when they finally parted ways. Chan said a common cause had connected three generations that evening, with the oldest driver approaching 60. "It was the first time we met, but we had a strong bond because of what we went through together," he said.

Resilience or adrift

Compared with the 2014 Occupy movement, the extradition bill protests introduced an organization model with remarkable longevity, political scientist Edmund Cheng Wai of City University said. One of its distinctive features was the volunteering spirit of individuals, he added. "In the past, some people might find the value of their participation negligible and they might want to free-ride it," he said. "But this movement has made everyone feel they have more or less contributed to the cause. Everyone believes their participation matters." For instance, black-clad radicals on the front lines would take on police, while moderate supporters would join peaceful marches, donate gear, patronize protester-friendly restaurants and shops, or promote the cause to the international community over Twitter. "Such volunteer actions and community connections would be able to be sustained by people in their everyday lives even after the high tide of the movement has passed," Cheng said.

But decentralized leadership has obvious drawbacks. The lack of conflict resolution and deliberation within the movement has meant a lack of clarity on the path ahead. "Everyone has been urging the government to address their five demands, yet no one has the legitimacy and authority to articulate how the goals could be achieved," Cheng said. Supporters have been calling for universal suffrage, but the discussion has been muted on how exactly the oft-chanted demand should be defined. On the ground, frontline protester Kelvin also revealed how, without a clear leader giving directions, building consensus took time and sometimes led to wrong moves, such as being slow to retreat, enabling police to make arrests more easily. "There are bound to be people who insist on staying even if we are outnumbered by the police, but somehow it is meaningless to drag on if we do not have a concrete next move. It is full of conflicts," Kelvin said. "In the end, those who stayed would very often be crushed by the police's unexpected advance."

The 25-year-old decided to take a break from the front lines in October. He armed himself instead with a loudhailer and telescope and teamed up with sentinels monitoring police deployments to boost information flow, which he felt needed improvement. "People spent a long time debating which routes they should take. Those on the front line, in the middle or at the back had no idea what was happening on the other sides," he said. "The decision made by the frontliners might not pass through to the crowd. Even if it got through, those at the back might be skeptical of its authenticity and [ask whether] it is a trap spread by the police officers infiltrated among them."

Such weaknesses were laid bare on November 18, Kelvin recalled, the night thousands heeded calls to gather in areas outside PolyU in Hung Hom, a day after officers had besieged the campus, trapping hundreds of protesters and first-aiders inside. The aim was to divert police attention and help their trapped comrades flee. That night, Kelvin said, he tried to help spread the frontliners' calls to get his peers to the side streets after they assessed that it was impossible to overwhelm riot police on the main road, as the officers had water cannons and armored vehicles stationed there. But his call was met with skepticism. The lack of direction and strategic planning eventually led to the mass arrest and prosecution of more than 200 people for rioting. "My responsibility is to brief the crowd on the latest situation and what protest supplies are needed on the front line," said Kelvin. "I am not a commander and I have no right to command anyone." But despite the lack of coordination and communication at times, Kelvin still preferred having no "main stage" leading the movement. The absence of clear leaders made it harder for the government to dissolve the movement by arresting the ringleaders, he argued.

Veteran social activist Avery Ng Man-yuen, former chairman of the League of Social Democrats, agreed that while the movement had thrived because of such agility, the absence of short-term tactical planning and long-term strategies was lamentable. "We might have successfully killed the bill, but what worries me is no one seems to realize we are paying a huge price for this in terms of the legal costs," he said. A lack of a well-thought-out strategy and leadership could result in mass arrests and put protesters only in reactive mode, he said, adding many were painfully unaware of the legal consequences of their actions. "We need leadership, not a leader. The different cells or factions in the movement should come together and have better coordination, or else we will forever be fighting a losing battle," Ng said.

By early 2020, as the ranks dwindled because of arrests and physical fatigue, the movement ran up against another enemy, the coronavirus pandemic plaguing the city and the world. But protesters themselves were also coming around to realizing they would not be able to achieve their aims overnight, political scientist Ma Ngok, of CUHK, said. By November, supporters began to acknowledge the need for solid organization, rather than relying on spontaneous mobilization, he said. "They know now it is going to be a long fight and they need to boost their capacity and resources through organization," he said. Dozens of trade unions have sprung out of the movement. One outcome was a week-long strike in February by medical workers dissatisfied with the government's handling of the coronavirus health crisis.

Steve Cheung, who now receives few requests for financial assistance, has switched to sourcing surgical masks for the poor and elderly, amid a shortage the government failed to address. The "612 Reminder" Telegram channel, whose subscription grew from 20,000 in June to almost 180,000 by early 2020, also has a new focus. It is exploring the future direction of the movement through debate, as well as advising people on their legal rights upon arrest, cybersecurity threats and what to do when police come to search their flat. "People now already have a preliminary understanding of protest equipment and supplies after rounds of frontline actions and have also floated different strategies. We believe this is no longer the information that they need the most," said Havertz, a channel manager in his 20s. Political scientist Cheng said the past months had further "normalized" the idea of protest among Hongkongers, who have taken it in their stride. That studied fortitude, he said, "is not going to go away unless there is a structural revamp in the political system."

Teenage tear gas soldiers

Jeffie Lam

High school teens are the arms and legs of the movement; full of idealism and willing to risk it all for their cause: a vision of an old Hong Kong they are too young to remember.

On weekends, Sophia never leaves home without a collapsible grey bucket in her backpack. It is not that she is an avid gardener or needs the pail to wash up after a picnic. Sophia* is a teenage tear gas soldier. During clashes with police, she swoops in with her bucket filled with water and coolly throws hot canisters into it, her hands protected by heavy industrial gloves. Barely exchanging glances, her squad of black-clad comrades move in a coordinated fashion to snuff out the rounds as they land.

Given that police have fired more than 16,000 rounds since the protests began, it is back-breaking work. Sometimes, when she has time to look up and suss out the riot police on the other side, she flings a canister back at them. "I want to protect others as I know how painful it is to be gassed," she said.

Sophia, 17, is one of the tens of thousands of teenagers who make up the backbone of the movement. They give up their weekends to press on with the protests, week after week, risking tear gas, beanbag rounds, rubber bullets, sponge-tipped pellets and the metal batons of police. What about the arrests of thousands of their comrades and the injuries sustained by hundreds of others? Bring it on, they seem to say.

"I can't sleep and can't eat, my heart is tired," said Pang, 15, who

136

has joined thousands of his fellow secondary students at a school boycott rally in Edinburgh Place, Central.

He covers his face with a full mask and dresses in black with shoulder, arm and shin pads above his grey Nike trainers. On his arm is a shield he made from a road sign on which he has etched the word "revolution."

Pang said that he and many of his peers have prepared wills. "If you haven't written one then you shouldn't be on the front lines."

Innocence, idealism and burning together

University students have long been at the forefront of social movements and in Hong Kong it is no different – except that the undergraduates are joined by spirited teens like Sophia.

Secondary school students, some as young as 12, fuel the protests with idealism and innocence – if not naivete – that in turn draws both sympathy and guilt from older, more jaded adults who fear the city's youth are trading their future for the impossible dream of democracy.

Among the shared principles sustaining the protests is one that comes from the phrase "If we burn, you burn with us" – a rebellious line borrowed from the young adult book and movie series *The Hunger Games*, where at the end, the capital city is vanquished. In Cantonese, the phrase used is *laam caau*, meaning "burning together" or "taking you down with me."

Google searches for the Cantonese phrase *laam caau* had been steadily rising since the first mass protest on June 9, 2019, but spiked in the week of August 11, one of the movement's darkest days. This was when protesters were arrested in Causeway Bay by undercover police who had infiltrated their ranks. It was also when a young woman suffered a severe eye injury during a protest outside a police station.

The circumstances are disputed – protesters say police shot her with a beanbag round; police insist the cause is unknown but under investigation. Regardless of the facts, she became an icon of the protests, her picture appearing in posters as a testament to "police brutality."

Driving the protesters on is an amalgam of emotions: nostalgia for an idyllic Hong Kong that had been erased by rapid development; unease at the runaway wealth of some while others suffer; and a sense of displacement over the influx of mainland Chinese. So they are happy to see the economy soften and the streets fall quiet as the tourist crowds grow thin because of the protests. They imagine a Hong Kong where people speak Cantonese and patronize family-run shops rather than chain stores and pharmacies catering to shoppers from the mainland; and a place where people care for one another as neighbors in close-knit communities.

"I am so looking forward to witnessing the closure of all those pharmacies," said Vincent Lo, a graduate in visual arts. "So what if you are an international financial city but have no substance inside? Hong Kong has been losing its character. I care about its substance, not titles."

For now, though, the heady romance of this reimagined Hong Kong must reckon with the harsh reality of the front lines. Two teenagers, aged 18 and 14, have been shot, one in the chest, the other in the leg, and thousands of others have been injured. For these young, self-styled soldiers, the risks to life and limb are real and immediate. For the establishment they are fighting, the risks are just as real now and in the longer term. Clamping down a protest movement made up of the young without winning them over will just provide fertile ground for a permanent opposition well into the future.

Extracurricular activities

On weekdays, Sophia is a bookish secondary school pupil in her pristine white uniform. Bespectacled and barely five feet tall, she keeps her hair in a ponytail and on her backpack she hangs a soft toy pig keychain. She enjoys reading Chinese literature when she is not busy with her school's debating team. She wants to be a lawyer someday.

On weekends, tear gas soldier Sophia dons her ballistic hat, helmet, and black outfit and speaks like a detonation expert. "The fastest way to cool down a round, actually, is to place the canister in a bottle and shake it with mud," she said, adding that she can tell the difference between tear gas canisters and other pellets fired by police just from the sounds they make when exploding.

Like taking a favorite subject at school, it is common for protesters at the front line to specialize in a core skill. Sophia has chosen extinguishing tear gas because she is too small to hurl bricks. She was among the protesters who stormed the legislature on July 1 when the city marked the 22nd anniversary of its return to Chinese rule. "I knew I was not gutsy enough to deface the city's emblem and so I decided to stay in the antechamber and remind our comrades not to vandalize the antiques there," she said.

In the early days of the protests, the government had hoped some normality might be restored with the start of the new school year. It wasn't. Instead, secondary school students organized class boycotts and human chains outside their campuses. After school, they flooded shopping malls, blanketed the city with protest art and organized flash mobs, singing the protest anthem *Glory to Hong Kong*.

For both Sophia and fellow protester Bosco, 16, everything changed on July 21. That was the night when a mob of white-clad men attacked protesters and ordinary passengers inside Yuen Long MTR station. Police were late to the scene, prompting vehement accusations that they were in cahoots with triads believed to be behind the attack.

Since then, both Sophia and Bosco have felt that violence is justified. "If the law enforcers are breaking the law, I don't think they are qualified to say what we do is wrong," Bosco said.

This is our moment

Bosco's mission goes beyond holding police to account. He is pushing for a Hong Kong in which the freedoms and democracy promised in the city's mini-constitution, the Basic Law, are preserved. For him and most of his friends, the highest prize is Hong Kong's identity, rather than its independence.

Most of today's teenagers are too young to have taken part in the Occupy protests of 2014, when democracy supporters staged a 79-day sit-in, paralyzing roads in the city's business districts. Instead, they see the 2019 protests as their defining moment, a chance to make a difference.

So, sacrifices have to be made. Lunch and pocket money are squirreled away to buy protest gear. Hobbies must wait and weekend activities lay hidden from the prying eyes of parents and friends. Arguments with family are frequent. Beatings from police are an unavoidable risk.

Henry*, 17, dreams of studying for a sports science degree and hopes to join the basketball team in university. But throughout the summer he did not attend a single training session. Fresh in his memory is him begging his father to delete from his phone all the conversations and photos they had shared. His father had been traveling to mainland China, where immigration staff were reportedly checking phones for evidence of protest activity, and Henry had been spooked. "He only deleted it after I refused to let go of his arm. I had never before grabbed my dad's arm like this. I wanted to cry," he recalled. "He is supposed to be a good citizen in the eyes of Communist Party and should not be dragged into any trouble." Henry's father, a law-abiding businessman, is firmly against any attempt to take on Beijing.

Sophia, too, has had her share of scrapes. At a protest in Kwun Tong, she was hit by Special Tactical Squad officers with batons and injured her waist. She wrestled free but dared not visit a doctor for fear of being reported to police. She turned instead to a volunteer Chinese medicine practitioner through the encrypted messenger app Telegram. "It would be imprudent for me to say I am ready for a 10-year jail sentence," she said. "I dare not say it would be worthwhile, but I will say I have no regrets if this is the risk I must bear."

Teenage kicks

Still, there is another side to protest life that even the most idealistic student would find hard to deny. Stand-offs with police are not only dangerous, but also thrilling. Weekends at the front lines have taken on an addictive quality.

Henry, an athlete, smiled sheepishly as he recalled feeling like he was in a "Korean drama" when he swept a female teammate into his arms and rescued her from smoldering tear gas. Even Bosco, who described himself as an introvert, said the feeling of unity on the front lines was intoxicating. No one from his school or family would have thought he would be a hard-core protester, he said. "In a group, we hurl bricks together," he said. "Wouldn't you be happy if you got to hit a police van?"

For some, the adrenaline rush may be an even greater motivation than the cause. Henry, who used to manage supply stations at protest sites, said he had received more than 100 requests for gas masks from junior pupils that he had turned away – including some as young as 12. "As we chant slogans in school, some of the pupils who have no idea about what's going on would also join in. I am not hardhearted enough to let them go this far," he said.

Of course, there is no adrenaline without danger and their readiness to take part in increasingly violent clashes is one of the most troubling aspects of the protests. On October 1 when China celebrated its 70th

National Day anniversary, an 18-year-old Form Five pupil was shot in the chest while he was attacking police with a rod during a clash, the first protester to have been hit by a live round. Less than two weeks later, another 18-year-old was arrested on suspicion of slashing a policeman's neck with a box cutter.

Such dangers do little to put off these young fighters. A survey of more than 12,000 protesters conducted between June and August by political scientist Samson Yuen Wai-hei of Lingnan University and other researchers found almost two-fifths were younger than 24, and about 12 per cent were 19 or below. In another study, Yuen found that since August extradition bill concern groups on Instagram were linked to more than 390 of the city's 472 secondary schools. "The findings suggest that secondary school pupils have participated in the movement at a fairly early stage in their personal capacity and they have tried to bring the cause to school campuses," Yuen said.

He said high school students were arguably the most organized supporters of the supposedly leaderless protests and that, unlike adults, they had a very clear "black-and-white" point of view.

Of the 7,613 arrested – aged between 11 and 84 – as of February 28, 2020, over the protests, 1,206 of them had been charged while 512 people were unconditionally released. The offenses included taking part in a riot, unlawful assembly, wounding, criminal damage, assaulting a police officer and possession of offensive weapons, among others.

More than 17 per cent of them, or 1,335 people, were aged below 18. Around 7 per cent of the arrestees, or 534, were under the age of 16. Anecdotally, protesters say up to 40 per cent of people on the front lines are secondary students.

These young frontline soldiers move between two conflicting worlds, of purposeful study and protest staging, making time for university open days to seek out higher education options they know they might not take up if they land in jail.

"Secondary school students are here because the city's future belongs to them," said Bosco, who like Sophia will face a university entrance exam in 2020, if all is well.

"Go ask people why they take to the streets. They are still here despite knowing the cost. That's because they know the consequence is not just about a 10-year jail term [for rioting] but the possibility that the Chinese Communist Party will continue to oppress Hong Kong."

Old hearts break

While the boldness of young students willing to risk it all is hard to doubt, many among the city's older generations – even those who support the protests – question their wisdom.

For Ho, 38, a nurse with a six-year-old son, it is the wills that trouble her the most. "Young people decide to stand up because they have learned what justice is and they envision their future with hope," she said. "But the moment they put wills in their school bags before going out, they contradict their goal of achieving a beautiful future."

Chan, a retired church employee, feels both heartbroken and guilty when she sees young people sacrificing themselves on the front lines. Her two daughters, aged 27 and 31, are often among them.

She said she understood that protesters who vandalized shops linked to the mainland were trying to send a message, but she could not support such actions. "We should focus on the authorities," she said.

Young people were more willing to engage in confrontational tactics not because they were immature, but because they had less life experience and were, therefore, more willing to sacrifice for their cause, according to sociologist Dana Fisher. However, she warned that violent protests would yield only a more violent response. "Nobody wins when a movement gets violent. Everybody loses," said Fisher, a University of Maryland professor and expert on activism.

Meira Levinson, a professor of education at Harvard University, said young activists were creative, idealistic and not bound by past experience, which made them more likely to push for change. But it was also easy for adults to dismiss them as young, foolish or being manipulated by other adults.

She cautioned young protesters against impatience, citing how activists in the Black Lives Matter movement in the US had learned the need to pass on the torch. "You will just end up killing yourself and you should not do that, especially when those changes will take a very long time. You want to be there for the long change," she said.

The long game

As the violence escalates, even protesters like Sophia recognize that too many of her brothers-in-arms are at risk of losing the plot. Violent rampages in which police and metro stations are petrol-bombed, roads set alight, banks and shops vandalized and people beaten up for holding different views are obvious signs that things are spinning out of control.

"Some frontliners are so emotional these days and I seriously don't know what will happen if they catch an officer," said Sophia. "I'm worried not because I think public support is important, but because I don't want to see us going further away from our original goals."

She estimated that more than 20 of her 27 classmates had joined the protests and that around half of them were hard-core participants, ready and willing to use violence. She herself is opposed to institutional violence but wishes protesters would leave the innocent alone.

The teenager has become less active recently, after a timely reminder. "A teacher asked us to think clearly about whether what we are doing now could help us play a more influential role in society in the future as it is going to be a long fight," she said.

But she has not given up the struggle, even if she has had to put her dream of being a human rights lawyer on hold.

For now, Sophia has a job to do, collapsible bucket in hand. "What I am doing and what lawyers do are actually for the same ends – justice. So even if I can't be a lawyer, I have done my part."

Names have been changed to protect identities.

Epilogue: Tear gas soldier reviews university ambitions

Jeffie Lam

H er feet stuck in the heavy, muddy ground, Sophia realized she could stand the burning sensation no longer.

It was November 17, 2019, and protesters were locked in a pitched battle with riot police outside the Polytechnic University (PolyU) campus in Kowloon. Sophia had been snuffing out tear gas canisters on the front lines for the past two hours, while a fellow protester tried to shield her from the pepper-based solution being fired at them by two police water cannon trucks. Protesters had dug up most of the bricks in the nearby pavements to use as weapons, leaving behind a waterlogged, muddy ground drenched with the noxious liquid.

Seventeen-year-old Sophia was wearing the same favorite pair of running shoes she had worn for an inter-school track meet that morning and they were making things worse. Her feet were completely soaked.

Months after what is generally regarded as the fiercest battle of the Hong Kong protests, the images of that day remain etched in Sophia's mind. "My comrade told me, as a girl, I had already done a good job bearing it for so long," she recalled in our conversation in early 2020.

"That day I realized I was screwed when I found my feet continued to burn even after first-aiders poured saline over them."

There was a widespread feeling in those surreal hours that the

146

protests were coming to a head and that both sides had stepped up the violence. Hard-core protesters were shooting arrows and hurling petrol bombs and bricks, at times using improvised catapults they had built on the roof of campus buildings. Police returned the barrages with seemingly endless volleys of tear gas, deploying an armored vehicle and two water cannons.

By now, Sophia was already a veteran in the war of fire and water. Just days earlier the sixth former had been at Chinese University (CUHK) where a similarly fierce battle of petrol bombs versus water cannons had raged.

"The scene was powerful yet dreadful. It was really like we were at war," she said. A rubber bullet hit her helmet. Two were found on the flak vest of her friend. His face turned pale and his lips were purple, Sophia recounted, fearful at the time that this was an effect of tear gas.

As a veteran, Sophia did not panic or run when, shortly before 6pm, police declared the clashes at PolyU a riot – effectively serving notice to all participants that they now faced up to 10 years in prison if caught.

Instead she immersed her feet in aloe vera gel, wrapped each foot in a plastic bag and put on a white pair of cheap white canvas sneakers she had found at the communal supplies booth.

Then she returned, once more unto the breach.

"I knew those outside were struggling hard to withstand the onslaught," she said. "I felt worthless."

For half an hour more she fought until she could no longer bear the pain and collapsed. A close comrade carried her away and, posing as a first-aider, spirited her out of the campus under the noses of police.

Sophia escaped home. Hundreds of other students remained trapped. The police siege lasted more than a week.

Unbroken

Ironically, the law finally caught up with the petite pupil at the most peaceful of protests she had attended, a flash mob in a shopping district.

Sophia and about 200 other mostly young people were surrounded by police at the protest in Mong Kok in December. "They asked me to hold my identity card and read my name aloud and then body-searched me. I was in a panic and my friend started to cry."

Yet Sophia's luck had not entirely deserted her. She had hidden her protest gear – a gas mask and a pair of black motorcycle pants with thick knee pads – in the firehose box of a nearby shopping center beforehand. With no such evidence giving her away, police only took down her details and let her go.

For weeks after that incident she laid low, planning to return to the front line only after taking her Diploma of Secondary Education examination in April 2020.

But in January, following the pro-democracy bloc's landslide victory in the district council elections two months earlier, she noticed that turnout at protests had started to dwindle and so she decided to return.

"I understand the movement could not keep going on forever but I do not want to see it end just like that. I realized how much I was willing to give for the drive after December."

Her ambition to become a lawyer had not wavered, she said, even if watching the arrest and punishment of so many young people over the past year made her re-think her views on the city's justice system. It should not mete out such harsh penalties to youth, she insisted.

Among the top students in her class now, she wants to take a dual degree in literacy studies and law at the University of Hong Kong, one of the most competitive programs in the city. If she cannot get in, she hopes instead to take a bachelor's degree in government and public administration at CUHK, which has a reputation as a breeding ground for activists.

Her involvement in the protests had only reinforced her convictions and made her more determined to succeed, she said.

"I think it would be great if there are more pro-democracy lawyers in Hong Kong," she said. "Many of my friends from elite schools whom I know from debate competitions place studies ahead of everything else but never apply what they have learned from books in real life."

"They are 'Hong Kong pigs'," she said, using a term for people who are politically apathetic and concerned only with making money, dining out and traveling.

With the experience she gained at the front lines, she said she realized that however her university dream panned out, there was more to life and, even if she did not make it there, she would be alright. She said when some of her fellow aspiring classmates discussed their future, "you can tell they look down at if not discriminate against those who cannot make it to university … it's disgusting."

She wished they knew of her comrade on the protest lines, who stood by her through thick and thin. He was not a top student, she said, but he knew how to stand up for what he believed in. He knew what to wear when you stood in a pool of muddy, noxious water and what to do when a tear gas canister landed next to your foot. He knew when to charge, when to retreat and how to escape when your enemies are closing in. He knew how fire could fight water.

"This movement has made me realize the definition of success," said Sophia. "Getting into university used to be my priority, but not any more. I know now in my heart what I treasure the most."

 # ProtestToo: Women on the front lines

Raquel Carvalho

Defying the stereotype of the materialistic 'Kong girl', women have headed to the front lines. But there lurks a dark side.

At night, Jordyn cuddles her teddy bear as she sleeps, surrounded by dolls. She generally keeps her voice low – and is easily startled by loud noises.

"I am not a brave person at all," the 23-year-old said.

But on weekends during the past several months, she has mustered the courage to take to the streets – sometimes by herself – equipped with goggles, a respirator, filters and bottles of water to extinguish tear gas canisters.

"I feel quite surprised how girls, including myself, have reacted in these situations," she said. "I think we have all toughened up."

Jordyn, an NGO worker, is one of many Hongkongers who have protested against the city's government since June 9, 2019. The seemingly leaderless movement has been mostly represented by male faces. But women joining the protests have become more daring, with many increasingly willing to go to the front lines and face off with police. Demonstrators and scholars say one positive aspect of the unrest is that it has empowered Hong Kong women and smashed lazy stereotypes, such as that they are materialistic. Yet there is a dark side to women's growing involve-ment. As the movement progressed over the months of 2019, some female protesters complained of sexual violence and other forms of harassment being used against them, including by police.

To the front lines

In 2014, Jordyn joined the "umbrella movement," when thousands occupied the city's streets for 79 days to demand universal suffrage for the 2017 chief executive election and 2020 Legislative Council election. She was left disappointed when the sit-ins ended with little to show for their efforts. Five years later, she finally saw hope in Hong Kong again. That was the day 1 million people, according to organizers, attended a protest against the extradition bill.

Jordyn began the summer of 2019 by going to protests with her parents. But as the movement evolved, she started taking to the streets whether she had company or not. "I will get closer to the front line and try to help. I believe that if you want justice, you need to fight for it," she said.

The first time she was tear-gassed, she was wearing only a surgical mask. Since then, she has learned how to build roadblocks and extinguish tear gas canisters by covering them with a traffic cone and pouring water over them. "I am not afraid of getting arrested – perhaps because I think that I will be lucky enough to get away," Jordyn said. "But I am scared of being beaten up."

When she thinks back to her weekends, all she hears are sounds of protesters groaning after being hit by tear gas, and the rhythm of riot police boots chasing after her. But she intends to continue taking to the streets until the government meets the protesters' five demands, which include an independent inquiry into police's use of force. "I did not hate anyone this much in the past," she said. "I blame it on police and Carrie Lam," she said, referring to the city's chief executive.

Testing their limits

What began as a protest to halt the extradition bill – which the administration eventually withdrew – morphed into a mass anti-government movement and a resistance to what is seen as Beijing's encroachment on Hong Kong's rights and freedoms. And according to a study by scholars from three Hong Kong universities, about 46 per cent of those taking to the streets were female.

Among them is Stephy, who is often at the front lines with a group of about 20 friends, who include three women in black full-body motorcycle armors and grey fabric masks to cover their faces. She has grown used to seeing her friends arrested and hurt.

Since the protests began, the level of violence has escalated. More than 7,000 protesters have been detained, a third of them women, and more than 16,000 rounds of tear gas fired. Police have also used live ammunition, water cannons, rubber bullets and beanbag rounds, while protesters have graduated from throwing water bottles to hurling petrol bombs, bricks and bamboo poles. Far from being cowed by the violence, demonstrators like Stephy, a 21-year-old designer, have only become more determined to fight for their cause.

"After two or three protests, I started seeing many more girls coming out and standing in front, instead of hiding in the back," said Stephy, who has taken on multiple roles, including assisting the injured and scouting out protest areas. Yan, 23, a graduate working in property management, said her company monitored those who took days off to join the protests, but she was willing to lose her job if necessary. "I am still young and I can pay the price," she said. "We need to protect Hong Kong's freedoms."

Yan said women had become more daring as the movement evolved. "We are still exploring our limits on how and what we can do," she said. "Most women are not as physically strong as men. I see how men can play an important role, like moving materials and protecting others." A couple of months into the movement, she and a female friend tried to extinguish tear gas canisters for the first time and Yan realized that "women can do more."

Cheung, 17, a student new to the protests, compared them to a "battlefield" where everyone, regardless of gender, had a role to play. One of her first jobs was to prepare a defensive line by stacking up bricks on a footbridge in Tsuen Wan, and she said her involvement would only grow stronger. "We feel this movement is very important for our future," she said.

Gong nui no more

Women have long played a prominent role in social movements, including fights for their own suffrage. More recently in Sudan, they led protests that toppled the corrupt president Omar al-Bashir. In contemporary China, female activists have been outspoken voices for change. Their numbers include the Tiananmen Mothers, who are still demanding to know exactly what happened in the crackdown on protesters in Beijing on June 4, 1989. In Hong Kong, while gender parity in education was reached about a decade ago, "if you look at leadership in higher education, the judiciary and listed companies, the male dominance is still very pronounced," said Susanne Choi Yuk-ping, a professor with Chinese University's sociology department.

Despite the gap, she said, there was a high rate of female voting and engagement in community organizations. "I am not surprised that in this anti-extradition movement we have seen a lot of women taking to the streets and even being at the front line," Choi said, recalling that large numbers of women had also joined the umbrella movement. "All these experiences will certainly empower women, and make them feel they have a stake in society and that they can make change."

Choi said the movement had been marked by female-led initiatives, such as groups of housewives and mothers who organized petitions and rallies. At the same time, the city's female leader Lam positioned herself as a maternal figure to court public sympathy. But scholars said her strategy had backfired, as Lam's likening of herself and protesters at the start of the movement to a mother and her spoiled children angered many.

While Lam failed to gather public support as a woman, Choi noticed a positive shift in the way local women had been described. "Before, Hong Kong women were often ridiculed as *gong nui* [or 'Kong girl', usually a reference to being materialistic]." But during the movement, "I've seen some posts on [the online forum] LIHKG addressing their changing perception of Hong Kong women."

Darker side

However, University of Hong Kong professor Petula Ho Sik-Ying said women had been more vulnerable than men to abuse and attacks since the movement began. Ho was criticized when dozens of people were arrested at a protest outside a police station in August 2019, which was organized after a female protester was photographed with her underwear exposed as police dragged her away. Some activists blamed the arrests on Ho, saying she had told protesters to stop throwing stones and not run away. Ho denied saying any such thing, but found herself still being harassed online.

"It's been a masculine movement and very patriarchal," Ho said. "We all enjoy the romantic aspect of the movement, but there are more dangers than we are willing to talk about."

Allegations of sexual violence by police grew louder as anger and resentment toward the force increased. One female protester accused police in August 2019 of subjecting her to a humiliating strip-search following her arrest. She said she was ordered to squat while naked, as a female officer patted her thighs with a pen and instructed her to open her legs wider. A police spokeswoman denied the allegations, saying there was footage contradicting the protester's story.

On August 28, 2019, thousands gathered in Central to hear the accounts of various victims alleging sexual violence. Many in the crowd held posters with the hashtag #ProtestToo, a reference to the global #MeToo movement against sexual harassment and abuse.

An online survey conducted from August 21 to September 30 by the Association Concerning Sexual Violence Against Women found that 67 female protesters alleged they had experienced sexual violence, mostly at the hands of law enforcement officers and pro-establishment activists.

And in October 2019, university student Sonia Ng came out publicly to accuse police of subjecting her and others to sexual violence.

Throughout the protests, authorities have insisted all allegations will be investigated. Police have repeatedly stressed that the force follows strict guidelines and respects the privacy and rights of those in custody.

In January 2020, lawyers for a teenager who said she was gang-raped inside a police station in September accused authorities of trying to discredit her, after police said the woman's statement did not match their investigation results.

Fighting on

Many young men say they welcome the greater prominence of women protesters. Leo, 17, a student who joined the protests as a first-aider, is among them, but is also concerned about the mistreatment of female demonstrators. "At the beginning, there were not that many female protesters on the front lines, but more women have come up to fight for the cause," he said. "Unfortunately, some of them have been caught by the police and have faced unfair and rude treatment." Another male protester, Chan, 24, is surprised by the female protesters' fearless attitude. "They are very efficient and brave. Some even walk in front of us. I respect that," he said, adding that many had been hurt.

Among the more prominent examples of those wounded is a woman volunteer medic who suffered a serious eye injury on August 11, from what protesters say was a beanbag round shot by police. While the force denied the action and declined to take responsibility pending an investigation, the woman became a symbol of the movement.

Some protesters say every injury makes them stronger. Jordyn, the NGO worker, believes she has become more driven since the protests started. "In some ways, Hong Kong youngsters tend to be a bit passive, mostly because of our education system. I feel more empowered now," she said.

Hongkongers needed to find ways to sustain the pressure, she said, adding their demands were still achievable. "It's important to blend our protest ideas and core values into our daily lives. We can't lose hope. It's a long process that has to include education, propaganda, changes in our consumerism patterns." Whatever the final outcome, the movement had shown another side of Hong Kong's women, she said. "Some are now realizing that Hong Kong girls are not afraid of getting their hands dirty."

Unions on the march

Jeffie Lam

Trade unions have mushroomed to sustain the protest momentum. The civil service has not been spared as a tilling ground.

Michael Ngan Mo-chau was a student leader at the Chinese University (CUHK) in 2012 when he co-wrote an orientation booklet for freshmen, encouraging them to participate fully in activities on school governance and civil movements. He told them it was not good enough for them to sit on their hands while others spoke up. "Your days in university will shape your thoughts and determine your future," wrote Ngan, then a final-year student in government and public administration. "So treasure your time here and keep reflecting on yourself."

While at university, Ngan helped to organize a boycott of classes to demand the scrapping of a citywide school curriculum aimed at nurturing patriotism. So his peers and teachers were not entirely surprised when, in July 2019, the 29-year-old civil servant initiated the first rally by government workers over the extradition bill crisis, risking the wrath of his employer. A Labour Department officer, Ngan had faded from the social activism scene after graduation, and was the only student union leader from his year to join the civil service.

He had hoped the rally would provide those in the 180,000-strong civil service with a platform to express their views openly, after many had done so anonymously online. Hundreds of administrative officers,

157

executive officers and government lawyers had signed petitions and open letters urging the government to address the demands of protesters. They concealed their identities by showing photographs of their staff cards, with their faces and names covered. Some went a step further by participating in protests, even at the front lines.

The rally, on August 2, drew an estimated 40,000 people, including thousands of ordinary Hongkongers, and went ahead despite Chief Secretary Matthew Cheung Kin-chung coming out hours before it was due to start to advise those on the public payroll not to "do things in contrast with the government's views." Ngan addressed the crowd that day, saying: "It is not easy for civil servants, who are part of the establishment, to stand up. You can take away my identity as a civil servant, but not as a Hongkonger. Our future can be sacrificed, but not Hongkongers'."

The rare protest by public servants deeply embarrassed the embattled government of Chief Executive Carrie Lam Cheng Yuet-ngor. The head of the civil service, Joshua Law Chi-kong, said in an internal memo that civil servants had to remain politically neutral and avoid giving the impression that the civil service opposed the government. Beijing's Hong Kong-based mouthpieces *Wen Wei Po* and *Ta Kung Pao* published dozens of articles criticizing Ngan, branding him a traitor.

None of that stopped Ngan from co-founding the Union for New Civil Servants in November 2019, or vowing to advance the interests of government employees and protect their right to express their views freely. One among the dozens of new unions set up in the wake of the protests, it began 2020 by accusing police of restricting Hongkongers' rights by ending the New Year's Day protest abruptly. The government warned the union against violating guidelines on impartiality that was demanded of the city's civil servants. "The government calls on all civil servants to stay united in this difficult time, and continue to support the government's work to stamp out violence as a matter of top priority," it said. As of February 2020, the union had 3,000 members.

Former civil service secretary Joseph Wong Wing-ping, who helped draft the civil service code, said city leader Lam should have sensed the seriousness of the crisis when those working under her started to speak up in July 2019. "Civil servants are supposed to be the most conservative group, inclined to back the government and long for social stability," he said. "How can you be indifferent when they speak out?" He said the emergence of the new union was not necessarily a bad thing, but much depended on how Lam chose to perceive it – she could welcome the unionists' constructive opinion, or dismiss them as opposition forces.

As of February 29, 2020, 42 civil servants had been suspended for suspected involvement in "unlawful public activities" relating to the protests. In April, bureau chief Law was replaced by constitutional and mainland affairs minister Patrick Nip Tak-kuen after he was said to have resisted Lam's order to enforce tighter discipline on the civil servants.

Ninety-one new trade unions in 15 months

The civil servants' union was among dozens of trade unions that sprang up in 2019 as Hongkongers looked for new ways to sustain the social movement behind months of anti-government protests from the middle of the year. There were 25 new unions registered in 2019, almost double the 13 set up in 2018, according to Labour Department figures. By mid-March 2020, another 66 had been formed, with more in the pipeline. They represented employees in a wide range of sectors, including the hotel, medical, optometry, dental, construction and information technology sectors, as well as bartenders and beauticians. Some were for workers previously not covered by any registered labor bodies.

The proliferation of new unions turned a page for Hong Kong's labor movement. For a long time, the unions of mainly blue-collar sectors were dominated by the influential pro-Beijing Federation of Trade Unions, an umbrella body with 253 affiliates and more than 420,000 members. It was almost three times larger than its opponent, the Confederation of Trade Unions, which had 93 affiliates and 145,000 members. The Hong Kong Professional Teachers' Union, founded by the late pro-democracy icon Szeto Wah in 1973, was the biggest trade union from a single sector, with more than 100,000 members.

"We want to introduce a new culture of trade unions that are not just about labor rights, but also consolidate the voices of industry to resist the authorities," said Alex Tsui, 24, chairman of the new Hong Kong Hotel Employees Union. A chef in a restaurant with two Michelin stars, he co-founded the union in November 2019 with dozens of others he had met via the encrypted messaging channel Telegram. He said clashes with police were necessary occasionally, but there was a need to bring Hongkongers together for the long-term battle to force the government to address their demands.

CUHK sociologist and former labor organizer Chris Chan King-chi, who specializes in unionism, said Hong Kong's trade unions were traditionally set up after labor disputes and tended to involve mostly blue-collar workers. He pointed out that the new wave had encouraged even those in the financial industry and information technology sector to unionize. He also noted that in the past, labor disputes required the intervention of external parties such as the Confederation of Trade Unions, and were handled by paid union organizers. "Now these novices from different sectors have volunteered to do the job themselves, instead of relying on salaried organizers. This is what Hong Kong has lacked over the years," he said.

Carol Ng Man-yee, chairwoman of the Confederation of Trade Unions, said Hongkongers used to have reservations about trade unions and were reluctant to go against their employers, but the 2019 protests changed that. "If we want to organize a real general strike, we have to form unions in various sectors," said Ng, who had been offering advice to the new unionists. Also, having seen a rising number of frontline protesters arrested, people began to feel that strikes were a way to take the movement forward, she added.

Pandemic sparks a change of plans

The new unionists' main aim may have been to unify pro-democracy forces in their sectors and prepare for a powerful strike, but 2020 brought an unexpected enemy, the coronavirus crisis that affected workers across the economy. At the front line of this new battle were the city's health workers, who were worried about Hong Kong's proximity to mainland China where the pandemic was thought to have originated.

February 2020 witnessed the city's largest health workers' strike ever, organized by the Hospital Authority Employees Alliance formed only in December 2019. Leaders of the alliance were at the forefront of the protests over the summer and had taken part in the Occupy protests of 2014. As a result of their action, 9,000 hospital staff members left their posts for five days after the government refused to shut Hong Kong's border with the mainland completely.

The new union's membership soared in just two months to more than 18,000 – or 22.5 per cent of the 80,000 employees with the Hospital Authority, which manages all public hospitals and clinics and was the second-largest employer after the government. The medical sector had other established unions, such as the Hong Kong Public Doctors' Association and the Association of Hong Kong Nursing Staff. But before the alliance was set up many health care personnel, including allied health workers and clerical support staff, were not unionized.

The Hospital Authority blasted the industrial action, saying it had severely disrupted services at accident and emergency departments and put patients at grave risk. Midway through the strike, Ian Cheung Tsz-fung, chief manager of cluster performance, said 3,100 nurses and 300 doctors were absent from work. Services had been affected at the neonatal intensive care unit, operating theatres and cancer departments, as well as at the obstetrics and gynaecology departments. There had been no blunders so far, but he added: "If this carries on, I dare not guarantee that nothing will go wrong." Some workers returned to help look after infants before the strike ended.

City leader Lam, who refused to meet the union leaders, said the "extreme" action of the striking workers would not force the government's hand. In the midst of the strike, however, she announced the closure of four more border crossings, but stopped short of demands to seal the entire border. There were fears of reprisals against those who went on strike. Two medical associations – the Hong Kong Public Doctors' Association and the Frontline Doctors' Union – supported the new union and urged the Hospital Authority to respect workers' rights to strike even though their own members did not join the action. "If any colleague is meted unreasonable treatment, we will respond in unity and provide relevant legal and other support," they said in a statement.

The pandemic brought chef turned unionist Tsui a growing pile of work as the hotel sector was hit hard, with workers being laid off or told to go on unpaid leave. Tsui accused tourism sector lawmaker Yiu Si-wing of mostly speaking up for travel agencies or hotels hit by the pandemic, rather than hotel employees.

The union demanded a more vigorous response from the hotel industry, including mandatory temperature screening for guests, turning away those with a fever, providing sufficient protective gear for staff and 14-day self-isolation leave with pay for employees who came into contact with infected people.

Membership of the union grew from 130 in December to about 500 by March, although that was a fraction of the estimated 40,000 people in the sector. "Most are adopting a 'wait and see' attitude," Tsui said. "They do not want to speak up publicly against their employers, for fear of jeopardizing their future." When a hotel abruptly laid off 200 staff, none of the 20 workers he approached had been willing to come forward to act against what he considered an unfair termination of their services. "It is going to take a long time to educate them about why we should unionize," he said.

Civil service union leader Ngan also had to turn his attention to the Covid-19 pandemic. In February 2020, his union organized a rally to criticize the government's handling of the outbreak, accusing it of allocating protective gear unfairly among different departments. Ngan, the union's spokesman, brushed aside fears of possible retaliation, saying: "The government has repeatedly warned that civil servants should stay politically neutral and not hold opposing views, but civil servants should also fight for citizens' support and reflect their opinions to the chief executive."

The various developments left activist and campaigner Johnson Yeung Ching-yin feeling optimistic that the new unions would allow pro-democracy Hongkongers to reclaim the narrative. Using the tourism sector as an example, he said: "There used to be only one voice, and it was pro-China, always calling for closer ties with the mainland. Now, these new unions can offer a very different voice."

Sociologist Chan was more circumspect, saying that it was a positive development for the labor movement that new unions were focusing on workplace issues, and not pursuing the political agenda only. He cautioned the new union leaders that successful unionism was a test of patience and could take years to bear fruit. Sustaining their organizations would be a challenge too, especially if there were no issues to pursue in a particular sector. "I would not be too optimistic," he said. "Not everyone has such patience, especially when people in the street protests want immediate results."

We are all Hongkongers ... even ethnic minorities?

Raquel Carvalho

The protests have reminded Hong Kong that non-Chinese residents are part of its political fabric. But a gap remains.

Arianne Baldesimo's heart sank when she saw a notification on her phone claiming ethnic-minority men had been involved in an attack on Jimmy Sham Tsz-kit, the leader of a pro-democracy group behind some of the largest protest marches in Hong Kong. Her fears were not only for Sham, who had been beaten with hammers and spanners, but that a vulnerable, easily scapegoated community had now become a target for anyone seeking revenge.

The October 16 attack on Sham was not the first time protest-related violence had been blamed, sometimes on the scantest of evidence, on the city's ethnic-minority communities. Just weeks earlier, rumors had swirled that paid thugs of South Asian descent had played a part in a gang attack on commuters at Yuen Long MTR station, apparently aimed at protesters returning from a demonstration near the city center. With the latest attack, "enough was enough," thought Baldesimo, herself an ethnic-minority Hongkonger of Philippine descent, and married to a third-generation Indian born in the city. "We had been talking for a long time if we should come out and say something. This time we felt we had to show that a lot of us were not part of that."

Four days later, Baldesimo headed to Tsim Sha Tsui, where Sham's group, the Civil Human Rights Front, was planning to march. Though for all the wrong reasons, the attacks on Sham and in Yuen Long served as reminders to Hong Kong that its ethnic minorities are a part of the city's social and political fabric. Suddenly, communities that had long struggled to get their voices heard were front and center of the most divisive political issue the city had faced in decades. And it was at the march in Tsim Sha Tsui that the glare of the spotlight was at its most intense. Rumors surrounding the attack on Sham had led to speculation that hard-core protesters would seek retribution by targeting two sites on the area's main artery of Nathan Road: Kowloon Mosque and Chungking Mansions, a hub for South Asian and African communities.

If the aim of the rumors was to sow division, they failed. Instead, what ensued was one of the more heart-warming episodes in the long months of simmering discontent. As thousands of Hongkongers descended on Tsim Sha Tsui for the march, some protesters headed to the mosque not to attack, but to guard it. At nearby Chungking Mansions, a group of ethnic-minority residents, including Baldesimo, handed out bottles of water and egg tarts to the protesters and gave speeches to the growing crowds. The mood was more celebration than fear; more unity than division. There were hugs and rounds of applause, and a new-found appreciation for the city's non-Chinese residents. And while the day was not all sweetness and light – Chief Executive Carrie Lam Cheng Yuet-ngor was forced to apologize after a police water cannon sprayed the entrance of the mosque with blue dye during a clearance operation – a sense of hope was palpable. "We do get a lot of racism in Hong Kong, but we stand here to show you that we are one," said Baldesimo, wearing a black T-shirt which read: "We love Hong Kong."

Signs of change

Like Baldesimo, Louise Bedaña, who was born and raised in Hong Kong after her father migrated to the city from the Philippines, is among the many who hope the protests could change the way society views ethnic-minority residents such as herself. Fluent in Cantonese, she knows more about Chinese culture than she does about her father's home country. Yet growing up, she often felt alienated and that she was "not a true Hongkonger." "Ethnic minorities have been systematically segregated. We attend different schools, we are separated from other Hongkongers, and we experience plain racism," said Bedaña, 20, who blamed the government for the lack of integration. Despite these feelings of alienation, the philosophy and politics student at the University of Hong Kong (HKU) was keen to take part in the protests. She had heard various rumors linking ethnic-minority men to the violence – not least among them a claim that triad gangs were recruiting them after the Yuen Long attack to "carry out their dirty work."

While the rumors were damaging and harmful, Bedaña said the protest movement had also been an opportunity for change. At a protest a day after the Yuen Long attack, she suffered heat stroke and was on the verge of fainting when a group of Chinese Hongkongers stepped in to help her – something she did not believe would have happened three months earlier.

She said "systemic and internalized racism" had not ceased to exist in the span of a few months, "but with the way that things are looking now, I am hopeful."

'We are all Hongkongers'

This sense of optimism that the protests could be a unifying rather than a dividing force was a common theme among ethnic Chinese who stepped forward to defend the city's minorities in Tsim Sha Tsui that weekend in October. As the protesters poured onto Nathan Road, Eddie Cheng, 76, stood for hours in front of the mosque with a banner that read "Be nice to religion." A few meters along, another ethnic Chinese protester, Chan, 22, also held a banner. "We are all Hongkongers," it read. "I am sorry if you have ever felt discriminated against. I am gay so I know how it feels. Please give Hong Kong some time, she is improving." The student said the attack on Sham and the rumors about ethnic minorities had prompted him to speak up. "I know they might face discrimination when they are looking for jobs or when they are dating or just in general," he said. "As the majority we have the privilege that, if we speak, our voice will be louder ... this is my responsibility."

That weekend, protesters had also plastered walls and traffic poles with messages in English and Arabic, vowing that South Asians would not be attacked. At Chungking Mansions, ethnic Chinese protesters applauded and sang Cantonese songs as the group that included Baldesimo and her husband Jeffrey Andrews led a powerful chant. "We are all Hongkongers," they shouted, in English and Cantonese.

For Andrews, 34, the city's first ethnic-minority social worker, the event was a "life-changing experience." "Whoever thought of causing the worst race riots in Hong Kong did not anticipate this. The community is even closer and people know that we are here for real," said Andrews, whose grandfather arrived in Hong Kong in the 1960s from southern India.

Of paradox and forgotten contributions

Puja Kapai, a law professor from HKU, said ethnic minorities faced a "paradox" in trying to show they were Hongkongers, because the media tended to show them as outsiders or as a burden. "During the 'umbrella movement' in 2014 and most recently during the movement for democracy or against the extradition bill, ethnic minorities who participated felt welcomed, celebrated," she said. However, they were "welcomed because they are standing with Hongkongers, as people showing international solidarity with the movement – not as Hongkongers ... People feel a sense of solidarity and inclusion, but the premise of it is still grounded on that lack of acceptance."

"We don't count as Hong Kong people in our own right, but when there is violence and trouble, we are ready to be scapegoated – largely because of this idea that we are so poor that our political affinity can be bought," said Kapai, whose family, of Indian descent, arrived in the city in 1953. She said it was hard to pinpoint the source of rumors linking minorities to the attacks, but the question to ask was: "Who does this narrative serve?"

"Obviously, those who are against the protesters ... It could distract the energy of the vandals away from the Chinese-owned businesses and government facilities and redirect anger to South Asian businesses, work or religious places," she said. It was common, she added, for ethnic minorities to be used for political ends, especially during periods of protest and ahead of elections. "It's a regular pattern and some politicians have been very deliberate at engaging with the ethnic-minority community at the right time."

Although their contributions to the city may often be overlooked, ethnic minorities have played an important role in Hong Kong society for more than a century. Many Nepalis and Indians were employed as policemen and soldiers under British colonial rule; and non-Chinese residents contributed to institutions such as the Star Ferry, HSBC and HKU.

While some families have been here for several generations, others arrived far more recently. In 2016, Hong Kong had 584,383 ethnic-minority residents – most of them from the Philippines, Indonesia and South Asia – making up 8 per cent of the total population, according to government figures. Foreign domestic workers, who cannot qualify for permanent residency, account for more than half this figure. Hong Kong also has a population of a few thousand asylum seekers, mostly from African and Asian countries, who cannot be resettled in the city. While Hong Kong grants religious and cultural freedoms, the city's relationship with its non-Chinese groups has long been marked by misconceptions. Several studies have identified systemic and structural problems facing such groups, including lack of equal access to education, public services and employment.

No unifying stance

Much like the population at large, Hong Kong's ethnic minorities hold no single view of the protests. "The ethnic-minority community is also torn apart," said Yasir Naveed, 29, who was born in Pakistan but has spent half his life in Hong Kong. Naveed joined the first protests against the extradition bill, but stopped after they descended into violence. "Many think it's better not to be part of the matter because whichever side you take, it can be dangerous," he said. Many ethnic minorities feel protesting or being too vocal politically would be more risky for them than for ethnic Chinese. Some fear being profiled by police, while others fear isolation and stigmatization within their own community. Alizai, 45, a trader from Pakistan married to a local Chinese woman, stopped protesting after attending the first demonstrations in June. "My wife and I have a five-year-old son. As an ethnic minority, I know I can be easily profiled by the police, so I can't be out there," he said. The concern that one arrest would reflect badly on the whole community tended to make minorities acutely aware of legal boundaries, said social worker Andrews. "Many of us worked so hard to be part of the so-called mainstream society that we don't want to risk that," he said.

With the protests evolving into wider calls for democracy, some hope Hong Kong can start a conversation that reflects the city's diversity. Amod Rai, 40, a teacher from Nepal who has been in the city for about two decades, was among those who stayed away from the protests but watched their evolution with interest. He said Hong Kong's system "oppressed ethnic minorities" because non-Chinese faced more hurdles in winning top political jobs – a point missed by both government supporters and protesters demanding democracy. But "diversity and multiculturalism should be fundamental elements" in any such system, he said.

"Everybody's rights should be secured," Rai said. "What kind of democracy are they asking for if we are not represented?"

Migrant workers in the danger zone

Fiona Sun, Chris Lau and Phila Siu

Sundays once made life bearable for Hong Kong's migrant workers. That changed in 2019.

After five years in Hong Kong, Daisy Martinez, a domestic helper from the Philippines, has decided that enough is enough. When her contract ends sometime in 2020, she will head off in search of a new, and hopefully safer, life in Dubai.

Leaving is no easy decision. Moving to the Middle East will take her even further from the eight-year-old son in the Philippines she works to support. But her mind is made up. "I'm so scared about what is happening here in Hong Kong," said Martinez, a single mother. "For the past five years, I could go everywhere and do whatever I wanted on my day off. I could enjoy my Sunday, but now I have to go home early because I'm scared about what will happen."

Months of anti-government protests have taken a toll on one of Hong Kong's hardest-working communities – the nearly 400,000 foreign domestic helpers, mostly from the Philippines and Indonesia, who eke out a living by keeping many of the city's households ticking over.

Even before the protests, their lives were notoriously hard. Most work six-day weeks and 12-hour days for a wage that, at a statutory minimum of HK$4,630 (US$600) a month, is less than a third of the citywide average. Since the unrest kicked off, their lives became harder still. For many, what made work bearable in the past were the Sundays spent congregating with compatriots in parks and public spaces to eat, pray and sing. But for the better part of 2019, the most popular spots – Causeway Bay for Indonesians and Central for Filipinos – no longer felt so safe or welcoming.

Instead, these places were scenes of often-violent clashes between protesters and police. Domestic helpers or other foreign workers who hung around risked being caught in the crossfire. In September, an Indonesian journalist was blinded by a rubber bullet; in December, a helper who wrote about the protests was deported.

The tense, volatile situation left Martinez and her friends with a dilemma. The 31-year-old likes her employers and regards their nine-year-old daughter as her "baby." But she is too scared to stay in Hong Kong, and too poor to return to the Philippines. "We are worried about our safety and also our jobs," she said. "But we can't just go back home, because our families need us to support them."

During the months of protests, some workers ended up just staying home. Lamie, 35, a Filipino helper who has been in Hong Kong for almost four years stopped going out completely. "I was afraid that I won't be able to go back home, so I just stayed in the lobby of the building where I live, to watch the news and YouTube and to keep myself safe."

The seven-day week

Staying at home like Lamie became the norm for many helpers, whose modest budgets limit entertainment options in one of the world's most expensive cities. But shunning the outdoors created another set of problems not least the sense of always being on duty. Support groups said unscrupulous employers exploited helpers stuck at home and pressured them to work without compensation. Some even barred their helpers from going out, they said, on the pretext that they might run into trouble if a protest broke out.

"Some employers truly care about domestic workers, but there are others who take advantage of the situation," said Shiela Tebia-Bonifacio, chairwoman of Gabriela Hong Kong, an organization that supports Filipinos in the city. The 35-year-old, herself a domestic helper with 13 years' experience in Hong Kong, added: "If the issue is safety, then domestic workers should be allowed to enjoy their rest days at home or anywhere else that is not near a protest site."

While the law offers protections for helpers, the reality is that many do not have proper rest areas. The government's sample contract for helpers says that employers should provide "reasonable privacy," but many end up sleeping on sofas or sharing rooms with the children they look after. And without a dedicated private space, it is hard to escape the employer's glare. Hong Kong's Employment Ordinance is supposed to guarantee that helpers have at least one rest day a week and stipulates that if there is an emergency requiring work on a rest day, the helper should be given another day off within 30 days. Employers who break the law are liable to prosecution and a fine of HK$50,000.

But Tebia-Bonifacio said helpers were often too afraid of losing their jobs to rock the boat. Others struggled with language barriers that prevented them from learning the latest official advice on the protests. "Most of the news is in Chinese and English, but many domestic helpers can read only in their own languages," said Lau Ka-mei, organizing secretary of the Hong Kong Federation of Asian Domestic Workers Unions.

While both the Philippine and Indonesian consulates would provide updates on coming protests, Lau said, they and the Hong Kong government needed to give better information and advice to help domestic workers assess the situation.

Cautionary tales

One of the few local outlets that cater to domestic helpers in their own language, the Indonesian Suara Hong Kong News, itself became an unwitting symbol of the dangers facing migrant workers who strayed too close to the protest front lines. The outlet hit international headlines when one of its journalists, Veby Mega Indah, 39, was partially blinded by a rubber bullet fired by police as she covered a protest in Wan Chai on September 29.

Veby should have been safe. She was an experienced journalist, trained in working in hostile environments, and had been doing everything by the book. She was wearing safety goggles, a helmet and clothes that clearly identified her as press and was standing with a dozen other journalists observing at a distance.

All of a sudden she heard a reporter shouting "journalist" in Cantonese and then felt a searing pain in her right eye, before collapsing into the arms of another journalist behind her. She heard voices urging her to stay awake and thought: "It's going to be my end." Despite surgery, doctors could not save the sight in her eye. A committed Christian, she has forgiven the officer who fired the shot, even though she is pursuing legal action to have him identified so she can initiate a civil action and possibly a private prosecution.

"I am pursuing justice in this case not only for me but for all the injured people in Hong Kong who cannot do the same," she said. "I hope there will be justice, so the officer who shot me will face consequences according to the law, so police officers understand what they cannot do."

At least for now, Veby must wait. Police said a "comprehensive investigation" had been launched and denied the officer was being protected, but it is unclear when or if he or she will ever be named.

Asked if she would return to the protest front lines, tears ran down

Veby's cheeks. Until the incident, she had written regularly about the rights of Indonesian migrant workers since arriving in Hong Kong in 2012. "It's one of the things that keeps me up at night, wondering whether I can continue to be a journalist."

An unspoken threat

Many helpers see another cautionary tale in the case of Yuli Riswati, 39, an Indonesian domestic worker who covered the protests as a citizen journalist once a week on her day off and was later deported under murky circumstances.

The government deported her in December 2019 on the grounds she had overstayed her visa, but her supporters believed the real reason was that she had reported on the social unrest for the not-for-profit Indonesian online news outlet Migran Pos, which she launched in March.

Fish Ip Pui-yu, a regional coordinator of the International Domestic Workers Federation, a labor rights group, said it was true that Yuli had forgotten to renew her work visa, which expired in July. But even so, she said, something did not seem right about her arrest. "During my 20 years as an activist, I have never heard of immigration officers arresting domestic workers at their employers' flats for expiry of their visas," Ip said.

Neither had Teresa Liu Tsui-lan, managing director of the Technic Employment Service Center, who has been in the business for 30 years. And neither had Yuli's lawyer, Chau Hang-tung, even as she conceded that technically the arrest was within the law. The Immigration Department, while it declined to comment on individual cases, emphasized that it has the power to arrest, detain, prosecute and deport anyone for violating their conditions of stay.

But various industry sources said the standard practice was that, as long as employers wrote to the department explaining they wanted to re-employ a domestic worker – as Yuli's employer had – then expired visas were usually overlooked. Yuli's case became even murkier when she appeared in court. Prosecutors offered no evidence and withdrew the overstay charge. A month later, she was on a flight home.

The very real ordeals of both Veby and Yuli coincided with fake news reports and rumors that foreign workers had been arrested for attending the protests, creating further doubts and fears in many minds. "We can't vote, we live on temporary visas, our voices don't count … Yet there have been false news reports about some of us being detained," said Eni Lestari, who has spent half her life as a domestic helper and chairs the International Migrants Alliance, which advocates for the rights of migrants and refugees. The Indonesian, who is in her 40s, said: "This creates panic and everyone is uneasy."

Suffering on the margins

Fiona Sun and Crystal Tai

As the protests wore on, those paying the biggest price were the working poor, the disabled and the elderly.

It was late afternoon on a Sunday in Wan Chai and street cleaner Tsui was heading home, when he found the nearest MTR station had closed because of anti-government protests. So he walked half an hour and two stops along the line to Tin Hau, taking care to avoid Causeway Bay, where police and protesters were locked in a violent clash. He thought he had given the disturbance a wide berth, but it was not enough to spare him the tear gas. "It must have been brought by the wind," he recalled. "My eyes and skin were burning."

The gaunt-looking 60-year-old made it home safely that night, but had to return to Wan Chai for another shift the next morning. When he arrived, the scene was unlike any he had seen in 10 years of cleaning the city's streets. Broken glass, torched rubbish bins and metal pipes were strewn across the roads, left over from the night's mayhem. "The glass was everywhere," he recounted. "We had to sweep it by hand. It took hours."

The months of anti-government protests in Hong Kong polarized society and, in many cases, even families. But among the many divisions there was one thing few would dispute. In a city where one in five people, or 1.37 million, lives below the poverty line of HK$4,000 (US$511) a month, life has become far more difficult for Hongkongers like Tsui. As tourists stayed away and retail sales plummeted, along with the impact of the coronavirus epidemic in early 2020, the city's economy has been severely hit. Those paying the biggest price are the people already on society's margins: the working poor, the disabled, migrant workers and the elderly. Closed restaurants, canceled events and delayed construction projects have meant less work for people in low-wage and part-time jobs. MTR closures throughout the more intense months of the protests made travel hard for those with mobility problems, and turned long commutes from far-flung working-class districts into costly, complicated affairs. Elderly patients missed hospital appointments, unable or too scared to keep them.

Picking up the pieces

Tsui and his colleagues often found themselves, quite literally, on the protest front lines. Unlike the black-clad protesters or uniformed riot police, Hong Kong's 11,900 cleaners rarely featured in the newspapers' front-page photographs, though they often found themselves unintentionally at the center of the action. And not only because it was they who must deal with the detritus when protesters hurled petrol bombs or trash metro stations, or police fired tear gas into the streets. But also because, poorly paid and with little job security, many felt they had no option but to continue cleaning those streets, even amid the violence.

A survey by the Cleaning Workers Union in August 2019 found 53 of 75 cleaners in nine areas regularly hit by protests – including Causeway Bay, Wan Chai and Sheung Wan – had been exposed to tear gas while working. Resulting health problems included breathing difficulties, eyesight damage and skin irritation. Not one had been equipped with protective gear such as a respirator, goggles or gloves. The government's Food and Environmental Hygiene Department said cleaners had the right to stop working when clashes broke out, but the union countered that, in reality, any cleaner who did so risked being seen as absent without leave and fired without com-pensation. "Most cleaners don't dare leave their shifts when clashes break out, even when tear gas is being fired. They are concerned about being punished or fired," said union organizer Leung Tsz-yan.

Cleaners earn an average of HK$9,643 per month, well below the city's average of HK$17,500, leaving them vulnerable to pressure from unscrupulous employers. Dick Lam, 50, a cleaner who works evenings in the Causeway Bay shopping district, was among those who kept calm and carried on. "I have to stay at work until my shift ends, no matter what," he said. As a consequence, he was often caught in the crossfire. "One time, rounds of tear gas were being fired nearby, and I didn't have any protective gear except for a surgical mask, which was useless against tear gas. So I wetted a towel and covered my nose with it. Then I rinsed my eyes." Usually, he would wait until the protesters left before he started cleaning. On days when the chaos extended late into the night, he was often left stranded, missing the last train home or finding that public transport had been suspended. On those occasions he spent the night at the refuse collection point, curled up on the hand cart he uses to transport bags of rubbish.

Not all contractors and managers were heartless. Kwok Chi-wah, 64, who is in charge of cleaning services in a part of Mong Kok, told employees reporting to him to stop immediately whenever clashes erupted. "Their safety is of the utmost importance," he said. But then, even workers with enlightened bosses had problems. Cheng, 73, a cleaner operating in Prince Edward, said his refuse collection site had shortened its hours so cleaners could avoid late-night clashes. Yet still he had to face the aftermath of the night's wrecking spree in the morning. His patch, near Prince Edward MTR station, was the site of a notorious run-in between police and protesters that sparked a rumor

– later debunked – that three people had died and their deaths had been covered up. For Cheng, the makeshift shrine to the imaginary martyrs, which for two months would be destroyed every few days and repeatedly rebuilt, only created more work. Along with the everyday garbage, he dealt with what the shrine's visitors left behind: bricks, burnt rubbish bins and bouquets and stands of flowers. Bins proved popular with protesters, who set them on fire to use as roadblocks, but again this only meant the cleaners had one more chore – hiding them away whenever protests loomed.

Trapped with no transport

Cleaners were not alone in their suffering. Closures of the MTR and cross-harbor tunnels and bus diversions affected most commuters and, as usual, the burden was greatest on the poor. Travel restrictions hit cleaners, laborers and builders hardest, said Samson Tse, a professor in social work and social administration at the University of Hong Kong (HKU). "These are people who have to travel for work from poorer neighborhoods such as Sheung Shui to Central, where they wash dishes, clean, do security work," he said. "They make HK$350 to HK$400 on a good night, but because the MTR is closed and bus routes have been blocked, they have to bribe taxi drivers with HK$500 to get home. They are losing money every day, but can't afford to lose their jobs either." The poorest, said Tse, struggled to stay afloat. "There's no safety net, there's no cushion," he said.

A security guard in his 30s, who was working on the HKU campus when it became a protest battleground in October 2019, painted a similar picture. "I live in Kowloon and the commute to work is very difficult. We're paid HK$100 to HK$150 per hour, but this barely covers lunch and transport on a protest day." And what money was left over provided cold comfort, given his safety concerns. "The worst is working the night shift – you don't know if you could get hurt during the clashes," he said.

For some groups, transport concerns were about more than increased costs. When services went down, disabled and elderly residents could find themselves trapped.

"My wife uses a wheelchair and has had to work from home many days because she is unable to navigate the roadblocks and sidewalks with broken and overturned bricks," said Duffy Tam, who lives in Jordan and is in his early 30s. "Working from home is not feasible in the long run." When protests disrupted traffic, many elderly found it hard to keep medical appointments, said Eugene Chan, a former district council candidate in Shau Kei Wan, where more than 30,000 people are elderly.

"They keep their eye on the TV to check if there are traffic disruptions and whether minibuses and buses are running, and whether hospitals are still open for check-ups," he said.

Struggling to survive

Low incomes exacerbated the problem, in a city where many elderly people's finances are growing more precarious. Lee, a former dishwasher in her late 60s who moved to Hong Kong from Guangdong province two decades ago, sleeps on an adjacent bed to her adult son in a one-room flat in Shau Kei Wan. Meeting the monthly rent of HK$1,400 had always been tough, but it became almost impossible when her son lost his job in the kitchen of a dim sum restaurant that blamed its dwindling custom on the protests. "I don't work anymore, but if someone had a job I'd take it in a heartbeat," said Lee, who lives on savings and government aid and has just HK$900 left each month after paying her rent.

Around the corner from her flat, the Ho Win Roasted Meat Restaurant distributes free lunchboxes three times a week. It is not unusual to see elderly people queuing for hours to receive one of the boxes, which would usually sell for HK$28. Another elderly lady, Lo, rations hers into two meals to last a full day. "Of course my life has been impacted by the protests," said Lo, who found it hard to leave her one-room flat in neighboring Chai Wan. "The tear gas makes me feel sick, and young people are getting hurt."

Many of Hong Kong's poorest feel the increasingly violent protests have highlighted just how trapped they are. "I'm all alone without family, so at least I don't have anyone to worry about me," said Mak Hon-kau, 68, a gardener at HKU who has been working since he was 13. "Life has always been difficult in Hong Kong. I don't have skills or an education, so what else can I do?"

Paul Yip Siu-fai, chair professor in social work and social administration at HKU, warned that the "life trajectories" of many workers would be affected if the government did not begin to do more for those in need. "If you go to any restaurant, they will tell you they are hiring fewer part-time and weekend workers," he said.

But it is not all doom and gloom. Yip pointed to restaurants that allowed the needy to use their kitchens in the morning to boil herbal teas and sell them, boosting not only their income but their self-esteem and sense of belonging. He said that, in cases like that, "it's all win, win, win. So don't tell me you can't do anything for them." He added that there was much to be done to help the elderly, poor and disabled, even in less politically febrile times. With the city's social discontent still simmering, it desperately needed to solve its social problems, he warned. It could start, he suggested, by learning to appreciate the contribution of sectors of society beyond finance and trade, and showing more compassion to the less well-off. "This inequality is real, and it hurts," he said. "It's not being acknowledged widely or tackled effectively. And at the end of the day we live with the consequences."

A song, slogans and Lennon Walls

Kimmy Chung and Jeffie Lam

A song, walls of fluttering post-it notes and slogans are part of the protest movement's identity, but not everyone is a fan.

Joyce Chow had never understood why people cried for their national anthems. How world-beating athletes and international footballers – not to mention their adoring, patriotic publics – could be brought to tears by the banging of a drum. Whenever she heard the Chinese anthem, *March of the Volunteers*, Chow could barely comprehend it.

Then one day in September 2019, at a suburban shopping mall in Tsuen Wan, it all fell into place. Chow, 33, a company director, had gone to the mall to take part in a flash mob protest organized over the Telegram internet messaging service. She hoped that, at precisely 9pm, hers would be one of hundreds of voices rising in unison to belt out a popular, newly penned protest song. But she could not be sure.

As is the nature of flash mobs, there was no guarantee the other chat group members – all of whom were anonymous – would even show up. There was always the terrifying possibility she would find herself alone, singing at the top of her voice in the middle of a mall.

Chow need not have worried. By 9pm, crowds of five or six people deep had gathered on four floors overlooking the central atrium in a shopping centre in Tsuen Wan. Some were dressed in black, some wore masks and some waved flags. All were there for the same reason. As the opening bars of *Glory to Hong Kong* rang out, hundreds of

Hongkongers started to sing as one. Chow, who said she seldom cried in her life, could not stop the tears.

"The scenes of the clashes kept popping into my mind as I sang," Chow said. "I finally realized how it felt to have a song representing you and your hometown."

Within just days of its release on the popular Hong Kong internet forum LIHKG, *Glory to Hong Kong* had been adopted as the protest movement's anthem. Soon it was being sung as spontaneously as it was passionately in pockets of protests across the city. Residents young and old, masked and unmasked, would gather at parks or malls to sing its four verses, pledging no more tears and vowing that freedom would reign. At first, people needed smartphones or sheets of paper to remind them of the words; soon they knew them by heart.

In 2019, *Glory to Hong Kong* was just one of the many ways in which protesters weaponized their creativity against the government. Across the city, Lennon Walls featuring brightly colored Post-it notes and anti-establishment graffiti popped up; in residential areas, high-rise apartment dwellers took to chanting the latest protest slogans to each other in "late night concerts." And the significance of all these efforts, songs or walls or slogans, was not merely a matter of artistic merit.

"*Glory to Hong Kong* itself is important, but even more so is the way people sang it in malls peacefully, yet creating a social disruption at the same time," said Sampson Wong Yu-hin, who has been collecting protest-inspired street art since the Occupy protests of 2014. "It empowered the movement."

Beyond the clashes, the movement had sought to attach more emotional meanings to unite supporters.

Stronger than helmets

The protests had been in their fourth month, stuck in a predictable pattern and in need of a boost when *Glory to Hong Kong* arrived on the scene. Its composer, a 20-something musician using the pseudonym "Thomas dgx yhl," said he had been trying to write a song for the movement since June as he believed that the power of a song could do more than anything else to strengthen Hongkongers' resolve to fight against the unpopular extradition bill.

"This might be the first song that gives people in the city a sense of belonging in this era," he said.

A slick video version of the anthem, featuring a 150-strong orchestra, became a hit on YouTube, gaining more than 4.3 million views in six months. The two-minute clip begins with a drum roll before panning across a dark, smoky hall occupied by a full orchestra and choir, all masked and in black, some wearing goggles and helmets, the signature look of the protesters.

The imagery is spliced with scenes of protesters in streets blanketed by tear gas; the lyrics pay tribute to those who defend values that protesters and their supporters believe have been eroded amid despair and darkness, and those who yearn for the city to regain its seemingly lost glory.

Thomas described the process of writing *Glory to Hong Kong* as a team effort involving lyricists, musicians, backroom producers and the protesters themselves. He came up with the melody and worked with others on the early Cantonese lyrics. They produced a demo which he posted on LIHKG, a Reddit-like forum popular with protesters, and invited suggestions for improvements. Forum users obliged, and he took in their ideas, adding the movement's clarion call, "Liberate Hong Kong; revolution of our times" into the last verse.

Unlike the hymns and pop songs previously adapted for the protest movement – especially during the days of Occupy in 2014, when student demonstrators blocked streets for 79 days – the anthem has a touch of a martial beat to it. A member of the song's production team said the idea was to fit the tone of the protests. "No more sentimental softness, but strength in determination," he said.

Its popularity even earned it comparisons to *Do You Hear the People Sing?* from the musical Les Miserables, which has itself been used as a protest song. Composer Edmond Tsang Yik-man said both songs consisted of notes of unequal length – something that would arouse emotion and fit the mood when people marched.

"It is easy to put yourself into the music while singing or walking, which is why the song resonated with many Hongkongers so swiftly after it came out," said Tsang.

That such comparisons were being made, and the anthem's runaway success, left many of those involved in its production taken aback, and almost wary that it might have become too successful. "It is not bad to boost morale," said the orchestra's conductor. "But we hope people do not forget to fight on."

Not everyone, however, was won over by the song. Critics said the so-called anthem was subversive and challenged the idea that Hong Kong was a part of China. Some displeased residents also responded by heading to the malls for their own flash mobs, this time waving the Chinese national flag and singing *March of the Volunteers* to demonstrate their loyalty to the nation.

Simon Zhang, who moved to Hong Kong from the mainland five years ago, took part in one such flash mob at Pacific Place in Admiralty. He attended because he found the protesters' anti-mainland sentiment unbearable and worried for the city's future. "I had goosebumps after hearing everyone sing the national anthem," he said.

"We must use our voice to stand up for China."

Lennon Walls: Venues for expression, and clashes too

Other observers saw the success of *Glory to Hong Kong* as an echo of the success of *Raise the Umbrella*, the anthem of the Occupy movement of 2014. Other forms of protest art, too, appear to have built on work that began five years ago.

The most visible examples are the many Lennon Walls that have sprouted up across the city on everything from shopfronts to underpasses to overhead pedestrian bridges. The walls are characterized by seas of pastel-coloured sticky notes with handwritten messages, sometimes even written in simplified Chinese characters to appeal to visitors from the mainland, as opposed to the traditional characters used in Hong Kong.

"Carrie Lam, step down" and "My dear, democracy is a good thing" are the sort of messages that are typical, while offensive caricatures of police officers are another favorite.

More recently, some of the messages advised people to take care during the coronavirus pandemic, expressed support for health care workers and urged the government to close Hong Kong's borders with the mainland.

The walls are named after John Lennon, of the 1960s British band The Beatles, who was an anti-war activist in later life. The original Lennon Wall sprang up spontaneously in his honour in Prague following his assassination on December 8, 1980.

In Hong Kong, the first Lennon Wall appeared during the Occupy protests along an outdoor staircase leading to the government headquarters in Admiralty. In 2019, it reappeared at the same spot after an estimated 1 million people marched on June 9 against the extradition bill. Soon after, similar walls appeared in all of Hong Kong's 18 districts.

The walls gave protesters an outlet to express their frustration, said Samuel Chu, a student who volunteered to manage one such board in

Tai Po. "It might just be a Post-it memo, but it is also a blessing to all Hongkongers," Chu said.

Significantly, the Lennon Walls of today are noticeably larger, more sophisticated and organized than those during the Occupy movement.

"In 2014, protesters mostly put up Post-its on the wall to vent their emotions. It was relatively passive," said Abaddon, a designer in his 40s who has been creating protest art since 2012.

"But now, people have organized among themselves through Telegram and deliberately come up with posters to sway public opinion."

He gave the example of a series of posters created in July that depicted protesters as "valiant" and highlighted images of alleged police brutality. These were expressly targeted at middle-aged residents who might otherwise hesitate to support the violence of hard-core protesters.

Abaddon said that as in the protests themselves, there was no leader directing the art. Instead, those who wanted to be involved met on Telegram. Political cartoonists, illustrators, designers and producers would create the posters, then volunteers including housewives and students would distribute them in their neighbourhoods.

The posters would be updated frequently to account for the latest developments and tended to fall under one of three classifications: infographics, protest schedules and emotional appeals to encourage supporters to keep up the fight.

Abaddon, who designed several meters-tall posters in the Kwai Fong Lennon Wall – including one titled "Fighting against our destiny is our only weapon" – said poster art was more powerful than traditional media because of its reach. "It catches the attention of passers-by. They take pictures and share with others," he said. Supporters also share protest art and information with strangers using Apple's Airdrop.

Much like *Glory to Hong Kong*, however, it is an art form that is not to everyone's taste. Pro-establishment residents complain that the walls are an eyesore and the areas around them have become flashpoints for clashes when other citizens try to take them down.

In August, a 50-year-old tour guide, whose earnings had been hit by the protests, was arrested for stabbing three people at a Lennon Wall in Tseung Kwan O. Ahead of Hong Kong's district council elections in November, the pro-establishment camp complained that Lennon Walls were being used unfairly for political advertisements.

Slogans and late-night concerts

Over the summer of 2019, protesters came up with many other creative ways to get their points across. On August 7, hundreds of mostly young protesters gathered outside the space museum in Tsim Sha Tsui for what might have looked to the uninitiated like an impromptu disco, shining laser pointers at the building while dancing to loud pop music.

The event was an ironic condemnation of the arrest of a student leader found in the possession of numerous handheld laser pointers, referred to by police as "laser guns."

Two weeks later there was another light show when about 210,000 people joined hands to form a 60km human chain across the city in an action inspired by the 1989 Baltic Way protests that contributed to the collapse of the Soviet Union. One of the more striking images to emerge was that of hundreds of hikers scaling Lion Rock, lighting the contours of the emblematic mountain head with torches that could be seen for miles around.

Popular slogans have also emerged as an enduring legacy of the protests. These began largely upbeat and cheerful but have evolved in lockstep with the mood, gradually taking on darker tones.

"Hongkongers, add oil" was one of the more popular ones in the early days, though after the government evoked an emergency law to ban masks "Hongkongers, resist" began to eclipse it. And after the death of undergraduate Chow Tsz-lok, who fell in unexplained circumstances from a car park in Tseung Kwan O near a police clearance operation, an even darker slogan, "Hongkongers, revenge," took hold. The undergraduate's death, blamed by protesters on police, also led to calls for the force to be disbanded.

Slogans also played a key role in another protest phenomenon, the "late-night concerts" that became popular in some high-rise residential areas and can still be heard on occasion today. The concerts worked on a basis of call and response: one resident would shout a slogan from their open window at 10pm every night then others would call back with slogans of their own. Among the more popular ones was "Liberate Hong Kong; revolution of our times," the same line used in the last verse of *Glory to Hong Kong*.

These "late night concerts" soon spread across Hong Kong and could eventually be heard throughout the week. To this day the concerts can break out spontaneously in shopping malls or at gatherings in people's homes.

"In 2014, the resistance mainly took the form of occupation, right in the city center," said the protest art collector Sampson Wong. "But since 2019, protests have appeared in different parts of Hong Kong, at different times, using all sorts of urban spaces.

"It is a unique expression. It works only in Hong Kong."

Unpacking 'Liberate Hong Kong; revolution of our times'

Jeffie Lam and Gary Cheung

A slogan calling for revolution has become a battle cry, with its jailed author seen as the spiritual leader of the protest movement.

When an earnest pro-independence activist with distinctive owlish glasses chanted "Liberate Hong Kong; revolution of our times" on the election stump in 2016, supporters cheered him on. The phrase, like so many campaign slogans, was soon forgotten.

But the words of Edward Leung Tin-kei became one of the most commonly heard chants during anti-government unrest three years later. Young black-clad protesters spray-painted the catchphrase all over the city from about July 21, 2019, the night scores of them vandalized Beijing's liaison office in Sai Ying Pun and defaced the national emblem on its front entrance.

The chant's popularity prompted city leader Carrie Lam Cheng Yuet-ngor to cite it as solid proof that the nature of the movement had changed, from anti-extradition bill to anti-China. She quoted the slogan twice in a news conference on August 5, two weeks after it first was widely chanted. "They ... called for a revolution to liberate Hong Kong. These actions challenge national sovereignty, threaten 'one country, two systems', and destroy the city's prosperity and stability," she warned.

Leung, who turned 28 a week before the unrest kicked off, rose to prominence as the poster boy of the localist movement born in the aftermath of the Occupy protests of 2014. Localists argue that Hong

Kong must retain its unique values, including its culture and language, and thwart mainlandization, by resisting the influx of mainland Chinese tourists and cross-border traders who they say bring inconvenience to certain northern neighborhoods.

A spokesman for localist group Hong Kong Indigenous, Leung revealed during a rally in 2016 that in crafting his new slogan he was torn between the phrase "Revolution of the generation" and "Revolution of our times." He eventually opted for the latter as his campaign refrain during a by-election for a Legislative Council seat that year.

"An era is not categorized by one's age. Even if you are old, you would belong to a new era as long as you believe in and embrace freedoms. But you would be in the old era if you can't get rid of the old framework, even if you are very young," he declared.

He was representing an era of people, he said, who were willing to use their "blood and sweat" to fight for their freedoms. Leung did not win the seat, but garnered 15 per cent of the vote, a warning to opposition veterans that young localists could eat their political lunch.

In 2018, Leung was sent to jail for six years for his role in the Mong Kok riot two years earlier, which began as a protest to defend illegal street hawkers. While the phrase was not in use during that riot, the use of the Cantonese word *gwong fuk* – pronounced *guang fu* in Mandarin, and meaning "liberate" or "reclaim" depending on your translation – first became popular in 2015 amid the rise in localist sentiment. Protesters in border towns, unhappy with mainland visitors, would walk the streets chanting the slogan, urging them to stay away.

But *gwong fuk* actually has a precedent in Taiwanese political culture. At the end of the second world war in 1945, when Japan surrendered having occupied the island for 50 years, the Chinese Nationalist Party's Chiang Kai-shek used it to celebrate victory. In 1949, the party resurrected the phrase when it called for *guangfu dalu*, or retaking the mainland, which it had just lost to the communists in the Chinese civil war.

In the summer of 2019, just as his slogan was taking off, Leung wrote a letter from Shek Pik Prison, beseeching anti-government protesters not to be consumed by hate. He was grieved and pained by the bloody scenes, he said. He advised them that "one should always stay vigilant and keep thinking when in peril" and added: "I think we should also be mindful of our own words and actions – whether they would get us closer to our goals, or further away?"

Throughout the months-long protests, Leung's posters could sometimes be spotted in the sea of banners. But more than that, his slogan became the soundscape of the movement, galvanizing participants at rallies or marches. Smaller groups would chant the first line, to hear the rest of the crowd respond even more loudly with the second.

While Lam and Beijing were angered by the slogan and its perceived implication of a campaign to break away from the mainland, not all protesters saw the slogan that way.

Engineering worker Tony Cheung, 28, who was protesting one weekend in Mong Kok in late summer, said it just meant that protesters felt "the government is rotten," rather than being a call for independence. "If we wanted independence, then we would have called for independence," he said.

Matthew Chung, a 29-year-old music company owner, said they shouted the slogan because they wanted to revive the Hong Kong spirit and call for freedom and democracy.

But Ip Kwok-him, a pro-establishment former lawmaker now an adviser to Lam on the Executive Council, saw it as a separatist slogan aimed at overthrowing the central and local governments. "This small group of people still want to live under colonial rule," he said.

A mainland Chinese expert familiar with Hong Kong affairs said that the protesters must know that the slogan irked Beijing no end. "Hong Kong people must recognize the severity of the implications when many young people chant slogans such as 'Liberate Hong Kong;

revolution of our times'," said the expert, who spoke on condition of anonymity.

"If you look at the history of Tibet and Xinjiang, it is impossible to break Hong Kong away from mainland China."

In November's district council elections, officials queried the use of the slogan by four election hopefuls, raising fears they would be barred, like the dozen others in recent years on the grounds that they advocated independence or self-determination. The four, who had posted the slogan on their social media accounts, insisted that they were not advocating independence, and were eventually allowed to contest the elections.

Political scientist Ma Ngok said the slogan itself was vague and open to interpretation. He suspected that people agreed with the term "revolution" as a call to rid the city of Lam's government, which they disliked, rather than as a cry for independence. Some protesters, he said, upheld the slogan in solidarity with Leung, imprisoned after fighting against what he saw as injustice.

At the end of 2019, *Time* magazine put Leung on its annual list of 100 influential people, describing him as "a spiritual leader of the city's months-long unrest." Nora Lam, a filmmaker who created a documentary on Leung called *Lost in the Fumes*, was quoted as saying: "He has a way of sounding like he always has something new, something provocative and interesting to say."

"IN THE PAST, SOME PEOPLE MIGHT WANT TO FREE-RIDE. BUT THIS MOVEMENT ... EVERYONE BELIEVES THEIR PARTICIPATION MATTERS."

Edmund Cheng, political scientist, City University

IN THE CROSSFIRE

"WE ARE FIRST AND FOREMOST HUMAN BEINGS AND HONGKONGERS BEFORE WE ARE PROTESTERS OR POLICE OFFICERS."

Dr Christian Chan, *psychologist*

The dynamics of demonization

Jeffie Lam

Every summer evening at Muk Lun Street in Wong Tai Sin, families leave their cramped flats for the fresh air and greenery downstairs. Teenagers shoot hoops at the basketball court, young couples dawdle en route home and toddlers take turns on the slide in the park. But on August 5, 2019, their quiet heartland life was turned upside down when the protesters held their first citywide strike. Muk Lun Street Playground became a battlefield.

Hundreds of agitated young protesters, who had gathered there hours earlier, were contemplating their next move as the sun went down. They had gone to the neighborhood, home to living quarters of police officers and their families, for a second siege after a first attempt two days earlier. With their helmets, masks and cling film as armor, they lobbed bricks at the second and third floors and began breaking multiple windows. "Shame on the dirty cops!" they chanted. "Police are triads!" others yelled. During the first siege, residents had fought back with their own projectiles, flinging water bottles, glass objects and even plastic bags filled with excrement at the protesters below.

What had begun as a protest against the controversial extradition bill had by August metastasized into deep anger and hatred toward the police force, the government's lightning rod as officials refused to accommodate any of the protesters' demands. It only suspended the bill and then declared it "dead," denying demonstrators' wish for it to be withdrawn.

The clashes between protesters and police were becoming predictable: tense illegal or legal gatherings would descend into chaos amid the road-blocking and brick-hurling by violent demonstrators and the tear gas-firing and beanbag-shooting by the officers. But the tensions were not just between police and protesters. Antipathy had seeped its way into many spheres of society, cementing divisions among colleagues, schoolmates, mainlanders and Hongkongers, friends and families. Either you were for the protesters and outraged by police's harsh treatment of them, or you were against the protesters and disgusted by their blatant disregard for law and order.

The divisions were reminiscent of the tensions during the pro-democracy Occupy movement five years earlier. This time though, the enmity seemed more intense. This was partly because the wounds of Occupy never fully healed, said psychologists and political observers. The hate of 2019, they warned, would take even longer to dissipate. Another key difference between 2014 and 2019 was a perceptible shift in Hongkongers' attitudes toward aggression. Where before city residents were known for their peaceful demonstrations, analysts and surveys by August were suggesting they could now stomach the use of force.

During the clashes, the MTR Corporation, the city's railway operator, began closing stations to avoid being caught in the mayhem and, once tear gas was actually fired inside one of them, found itself accused by protesters of colluding with police and became a direct target. Reckless demonstrators trashed stations, paralyzing operations countless times. The hard-core radicals also took aim at state-owned

Chinese bank branches and shops and restaurants with Beijing links, smashing windows, hurling petrol bombs and daubing graffiti on storefronts in what they nicknamed as "renovations." The message was clear: you were either with us or against us. Police supporters felt the same way. "It is very easy for us to be trapped in the 'us versus them' binary oppositional mindset amid this type of inter-group conflict," Christian Chan, an associate professor at the University of Hong Kong (HKU)'s psychology department, said. "That is not helpful because most political conflicts are complex and do not only entail two parties, one all good and one all evil."

'Us versus them'

Unattached for more than two years, human resources worker Joe, 30, was thrilled when he had a perfect first date in August, followed by a few more meetings with the same woman.

He thought he was heading for a serious relationship, until he got dumped weeks later. It was about the time he had posted this message on his Facebook: "You should unfriend me if you support the police." He guessed the two events were related. He had met his love interest on dating app Bumble.

With nearly one in two Hong Kong millennials using dating apps, according to a 2017 study, this space too exposed the depth of the political divide across the city. "Revealing your political stance has become a must on these apps," said Joe. Profiles came with phrases such as "No blue ribbons" or "No yellow ribbons." Romance and love, in a city with one of the world's lowest fertility rates, faced a new barrier: political leanings.

They colored everything. For younger students, school became especially difficult to navigate. Protester Mei, 16, found arguments with teachers and principals wearying, as her views could hardly prevail over theirs. "I am tired, exhausted … I really struggle to focus," she said. For those students from families of police officers, the strain was also evident, according to Eliza Cheung Yee-lai, a clinical psychologist with the Hong Kong Red Cross, which reported relatives of officers being among those seeking help. "The conflicts at home are even more severe," Cheung said. "It's quite complicated for them. If they don't join certain activities, they feel guilty. They feel they betray their friends."

Then there were the quarrels within families, like in Kit's. His heart sank whenever he saw a pop-up notification on his cellphone. It would probably be another message shared by his stepfather in their family WhatsApp group. The stepfather had been assiduously forwarding articles, photos or videos that described the protesters as thugs. Kit, a 38-year-old editor, who would only tell us his first name, had taken part in at least half the protests since June 12.

"I'd always been restrained, until he said those who support the protesters should die," he said as he recalled one of his rows with the retired policeman. "I tried to rebuild the trust over the dinner table – but it's useless. As soon as we bid goodbye, he would go back to those pro-police videos circulating online." Eventually, he quit the family WhatsApp group.

Jacky Lam, a police inspector turned law student, found himself wrestling with another form of social pressure. Facebook friends who sympathized with the protesters kept tagging him in videos or posts of what they saw as police brutality. "I would just hide them," he said, saying he wanted to avoid arguing with his friends.

Over the course of the summer as the protests wore on, social media amplified the city's divisions, said Paul Wong Wai-ching, a social inclusion academic at HKU's department of social work and social administration. "Protesters and their supporters would post the eye-catching wrongdoings of the officers while the police's supporters would play up the misdeeds of protesters," he said. "We used to say 'a photograph is a representation of reality' – but now even video cannot tell the truth."

On July 30, for example, hundreds besieged Kwai Chung Police Station, where 45 protesters arrested a day earlier were being detained. In the melee, a sergeant was live-streamed pointing a Remington shotgun at the crowd. He looked like he had gone berserk. But other videos circulating later showed that the protesters had surrounded him and another officer, flinging projectiles and flashing laser pointers at them. He then fell to the ground and had his helmet snatched from him, according to other videos. And the shotgun held beanbag, not live, rounds. The Rashomon effect was created by different camera angles and would rear its head over many, many other clashes.

Lokman Tsui, assistant professor at Chinese University's journalism school, said the algorithms of Facebook and most social media platforms were offering people what they wanted to see, to encourage them to stay longer on the site. "This makes the social divide worse, because you don't see the viewpoints of the other side, therefore making it more difficult to develop enough of an understanding or common ground," he said. "It might also overstate the extent you think your side is 'right' because you see primarily people you agree with."

Given that 4.4 million out of 7.5 million city residents – almost 60 per cent – were on Facebook in 2018 according to Statista figures, there was little doubt online media deepened the offline cleavages. The echo chambers produced by social media only served to intensify the polarization of society, Chan said. "Both protesters and police would think that their side is the righteous one and that everyone in their in-group is doing the right thing for Hong Kong," he explained.

"The problem is, on top of the nebulous nature of the current situation, we are only fed a narrow facet of the complex reality. Everyone thinks they are seeing the full and complete picture when in reality no one actually does."

Social psychologists describe this phenomenon as the "out-group homogeneity effect," when people tend to perceive those outside their circles as more similar to one another – and therefore easier to reduce to a stereotype – than those in their own circles, whom they view as more diverse. So protesters might see all police officers as equally brutal in handling clashes, whereas the officers regard all protesters as thugs. Such single-lens perceptions only harden each side's position, removing any room for reconciliation.

While the selectivity of information being shared among groups might be an unconscious reflex for many with no ill intent, others with more sinister motives did engage in wilful disinformation, as part of a campaign of "psychological warfare" waged to control the narrative of the social unrest.

"It is really hard to win somebody's heart with just facts and accurate information," said journalism academic Masato Kajimoto, who is leading an HKU team scrutinizing images, videos and any information from the protests, trying to tell which are real, misleading or fake. "You have to appeal to people's emotions."

To do that, one might have to engage in deliberately presenting an incomplete, misleading or false picture of what was happening on the ground, he said. Even at the best of times, calling out disinformation is difficult. But doing so during the protests had proven even more challenging because of plummeting trust in the force and the government, Kajimoto said.

On August 31, for example, protesters and police clashed inside Prince Edward MTR station, with injuries on both sides. When the number of people hurt was revised several times, a rumor spread that police had beaten some protesters to death. Photos of dead bodies were shared online. Government officials, police, the MTR Corp and the fire service explained multiple times there were no deaths that night, but protesters kept returning to the station demanding "truth and justice."

In December, local news outlet Factwire traced most of the 52 people arrested that night, including six allegedly killed by police. All six had been taken either to a police station or hospital that night. A memorial shrine outside a station exit remained for weeks after and to this day, some still believe the rumor. Kajimoto said the episode revealed the depth of mistrust toward police. "If somebody floats conspiracy theories on social media and you're against the police, you believe that. Or you don't care if it's true or not."

Mental well-being at stake

The mutual fear and loathing – or, as some call it, hate – exacts a cost. And for many city residents, the cost was their mental well-being. A study published by medical journal *The Lancet* in January 2020 assessed the situation to be six times worse than during the aftermath of the Occupy movement of 2014. Researchers found that more than 2 million, or almost one in three, Hong Kong adults had shown symptoms of post-traumatic stress disorder (PTSD) during the prolonged unrest.

Conducted by academics from HKU, the survey was the largest population-wide mental health study done – with questionnaires sent to more than 18,000 residents aged at least 18 – and the longest observational one as it studied data across a decade, from 2009 to 2019.

In March 2015, PTSD symptoms were only reported by 5 per cent of respondents, but that figure rose to almost 32 per cent from September to November 2019. The study also found that 22 per cent of residents surveyed during the 2019 protests reported probable major depression or suspected PTSD – a situation the researchers described as "comparable to the prevalence of mental health conditions observed following large-scale disasters, armed conflicts or terrorist attacks."

The findings were consistent with another study co-authored by Hou Wai-kai, director of Education University's center for psychosocial health, which found that 25.7 per cent of 1,112 respondents polled in July 2019 – or one in four Hongkongers – had reported symptoms of depression, with 9.1 per cent even reporting suicidal ideation. Hou's study also discovered that people of lower socio-economic status were more vulnerable to depression as their daily routines were more likely to have been disrupted. "The scale is unprecedented," he said.

Responsive and cost-effective strategies were badly needed to supplement the under-resourced public mental health system to aid long-term recovery, he said. "Even though Hong Kong is affluent as such, there are only 11 psychiatrists per 100,000 people," Hou said. "The government should consider introducing a step-care model to allow non-specialists – such as psychology graduates – to provide care."

But clinical psychologist Chan said the situation might not be as severe as portrayed by the recent epidemiological studies, arguing that it was normal for people to show symptoms of distress in the midst and immediate aftermath of a crisis. "The good news is, most people will manage to bounce back with time. Some might require a bit more help, but not all 2 million, as cited in the [HKU] study," he said. What was more worrying, he said, would be the pervasive and persistent sense of hopelessness and mistrust that was emerging, especially among young people.

HKU's Wong warned no one was immune to psychological trauma, even those who had stayed silent during the protests. "The people around them, who have taken sides, might slam their inaction as 'not caring about the city'. One wouldn't be better off by staying silent," he said. Also a research fellow at the Hong Kong Police College, he argued it might be unfair to expect frontline officers to manage their emotions around the clock just because they were trained to maintain law and order.

"It would be a legitimate expectation if the society was calm. Officers now, however, are subject to physical and mental abuse, threats and bullying of their family members," he said. The provocations they faced required them to possess a very high level of self-control and emotional management, qualities not easy to summon in a highly charged environment, he said. Seeing officers swearing at protesters or even reporters suggested they were at the end of their tether, he said. "They could not or did not bother to control their emotions or take the feeling of citizens into account," the clinical psychologist said, citing such incidents as evidence that more attention needed to be paid to officers' mental well-being and training.

Chan, also a clinical psychologist, said that for society to heal, Hongkongers needed to put aside their political armor and reach out to their social circles for emotional support, spend time with family and friends and re-establish healthy everyday habits. Those still reeling from months watching the never-ending loop of clashes and clearances should take regular breaks from social media and tune out sensational feeds from their news diet, he advised.

Both sides also just needed more sleep, he said back in late summer. Young demonstrators had been staying awake at all hours of the day, keeping track of their activities on encrypted messenger Telegram and Reddit-like site LIHKG – an online forum that is effectively a virtual command center of the movement.

Similarly, police officers, who had been mobilized to multiple locations and sometimes on 17-hour shifts, were also often seen slouching on the ground, resting wearily after clashes with protesters. "Numerous scientific research data have suggested that sleep deprivation could amplify biases and affect our ability to think. It also hampers our ability to regulate emotion," he said. "We err more easily when we don't get enough sleep."

Chan also appealed to Hongkongers to stop dehumanizing each other and refrain from calling police officers "dogs" or protesters "cockroaches" or "yellow zombies," a derogatory term first used during

Occupy. Dehumanization, or the process through which people see the other as less human than their own group, would help justify the use of violence and extreme means, he warned. "We need to retrieve our common identity," Chan said. "We are first and foremost human beings and Hongkongers before we are protesters or police officers, or supporters of either side. Let us remind ourselves of our common humanity." He quoted a line from a favorite hit by English rock band Pink Floyd: "And after all, we're only ordinary men." The title of that song? *Us and Them.*

So, when can all sides come together and society be healed again? Psychologists like Chan had no answer when we first spoke to them in August 2019. But in early 2020, he lamented that the government had lost an opportunity to mend the rift as the city battled its biggest public health crisis in 17 years with the coronavirus pandemic.

"The outbreak of Covid-19 could have been an opportunity for the society to come together and mend our rifts as we face this common threat. Unfortunately, the government has managed to further lose the trust and support of its people," he said, referring to the early indecisive actions of the administration in combating the highly contagious disease.

While the protests remained in abeyance in early 2020, there was little to suggest the virus would unite rather than divide. Cockroaches and dogs and a litany of expletives to describe the other remained very much part of the local vocabulary.

Perhaps when things get back to normal, the Wong Tai Sin playground where violence broke out on August 5 can once again live up to its Cantonese name, *muk lun.* It means: "harmonious neighborhoods."

— *With reporting by Linda Lew and Raquel Carvalho*

The unwelcome mat for mainlanders

Tens of thousands of mainland professionals call Hong Kong home but the protests have left many questioning their place in the city.

David Feng once considered Hong Kong the dream destination to study and work in, but not any more. In the summer of 2019, after weeks of anti-government protests revealed Hongkongers' deep anti-mainland sentiments, he reached the point of no return.

"My heart aches and I am really disappointed to see the city descend into a place that's highly politicized and no longer suitable for study and research," said Feng, 26, who started his doctoral studies in September 2019 in computer science.

Unable to support protesters who vandalized public property and attacked police officers, he said he was looking forward to graduating and returning to his hometown in northern China to work there or in Beijing, where opportunities have expanded significantly.

He found it painful that Hong Kong, once a place where people got along regardless of their origin, had changed for the worse. "For me, it is like a wound. Even if it heals on the surface, it still hurts below," he said.

From support to shock and despair

Feng is one of tens of thousands of young mainland Chinese known as *gangpiao*, or drifters, who have made Hong Kong home in the past decade, attracted by the city's job opportunities, shared culture and tolerant society. Unlike mainlanders who arrived decades earlier as refugees or entrepreneurs, *gangpiao* are mostly well-educated Chinese who arrived through Hong Kong Immigration Department programs targeting young professionals.

There is no official data on the number of *gangpiao*, but according to Hong Kong census statistics from mid-2016, there were about 77,000 mainlanders who had lived in Hong Kong for less than seven years. About 80 per cent of them were aged between 18 and 30, and more than 60 per cent held postgraduate qualifications. After living in the city for seven years, Chinese citizens – like other nationals – can apply to become permanent residents, but the census data does not indicate how many have done so.

Before the protests erupted in 2019, most *gangpiao* were happy to call Hong Kong home. But the anger and tear gas that swept through the city in the second half of 2019 left many disillusioned, turning their relationship with the city upside down and prompting them to wonder if they had a future there. Many were shaken by the violence over the summer including the ransacking of the Legislative Council building on July 1 and the siege of the central government's liaison office.

Leon Liang, 33, from Shanxi province in northern China, said the day masked radicals attacked two mainland men at Hong Kong's airport in August was the saddest, darkest day of his nine years in the city. "What a shame for Hong Kong," he wrote in a social media post. "I never imagined that such a personal assault could happen in a city that prides itself on upholding law and order."

As a Hong Kong permanent resident working in the finance

industry, Liang said that, at first, he had supported the peaceful protests. Later, however, he took part in a rally and crowdfunding campaign for advertisements supporting police. "I really value this space where we can make our voices heard – it's something we can't do on the mainland," he said. "But now, things have degenerated to the stage where the righteous police have to take the blame for worsening law and order, and radical protesters can go on a rampage, vandalizing public property and attacking law enforcement with some noble excuse, but without punishment."

Zhu Jie, a specialist in Hong Kong affairs at Wuhan University, said many *gangpiao* were offended and felt the protesters crossed the line in disrespecting their country. For many, the storming of Legco was a shocking act, and the attack on the liaison office was a direct assault on Beijing's sovereignty. "Many of the *gangpiao* were educated in mainland China and patriotism is a key value they shared," Zhu said. "That is why so many *gangpiao* joined activities to support police."

Alicia Liu, 36, a senior banker at a Chinese investment bank and a long-term Hong Kong resident, was taken aback by the attack on the liaison office. "I used to think that I was a local in Hong Kong, but now I consider myself more a mainlander," she said.

The months of unrest saw protesters targeting mainlanders for abuse. One of the first casualties was Hong Kong's tourism industry, which took a major hit when mainlanders, the city's largest group of visitors, began staying away.

Gangpiao were shocked when some University of Hong Kong students painted derogatory slogans outside the residence of their vice-chancellor Zhang Xiang, a respected mainland-born scientist. The mainland group saw it as "Red Guard-style" tyranny, a reference to the notorious youthful terrors of Mao Zedong's Cultural Revolution in the 1960s.

When the assistant principal of a Hong Kong school went online in July to wish death on the children of policemen, it sent chills down the spine of many a *gangpiao*, especially those with children. Some drew up a "white list" of preferred Hong Kong schools whose administrators had taken a conservative position on the protests, while others moved their children to schools on the mainland.

No Mandarin, please

Lynn Lin, 37, a human resources officer at one of China's leading internet companies, said she began to think hard about remaining in Hong Kong. "My child was born here, but I don't want her to grow up in a hostile and divided society. I now prefer to send my child to Beijing, my hometown, where she can study in an international school and can get a broader understanding of China," she said.

Mainlanders in Hong Kong became alarmed when masked radicals began targeting Chinese nationals, businesses with Chinese links and anyone perceived to be pro-Beijing. These fears were heightened on October 6, when a Xiaomi smartphone shop in Mong Kok was set on fire, a Fulum restaurant in Cheung Sha Wan linked to a Fujian clan was wrecked, and a branch of China's state-owned Bank of China in Wan Chai was damaged badly. A branch of the China Construction Bank (Asia) near Prince Edward MTR station was also vandalized.

The *gangpiao* community also became afraid of using Mandarin in public because that made them stand out immediately in Cantonese-speaking Hong Kong. Mary, a 35-year-old working in the finance industry, recalled that she was with a friend and had been speaking in Mandarin when a stranger began shouting obscenities at them, saying: "Go back to mainland China!"

She said: "I was so shocked. I couldn't understand what prompted him to do such a thing to us, as my friend and I were just talking about my newborn baby."

The mother of two, who is married to a Hongkonger working in the finance industry, said: "It's ironic. I've always told my elder son that he is a Hong Kong citizen and also Chinese, but my mother-in-law told me I shouldn't say things like that in public now as it might bring us trouble." She added: "My husband also asked me not to speak Mandarin in the street. The protests were politically driven at first, but now they seem to have evolved into a hatred of people with links to the mainland."

Geng Chunya, 40, president of the Hong Kong Association of Mainland Graduates and a permanent resident since 2001, also experienced hostility firsthand. "My 70-year-old father and I returned to Hong Kong after a day trip to Shenzhen in early July," he recalled. "Almost as soon as my father sat down in the MTR and began to speak in Mandarin, the man next to him shouted obscenities and told my father to get out of Hong Kong."

Other mainlanders said they had a larger concern about the impact of the protests on Hong Kong's long-term role in the region. Among them was Lin Yuxi, from Shenzhen, who runs a 6 billion yuan (HK$6.5 billion) private fund out of Hong Kong, investing in mainland Chinese start-ups.

He said the political unrest itself did not put him off because "freedom of expression within the boundaries of the law is part of Hong Kong's society." His main worry was the prospect of Hong Kong having a diminished role in the ambitious Greater Bay Area project to connect it with Macau and nine cities in Guangdong province, creating a massive hub of innovation and technology.

"Hong Kong was supposed to play a leading role in the Greater Bay Area, where its legal framework, financial system and services were supposed to be the role model for the rest to aspire to," Lin said. "If Hong Kong's role is diminished, the question for recent arrivals like me will be: why bother to put up with the higher costs in this city? We might as well stay in Shenzhen, or move to Guangzhou, closer to the action, and where the cost of living, operations and everything else is cheaper."

In the 20 years after Hong Kong returned to Chinese rule in 1997, about 1.5 million mainlanders moved to the city. Even though there were brief periods of harmony, there has long existed friction between Hongkongers and the mainlanders, with the latter stereotyped as a drain on the city's scarce public resources..

The disconnect between the two sides runs deep. Most of Hong Kong's native inhabitants also trace their roots to mainland China, but a survey by the Chinese University (CUHK) published in August 2019 found that more than 40 per cent of Hongkongers had a "low" or "very low" sense of belonging to China, and nearly 60 per cent of those whose ancestral hometown was on the mainland had not been there in the previous three years.

Victor Zheng Wan-tai, assistant director of CUHK's Hong Kong Institute of Asia-Pacific Studies, which carried out the study, said the results reflected "an alarming rise in anti-mainland sentiment" and were cause for concern. "But those feelings may also stem from a lack of understanding of, and social interaction with, mainland China, where their parents and grandparents came from," he said.

Lau Siu-kai, vice-chairman of the Chinese Association of Hong Kong and Macau Studies, a semi-official mainland think tank, had another take. He felt the increase in animosity toward those with links to the mainland reflected an insecurity across Hong Kong society. "Hong Kong's social unrest triggered some people's long-held anxieties and fears regarding immigrants from the mainland," he said.

To stay or to go?

With no end in sight to the protests in 2019, some mainlanders decided to pack up and leave despite having put down roots in the city. Zhang Ning, 35, spent eight years in Hong Kong and, like her husband, worked in the civil aviation industry. In November 2019, her husband took a job in Toulouse, France, and the family made the difficult decision to move. "What happened in Hong Kong made me feel unsafe," Zhang said. "The mass sit-in at the Hong Kong airport severely disrupted my work and life and made me determined to leave."

Others were more sanguine and planned to stay despite the tensions. Eric He, 31, a mainlander and a salesman in a Chinese-owned securities company, decided to stay put. "A lot of friends say drifters like me have to leave and return to the mainland as soon as possible due to the crisis, but I still think Hong Kong is a place I love, a place that has good public order, future prospects and valuable wilderness to explore. I don't want to waste the nine years I've spent here," he said.

Henry Ho, chairman of the One Country Two Systems Youth Forum, a Hong Kong think tank, said the departure of *gangpiao* was a loss for the city. These were people who understood both mainland China and Hong Kong and could be the bridge to better ties, apart from being an important source of talent for the city, he said.

Agreeing, Alexa Chow Yee-ping, managing director of AMAC Human Resources Consultants, feared that Hong Kong's economy would suffer if mainland professionals left. "Hong Kong has a greying population and we are already at risk of a shortage of manpower as the population from the post-war baby boom reaches retirement age. Mainland workers have provided an important source of human capital for Hong Kong," Chow said.

Wuhan University's Zhu Jie said any exodus by the *gangpiao* would be like the loss of a bridge between mainland China and Hong Kong. The anti-Chinese sentiments of the protests had "severely eroded trust between the two sides," he said.

"Without enough communication and exchange, misunderstandings are bound to arise, which will fuel nationalist sentiments both on the mainland and in Hong Kong and make it more difficult to solve problems."

'Renovation' and 'decoration': Mainland-linked firms under attack

Kinling Lo and Phila Siu

Over the summer, demonstrators began attacking mainland-linked businesses to vent their anger and to hurt their bottom-lines.

Annie Wu Suk-ching is known for being part of a fabled Hong Kong success story – Maxim's, the sprawling catering empire founded by her father, James Tak Wu. It runs a massive in-flight catering operation, a chain of restaurants, bakeries and cafes, and the Hong Kong franchises for Starbucks and Genki Sushi. But in the midst of the social unrest that rocked Hong Kong through much of 2019, the prominent businesswoman's blunt criticism of anti-government protesters turned her into a hate figure, and made outlets linked to Maxim's a target of widespread attacks and vandalism.

Her invective included calling protesters "brainwashed zombies" spoiled by their parents. Outraged black-clad radicals responded by trashing outlets related to Maxim's, including its dim sum, coffee and sushi chains. Most of the time, they would charge into a restaurant, overturn tables, smash fixtures and tell customers not to dine there. Maxim's, a household name anglicized from its Chinese moniker meaning "beautiful heart," was mocked as the "black heart" conglomerate.

The septuagenarian, however, shrugged off the attacks. A former standing committee member of the Chinese People's Political Consultative Conference, the country's top political advisory body, she continued to lambast protesters, criticize their upbringing, and blame Education

Bureau officials, teachers and parents for young Hongkongers' lack of national pride. Wu and Maxim's clarified that she was not involved in running the business, but the trashing did not end. Outlets connected to the group were hit hardest as radicals targeted businesses backed by the Chinese government or perceived to be pro-Beijing.

Targeting the black heart

The protesters had euphemisms for their actions. The premises they trashed were "renovated" by having windows smashed, tables overturned and goods destroyed. Others were merely "decorated," by having their exteriors covered with graffiti and expletives, or plastered with sticky-notes filled with pro-protest messages.

JC, a 26-year-old chef who took part in "renovations" as a frontline protester, said such actions were a demonstration of anger toward Hong Kong's coterie of tycoons and their cronies who had accumulated enormous wealth and political clout through their cozy relationship with Beijing. Explaining their so-called strategy, she said: "We need these anti-protest businessmen to bear economic losses in order to turn them against the government. If the destruction we cause makes them lose money, they will begin to pressure the government and that will help us get a step closer to attaining our demands."

On July 1, 2019, violent protesters stormed the Legislative Council, and that marked the start of vandalism at public buildings and facilities. From around mid-August, the national flags became a target to vent their anger against the Communist Party. In September, a group of protesters in a shopping mall in Sha Tin trampled on a Chinese national flag – which they took from a nearby town hall – and later threw into the Shing Mun River. A 13-year-old Hong Kong girl was also sentenced to 12 months' probation after she, and two others, pulled down the national flag outside Tuen Mun Town Hall and set fire to it with a lighter.

The wrecking widened to include businesses linked to Beijing from October 1, China's National Day. After an 18-year-old protester was shot in the chest that day by a police officer during an intense clash, many shops run by Maxim's were attacked. ATM machines at some Bank of China branches were smashed, as was a mahjong house whose management was accused of having links with triads who attacked protesters.

The Maxim's group was targeted not least because of Annie Wu's firm stance against the protesters and her unabashed patriotism. She was 30 when she joined a pioneering Hong Kong business delegation to visit the mainland in 1978. The group was on its way back when China's paramount leader Deng Xiaoping made the momentous announcement that China was embarking on reforms and opening up to the outside world, and that Beijing would welcome foreign investment, including from Hong Kong, Macau and Taiwan.

Wu and her father were drawn into the new China story, which brought massive business opportunities in the years that followed. She convinced her father to help upgrade China's backward in-flight catering industry, in time for the first non-stop flight between the United States and China, following the normalization of relations. Deng hoped it could take place in early 1981.

James Wu took a leap of faith when the mainland's Civil Aviation Administration chief Shen Tu asked him to spend HK$5 million (US$645,000) of his own money on the equipment for the joint venture, before Deng had even approved it. Recalling the moment that would change the fortunes of Maxim's, Annie Wu said in an interview later: "After 30 seconds, my father told Mr Shen, 'We are Chinese. We trust Mr Deng Xiaoping and we believe China will open up.' Shen shook my father's hand and then we went back to Hong Kong to order the equipment."

In March 1980, she learned that Deng had given the green light for the joint venture after asking Shen what sort of business her father did in Hong Kong. "Does he know how to make croissants?" asked

Deng, who had acquired a taste for the crescent-shaped pastries as a student in France in the 1920s.

Shen replied: "He knows how to do it very well."

Deng said: "Then why not approve it?"

Beijing Air Catering, the first joint venture company on the mainland, was registered in 1980 as "Sino-foreign Joint Venture 001," earning the young Hong Kong businesswoman the nickname "Miss 001."

Wu had a deep sense of being Chinese, and she was appalled by the protests of 2019. The unrest was in its fourth month in September 2019 when she upbraided students at the Chinese Foundation Secondary School, which she founded, for planning to join a boycott of classes. She warned them to drop the idea or quit the school, telling the youths that their parents paid fees for them to study, not strike.

Cue uproar. A group of about 100 protested outside the school, vandalized its facilities and blasted Wu for threatening to expel students and staff who supported a boycott. The school clarified that students with parental permission to boycott classes would not be punished.

Wu was unmoved. Later that month, she flew to Geneva with Macau casino heiress Pansy Ho Chiu-king for a UN Human Rights Council session as representatives of the pro-government Hong Kong Federation of Women, which claims more than 100,000 members. The pair defended the Hong Kong government's handling of the unrest and criticized the protesters, saying they did not represent all 7.5 million people in the city.

Angry radicals began venting their rage on cafes, restaurants and shops linked to Maxim's, which had more than 500 outlets across Hong Kong. That upset Wu, who declared she had lost all faith in the city's young people for becoming anti-government and anti-China. "I think we have lost two entire young generations," she told the nationalist mainland tabloid *Global Times* in November 2019. "I have given up hope and will not waste my time talking to them, as they have no idea what they are doing and what they should do ... Their brains have been occupied by other ideas and that is irrevocable."

Beyond Maxim's

Another company that came under ferocious attack was Hong Kong-listed Best Mart 360, a chain with 102 outlets selling imported snacks, confectionery, dried fruit, baby foods and products, as well as health foods and supplements. The company became a target of radicals accusing it of having ties to suspected triad members who fought a violent street battle with black-clad protesters in North Point on August 5, 2019. The men armed with bamboo rods were said to be part of the city's close-knit Fujian community, many of whom lived in the area in the east of Hong Kong Island.

Best Mart 360's founder and chairman, Lin Tsz-fung, a native of the southern Chinese province of Fujian, was also permanent honorary president of the Hong Kong Federation of Fujian Associations, which held several pro-Beijing and pro-police demonstrations. Although the company denied any connection with the so-called Fujian gangs who attacked protesters, 70 Best Mart 360 outlets were attacked more than 180 times by November 2019 and the company's share price took a major hit.

Describing the attacks as a "very, very big blow," Lin said: "I've never seen anything like this. Hong Kong now feels unfamiliar to me. I don't know why Hong Kong has become like this, like a war zone. Now that we've reached this stage, I think the government should set up an independent inquiry to look into the whole issue and to give 7 million Hongkongers an explanation." He said the company was looking to expand in Macau and the mainland, in order to rely less on Hong Kong.

Lin insisted that he was innocent and defended the city's Fujian community, saying: "Hong Kong is home to 1.2 million Fujian people.

For every six Hong Kong people, there's one Fujian person. You cannot just tie Fujian people and gangs together because of the clashes in North Point in August. I think that is very irresponsible."

Other businesses also became targets for "renovation" and "decoration." Japanese fast-food chain Yoshinoya had been singled out since June, when pro-establishment Marvin Hung Ming-kei, CEO of the Hop Hing Group, which owns the Yoshinoya franchise in Hong Kong, told the media that he was angered by a post on the restaurant's Facebook page mocking police. The chain remained a target of vandalism by the mobs for months to come.

Chinese state enterprises or Chinese government-funded companies including China Travel Service and China Mobile also came under attack. China's oldest lender Bank of China was hit hard and forced to shut all but one of its 200 Hong Kong branches on the Saturday in early October after the government announced a ban on face masks. Its facilities were set on fire and wrecked. Other major Chinese banks that were vandalized included the Industrial and Commercial Bank of China, China Citic Bank International and Bank of Communications.

Companies owned by mainland Chinese, such as lifestyle retail chain Miniso, electronics brands Xiaomi and Huawei, also saw their branches damaged. In the first three weeks of October alone, police recorded more than 80 cases of arson involving shops believed to have links to the mainland, with some owners reporting losses of property as well as damage to their premises.

Although such destructive actions became a regular feature of protests from then on, no large-scale incidents of looting occurred. The radicals who left so many premises seriously damaged also issued reminders to protesters not to help themselves to anything.

Backing for the trashing

Despite shocking the public, the protesters enjoyed some support from Hongkongers for their new strategy of vandalism and destruction. An opinion poll commissioned by the *South China Morning Post* in December 2019 found that "damaging private property including mainland businesses" ranked fourth among protest methods with the most support from respondents. The top three were the use of laser pens against police, blocking major roads and disrupting the MTR.

Of the 832 people surveyed, 42 per cent of those who identified as pro-democracy supporters backed the use of vandalism against private property such as mainland Chinese businesses. That scored higher than the 32 per cent who supported vandalism of public property such as the MTR.

At first, there was some debate among protesters on whether these acts of mayhem and wreckage were justified. Lengthy discussion threads on the movement's virtual command centre, the Reddit-like online forum LIHKG, saw many questioning the rationale of attacking businesses.

One forum user said: "Only dictators are intolerant of dissenting views. What's the difference between the Communist Party and us, if we 'renovate' the stores just because their owners have a different point of view?" Others wanted the violence scaled back to retain international support for the protest movement, particularly from the US. Opinions remained divided until someone came up with a color-coded system to coordinate protesters' actions.

Only businesses and entities considered "black," such as those run by gangsters, government premises and the offices of pro-Beijing politicians, deserved to be "renovated." "Red" shops and restaurants owned by Beijing-friendly businessmen would only be "decorated" with graffiti and so-called Lennon Walls comprising colorful sticky notes bearing anti-government and pro-democracy messages. "Blue" businesses, whose owners were known to be anti-protests, should be boycotted, and "yellow" ones, run by people who backed the protests, deserved active support.

As these messages circulated widely, police warned that anyone charged with causing criminal damage in Hong Kong could be jailed for up to 10 years. "Some people are romanticizing the moves to damage certain shops. So-called 'renovation' and 'decoration' are purely destructive and just meant to vent anger," police said.

The new year brought a respite from protests as a larger menace swept Hong Kong and the world. After the city's first two cases of coronavirus infection were recorded on January 22, 2020, protests, gatherings and marches were called off.

Radical protester JC, however, maintained that the pandemic did not spell the end of the protests. Rather, he said, the severe economic damage wrought by the pandemic offered protesters a glimpse of the impact they could have. "If we are able to use this time to rethink our strategy, and work out how to keep up our momentum by focusing on the right business targets and making vandalism our most important strategy, I believe we will still have a chance," he said.

Annie Wu, meanwhile, continued to lament the state of young people in Hong Kong, and blasted the Education Bureau for failing to teach youth about their Chinese identity. There were anti-China textbooks, and some teachers were anti-mainland too, she told state broadcaster China Global Television Network.

She said the bureau should have encouraged government schools to help students understand that Hong Kong was part of China, and appreciate that they were Chinese nationals. "The Education Bureau has never been interested in promoting this national education," she said. "So for the last 20 years, young people in Hong Kong have only been trained to say they're born in Hong Kong."

The bureau said it shared the responsibility for fostering students' values, but added that the reasons young people took part in illegal activities were complex. While some agreed with Wu, others believed that national education could not be forced on the young. Wu's unwavering stance earned her praise on the mainland, and the state-run China News Service named her a person of the year in January 2020 for her dedication to teaching Hongkongers to love their homeland. Opinion polls toward the end of 2019, however, continued to show teenagers' sense of national identity at rock bottom.

Dark clouds over Cathay

Danny Lee

Hong Kong's favorite airline found itself on a collision course with Beijing when it failed to reign in staff over the protests.

I t is something soccer fans have known for years: that, when a troubled team manager announces he has the "full backing" of the board, his head is about to roll and those of others will follow shortly. While it is hard to know how many soccer fans there were among the 32,000 staff the Cathay Pacific Group employed in August 2019, it was a safe bet that many of them would have had a similar sense of foreboding when the airline's chairman John Slosar told them this line.

Hong Kong's flagship carrier had landed itself in the middle of the anti-government protests rocking the city, its staff having drawn attention for all the wrong reasons. Not only was the airline's home, Hong Kong International Airport, a focal point for protesters whose repeated occupations were making headlines across the world, but a trade union representing Cathay's flight attendants was backing them. Even worse, an off-duty pilot was accused of rioting, another of passing company information to protesters, and two airport ground staff were alleged to have leaked the travel plans of "dirty cops" online.

Still, Slosar seemed reassuring. At a twice-yearly press conference to discuss the company's financial performance, a journalist asked him whether Cathay would rein in staff who expressed political views. "We certainly wouldn't dream of telling them what to think about something,"

Slosar replied. "They're all adults, they're all service professionals. We respect them greatly." The exchange lasted little more than 60 seconds, but was significant. Within 72 hours the heads began to roll.

'Don't mess with Beijing'

In the days and weeks that followed Slosar's comments, an estimated three dozen Cathay staff either lost their jobs or resigned, from cabin crew to pilots to the CEO and finally Slosar himself. The problem for Cathay was that Beijing decided to make it into an example for any other big company that failed to toe its line. And with the airline reliant on business from flights to mainland China, it swiftly found itself unable to withstand the pressure. Within minutes of Slosar's press conference the influential Chinese tabloid *Global Times* – known for its nationalist tone – began to weigh in. The state-run paper said the airline would "pay a painful price" for the actions of its employees, leading the rest of the mainland media in a chorus of disgust against the company.

More worrying for Cathay was the intervention two days later of the mainland's aviation regulator, the Civil Aviation Administration of China (CAAC). Without giving the airline prior notice, the CAAC announced publicly that it had issued a major safety warning against the carrier and demanded sweeping changes that included barring its staff from taking part in the protests. It said staff involved in the "unlawful" actions would be banned from flying to mainland China and even from working on planes that entered its airspace. It also said the airline would have to supply lists identifying all crew members working in mainland Chinese airspace for approval, and that planes without prior permission would be denied entry.

The announcement was explosive. Not only would being shut out of mainland airspace have put an end to a fifth of the carrier's daily flights, it would have meant diverting long-haul flights to Europe and the US. Within hours, Cathay confirmed that it had received the directive from Beijing and was "studying it very carefully." It was dumbfounded at first, though as the shock settled it released statements stressing the safety of passengers was its "top priority" and vowing "zero tolerance toward any inappropriate and unprofessional behavior that might affect aviation safety."

Albert Lam Kwong-yu, Hong Kong's director of civil aviation from 1998 to 2004, said the message was clear: "Don't mess with Beijing." He said the escalation of the protests, from opposing the extradition bill, to calling for universal suffrage and, in some more radical quarters, demanding Hong Kong's independence, had touched a nerve with the central government. It was in no mood to pull its punches. "The Hong Kong government had a very lukewarm attitude [to Cathay's position] but there was an opportunity for China to clamp down on, not exactly Cathay, but to do something to demonstrate the Chinese government was in control," Lam said. "Cathay presented itself on the table as a lovely dish."

Turning the screw

The hours and days following Slosar's press conference made it clear that Beijing would be appeased by nothing short of regime change. On August 10, just 24 hours after the intervention by the CAAC, Cathay announced it was firing the two members of airport ground staff and removing the pilot who had attended the protests from flying duties. It also warned staff to expect greater scrutiny when on mainland soil. Mainland authorities said Cathay aircraft would face extra inspections to ensure their safety; skeptics suggested it was a naked attempt to disrupt and delay the airline's flights.

But Beijing was not satisfied. On August 11, *Global Times* weighed in once more, insisting the airline "draw a clear line" with radical employees. It quoted experts warning of "further risks if the company fails to root out its management problems." The following day Cathay's CEO Rupert Hogg warned that staff could lose their jobs if they were found "supporting or participating" in illegal protests.

But Beijing still was not satisfied. On August 13 both Cathay and its controlling shareholder Swire Pacific announced in separate but identical press releases that they "strongly supported" the Hong Kong government and called "for the restoration of law and order" in the city. The announcement was overshadowed by another demonstration at the airport, with protesters for the first time physically clashing with travelers.

And that was when the dominoes began to fall. On August 15, the two pilots were dismissed and the following day, exactly one week after the CAAC's intervention, Hogg resigned, along with his deputy Paul Loo Kar-pui. The announcement drew gasps, tears and bewilderment in Cathay City, the airline's headquarters, as staff mourned two popular and energetic leaders who had helped return the airline to profitability in 2018 after two difficult loss-making years. It also raised questions as to who was pulling the strings, not least because China's state broadcaster China Central Television broke the news of Hogg's resignation 15 minutes before the official announcement was made to the Hong Kong stock exchange. Installed in Hogg's place was Augustus Tang Kin-wing, only the third ethnic Chinese CEO of the airline since its founding in 1946 and a man who had been just weeks away from retirement. Tang was a Swire lifer who would be seen as a steady hand to shareholders. His remit was to bring the airline out of its crisis with Beijing. It later transpired that the shake-up of the airline had been planned for days. At the start of the week, the chairman of Cathay's parent, Merlin Swire, had been summoned to Beijing to meet the CAAC's deputy chief Cui Xiaofeng, who told him in unvarnished language that management changes would be needed if it wanted to continue to do business in China.

Achilles' heel

What the whole sorry saga laid bare was just how much Cathay had come to rely on the mainland Chinese market. Faced with losing access to its airspace, and a possible boycott from angry mainland customers, its vulnerabilities were exposed. In recent decades the airline's growth has gone hand in hand with that of China, to the point that today, with almost two dozen destinations and approximately 400 flights a week to the mainland, far more than its foreign rivals, its access to the country is essential to its business model. Revenue from Hong Kong and mainland China now account for 50 per cent of the airline's total.

In the boardroom, Cathay has two dominant investors. Swire Pacific is the controlling shareholder with a 45 per cent stake, ahead of Air China, the mainland's national carrier, which has a 29.99 per cent holding. Air China stayed conspicuously silent throughout Cathay's ordeal.

Swire, like Cathay, has grown increasingly reliant on mainland China. A third of the British-controlled conglomerate's revenue comes from China and its history is steeped in Hong Kong's colonial past. Of the 50 companies tracked by the Hang Seng index, few are as closely knit to the mainland market. If anyone had ever been in doubt, the sackings at Cathay underlined that doing business with that market was as much about politics as it was about passengers.

'White terror'

The job losses did not end with the sackings of Hogg and Loo. One week later Rebecca Sy On-na, the union leader for flight attendants with the carrier's sister airline, Cathay Dragon, became the next high-profile casualty. Unlike some who had gone before, she was not prepared to do so quietly. The 40-year-old's firing proved particularly controversial because of the proliferation of messages of support for the protests she had posted in a personal capacity on her Facebook account. She believed a colleague brought the postings to the attention of Cathay's management. Two HR managers showed her screengrabs from her social media account before she was fired. "I didn't think they would announce my dismissal," said Sy. "I warned them it would be a big issue and it was." Her abrupt departure perhaps did more than any other to fuel worries, justified or otherwise, that Beijing was pursuing a strategy of "white terror" to produce a culture of fear within the mainly pro-protester cabin crew community.

After her sacking, many Cathay employees rethought their presence on social media, using pseudonyms, screening their posts and friends more thoroughly and even deactivating accounts. Many Hongkongers followed suit, seeing the Cathay experience as a litmus test for their own employers. Jeremy Tam Man-ho, a pilot elected to the Legislative Council in 2016, was another prominent exit from the group. He remained employed by Cathay Pacific until soon after Sy's sacking, when he opted to resign. Tam, a prominent pan-democrat lawmaker, had spent many months on the front lines of the protests. He and his colleagues could regularly be seen sandwiching themselves between riot police and protesters, pleading for officers not to use force.

Tam felt that the company's neutral stance had been compromised the moment a young Cathay pilot was arrested at a protest. Soon after, there was an avalanche of "fake news" stories linking the airline to the protests, Tam claimed, saying Cathay's failure to act sooner in rebutting the claims only fueled the outrage of netizens on the mainland. The problem was exacerbated by the fact that the Cathay Pacific Flight Attendants Union did indeed support the protests. The union represents most of the company's 10,000 cabin crew but is independent of the company, despite including its name in its official title. Still, that was a subtlety lost on the legions now voicing their outrage.

Suddenly, the airline faced a boycott by mainland travelers and state-backed corporations, who ordered staff not to fly with the carrier on the grounds that its agitated cabin crew were a safety risk. Then, "when the CAAC issued its warning to Cathay, everything went completely downhill," said Tam. He knew as well as anybody that the CAAC was used to getting its way. In the summer of 2018, it had ordered 44 international airlines, including Cathay Pacific, to amend references suggesting that Taiwan and Hong Kong were independent countries. It warned any who failed to comply could have their websites blocked or lose access to one of the world's biggest air travel markets. As in 2018, Tam realized the writing was on the wall. "Cathay had to fire people. They had a gun to their head," Tam said. The 44-year-old pilot-politician surmised that he too would be in the line of fire and gave up his 17-year career to save the company from further attacks. "When Hogg and Loo resigned, I realized it was time for me to go. If the major reason was they needed to take the heat, the China government would think 'What about this Jeremy Tam?'"

Tam was not the last to go. That distinction fell to Slosar, whose ominous backing of staff did not save them but was the start of the chain reaction. Slosar finally announced his departure on September 4, but, as with Hogg, the mainland media had already beaten him to the punch, this time by 24 hours. It later emerged that he had offered to resign much earlier, but his scalp had not been seen as significant enough and the offer had been rejected. In the end, he opted to "retire" instead. With Slosar dispatched, the exercise in regime change was complete, but it was not entirely the end of the matter.

Sunny skies ahead?

While the immediate turbulence appeared to have passed for Cathay and its majority stakeholder, politics continued to rear its head. In a sign Swire might not have entirely learned its lesson, in November it appointed Shirley Lin, a leading academic on Taipei-Beijing relations and a noted critic of the Hong Kong government's handling of the civil unrest, as an independent director starting January 1, 2020. The pick passed under the radar. But within a month, Lin's daughter, the playwright Stefani Kuo, was in the headlines for expressing her heartfelt support for the protesters in a viral video. Given the sensitivities over both Taiwan and the protests, the appointment had crossed the very lines that Beijing was most sensitive to. By February, Lin had agreed to resign from the lucrative job, worth HK$690,000 (US$90,000) a year for just a few days' work. Swire's subsequent explanation suggested it was, finally, on message. "Over the course of [Lin's] appointment, it has emerged that her roles as an independent commentator and scholar could potentially be at odds with the operational realities of Swire Pacific's businesses," it said.

Other appointments, too, suggested a shift in mindset. In November, Patrick Healy was announced as Slosar's replacement. Another Swire lifer, Healy, 53, had spent most of his career working in mainland China. Unlike Slosar or Hogg, he was fluent in Mandarin.

Another addition to the Swire board, announced in January, was Zhang Zhuoping, 48, who returned to the company after leaving to start his own business. Part of Zhang's appeal, insiders said, was his effortless understanding of both Western and Chinese cultures. Both men will now be critical to whether Swire and Cathay can turn around relations in their most important market. They will have a lot on their plates in 2020, from picking up the pieces after the devastating impact of the coronavirus pandemic to, when the situation eases, honing their ability to navigate Hong Kong's politics while paying heed to business imperatives on the mainland. For Cathay, the city's "one country, two systems" governing principle may bring lush rewards, but it also comes laden with risks.

For now, the duo have the full backing of the board.

Trainwreck

Cannix Yau

The MTR was sent shuttling into a dark hole when protesters decided it was an enemy of the people. Months on, vandalized stations are a reminder of its problems.

The scene was hard to imagine almost anywhere else in the world. Members of the public leaving thousands of dollars in cash at metro stations in case fellow citizens needed a ticket.

But in Hong Kong, even when anarchy descends, people like to show solidarity with the defiant ones in their midst.

People would donate spare dollars so that protesters returning from demonstrations could buy tickets, rather than risk police tracking their movements via cashless payment Octopus cards. Staff of the MTR Corporation, the city's sole rail operator, would turn a blind eye to the practice, just as they often did to masked men dressed in black who jumped the turnstiles without any ticket at all. Indeed, if anything, it sometimes seemed as if the MTR was helping the cause, putting on extra services so members of the public had a convenient way of traveling to and from protest sites.

As shareholder activist David Webb recalled: "Until August 24, the MTR Corp was behaving in a politically neutral manner, providing its normal service to the public, including protesters. It occasionally suspended access if platforms were dangerously overcrowded but that was on valid public safety grounds."

Yet months later many MTR stations still bear the scars of vandalism caused by those very same protesters. Battered ticket machines and broken turnstiles remain unfixed, and faint markings of graffiti and charred marks on floors are still visible in some stations. A sense of unease hangs over its staff. Somewhere along the line, a service that was once the pride of Hong Kong became a symbol of how the city was unraveling.

Mid-life crisis

The MTR Corp was already in trouble before the protests came along, reeling from a series of management crises and scandals that included a train crash and delays to the multibillion-dollar Sha Tin-Central rail link project. Still, it harbored reasonable hopes of turning a page as its 40th anniversary approached.

Instead, anti-government protests unlike anything the city had seen in its post-colonial history sent the rail operator shuttling into a dark hole from which it is still struggling to emerge. The MTR Corp's initial softly-softly approach to the protesters angered Beijing, which put it under intense pressure to toughen its stance. The pressure was made worse by the fact that the corporation is 75 per cent owned by the Hong Kong government. Media on the Chinese mainland fired a barrage of criticism at the firm for handling the protesters with kid gloves – even when demonstrators began crippling services by, for example, jamming train doors during rush hours.

"The 'black-clad people' breach the law but still receive the 'nice treatment'. What's wrong with the MTR?" asked the *People's Daily*, a mouthpiece of the Communist Party. A subsidiary, the *Global Times*, accused the MTR Corp of showing a "smiling face to the radical protesters and giving a cold eye to police," adding to the city's turmoil. State broadcaster China Central Television went further, warning the rail operator not to help the "rioters" or risk the company "derailing and slipping into the abyss."

Facing such pressure, the rail giant hardened its stance, obtaining a court injunction to prevent disruptive acts on its network, closing stations in advance of demonstrations and curtailing services. Such actions not only made it harder for protesters to get to demonstrations, it also cut off their available escape routes. On various occasions, police cornered protesters after chasing them into MTR stations.

"The MTR Corp started behaving differently, including the pre-emptive shutdown of stations ahead of lawful assemblies, making it harder for the public to attend and exercise the freedom of protest … That's what made the MTR Corp a target for extremist protesters, because it became a proxy for the government," Webb said.

In a play on the firm's Chinese name *Gong Tit* (Hong Kong's Railway), protesters labeled it *Dong Tit* (Communist Party's Railway) and it became the main target for the destructive fury of radicals who blamed it for bowing to pressure from Beijing and colluding with the same police force they had been battling in the streets.

They trashed stations and set facilities on fire, hurled petrol bombs at entrances, spray-painted graffiti on walls, and threw obstructions onto tracks. Things seemed to hit a nadir on the night of August 31 when a rumor spread that riot police had beaten three protesters to death after charging onto a train at Prince Edward station.

The rumor turned out to be false, but the decision to bar journalists and first aid attendants from the scene only served to fuel public suspicions. The station was subsequently shut for two days and despite attempts by police to debunk the unfounded rumors, one of the exits became a makeshift shrine and an emblem of resistance. Again, the MTR Corp did not exactly help itself, resisting calls to release the relevant closed-circuit television footage, saying it would be kept for three years and only authorized persons would be allowed to see it.

The controversy was a baptism of fire for the MTR Corp's new chairman Rex Auyeung Pak-kuen, who had taken the top job just two months earlier on July 1, the same day protesters stormed and vandalized the city's legislature. Until the Prince Edward incident, Auyeung, 67, had managed to keep a low profile.

In an interview in September, he tried to quash claims the firm had kowtowed to Beijing in taking a harder line with protesters, insisting the MTR Corp was merely a commercial entity that had nothing to do with politics.

However, he defended police's actions inside metro stations. "We are a law-abiding listed company that follows the rules and regulations. If police want to enforce the law in our premises, who are we to refuse them?" he asked.

He admitted the challenges he faced were unprecedented, saying he felt an overwhelming sense of "helplessness" at being embroiled in the political storm. A businessman all his life, he was non-partisan and did not know politics, he said. "I don't know how to ease the tension," he confessed.

"I respect that the protesters have their sense of frustration. We can only appeal to them to treasure the MTR facilities, and think hard whether it is in everybody's interest to damage those and cripple the service."

Turn for the worse

In October, rail stations were targeted anew by extremist protesters. When the government announced a ban on face masks on October 5, rampaging mobs attacked stations, causing extensive damage and forcing the closure of the entire rail network for the first time in its 40-year history.

Through most of the following two months, the rail operator closed its stations early, saying it needed the time to fix damaged facilities.

Critics accused it of imposing a de facto curfew on the city.

Whatever the truth of those accusations, the damage was visible. Countless turnstiles, ticketing machines, surveillance cameras, lifts and escalators had been wrecked, as had 54 heavy railway trains and 16 Light Rail vehicles.

The rail firm said that, as of November 24, 85 of its 94 MTR stations and 62 of its 68 Light Rail stops had been vandalized, with the damage to University station so severe that it would require works on a scale similar to rebuilding the whole station.

Amid the damage, passenger numbers plummeted, falling 27.4 per cent in October and 27.2 per cent in November, year on year. In December, the MTR announced more bad news, saying its protest-related costs would hit HK$1.6 billion (US$206.2 million) as a result of lower revenue from services, a HK$500 million bill for repairing facilities, extra spent on security, and concessions for retail tenants.

So steep was the price of incurring the wrath of the protesters that questions have been asked about the future of the company – a stunning reversal of fortunes for a firm that serves more than 5 million passengers a day, once boasted a punctuality rate of 99.9 per cent, and had reaped a net profit of around or above HK$10 billion in each of the five years leading to the protests.

The MTR's own financial report released in March 2020 showed its transport operations had made a loss of HK$591 million in 2019, down from a profit of almost HK$2 billion in 2018. The firm said the impact of the protests amounted to about HK$2.3 billion in losses, of which more than HK$600 million was spent on repairing facilities. Passenger numbers fell 6.4 per cent last year, with a 14.8 per cent drop in the second half.

Consequently, many critics are now bearish on the MTR Corp's future standing. Francis Lun Sheung-nim, chief executive of Geo Securities Ltd, sees no end in sight to the protesters' fury and defends his position to put a "sell" rating on MTR stock. "The problem is – like police – the MTR has become the enemy of the people. I put a 'sell' rating on MTR because I don't have any confidence in its management."

Lun argued that the firm's corporate image had been irreparably damaged as it toed the line from Beijing and shut down services. "I think they have to put common sense before just blindly following orders," he said. "It's a public service provider, it should never abandon people in the middle of nowhere."

Quentin Cheng Hin-kei, spokesman for commuter concern group Public Transport Research Team, agreed: "The MTR has given the public the impression that it toes the line of the government instead of serving the public."

He said the early station closures had driven away passengers, who had turned to buses and ferries instead. Cheng warned that, now that protesters had linked the MTR Corp to the government, the rail company could expect more trouble as the "protesters will continue to vent their anger."

"I feel pessimistic about the MTR," he added. "It has become complacent with its monopoly of the rail service. It just keeps blaming other parties without improving itself."

The government should either sell its 75 per cent stake in the corporation to investors and give it complete autonomy, or buy back the remaining 25 per cent and take full control, he said. "The MTR is a monster. It is only partially privatized but controlled by the government. Who is it accountable to – the government or its customers?" he asked.

Light at the end of the tunnel?

Not all are so pessimistic. Jason Chan Wai-chung, head of research at uSMART Securities, said the protests were a minor setback for the MTR Corp, as commuters still had to rely on it as their main mode of transport.

"The MTR holds a monopoly on the city's railway services. Despite its tarnished image, there won't be a big impact on its future patronage. The recent slowdown in protests and resumption of normal services will help restore its profits."

Tam Kin-chiu, vice-chairman of the pro-Beijing Hong Kong Federation of Railway Trade Unions, said staff morale was now the biggest issue facing the MTR Corp. "There's a real need for the company to hold regular talks with the frontline staff, to learn their difficulties and concerns," he said. However, he felt that while protest-related vandalism had affected the operator's service, its reputation as a reliable, if not indispensable, mode of transport was undimmed.

Lawmaker Michael Tien Puk-sun, former chairman of the Kowloon-Canton Railway Corporation, was similarly upbeat, but citing the support the MTR Corp received from the government and its business model, which is built as much on property development as transport.

Under the model, "Rail plus Property," the government grants the MTR Corp development rights at stations or depots when it builds new railway lines.

Tien said that while the social unrest was a "single incident that won't happen every year," property was the main source of the MTR Corp's profits, and development rights on rail projects, including the Tuen Mun South extension, would "generate huge profits for the MTR in the long run."

His point was backed up by the MTR Corp's own figures: the same report that revealed that the firm's transport operations had posted a loss of HK$591 million in 2019 also revealed that, even so, the firm had made an overall net profit of HK$11.93 billion. Not bad for what was supposedly an *annus horribilis*.

"Actually the MTR is a real estate firm with a side business as a transport operator," Tien said.

Side business or not, its rail services remain the focus of hostility for radical protesters. They and some others claim they will continue snubbing the rail network.

While it would appear impolitic for protest organizer Ventus Lau Wing-hong to admit to using the trains as he had vowed to avoid them unless he had no choice, others down the line insist they are doing the same. Black, 21, a university student and peaceful protester who would only give his first name, is one of them. Still unhappy at the MTR Corp's refusal to share the security camera footage of August 31 and cutting back services during protests, he is boycotting the operator. "Unless I am in a rush, I won't take the MTR now. Most of the time, I will take a public bus."

As it sought to grapple with such sentiments, the MTR Corp, like other things in Hong Kong, was hit by the crushing impact of the coronavirus that forced commuters to stay home. In February 2020, patronage of its domestic services fell 43 per cent from a year ago, to 71.4 million, a new low since April 2007.

At the height of the protests, MTR chairman Auyeung and chief executive Jacob Kam Chak-pui wrote a joint open letter appealing to all sides to treasure and safeguard the railway network that has been "carrying our collective memories over the past few decades."

It would appear that they have their work cut out for them to renew that emotional connection between commuter and operator.

Tycoons caught in a political tempest

Gary Cheung

They are Beijing's trusted allies but is the honeymoon between the central government and Hong Kong's property tycoons over?

Well before Hong Kong returned to China in 1997, the city's tight group of property developers were Beijing's main political allies. China's preoccupation, as the handover approached, was to ensure the city's continued stability and that meant retaining the confidence of the business community.

"Winning the support of major property developers was its top priority," said Anthony Cheung Bing-leung, a political scientist and former secretary for transport and housing. The post-handover political system was in fact designed to protect the interests of the business sector, he added.

The colony's richest man, tycoon Li Ka-shing, was said to have helped shipping magnate Tung Chee-hwa land the job of Hong Kong's first chief executive. The *South China Morning Post* learned that in late 1995, Chinese president Jiang Zemin received a letter recommending Tung for the role. It was penned by Li and Beijing princeling Larry Yung Chi-kin, head of CITIC Pacific, one of the first mainland companies to set up in Hong Kong. Yung's father, Rong Yiren, was China's vice-president and had been on good terms with the late paramount leader Deng Xiaoping.

A source close to Beijing who revealed to this author the existence of the letter said that Jiang had viewed its contents positively. In January 1996, the Chinese leader set off a storm of speculation when he crossed a crowded room at the Great Hall of the People, where a handover preparatory meeting was taking place, to shake Tung's hand. Exactly 11 months later, Tung was picked for Hong Kong's top job.

That Li so confidently offered his view to Jiang revealed how close Hong Kong's tycoons were to the Beijing elite at the time. In the years after the handover, the city's property giants thrived and massively expanded their wealth, all while remaining firm supporters of both the central and city governments.

Dominating the city's property scene are four families, each running a sprawling conglomerate involved in everything from housing to transport, education, retail, telecommunications and utilities. Aside from Li's Cheung Kong Asset Holdings, there are the Lees of Henderson Land Development, the Kwoks of Sun Hung Kai Properties (SHKP), and the Chengs of New World Development.

In 2020, for the first time in decades, Henderson Land's Lee Shau-kee, 92, was listed by Forbes as Hong Kong's richest man after his wealth rose 3 per cent to US$30.4 billion (HK$235.7 billion). That put him HK$1 billion ahead of Li, long the city's wealthiest billionaire used to the media limelight and the attention of powerful visitors to the city. The third-richest man, Henry Cheng Kar-shun, 73, is chairman of New World Development and the Chow Tai Fook Jewellery chain, while SHKP is run by brothers Raymond Kwok Ping-luen and Thomas Kwok Ping-kwong.

Strains in the tycoons' close relationship with Beijing appeared during the pro-democracy Occupy protests that shut down parts of Hong Kong for 79 days in 2014. At first, most of the city's wealthiest men remained silent. Then, on October 25, 2014, the official Xinhua news agency issued an English-language report at noon, pointing out that many Hong Kong tycoons had stayed "mute" on the Occupy movement.

It named four – Cheung Kong chairman Li, Henderson Land's Lee, Wharf Holdings chairman Peter Woo Kwong-ching and Malaysian billionaire and retired founder of the Kerry group, Robert Kuok Hock-nien – and said they were "reluctant to take sides" over the protests. Xinhua noted that Li had issued a statement on October 15 urging the protesters to go home, but added: "Asia's wealthiest man did not make it clear whether he agrees with the appeals of the protesters."

Seven hours after it appeared, the Xinhua report was retracted mysteriously, with no explanation. But it clearly had done its job of reminding Hong Kong's rich and powerful of what Beijing expected. One by one, the city's billionaires spoke up, stressing the need for stability to ensure Hong Kong's continued prosperity.

A second-generation tycoon, speaking on condition of anonymity, said it was clear that some Beijing officials were frustrated at the time with "big families" in Hong Kong who made the bulk of their fortune from the property sector. "Beijing had many avenues and channels to influence behavior, such as this critical Xinhua report that was retracted hours later," the source said.

The tension between Beijing and the tycoons was on display again in 2019, as the extradition bill protests which broke out in June evolved into an anti-government, even anti-Beijing movement. Not a single tycoon spoke up in the first two months of the protests, and they remained silent even after clashes between protesters and police turned violent.

It was only in August that they went public, again one by one, to condemn the chaos and violence. If Beijing had once looked to the tycoons to help keep Hong Kong stable, it now appeared to believe that they had failed to deliver. China's state media criticized the city's developers who owned massive land banks, even as Hongkongers found property prices unaffordable. On the mainland, Hong Kong's exceedingly high property prices appeared to be a key reason for the protests.

Li found himself in hot water in September when he urged those in power to "provide a way out" for young protesters, and said that on political issues, justice might have to be tempered with mercy. He was accused of suggesting leniency for lawbreakers and condoning crime. Around this time, articles published by Xinhua, the official *People's Daily* and the nationalistic tabloid *Global Times* began to single out unaffordable housing as a root cause of the protests.

The message seemed clear – the tycoons ought to play ball and back the chief executive and government policies, or risk unstated consequences. Soon enough, the Democratic Alliance for the Betterment and Progress of Hong Kong (DAB), the city's largest pro-Beijing party, proposed that city leader Carrie Lam Cheng Yuet-ngor invoke the Lands Resumption Ordinance and acquire from developers large swathes of unused rural land to tackle the city's dire housing problem.

The idea won immediate backing in state media. A Xinhua commentary accused unnamed groups with vested interests of obstructing the Hong Kong government's attempts to boost land supply, by either hoarding or raising prices. A *People's Daily* commentary went further, saying: "For the sake of the public interest, it is time developers show their utmost sincerity instead of minding their own business, hoarding land for profit and earning the last penny."

A person familiar with Beijing's views on Hong Kong said the central government was unprepared to make concessions to Hongkongers' calls for greater democracy and preferred to focus instead on alleviating social ills, or the housing shortage, deeming these as legitimate concerns of the city as well.

The second-generation tycoon believed that Beijing had singled out the city's developers and was blaming them for skyrocketing property prices and the severe shortage of affordable public housing. When state media attacked the property tycoons, it gave Beijing the opportunity to show Hongkongers that it had identified the bogeymen, and that the central government cared. "Perhaps Beijing calculated that this could take some steam out of the situation," he said.

A source close to the city's developers believed that Beijing's liaison office in Hong Kong was behind the DAB call to seize land. "Many developers know that Beijing can't offer meaningful solutions to political issues in Hong Kong," the source said. "So it is shifting the focus to deep-seated problems like housing. The developers feel helpless as they can't do much, given Beijing's growing assertiveness."

In September, New World Development, whose portfolio included the Rosewood luxury hotel and shopping centers, said it would donate nearly a fifth of its farmland reserves to the Hong Kong government and to non-profit organizations to build public housing. Executive vice-chairman Adrian Cheng Chi-kong announced that it would hand over 3 million sq ft (27.8 hectares), and said: "We are very concerned about the housing problem in society."

By year-end, Henderson Land Development and Wheelock Properties had stepped forward too. Henderson Land gave 428,000 sq ft, while Wheelock loaned three plots of land, with a total area of 500,000 sq ft, for a nominal HK$1 each to the Hong Kong Council of Social Service and the Lok Sin Tong charity for eight years.

"It was too coincidental for all three developers to do that at the same time," said the second-generation tycoon. "They were reacting to the media pressure, the tense social atmosphere in Hong Kong." Pointing out that the developers' donations did not significantly increase the supply of land for housing, the tycoon added: "The question is, has it changed anything? Has it bolstered support for the central government and the Hong Kong government?"

The tycoon noted that Beijing had shown over the past decade that it wanted Hong Kong's business community, especially the major families running property firms, to toe the Communist Party line and close ranks around the Hong Kong government. It might have hoped that that would happen when protests broke out against the extradition bill, but there were wide differences of opinion over the issue.

"In Hong Kong where there is a competitive flow of information, do you think there would have been no riots if the tycoons came out to support the government? To hold high hopes that a bunch of compliant tycoons can change public opinion in Hong Kong, reflects a basic misunderstanding of how information flows and how Hong Kong works," the tycoon said.

As far as land ownership in Hong Kong was concerned, the "Big Four" major developers – SHKP, Henderson Land, CK Asset Holdings and New World Development – held a total of 83 million sq ft as of 2019, according to their annual reports. A Bank of America Merrill Lynch report said they also held a total of 107.3 million sq ft of farmland in the New Territories. Henderson Land owned 46 million sq ft, followed by SHKP with 31 million sq ft, New World Development with 17 million sq ft, and CK Assets with 13 million sq ft.

A mainland expert familiar with Hong Kong affairs pointed to the developers' dominance across various sectors of Hong Kong's economy and said: "The government badly needs to tackle deep-rooted problems like unaffordable housing and the lack of social mobility for the young people."

Noting the way protesters vandalized MTR stations and trashed shops, banks and businesses with mainland links or considered Beijing-friendly, the expert said: "You can sense the frustration of the rioters who vandalized shops and public facilities. They think they have no stake in society and couldn't care less."

However, housing and property prices did not figure as a chief concern among younger Hongkongers who were polled in August 2019 by the Hong Kong Public Opinion Research Institute to find out the reasons for their discontent. Only 58 per cent of respondents aged 14 to 29 ticked off housing problems, compared with 91 per cent who blamed distrust of Beijing, 84 per cent who distrusted city leader Lam, and 84 per cent who were moved by the "pursuit of democracy."

Protesters interviewed by the *Post* over the course of 2019 indicated that a combination of factors drove them onto the street, including a long-simmering sense of social and political injustice. Aside from astronomical property prices, they listed insufficient help for the underprivileged, inadequate medical services, the stressful education system, the influx of mainland visitors, the difficulty of moving up the social ladder, and the gnawing feeling that Hong Kong's freedoms were under threat.

Muk Lam, 26, a doctor in a public hospital earning HK$970,000 a year said: "The narrative in the mainland media is that those taking part in the protests are *fai cing*," she said, using a term that means "rubbish teenagers," youngsters with no hope. "But Hong Kong's unemployment rate is only about 3 per cent. Are high property prices a reason for the unrest? We cannot blame this entirely on the economy."

However, Edmund Cheng Wai, a political scientist at City University, felt that housing woes did affect some protesters, particularly those born after 1990. Referring to these younger protesters, who made up nearly half of over 6,100 protesters interviewed by a research team including him and others from Chinese and Lingnan universities since June 2019, he said: "Many suffer from lower social mobility and their career prospects can't compare with those of older generations."

The question that remained was whether the Chinese state media attacks on Hong Kong's wealthiest tycoons signaled that a 40-year honeymoon could be coming to an end. The developers have long enjoyed considerable political clout, wielding considerable influence in the process to elect the city's leader.

They were represented strongly in the Election Committee, comprising the business elite, professionals, unionists and politicians, that picked the city leader. Checks by the *Post* found that the

1,194-strong Election Committee which chose Lam in 2017 included 96 members directly representing developers and their business associates. Forty-three of those 96 were directors, employees or business associates of six major developers – SHKP, CK Asset Holding, Henderson Land Development, New World Development, Wharf Holdings and Sino Land.

Many others with indirect connections to the property giants were to be found in the committee's sub-sector groups for transport, hotels, finance, wholesale and retail. This reflected the developers' dominant role in Hong Kong's economy, with their conglomerates involved in everything from telecommunications to public utilities and supermarkets.

Ray Yep Kin-man, a professor with City University's department of public policy, does not believe that the tycoons' cup of goodwill with Beijing is at risk of running dry. "Beijing just wants to rally their support in putting an end to the violence in the city," he said.

But others point out that ties between Beijing and the tycoons had been cooling ever since Xi Jinping became president in 2013, well before the protests in Hong Kong. It is noteworthy that Beijing leaders held fewer meetings with Hong Kong tycoons when visiting the city compared to the past, to avoid criticism that they cared only about the rich. In the past, Li Ka-shing's close ties with Jiang Zemin were well-known. Li played host to the former president during his visits to Hong Kong in 1997, 1998 and 2001.

Despite that cooling off, the property developers remained Beijing's indispensable allies. It would be unlikely that the central government would want to alienate them, especially with the Legislative Council elections due in September 2020, and the selection of the chief executive in 2022, the second-generation tycoon said.

Analysts and key figures within the pro-establishment camp expect candidates from the bloc to be punished at the Legco polls, as they were at the district council elections in November 2019. Seventy Legco seats are for the taking. In the 2016 Legco elections, pro-establishment candidates secured 40 seats while pan-democrats and localists won 30. Some analysts expect opposition politicians to win 34 seats or more in 2020, which would make it more difficult for the government to get its bills and policy initiatives passed in the legislature.

"In an ideal world, Beijing would want to diversify the political power base in Hong Kong. That would mean making it not so concentrated in the business community," the second-generation tycoon said. "But that is much easier said than done."

Hong Kong's tycoons may have less influence in Beijing than in the 1980s and 1990s, but they remain a force the central government cannot ignore. "Beijing must realize that the four big property families are at most only part of the problem in Hong Kong," the tycoon said. "What would it cost Beijing to no longer cooperate with the business community? If the cost is less than the benefit, they should do it. But is it?"

Superman and melon-picking

Denise Tsang

Hong Kong's richest man Li Ka-shing caused a stir when he invoked Tang poetry to end the protests and the violence. But who was he directing his message to?

I f ever a city needed a superhero, this was the time. It was mid-August, the height of Hong Kong's summer of discontent, and tensions were at boiling point.

Hardcore mobs were clashing with riot police; triads were beating people in the streets; police stations were under attack. Rampaging protesters had defaced the city's emblem, blocked the Cross-Harbour Tunnel and paralyzed the airport.

Asia's world city was well into its third month of chaos as it stared into the abyss and the abyss stared back. On one side, protesters vowed never to surrender unless their five demands were met. On the other, authorities in both Beijing and Hong Kong were equally adamant that would never happen. The battle lines had been drawn and there was no grey area in between.

Until "Superman" stepped in, as if on cue. Also known as Li Ka-shing, Hong Kong's favorite billionaire was exactly the kind of man Lois Lane might have asked for a quote, had the Daily Planet been following the story as closely as the rest of the world's press.

In Hong Kong, a city that worships wealth, the opinions of self-made supermen like Li are priceless. And Li's was worth more than most. Not only did his backstory of rising from teenage factory worker to plastic flowers seller to Asia's richest man have an obvious folk appeal, but in a quite literal sense nobody else had invested in the city's future as much as him.

The 91-year-old tycoon's empire of ports, property, energy and financial services had over the decades built much of the city – amassing a US$30 billion (HK$233 billion) fortune for Li in the process – while his flagship enterprises, CK Hutchison Holdings and CK Asset Holdings, were among Hong Kong's biggest employers.

And there was another, less obvious, motivation why Li might want to speak out. While the protests had often been framed as a fight for greater democracy, increasingly a strand of thinking was evolving that the real reason for the disenchantment of the city's youth were the sky-high property prices that prevented all but the most privileged from ever owning their own homes. Public opinion was shifting against the city's property developers, and Beijing – which had once backed them – appeared to be leading the grumblings against the tycoons.

Against this background it was only natural that when the oracle of Hong Kong's business world spoke, the city listened to every word. There was just one problem: deciphering what he said.

An oracle speaks

On August 16, Li took out two adverts in the city's newspapers, one in color and one in black and white, both of which he signed in true everyman style as "a Hong Kong resident, Li Ka-shing."

In the color advert, the Chinese character for "violence" had been crossed out in red and next to it were slogans about loving China, loving Hong Kong, loving freedom and loving oneself. At the bottom was the message: "Stop anger and violence in the name of love."

Even more intriguing was a line at the top saying: "The best of intentions can lead to the worst outcomes." Yet nowhere did the advert make clear whose good intentions Li was referring to.

The black-and-white advert was even more mystifying, featuring eight Chinese characters that translate roughly as: "The melon of Huangtai cannot bear being picked again."

It appeared to be a reference to a Tang dynasty poem, the moral of which is that some things have suffered so much that any further attack will ruin them.

Again, the advert did not make clear whose "attacks" were damaging the "melon" of Hong Kong. Was this – as much of the business community felt – Li's way of telling protesters the city could stand no more violent civil disobedience?

Or was it – as many protesters believed – a veiled reference to Beijing's increasing influence, a warning that if it kept encroaching on Hong Kong's freedoms it would soon spoil the very thing that had once made the city special?

Shades of grey

With speculation rife over the true meaning of Li's gnomic message, all sides were quick to claim him as their own. Protesters pointed out Li had once described democracy as "good for business" when in 2003 he spoke of his pride at a march against the infamous Article 23 – a Beijing-backed piece of legislation meant to guard against treason and secession but was widely seen by the Hong Kong public as an assault on the city's freedoms.

Others pointed out the tycoon had opposed the Occupy protests of 2014, saying at the time that "even if it just lasts for one hour, it will be harmful to the city." The Occupy protesters went on to cripple the financial district for 79 days, or 1,896 hours.

The internet, too, could not make up its mind. The social media forum LIHKG, heavily used by Hong Kong protesters, was swamped with endless debates over whether the tycoon was on their side or not.

Meanwhile, over on the Chinese mainland, the hashtag #LiKa-shingSpeakingOut became one of the most searched-for phrases on Weibo, China's Twitter. Even when censors disabled the hashtag, along with #LiKa-shing, users continued to find ways to discuss the nonagenarian's ambiguity and whether he was being a wily "old fox."

Appeals to Li's spokesman did little to clarify his meaning. The spokesman said Li believed the city's prosperity hinged on the principle of "one country, two systems" and that "investing in our next generation will always bear fruit."

To young ears that sounded like 1-0 to the protesters.

But the spokesman added Li's thinking was "in line with Hong Kong's mainstream values" and that the most pressing issue was to stop violence and maintain the rule of law. Now, that sounded like a score for the establishment.

As a mixed message, it was something of a masterpiece. Whose side was Li on? Was he on one or the other, both or neither? Was he even saying anything meaningful at all?

The spokesman did not seem entirely sure. "There is no need to read too much into it," he said.

One poem, two meanings

Of course, reading into it was exactly what most people were now eager to do. The more determined among them took the chance to refresh their memories of the Tang dynasty poem he quoted, penned by the crown prince Li Xian, who lived between 654 and 684 AD.

The sixth son of emperor Gaozong and the second son of the legendary empress Wu Zetian, Li Xian was known as an intelligent and capable prince. As his brothers fell one by one through court intrigue, he was made crown prince and the heir apparent.

But his ambitious mother concentrated all power in her hands as her ailing husband succumbed to illness. She became suspicious of Li Xian and put him under house arrest. In desperation, Li Xian wrote the poem as a subtle protest to his mother:

Growing melons beneath Huangtai,
Hanging heavily, many grow ripe,
Pick one, the others will be fine,
Pick two, fewer are left on the vine,
If you want to get yet another one,
That's where we must draw the line,
For if there is any more reaping,
You will end up with an empty vine. *

The prince's lament did not move his mother. The empress accused Li Xian of treason and he was sent into exile. In 684 AD, shortly after his father's death, the empress Wu drove her son to suicide.

"The melon of Huangtai" became a popular expression in Chinese culture, symbolizing suffering in the face of persecution.

Some protesters believed that under this deeper meaning, they were Li Xian, while Beijing was the empress. Others have suggested the tycoon's use of the poem was simply an apt description of Hong Kong, torn by violence and radical views.

A third option, favored by those of the "wily old fox" school of thinking, was that Li was indulging in a deliberate act of constructive ambiguity, playing all sides at once to keep everyone happy.

Lau Siu-kai, vice-chairman of the Chinese Association of Hong Kong and Macau Studies, a think tank associated with Beijing, said the tycoon might have deliberately chosen to be indirect to avoid being too provocative, but if that was the plan, it might have backfired.

The problem was, people were "not sure if the advertisements are aimed at the central government, the Hong Kong government or the rioters."

A message, but to whom?

Some observers put greater emphasis on the timing of the adverts, which were published shortly after about 500 Hong Kong businessmen and pro-Beijing politicians visited Zhang Xiaoming, then director of the State Council's Hong Kong and Macau Affairs Office, in Shenzhen. While Li did not attend that meeting, his elder son Victor Li Tzar-kuoi did.

At the time, the city's businesses had come under great pressure from Beijing to be more outspoken against the protesters and, sure enough, following their return from Shenzhen, several of the tycoons came out to condemn protesters for the chaos and violence roiling the city.

But political scientist Ivan Choy Chi-keung, of Chinese University, said given Li's influence, age and cultural background, he had the freedom not to join this chorus, though he might have had other reasons for his ambiguity. "He knows he can't be too specific on some issues; otherwise, there is little room for discussion," Choy said.

Some suggested Li's aim was to put pressure on the Hong Kong government and in particular its embattled chief executive, Carrie Lam Cheng Yuet-ngor.

They pointed to an address Li gave on September 8 to about 1,000 Buddhists at the Tze Shan Monastery, the HK$1.5 billion temple he built in Tai Po, just a few weeks after his adverts appeared.

Li spoke about the growing unrest and appealed to the city authorities to show humanity and provide a "way out" for young people involved in the protests, saying justice might have to be tempered with mercy on political issues. The speech appeared to be a veiled suggestion that the law should go easy on arrested young protesters, who could face up to 10 years in jail if charged with rioting.

"We hope Hong Kong will be able to ride out the storm. We hope the young can take the big picture into consideration. For those at the helm, we hope they can give the masters of our future a way out," Li said.

The speech did not go down so well with city leader Lam, who brushed off any suggestion of leniency in the eyes of the law, or with Stanley Ng Chau-pei, leader of the pro-Beijing Federation of Trade Unions, who mocked Li as the "king of cockroaches" – using the police force's term for protesters.

Meanwhile, mainland China's political and legal affairs commission accused Li of condoning crime and blamed him explicitly, as a real estate tycoon, for the housing crisis facing young Hongkongers. It added sarcastically that as a major developer, Li ought to be the one providing a "way out" for young Hongkongers.

A power play?

These criticisms appeared to have stung the tycoon, who responded that his remarks had been misinterpreted and that he was used to "unwarranted accusations."

They also hinted at the changing power dynamics between Beijing and Hong Kong's once untouchable property magnates, something Li was all too familiar with.

He had once enjoyed close ties with both Deng Xiaoping and Jiang Zemin, who between them led China from the late 1970s to the early 2000s. Indeed, Li hosted Jiang during his visits to Hong Kong in 1997, 1998 and 2001. Each time, the Chinese leader stayed at CK Assets' Harbour Grand Hotel in Hung Hom, and would have breakfast with Li and his sons.

Such coziness came to an abrupt end when Xi Jinping became president in 2013 and Beijing began to be more detached toward Hong Kong's developers.

Since then, Li had often incurred the wrath of the mainland Chinese media, usually whenever he sells assets. In 2015, the Liaowang Institute think tank, which is linked to the state-run Xinhua news agency, denounced him for moving his capital out of China, accusing him of forgetting the favors the motherland had done him, and of running for the exit at the first sign of trouble in China's economy.

It said Li had not grown rich from a level playing field in a market economy, but owed his success to his connections with top officials, who had given him access to prime locations, often at hugely discounted prices.

The *People's Daily* said Li was happy to "enjoy the benefits when things are good" but could not be counted on when the going got tough.

The vitriol against Li was part of a wider picture in which Beijing was rethinking its approach to the city's property developers.

Lau of the Chinese Association of Hong Kong and Macau Studies said while Beijing had once relied on the tycoons to maintain investment confidence in the city following its return to Chinese rule in 1997, this was no longer the case.

Instead, Beijing was now increasingly alarmed at how monopolies in the sector had contributed to the widening wealth gap that it saw as a root cause of the unrest.

One week after Li's address to the monastery, various state-run media outlets on the mainland urged the Hong Kong government to seize land hoarded by developers and use it for public housing.

Evil tycoon to man of the people

At this point, it would have been tempting to liken Li's newspaper adverts to kryptonite. In wading into the most polarizing debate seen in Hong Kong since its return from British rule, Li appeared to have laid bare his own weakest point.

It was almost as if he had invited Beijing to side with the long-standing community critics who had for years caricatured him as an evil developer who was milking Hongkongers in a game of supercharged, real-life *Monopoly*. So much for playing both sides with constructive ambiguity.

Over the subsequent weeks, several of the city's biggest developers – including New World Development, Henderson Land Development, Wheelock Properties and Sun Hung Kai Properties – took the hint, agreeing to contribute part of their land banks to build 10,000 transitional homes for people on public housing waiting lists.

But the "wily old fox" of Chinese internet fame was not to be so easily cornered, at least not yet. Whether or not it had been his plan all along, the effects of his newspaper adverts and speeches to the monastery had redefined his image among young Hongkongers on the protest front lines.

Suddenly, many of those very same youths who admitted to being disillusioned by the property market and income inequality were now proclaiming its greatest tycoon as "the strongest yellow ribbon" (after the color of the protesters) and urging their fellow citizens to support him by shopping in his pharmacies and supermarkets.

Even for a superhero used to costume changes in tight spots, it was a remarkable transformation. Evil tycoon to man of the people, Lex Luthor to Clark Kent, in a single bound.

While all this was playing out, the media was still busy dissecting Li's adverts, trying to divine a deeper meaning.

Some of the more probing reports discovered that he had fallen back on the poem about the melon before, using it in 2016 when asked whether Leung Chun-ying should run for a second term as Hong Kong's chief executive.

Much was made of the fact that subsequently, Leung did not enter the race, though the mystery of the melon's significance was never fully solved in that case either.

It may simply have been that people were stretching the analogy in the poem too far, reading too much into the superman and his myth.

Perhaps here was merely a man who cared deeply for his city and hoped for cooler heads to prevail as the summer of discontent segued into fall.

Li's old friend, the veteran nightlife entrepreneur Allan Zeman, said it was not in Li's nature to be political. "He does not need to gain favor from anyone, he has passed that point," Zeman said.

"Hong Kong is divided. He was speaking to both sides to bring them together. He wanted to bring some sense to both protesters and those who are pro-establishment. It was a wake-up call to them, asking, 'Why are you doing what you are doing? Think about the consequences for Hong Kong.'"

Still, even if Li's intentions had not been political, he had one last loose end to tie up and, like any good superhero tale, there was always going to be a winner and a loser.

While his rival developers were being cowed by the Chinese media, Li's firm, CK Asset Holdings, took a firmer stance. Even as it agreed to look into using some of its farmland for housing, the company warned that the transformation would take too long and suggested another solution instead.

In October 2019, Li's foundation announced it would give HK$1 billion in cash to smaller firms grappling with the economic downturn caused by the seemingly unending protests.

True to his word, within just two months the cash had been channeled to 28,000 small and medium-sized firms in the food and drink, retail and travel sectors.

The move won Li the approval and applause of the city, not least because it also highlighted the tardiness of the Hong Kong government, which had promised relief measures worth HK$25 billion back in August but had yet to deliver even as Li was dishing out the cash.

Once again, Li was the hero of the hour. Or, as Zeman put it, "the superman."

Poem translated by Chow Chung-yan.

Not the Michelin Guide: When restaurants are labeled 'yellow' or 'blue'

Fiona Sun and Cannix Yau

Many Hong Kong diners, cafes and bistros nailed their colors to the mast during the unrest, refusing customers from the opposite camp.

Yellow sticky notes posted outside the Lung Mun Cafe in Hung Hom carry a plain message: "Blue-ribbons stay away." It means those who support the Hong Kong government or police are not welcome. The *cha chaan teng*-style restaurant – with its Chinese-Western menu of *char siu* (barbecued pork), spaghetti and pork chops – is known to be a "yellow-ribbon" establishment which supports the protest movement.

In the turmoil of the city's political unrest, some businesses have found themselves branded "blue" and pro-establishment, while others are marked "yellow" for supporting the protesters. A "blue" label can mean being boycotted or even vandalized, whereas "yellow" businesses can count on backing from protesters and their supporters.

Lung Mun Cafe first became popular among protesters in August 2019, after it began offering free meals to students at all of its five branches. Owner Cheung Chun-kit, 40, decided to help young protesters after learning that some had been cut off financially by their parents who held different political views.

While protesters welcomed his support, others criticized him. Cheung had to deal with numerous harassing phone calls, hoaxers who made fake food orders, as well as vandalism. His Hung Hom outlet was attacked on October 24, 2019 by five masked men who smashed windows, computers, closed-circuit television cameras and furniture, causing damage of about HK$100,000 (US$12,900), Cheung said.

News of the incident brought a large number of people eager to show their support, and long queues formed despite the smashed windows and damaged facilities. It was a heartwarming sight to Cheung. He was undeterred by the attack. "I will always support young people. Society is unfair to them. They have lost their freedom, which they are now fighting for," he said.

For businesses that took sides, or were perceived to take sides, there was a price to pay. Radical protesters targeted businesses with mainland ties or which were considered pro-establishment. Companies such as Maxim's and Best Mart 360, Chinese state-owned banks, as well as mainland smartphone giants Huawei and Xiaomi, had their premises vandalized, torched, trashed and covered in graffiti.

Many smaller establishments were labeled "yellow-ribbon" or "blue-ribbon," and protesters urged their supporters to patronize "yellow-ribbon" shops only. They drew up lists of businesses to support or avoid, and circulated them online.

"Hong Kong's economy has taken a hit amid the political crisis, but 'yellow-ribbon' businesses have been growing. We can force more businesses to take sides, and increase the number of people on our side," said a post on LIHKG, the online forum popular with protesters.

At the height of the protests, so-called "yellow" cafes and their followers, however, brushed aside one hard reality of their business: most of their raw materials are imported from the mainland. "We have to start somewhere," said an online post, shrugging off the inconvenient truth.

Growing a 'yellow economic force'

The anti-government movement had hoped that, by encouraging and uniting businesses supporting it, a "yellow economic force" would emerge. "The yellow economic concept is heading in the right direction, with the boycott of 'blue' shops. This will lead to 'yellow' shops making more money and opening more branches," cafe owner Cheung said.

To help young people affected by the social unrest equip themselves with skills and become financially independent, he organized free vocational training sessions in hairdressing, beautician skills, leathercraft, baking cookies and making mini *fa pai*, traditional floral decorative plaques.

Using more than HK$1 million of his own money, Cheung launched more than 20 free classes in December 2019 with the help of volunteer instructors. Several hundred people signed up for courses that ran for a few days a week or a few sessions each month.

"Because of this unrest, many young people have become jobless, penniless, 'school-less' or even homeless, as some have been evicted by their families," Cheung said. "I want to make them feel that they can still find hope in their lives."

Chan Sing, 44, the boss of a company producing mini *fa pai*, was among a handful of "yellow" business owners who joined Cheung in his efforts. After his 19-year-old son was arrested in July 2019 during a protest, Chan declared on Facebook that he would refuse orders from police.

His business suffered, and then was hit further by the economic downturn. But a flood of orders came in after he joined Cheung and began running free classes teaching youngsters how to make mini *fa pai*.

At the start of the coronavirus outbreak in January 2020, anti-mainland sentiment was again on display. Restaurant chain Kwong Wing Catering posted notices at several of its outlets in late January, saying its staff did not speak Mandarin – a thinly-veiled hint that customers from mainland China were not welcome.

The Equal Opportunities Commission (EOC) – the anti-discrimination watchdog – advised the chain to remove the notices, but its defiant owners, who support protesters, insisted that their staff would only speak Cantonese and serve Hongkongers "and friends from Taiwan."

The EOC said it received nearly 600 inquiries and complaints about restaurants and other businesses that refused to serve mainlanders or Mandarin-speakers during the first few months of the Covid-19 pandemic.

A survey conducted by the Society for Community Organization (SoCO) in the second half of February found 101 restaurants displaying discriminatory content that targeted mainlanders online or in notices at their premises. They wanted mainland visitors, Mandarin-speakers and those who had visited the mainland within the past 14 days to keep away.

Paying the price for being 'blue'

On the other hand, businesses branded "blue-ribbon," such as those owned by the Maxim's group, Best Mart 360 and Japanese fast-food chain Yoshinoya, had their premises vandalized, torched or covered in graffiti. Smaller shops such as the Ngan Loong Cafe, in Lei Yue Mun, and Friendly Tasty restaurant, in Tai Po, were affected too, with their fortunes changing overnight after the owners expressed support for police.

Kate Lee Hoi-wu, 51, a single mother who runs Ngan Loong Cafe, became the target of online abuse and repeated complaints to the authorities after she put up signs in her restaurant in June 2019, supporting police. "For the first three weeks, I had very few customers. There was a day when I earned only HK$80," she recalled.

Her business picked up dramatically from late July 2019, after some police officers dropped in and thanked her for her support. Among them was Chris Tang Ping-keung, who became police commissioner later in the year. A stream of "blue ribbons" and mainland tourists started showing up, and some even volunteered to help Lee run the place.

"Now my restaurant is full of customers. I can tell you business has never been so good," she said happily. But her experience left her firmly against the notion of color-coding the economy. "This will only sow further discord in society," she said.

Widow and single mother-of-two Wong Lee-lee, 38, who runs Friendly Tasty restaurant, serving rice noodle rolls and traditional desserts, also paid the price for a Facebook post in June 2019 in which she expressed support for police. Online abuse flooded in, her shop was branded "blue-ribbon," and there were calls to boycott the place. Her business suffered, and she had to dip into her savings to make ends meet.

Wong did not regret stating her view, but said she was against dividing Hong Kong businesses by politics. "I don't care for this kind of labeling," she said. "I welcome all sorts of customers, 'yellow' or 'blue'. I woo customers with my food and service."

Businesses jittery about color labels

The swiftness with which protesters could wreak havoc by labeling establishments "blue" did cause jitters among some businesses. Chrisly Cafe, a *cha chaan teng*-style chain with seven branches in Hong Kong and one in Macau, had to issue a statement on October 25, 2019, denying online rumors that veteran Canto-pop star Alan Tam Wing-lun was one of its shareholders. Tam had found himself in hot water with protesters after he attended a pro-police rally earlier in June.

"The cafe has been color-labeled over the past months. We feel helpless," the chain said in its statement, posted on Facebook. It said its management supported demands for freedom and democracy, as well as the formation of an independent commission of inquiry to probe allegations of police brutality – one of the key demands of the protest movement.

On October 26, 2019, popular noodle chain TamJai Yunnan Mixian was quick to deny responsibility for notices that appeared outside its Yau Ma Tei and Kwun Tong Plaza outlets, saying: "Our restaurant is particular with hygiene and does not serve cockroaches and uncivilized customers." That branded the restaurant "blue-ribbon," because police officers had been known to refer to protesters as "cockroaches." The restaurant released screenshots of video footage of an unidentified man sticking the prank notice outside its shops.

Catering industry veteran Samme Cheng said most restaurant owners were lying low to avoid trouble. "Many eateries have been in a constant state of fear and are afraid of speaking up, especially on politics. We feel very helpless," he said. "We also ask our employees not to comment on politics, and to keep a low profile."

Simon Wong Ka-wo, president of the Hong Kong Federation of Restaurants and Related Trades, said restaurants that made their political positions known accounted for only a fraction of the city's more than 20,000 establishments. "Most restaurants do not want to be labeled with the so-called colors, or bring politics into business," he said. "We are a service industry, in which most businesses seek to serve all customers."

Simon Lee Siu-po, co-director of the international business and Chinese enterprise program at Chinese University, said that for the protest movement's "yellow economic circle" to succeed, much depended on the "yellow" businesses' ability to provide quality goods and services. "Using one's political stance to attract business may only work in the short term," he said. "In the long term, if firms fail to keep their customers happy with their goods or services, they may go. A successful business can never depend only on a political slogan."

Lee said "yellow" shops would have to unite in making long-term strategies, forming alliances and avoiding vicious competition. He thought it was not impossible for a "yellow economic force" to break the market dominance of pro-Beijing firms in Hong Kong.

"If yellow firms are united and dedicated to cultivating like-minded younger people through employment, vocational training and partnerships, they will have more bargaining power to counteract the blue camp's economic dominance," he said.

But others poured cold water on the notion of growing a "yellow economic circle." Billy Mak Sui-choi, associate professor of finance and decision sciences at Baptist University, dismissed it as "unworkable" and "stupid."

"To maximize profits, a business should attract a broader base of customers. To target a particular group of customers based on political considerations will only limit your customer base and eventually restrict business growth," he said. As for the "yellow" group's strong anti-Beijing stance, he asked: "How can a firm entirely cut ties from the mainland and refrain from using mainland materials?"

Economist Andy Kwan Cheuk-chiu, director of the ACE Centre for Business and Economic Research, said only certain sectors such as dining, retail, advertising and marketing, as well as IT, would be able to sustain "yellow" practices as these had individual firms.

"But for Hong Kong's four key industries – finance, tourism, trading and logistics – it'll be very hard for the 'yellow economic circle' to even make an entry. These sectors are all dominated by corporate clients and most of the firms have ties with the mainland," he said.

Pro-business lawmaker Felix Chung Kwok-pan warned that bringing politics into the workplace would hurt the city's overall business environment. "Businesses are concerned about the business environment," he said. "If Hong Kong's environment becomes so bad that an operator risks being attacked simply because it holds different political views, businesses will leave the city."

Message from the ballot box

November's local elections unleashed a political tidal wave. Can rookie representatives prove they are more than just a protest vote?

O f the 1,100 candidates running in the district council elections, Leung Pak-kin was possibly the only one who never put in an appearance at his constituency on polling day, November 24. Neither did he make much of an effort to personally connect with voters, not even standing on street corners to greet people in his neighborhood during the final weeks of campaigning.

Instead, Leung, 44, was focusing his energies on covering the ongoing protests against the government's extradition bill, hoping to "safeguard the truth" by recording the violence on the front lines as a freelance cameraman. A week before polling day, he entered the campus of Polytechnic University, where students would later hunker down as the movement mounted one of its most ferocious attacks against riot police. "My campaign team tried to persuade me to come out on polling day," Leung said, adding that they had even wanted him to get out early enough to allow for the maximum 48 hours of detention after leaving the site. "But in the end, I just could not let go of the protesters inside the campus." After the poll, Leung's team told him he had defeated his pro-establishment rival by 98 votes, and he emerged from the campus two days later. He now represents Tai Fat Hau constituency on Wan Chai District Council, having beaten the man he lost to four years previously, Kenny Lee Kwun-yee of the Democratic Alliance for the

Betterment and Progress of Hong Kong (DAB). He had more than doubled his 2015 vote tally, from 793 to 1,723. Calling the result "a surprise," he said: "They were protest votes for sure. They voted for me because I am not the pro-establishment person."

Leung's victory was part of a wave that crashed down on Hong Kong's political landscape that day. Riding on the anti-establishment sentiment fomenting over nearly six months of unrest, democrats scored victories amid a record-high turnout of 71 per cent, not only in their usual strongholds but also in the so-called deep-red constituencies which the Beijing-friendly camp had dominated for years. They are now in control of 17 out of 18 district councils, having taken 392 seats and left their rivals with just 60.

Beyond the stunning reversal in political fortunes, the elections upended traditional thinking about campaign strategies. A number of the winners were first-time candidates, but their lack of experience and resources proved little impediment to victory. Chan Tsz-wai, for instance, should not have had a chance. The 27-year-old lift worker mounted what could be charitably described as a modest bid for votes. He ran in the Jordan South constituency of Yau Tsim Mong district, against incumbent Chris Ip Ngo-tung. Chan's campaign materials consisted of a poorly lit photograph of him wearing a green soccer jersey with a manifesto scrawled by hand in Chinese. By contrast, Ip – who had served the area for 11 years – was advertising himself dressed in a sharp black suit, his hair carefully coiffed and he had a neatly printed bilingual message.

Yet Chan sent the 39-year-old rising star of the DAB packing, taking 65 more votes than Ip's 1,451. His strategy? Attack Ip's role as council chairman, by then a tainted position thanks to the protests of the past summer. Ip and 17 other chairmen of the district councils – all controlled by the pro-establishment camp – had earlier made a fatal miscalculation by issuing a joint statement calling on the government to fast-track the extradition bill. Ip's loss was repeated across the DAB slate, which won just 21 of the 179 seats it contested, a huge climbdown from the 119 it secured in 2015. Nine of the 13 pro-Beijing Legislative Council members who sought re-election at the district level were defeated, many losing by large margins.

De facto referendum

With the voting outcome, the majority of almost 3 million Hongkongers – 71.2 per cent of total voters – sent a strong message to Beijing and local authorities about their unhappiness with the status quo, turning the traditionally uneventful local contests into a de facto referendum on the protests. Housewife Koni Kwok, in her 30s, described what she cast as a "protest vote." "I used to choose whoever could deliver. Now I won't vote for anyone in the pro-establishment camp," she said. KY Wan, a 44-year-old nurse, booked her flight back from a holiday in Australia a day before the ballot, just to make sure she would not miss out on voting. "I had never planned so intentionally to cast a vote," she said. "There's a need for a fair way for citizens to express their feelings toward the government now. To me, this is a referendum."

Ip, the unseated Yau Tsim Mong chairman, agreed that the result reflected the depth of dissatisfaction with the government. Accusing Chan of parachuting into the constituency only recently, he lamented: "His victory does not make sense under rational analysis."

About 210 of the 392 pro-democracy winners, or about 54 per cent, were first-time contenders in district council elections, with little on-the-ground experience. While the pro-democracy camp has always enjoyed a bigger share of votes in the city, the district councils had been dominated for years by the more resource-rich pro-establishment bloc. Voters tended to place greater weight on a candidate's proven ability to manage their local communities – rather than gauge their political stance – when choosing representatives for the lowest tier of the city's administration. The latest elections threw out such assumptions. Civil Human Rights Front convenor Jimmy Sham Tsz-kit, who won the Sha Tin constituency of Lek Yuen, said Hongkongers were using the vote to punish Hong Kong leader Carrie Lam Cheng Yuet-ngor and the pro-establishment camp for refusing to listen to them. He accused the government of being dismissive of public opinion. "It's time for the government to address our five demands," said Sham soon after he won, referring to calls which included an independent probe into police's handling of protests and the implementation of universal suffrage.

Most importantly, the pan-democrats' sweeping gains could make them kingmakers at the next chief executive poll, due in two years. Since the camp holds power in the overwhelming majority of district councils, it is set to bag 117 seats on the 1,200-strong Election Committee that selects the city's leader. This is not an insubstantial figure when added to the other 325 seats it typically controls.

But for now, the bigger challenge for the pan-democrats is to not squander their success, like they did 16 years ago. In 2003, the bloc secured a similar landslide victory after 500,000 people took to the streets to oppose proposals for a national security law under Article 23 of the Basic Law. The Beijing-friendly camp soon made a strong comeback in the next polls, re-taking most of the seats it lost. Some defeated pan-democrats were blamed for focusing solely on political slogans and not putting enough effort into community work. "We need to demonstrate that the supporters of democracy are more outstanding than those who support the establishment," Sham said.

Reality check

That mission has been tough for some rookie councilors. "Even with the majority, it is not like the pro-democracy camp is taking up a ruling role," said Napo Wong Weng-chi, one of the 14 pro-democracy members on the 15-strong Central and Western District Council. "The district councils play only a consultation role. There has been no policy discussion with government officials as of March."

The closest they came to such a conversation was on January 16, 2020, when Commissioner of Police Chris Tang Ping-keung attended a council meeting. During a rowdy session with councilors, he rejected calls for the force to apologize for its alleged acts of violence during the social unrest. Tang and others, including the district officer and 10 officials from eight other government departments, walked out of the conference room while council chairwoman Cheng Lai-king was reading out an impromptu motion to condemn him for condoning "police violence." The officials had been scheduled to address the council members on the remaining items on the agenda, such as land use, epidemic prevention and public market management. But the government later supported their walkout, saying the motion had not been based on facts. "The government can use different strategies to sideline or dwarf the councils," Wong, 32, said. The motion condemning police passed that day. But as another councilor Jordan Pang Ka-ho, 21, noted, all district council motions are non-binding. "Even for democratically elected representatives, we're unable to express the people's views to the government," Pang said. "They will not act on your motions."

In the northeast of the city, Tai Po District Council set up a committee to focus on security and constitutional affairs, but the government deemed the new set-up illegal and outside the council's remit. In mid-February, as the coronavirus crisis gripped the city, the Home Affairs Department stopped offering secretarial support to the 18 district councils, to minimize social contact. But critics said the move was politically motivated and was intended to hobble the councils. "The government is trying to limit our operation with administrative methods. That's a political motive behind it, taking advantage of the coronavirus," said Clarisse Yeung Suet-ying, chairwoman of Wan Chai District Council.

Then there was the reality of dealing with their actions of the past year. As of March 2020, 15 district councilors – including three council heads – had been arrested for offenses mostly related to their participation in the protests.

Mask battle – distribute or not?

The public health crisis also meant district councilors had to solve more pressing livelihood problems for residents whose attention was no longer on the government's performance or police's use of force. After being repeatedly asked by residents, Chan Tsz-wai, the lift worker in Jordan South, ended up paying HK$10,000 (US$1,290) out of his own pocket to buy 25 boxes of masks. "All I can do is buy the expensive masks on the market and distribute them to residents. Luckily, it was the end of the month when I had just received my salary," he said. (Councilors are paid HK$33,950 a month plus a maximum reimbursement of HK$44,816 for operating expenses.) Many residents pressed him to hand out more masks. Another rookie councilor, Jocelyn Chau Hui-yan, 23, of City Garden constituency in Eastern district, flew to Tokyo at the end of January to buy masks from dozens of convenience stores. But that still proved inadequate. She expressed her frustration on her Facebook page, saying it was impossible to meet the needs of the area's 16,955 residents.

Leung, the photographer turned councilor, framed the question of whether to distribute masks another way. "Are we being populists here?" he said. "As we are now the majority, we should have a ruling mentality and better understand priorities in serving the people." He flew to France in February to help a businessman friend source 1 million masks for Hong Kong. Yet he refrained from handing them out for free to all residents in his constituency, giving them instead to cleaners and guards – people generally less likely to be his supporters. When pressed by residents for handouts, Leung said, he first tried to learn their background and see whether they were in a difficult situation. "If they are property owners here, it means they are rich enough to buy a box of masks," he said. "Then I would just tell them I have none." In his view, pan-democrats should learn from the crisis and act differently from the pro-establishment camp, which had been associated with the Cantonese phrase *se zaai beng zung* – literally "snake feasts, vegetarian feasts, moon cakes and rice dumplings," a mocking reference to handing out sweeteners to residents.

Pro-Beijingers in opposition

The pro-establishment camp had indeed been busy distributing masks in various districts since mid-February. A group of pro-Beijingers founded the United Hong Kong Community Anti-epidemic Initiative, with former Kwun Tong District Council chairman Bunny Chan Chung-bun, also a deputy to China's legislature, acting as convenor.

The group was later tasked with giving out masks donated by the Shenzhen municipal government, which announced near the end of February that it would send Hong Kong 100,000 masks every day via the central government's liaison office in the city, with the first batch consisting of 1 million pieces. DAB vice-chairman Chan Hok-fung said the party had handed out another 1 million masks, but insisted it was solely to help alleviate the burden on residents rather than to win votes. "The public grievance against the government and police is still very strong," Chan said. "It helps little for elections, no matter how many masks or how much bleach you hand out."

After losing his seat as deputy chairman of Central and Western District Council, Chan Hok-fung and other defeated pro-establishment candidates set up District Council Observers, a group to monitor the operations of all 18 councils. "We welcome any netizens reporting to us problems of the elected councilors," he said. One of the cases he took up was against councilor Leos Lee Man-ho, a 25-year-old political novice serving in Sham Shui Po district. Lee had posted a notice outside his office that read "Blue ribbons and dogs not allowed," a slur against police and their supporters. The group accused Lee of acting like an authoritarian and shared memes of him as Adolf Hitler. Chan said Lee's actions were disgraceful.

He cited other complaints from locals about being unable to contact their councilors. "Many of the newly elected are not humble in serving their residents," he said. "They don't know the art as they have little experience on the ground." Still, he did not see those grievances translating into victory for his bloc, given that the next round of local elections was four years away. For the time being, the challenge was to do well in the September 2020 Legco elections. But the camp's battering at the local level has left it with fewer offices and resources. "The offices serve as important hubs with resources for us to gather residents," he said.

There were more than 200 DAB offices across the city in 2019, including those for Legco and district council members. That figure has now halved, according to an insider. The party has been scrambling to find about 200 jobs for its out-of-work politicians and staff, with most still working in their district offices until at least September. The idea is to shore up their base and once again test the mood of the people, toward themselves and the government. Will it be another repudiation, or will sentiments against them have eased? The coronavirus pandemic adds another dimension to the question. For now, politicians know every misstep could cost them dearly come September.

— *With reporting by Sum Lok-kei*

The Beijing connection

Gary Cheung and Kimmy Chung

The central government was blindsided by the protests. Why did it have trouble reading sentiments in the city?

For a long time, in Hong Kong's Western district, a building that towers over the neighboring tenement blocks was closed to prying eyes. Only selected guests were invited inside. The office inspired, in equal measure, awe and curiosity, fear and loathing.

But in the spring of 2018, those in charge of the premises declared an open house, and 1,500 people who had booked limited tickets poured into the first five floors of the 41-story building. They found canteens serving subsidized food, a gymnasium, meeting rooms lined with tasteful beige sofas and wood carvings, and a library packed with 13,000 books. Works on Marxism competed for space with books by democracy scholars in Hong Kong.

The liaison office, the central government outfit that acts as a bridge in Beijing's relationship with the city – and which critics and anti-mainland voices have often accused of meddling behind the scenes – decided to open its doors to give Hongkongers a glimpse into its work. The aim was to "bring us closer together and break the sense of secrecy," office director Wang Zhimin said at the time.

Just over a year later, on July 21, 2019, the building became the target of extremist protesters' wrath. They pelted it with eggs and paint, and defaced the Chinese national emblem on its facade. The office condemned the attacks and placed the insignia behind plexiglass. It also fortified the building with two-meter-high water-filled barriers.

By January 4, 2020, Wang was gone, demoted to the history research unit of the Communist Party's Central Committee. Months earlier, rumors had swirled that top leaders would be held to account for the continuing social unrest and for not giving Beijing a correct reading of the situation on the ground in Hong Kong. Many made bets that city leader Carrie Lam Cheng Yuet-ngor would be top of the list. But it was Wang who became the first high-profile political casualty of the turmoil. Luo Huining, a former party leader in Shanxi and Qinghai provinces, was named as the new liaison office director. The appointment took many by surprise, as Luo had reached the retirement age of 65 the previous October and had only just moved into a post at the country's legislature, the National People's Congress (NPC), usually reserved for retired officials. More than that, he had never held any position directly related to Hong Kong.

The shake-up of Beijing's institutions overseeing Hong Kong affairs became even clearer a month later. On February 13, 2020, another former provincial party boss was appointed to head the Hong Kong and Macau Affairs Office (HKMAO), the central government's cabinet-level bureau that oversees its two special administrative regions. Xia Baolong, a vice-chairman and secretary general of the Chinese People's Political Consultative Conference (CPPCC), the nation's top advisory body, was named director of the HKMAO on February 13. Incumbent Zhang Xiaoming, a 34-year veteran of Hong Kong affairs who was liaison office chief before taking up the post in 2017, was demoted to executive deputy director. Xia, a former party chief in Zhejiang province, where he was a deputy chief to Xi Jinping for four years in the mid-2000s, was seen as a trusted ally of the president.

Given Luo and Xia's experience and seniority, along with the Xi connection, it was clear that Beijing saw the need to reset its relationship with the city and recalibrate the "one country, two systems" governing principle it had pledged for Hong Kong up to 2047. How exactly, it was not immediately clear, even as many equated the shake-up with Beijing's intent to exercise tighter control over the city.

Liaison office and the disconnect

On the day of Xia's appointment, Beijing officials stationed in Hong Kong sought to put a positive spin on the change. The central government was "upgrading" the office by appointing a state leader and therefore devoting more attention to the city, the liaison office said in briefing notes obtained by the *South China Morning Post*.

But Beijing loyalists with close connections to the central government said there was little doubt the reshuffle was sparked by the extradition bill debacle and the pro-establishment camp's crushing defeat in district council elections the previous November. The bloc won just 60 of 452 seats, while pan-democrats took 17 of 18 councils. The staggering losses were the final straw and Beijing knew it had to act to prevent a loss of seats at the Legislative Council elections in September 2020.

A pro-Beijing lawmaker, who declined to be named, said Wang had to be held accountable for both disasters. Trouble began with the liaison office's first misreading of the situation, seeing the extradition bill as a chance to bring the city and the mainland closer. "And had Wang not asked the pro-Beijing camp to support [Chief Executive Carrie Lam], Lam would not have dared to rush it in Legco," the lawmaker said.

In the middle of May 2019, weeks before the unrest began, Wang summoned local delegates to the NPC and the CPPC for a meeting at the liaison office, urging them to throw their weight behind the bill. He made this demand despite the business sector already having expressed serious reservations about the bill, arguing it would be a blow to the city's rule of law if people found themselves being sent to the mainland, where the same legal standards do not apply.

By June, the protests had gained momentum, and attempts by Lam to suspend the bill – later even calling it "dead" – did not puncture it. Amid the increasingly violent protests, the district council elections loomed, prompting an internal debate within government circles whether it would be better to postpone the polls.

A pro-Beijing lawmaker said Wang, however, supported the idea of pressing on as scheduled. "The district councils are not essential parts of the governance. Under the chaotic conditions, we had enough reasons not to hold the election as scheduled," the lawmaker said. "But the liaison office failed to use its authority to urge a suspension." He believed Lam had wanted to press ahead with the elections to provide an outlet for public grievances and Wang went along, thinking any losses would be modest. He had not expected the thrashing they eventually received.

Another veteran pro-establishment politician in Hong Kong accused top officials then at the liaison office of being so disconnected from reality that even on the afternoon of polling day, when a record 71.2 per cent of voters had cast their ballots, they were still confident of a respectable showing. Higher voter turnouts in the city often correlate with better performance for the opposition.

Another source familiar with the operation of mainland-funded institutions in Hong Kong said Wang then tried to put a positive spin on the results in his post-election report to the Beijing leadership. He highlighted that the pro-establishment camp won 1.2 million votes, 430,000 more than it won in 2015.

"Wang argued that the bloc managed to win 41 per cent of the valid votes cast against all odds," the source said. "But state leaders wanted a candid and no-nonsense assessment of the reasons behind the humiliating defeat."

The veteran pro-establishment politician said the demotion of Wang and later Zhang showed that the Communist Party did heed the voice of Hongkongers. "But the party did it at its own pace because it always wants to do things on its own initiative, rather than be seen to be doing something under pressure," he said. "Back in October, core leaders in the pro-Beijing circle knew the days of Wang and Zhang were numbered but Beijing kept on monitoring the situation in Hong Kong for some time," the politician said. "In the first few months of the protests over the extradition bill, Beijing leadership thought what was happening in Hong Kong was no big deal.

"But President Xi felt senior mainland officials handling Hong Kong affairs had failed to present him the true picture after learning the results of district council elections. So the ax fell."

Zhang's demotion was the bigger surprise, as he was considered an old, trusted hand. But Tam Yiu-chung, Hong Kong's sole representative on the NPC Standing Committee, believed Beijing saw the need for an overhaul of the entire set-up, rather than a piecemeal approach, after the unrest remained unquelled for months.

A mainland expert familiar with Hong Kong affairs, who spoke on condition of anonymity, said that during the fourth plenum of the 19th Party Congress in 2017, the Communist Party had produced a detailed road map to take the country into "a new realm" of good government and prosperity. But the predictors of that "new realm" had not anticipated an unruly city in the south being the source of violent protests that gained worldwide attention, and adding to the woes of a central government already battling a trade and technology war with the United States. "Despite the road map, more than 22 years after Hong Kong returned to Chinese rule, the central government is still having to explore ways to govern Hong Kong under one country, two systems," the expert said. "The reshuffle of the central government agencies that oversee Hong Kong affairs results from Beijing's thorough assessment of the experience in handling Hong Kong affairs in the past 22 years," the expert said. The bill fiasco and the election defeat were the "catalysts."

Getting Hong Kong wrong

Beyond the change of leadership, the question was whether there would be a change to the lens through which Beijing sees Hong Kong affairs. It was clear it was caught by surprise and embarrassed by the depth of anger unleashed by the protests. In May 2019, just a month before the protests began, Vice-Premier Han Zheng – China's top man on the city's affairs – told local delegates to the NPC that "the political atmosphere in Hong Kong is changing for the better" and the city was "on the right path of development."

This was not the first time central authorities had felt blindsided by the city. Beijing increased intelligence gathering on Hong Kong after July 1, 2003, when an estimated half a million people took to the streets to oppose a national security law that critics said would have limited residents' freedoms. The scale of the protest then caught the local and national governments off guard and forced the authorities to shelve the plan. Since then, Beijing has sent hundreds – if not thousands – of researchers and officials to talk to people from all walks of life in Hong Kong ahead of important political events, including elections. This is on top of the work of the liaison office, which has a "research office" tasked with monitoring public opinion and sending Beijing daily briefings on Hong Kong media reports. The office also regularly meets pro-Beijing figures and groups in political and business circles, as well as at the grass-roots level of society. The HKMAO has its own team of researchers who periodically visit the city to "catch the wind" and submit reports to the leadership. Other departments – such as the National Development and Reform Commission and the

Ministry of Commerce – also send people to Hong Kong from time to time, not to mention the Ministry of State Security and its agents.

Beijing also operates a listening post in Shenzhen, where high-ranking officials are dispatched during critical moments such as the Occupy protests of 2014. Being in the city closest to Hong Kong allows them to tap into the media and happenings more easily for a better reading of the ground. In 2019, Beijing again set up a task force there, at its office Bauhinia Villa, to monitor the situation closely. Sources said then that Vice-Premier Han met Carrie Lam there just before she suspended the bill on June 15.

But the labyrinthine information network spanning multiple ministries across the central government – each with its own lines of reporting – is confusing even to insiders. This wide range of channels and the vast scale of information collected do not always lead to a clear and comprehensive picture of public sentiment.

Experts blame the failure on a lack of coherent analysis and coordination among various central government departments. Tian Feilong, an associate law professor at Beihang University in Beijing, noted that information collection and reporting was slanted toward the pro-establishment camp while the voices of pan-democrats and young localists were marginalized.

The mainland expert said there was no question the central government did not have a good grasp of the situation in Hong Kong, given the information it obtained from various channels. "What we badly need is more accurate assessment and to do a better job in addressing the latest developments in the city," he said.

What next for ties with the mainland?

Anthony Wu Ting-yuk, a Hong Kong member of the standing committee of the CPPCC, believed that compared with "old Hong Kong hands" such as Zhang, the two former provincial party bosses Xia and Luo might offer fresh perspectives on handling the city. "Many provincial party secretaries are visionary and are inclined to look at the big picture. They are tempted to deliver something good for the people under their charge," he said.

The mainland expert said provincial party chiefs were also more strategic and could be counted on to think outside the box. "Xia and Luo's lack of previous experience related to Hong Kong could be an advantage. They won't have the baggage left by traditions and established lines of thinking," the expert said. However, he stressed that the central government's assessment was that Hong Kong's most pressing task was to revive its economy and tackle deep-rooted livelihood issues such as the lack of affordable housing. Central government officials were neither ready nor prepared, he said, to talk about political reform or greater democratization, all core issues for the protest movement.

Hence, analysts and Beijing loyalists warned against harboring high expectations that the two former provincial party leaders would relax the central government's oversight or control over Hong Kong any time soon.

Wong Kwok-kin, a veteran lawmaker from the pro-Beijing Federation of Trade Unions, said: "As the HKMAO is now chaired by a state leader, that means the central government can make faster and more flexible responses to Hong Kong and Macau affairs." Wong, also a member of Lam's advisory cabinet, the Executive Council, added: "Xia will spare no effort in implementing the central government's policies on Hong Kong as he is beyond the retirement age of 65 and has no need to be concerned about future career prospects. Similarly, Luo is also beyond normal retirement age."

"Provincial party chiefs might attach more importance to the possible impact on other mainland provinces and cities if a concession is made in Hong Kong," he said. "In general, provincial chiefs have a stronger political ideology."

Xia, 67, gained a reputation not just for delivering economic progress to Zhejiang but also as a hardliner overseeing the suppression of Christian churches in the eastern province five years ago. He became Zhejiang's deputy party chief in November 2003, first as Xi's deputy, and then later rose to be the top party cadre before leaving in 2017. "I am fortunate to have become a member of the 'Iron Army' in Zhejiang," he said in his official farewell speech, using a term to refer to officials who worked with Xi mostly in Zhejiang but also in Shanghai, Shaanxi and Fujian.

While Xia has not made public statements on Hong Kong, the liaison office has signaled a change of style with its new director. Just weeks after Luo took office, Hong Kong was hit by the coronavirus outbreak and calls grew for the government to close its borders with the mainland. Infections then were mostly from returnees from north of the border, but the call was also fueled by political sentiments. Unlike previous liaison office chiefs who kept a low profile for fear of accusations of interference in the city's affairs, Luo quickly became proactive and visible.

On February 17, he toured several major mainland-funded enterprises in the city, calling on them to ensure market stability, especially for daily necessities – toilet paper and rice had become scarce – and to offer financial aid to struggling local businesses. Luo's message was clear: the mainland was there to help the city weather the tough times.

Just over a week later, Luo, wearing a helmet and surgical mask, visited a quarantine camp in Lei Yue Mun and praised workers racing to expand the facilities and their employer, China State Construction Engineering (Hong Kong), a mainland-funded enterprise. While some pan-democrats dismissed his visit as an "image-building" stunt and others questioned how the contract was given to the mainland firm, Luo's tour showcased the front-foot approach of Beijing's top man in Hong Kong.

That month, he also sent a letter by email – a first for the liaison office – to local delegates to the NPC and CPPCC. He appealed for unity with the mainland in battling the coronavirus with "faith and love," pledging that Beijing would give its full support to the city in the fight.

But Luo, who double-hats as deputy director of the HKMAO and reports to Xia, also chastised those behind a strike of medical workers, accusing them of spreading a "political coronavirus." He lambasted those "few people, at this moment, still creating all kinds of conflicts for political self-interest, and even manipulating strikes to 'save Hong Kong'."

It is clear no olive branches will be offered to the radical core. For now, all eyes will be on the relationship between Lam and the two former provincial party leaders and how they harness the one country, two systems model to secure Hong Kong's future.

— With reporting by Nectar Gan

LAW AND DISORDER

"IT'S THE GOVERNMENT THAT SACRIFICED THE POLICE FORCE."

Steve Vickers, security specialist

Asia's finest in the dock

Christy Leung and Chris Lau

N elson Ng Kwok-cheung was a young man in the 1990s when he worked with journalist Kevin Sinclair to write a book about Hong Kong's police force. What stories they told in *Asia's Finest Marches On – Policing Hong Kong From 1841 Into the 21st Century*. The British colony's earliest policemen were a suspect bunch of Chinese, Europeans and Indians cobbled together and disorganized, before a proper force of under 200 was established and the first stations appeared in Central, Aberdeen and Stanley.

There were dark years of pervasive corruption in the 1970s, followed by a massive clean-up that transformed the force into a formidable one, capable of maintaining law and order and chasing down heavily armed mainland Chinese criminals who terrorized the city's goldsmiths and jewelry stores in the 1980s and 1990s.

Hong Kong's police force was Asia's finest, declared the late Sinclair, a New Zealander and veteran of the *South China Morning Post*, who was impressed by its professionalism. The phrase stuck for years to come. His assistant and co-author, Ng, was so moved that in 1997, the year their book was published, he joined the police force.

Now a senior superintendent, Ng recalled in early 2020: "In those years, many agreed that police had a noble status in society. When people saw an officer on the street, they felt safe." Ng never imagined that a day would come when Hongkongers would detest their 31,000-strong police force, curse and attack officers on the street, and unrelentingly hurl accusations of brutality.

Through the second half of 2019, as anti-government protests grew increasingly violent and rampant, the force became a target of abuse and derision. Angry protesters scrawled *hak ging* or "black cop" across city walls, using a derogatory Cantonese term referring to crooked policemen who collude with criminals. They accused officers of concealing the deaths of protesters and sexually abusing some of those detained, allegations the force rejected strenuously. On the street, protesters chanted: "Disband the police force now!"

'Tiderider' turns tide against police

In June 2019, police launched an operation codenamed Tiderider, to deal with the first street marches and protests against the government's unpopular extradition bill designed to send fugitives to jurisdictions with which Hong Kong had no exchange arrangement.

At first, the demonstrations organized by the Civil Human Rights Front were mostly peaceful. June was the month of two massive marches, attracting a million people at the first and twice as many at the second, according to organizers. As the protests continued for weeks and months, vandalism and violence became regular, almost predictable occurrences, along with intense clashes between black-clad extremist protesters and police officers at the front lines. The extradition bill was eventually withdrawn, but the anti-government protests did not end.

Deputy Commissioner of Police Raymond Siu Chak-yee, who was director of operations when Operation Tiderider was launched, said in early 2020 that the protests were an unprecedented challenge because police did not expect the unrest to continue for so long. Scenes of riot police slumped on the sides of streets, some lying flat on their backs and others leaning against each other, became commonplace. Worse, residents and passers-by would heckle them with expletives while they tried to rest.

The force was stunned by the level of violence and how organized protesters proved to be, despite their claims that theirs was a leaderless movement. Masked mobs destroyed public property, set fires at MTR stations, trashed businesses and shops belonging to those they believed to have mainland links, and attacked frontline officers trying to disperse protesters.

Siu said: "Some will call the level of force we used police brutality, but I do not agree. It is the sworn duty of officers to maintain law and order and ensure public safety. During the protests, people came out, committed crimes and caused serious disturbances. Violence invites a forceful response, and that applies to police forces all over the world. When violence occurs, we need to use an appropriate level of force to restore public order and bring offenders to justice. There is no police force in the world that would tolerate the violence used by the rioters in Hong Kong."

Protesters, civil rights campaigners and opposition lawmakers believed otherwise, accusing police of using excessive force and doing the government's bidding. Human rights group Amnesty International carried out an investigation, which included interviews with 21 people arrested during the protests, and claimed police used "retaliatory violence" while arresting or dealing with suspects in custody.

Others have pointed out that in Hong Kong's increasingly politicized social environment, police took a major hit on behalf of a hugely unpopular government led by Chief Executive Carrie Lam Cheng Yuet-ngor. "It's the government that sacrificed the police force," said security specialist Steve Vickers, a former head of the Criminal Intelligence Bureau, who runs his own consultancy. "Carrie Lam and her administration decided to stonewall the protest movement."

When radicals raised the level of violence, vandalism and direct attacks on police, the force responded more aggressively at the front line. Between June 2019 and February 2020, officers fired 16,191 rounds of tear gas, 10,100 rubber bullets, 1,880 40mm sponge grenades, 2,033 beanbag rounds and 19 live bullets. More than 1,700 people were injured, including three young protesters who were hit by live rounds. More than 550 police officers were injured too, including one who was shot in his calf by an arrow, and another who had part of his finger bitten off.

It all began on June 12, when the controversial legislation was expected to have its second reading at the Legislative Council. Thousands of angry protesters blocked streets around the complex that morning, bringing the surrounding areas to a standstill. That afternoon, police fired the unrest's first volleys of tear gas.

In April 2020, Assistant Commissioner Rupert Dover, among the first targets of protesters' wrath, revisited the orders he issued that day. As one of six ground operation commanders throughout Operation Tiderider, he said he had instructed tear gas be discharged in his area around Lung Wui Road, but was not certain if he was the first to do so.

Without going into detail because of an ongoing judicial review into the force's operations that day, Dover recalled that a few official vehicles, one of them carrying a government minister, were surrounded and trapped in an underpass. His mission was to rescue the individuals and clear the crowds.

Asked if he realized, before making the command, that those rounds of tear gas would change the course of the movement, Dover said: "Have I thought that? I was aware of it."

He said the alternative was to march the officers into the crowd knowing protesters overhead would hit them with bricks and other projectiles. "It could have been huge casualties to the police ... I stuck with the use of [tear gas], it is the most efficient way to do it."

He said his aversion to fighting in such close quarters was based on past experience. "When we had the Mong Kok riot earlier in 2016, there were a hundred police officers injured, because we got way too close to the crowds. They were hit by all sorts of missiles. As an organization, we learned: if we get that close, we will get severely injured. And also protesters will get severely injured."

Dover said he was quite sympathetic to the protesters' motives, but it was the police's job to uphold law and order. "I'm totally against how they're doing it ... I do understand some of the rationale behind this – the soaring property prices, the lack of social mobility, perhaps the impression that there is a decreased opportunity to move forward in life, I can understand that. There is still no excuse for smashing up your home and assaulting members of the public," he said.

Police's reputation takes a big hit

There was little sympathy for frontline officers from the wider community, let alone expressions of support. When protests spread into various neighborhoods and police tried to disperse the crowds of masked radicals thronging the streets, many booed them. Residents also complained that the use of tear gas was affecting their health.

By November 2019, the public satisfaction rate for police had sunk to a record low of just 27.2 per cent, according to the Hong Kong Public Opinion Research Institute. Over the previous decade, and even through the Occupy protests of 2014 that shut down parts of the city for 79 days, this satisfaction rate remained at 50 to 60 per cent.

As mutual hostility deepened, name-calling became common, with some officers referring to protesters as "cockroaches," while police were called "dogs." Complaints against police were a refrain throughout the months of unrest, but two incidents stood out and were immortalized in the protest slogan "721, nowhere in sight. 831, beating someone to death!" The numbers refer to the dates of events that many believe turned the tide of public opinion against police irreversibly.

On July 21, 2019, at Yuen Long MTR station in northwestern Hong Kong, a mob of white-shirted men armed with sticks, rods and rattan canes assaulted protesters and other train passengers for more than 45 minutes. Videos circulated widely over social media left many shocked by the vicious attacks on station platforms and even inside a train.

Police denied accusations that they had deliberately taken their time showing up, and that they had worked hand in glove with gangsters that night.

On August 31, police arrested 63 people aged 13 to 36 for causing criminal damage, possessing offensive weapons and explosive substances, and illegal assembly at Mong Kok and Prince Edward MTR stations in Kowloon.

At Prince Edward station, members of the elite Special Tactical Squad chased fleeing protesters through the station and stormed a stationary train compartment, using batons to beat four cowering protesters. Other officers wrestled suspects to the ground on the station platform.

A rumor began circulating soon after that some protesters died at the station that night, and that police had whisked their bodies away. Although the force and government issued strong denials – and despite a lack of any evidence – the rumor persisted and protesters returned to the station every month to remember the incident. The "721" and "831" dates helped entrench the view among Hongkongers that police were cruel toward protesters.

Icarus Wong Ho-yin, founder of Civil Rights Observer and an advocate for freedom of assembly, insisted that he and other activists did not just make up allegations of brutality against police. "We rely on various yardsticks, including international human rights conventions and different treaties which govern the way in which police may use force during their operations," he said. They also referred to past court rulings and guidelines issued by the Independent Police Complaints Council (IPCC), the police watchdog. Wong said the term "police brutality" went beyond physical violence alone, and included degrading treatment of suspects and the failure to follow criminal procedures.

Through the months of protests, there were numerous examples of excessive use of force by police, Wong said. There were scenes of officers firing tear gas inside a train station, beating protesters and firing pepper balls at them at the top of a long escalator, ramming a police motorcycle into a crowd of protesters, and using a water cannon in busy Tsim Sha Tsui, accidentally spraying the entrance to the mosque on Nathan Road with blue-dyed water. All these incidents added up, Wong said. "People expect protesters to be dispersed. But does that mean you can overstep the boundaries?" He accused police of damaging Hong Kong's freedom of assembly by halting largely peaceful protests and insisted only "a handful" of radicals caused disruptions. Critics like Wong saw the violence of protesters as a reaction, rather than premeditated action even though this did not often square with the facts.

'We were under attack'

Deputy Commissioner Siu rejected the accusations of police brutality, pointing instead to the escalation of violence by masked radicals. He also disagreed that police action against protesters affected Hongkongers' freedom of assembly. "Despite repeated warnings, they insisted on staying in an unlawful assembly," he said. "They claimed they were not radicals. In fact, we were under attack by them. They were hurling petrol bombs at us. We had to use an appropriate level of force to deal with them."

Siu pointed out that during the early protests in June 2019, demonstrators had thrown plastic bottles, metal rods and bricks at officers. Later, they used lethal weapons such as bows and arrows, petrol bombs, explosives and even firearms. Over the months of protests, some radicals became so violent that they set a 57-year-old construction worker on fire after he confronted them while they went on a rampage through Ma On Shan MTR station on November 11. Two days later, a 70-year-old cleaner died after he was hit with a brick during a clash with protesters in Sheung Shui. Two teenagers aged 16 and 17 were charged for his murder in April 2020. Despite such shocking incidents, the public appeared reluctant to condemn the violence and by their silence showed solidarity with the protesters.

The 2019 protests coincided with a period of leadership transition in the police force, as several of its most senior officers approached retirement age. Commissioner Stephen Lo Wai-chung was himself due to retire at the end of 2018, but had had his term extended by a year to let his successor prepare to take over. Chris Tang Ping-keung, a senior assistant commissioner, was identified as the next chief, but needed to first serve a stint as deputy commissioner.

Lo was 58 when he stepped down in November 2019, after 35 years in the force and amid some of the most violent protests the city had endured. There was a feeling a leader on his way out was slow and indecisive in galvanizing his men into action. He was the first chief in 175 years to leave without ceremonial fanfare. "There is simply nothing worth celebrating at this moment, as the city is on the brink of a total breakdown," a senior police source said at the time. "The sentiment in the force is not that good. Lo wants to keep a low profile." Opposition politicians were blistering in their criticism of Lo, but others pointed out that Hong Kong's crime rate maintained a steady decline during his tenure, achieving a 48-year low in 2018.

The new commissioner, Tang, 54, said in an interview before he assumed the top job that he wished Hongkongers would condemn protesters' use of violence, adding that their silence and tolerance only encouraged radicals to wreak havoc. He found it worrying that people only pointed fingers at police, but turned a blind eye to violence.

"Enough is enough," he said. "Whatever your beliefs, do not glorify and put up with the violence. Do not let the mob further motivate themselves and become more radicalized. If everyone had come out earlier to condemn the violence, society would not have turned into this state in five months. We can only end the unrest with society's condemnation, reflection by the rioters, plus our appropriate tactics."

Police compare violence to 'home-grown terrorism'

In its review of Hong Kong's 2019 crime situation, the force noted that online publicity for early extradition bill protests merely encouraged people to participate in processions or demonstrations. Later on, however, they included "weapon-making handbooks" and even "guides to killing police." A police statement said: "In order to express their dissatisfaction with society and the government, rioters chose to hurt the public and cause social panic, which is exactly the behavior of home-grown terrorism."

Siu said it was always difficult to apprehend the extremist protesters in the midst of chaotic circumstances. "When we try to subdue a suspect, it is not as simple as just putting him on the ground," he said. "We need to handcuff him quickly, because other protesters may try to confront and distract the officers. Some will try to snatch the suspect away. Even worse, as in a couple of incidents, some tried to snatch our officers' firearms as well. If we do not handcuff the suspect, he will put up a fierce struggle, it will be very dangerous to our officers."

He also maintained that the force displayed utmost professionalism through months of unending unrest, violence and attacks from citizens.

"I hope everyone in Hong Kong will understand the sort of stress officers have faced on a daily basis. They have been under physical and psychological attack every day," he said. The family members of police personnel were not spared either, and faced various forms of harassment. "We are human beings. We are not robot cops," Siu said. Acknowledging that some officers made "unnecessary remarks" while confronting protesters, he added: "We have been advising our officers to try to avoid that. We will have appropriate disciplinary reviews."

Battle of the info wars

If the police force suffered a hard knock to its reputation in 2019, security analyst Vickers blamed its failure to fight a sophisticated "information war" adequately. After all, this was not the first time Hong Kong's police force had found itself between the government and pro-democracy protesters. Even after dealing with the Occupy protests of 2014, police enjoyed a public satisfaction level of above 50 per cent. "What was new this time was a highly sophisticated social media campaign, a weaponized social media campaign which attacked the whole Hong Kong government," Vickers said.

Rumors and disinformation were rife. For events that actually happened, scenes of police officers pinning down bleeding protesters, swearing at angry bystanders, and pepper-spraying pedestrians in the face were broadcast and repeated over social media. These images spread widely over Facebook and the instant-messaging platform Telegram, which was used extensively by protesters to mobilize participants for their activities. There may have been breaches of discipline by some officers, Vickers said, but the extent was not as egregious or as widespread as social media made it appear. "In the end, the information war destroyed the police force's image," he said.

Senior Superintendent Kelvin Kong Wing-cheung, from the Police

Public Relations Branch, said that the PR task proved monumental because of the massive volume of false information that went viral, including attacks on police. "Fake news takes a second to create, but takes us up to two days to fact-check by looking at CCTV footage and questioning the officers concerned. In the meantime, public perceptions are formed and we appear passive," he said.

It was not until August 5 that police began to hold daily press conferences to provide an update on operations and rebut rumors. Kong acknowledged that the daily briefings ought to have begun sooner, because the onslaught of fake news succeeded in eroding citizens' trust in police as an official source of information. "Fake news is indeed influential. We have been the biggest victim," he said.

The Junior Police Officers' Association, which represents 80 per cent of the force, agreed that police fell victim to a "propaganda attack" by opponents. "They fabricated news and tried hard to smear us. I have never seen such a tactic used before," said association chairman Lam Chi-wai. But he disagreed that Hongkongers across the board had lost faith in the force, despite protesters' efforts to drum up hatred of police. "These people needed to find a common ground to nourish their violence and protests after the government officially withdrew the extradition bill. So they turned on police and smeared us. They painted us as evil in order to rationalize their violence," he said.

Lam said it was despicable that more than 2,000 officers and their family members had been targeted for doxxing, having their personal particulars exposed, and that officers' children were being bullied in school. "The only mistake of the force is that we love Hong Kong too much. We have been too devoted to exercising our duty and protecting Hong Kong people. We stood fast and people wanted to smear us." He was proud of the professionalism displayed by police throughout, despite the treatment they received from protesters.

Assistant Professor Lawrence Ho Ka-ki, of the department of social sciences at Education University, who specializes in the history and sociology of policing, said the work of the force had been much simpler in the past, when officers only had to deal with street-level crimes. In recent years, however, the force has found itself caught up in public order events related to Hongkongers' frustration with the government and Beijing, matters beyond its control. As much as citizens still valued stability, he added, they also demanded greater accountability and transparency, and felt that police had not responded accordingly.

Ho noted that a unique feature of the 2019 protest movement was the live-streaming of events and incidents. People were able to view events in real time and form their own opinions well before police provided their version of what had happened. "A lot of things done by police can be justified in legal terms, because Hong Kong law grants huge power to the executive branch and law enforcers. But while you may well be operating within the legal framework, the question is whether people think you acted reasonably," Ho said.

Democratic Party lawmaker James To Kun-sun said the perception of Beijing's increasing involvement in Hong Kong affairs also did not help the image of police. To, a member of the Legislative Council's security panel, noted that several senior Chinese officials, including President Xi Jinping, had come out strongly in support of Hong Kong's police force. The protesters were strongly anti-mainland, and targeted shops and businesses with perceived links to Beijing. So when some junior Hong Kong policemen began using China's popular social media platform Weibo to appeal to sympathizers on the mainland, what came across, To said, was the perception that "you are no longer the police of Hongkongers."

Assistant Commissioner Dover, who was singled out for public attention along with a few other foreign-born policemen and even had his role mentioned in the UK Parliament, brushed off accusations of British officers doing Beijing's dirty work.

"I don't work for China. I don't work for Beijing. I work for the Hong Kong government. That's why my oath of allegiance was never to the queen, it was to the Hong Kong government. So I work for the Hong Kong people," said Dover, who was born in Hertford in the UK and joined the Royal Hong Kong Police Force in 1988.

"My job is to ensure this place is safe. There have been a lot of mistruths stuck out on social media about the police officers, the expatriate police officers and about me. It is quite amazing."

'The government is to blame'

Vickers blamed the Hong Kong government for leaving police to bear the brunt of protesters' wrath for months on end, instead of coming up with a plan to end the unrest. "You can get away with hiding behind the police force for a month or two," he said. "Most governments would use that time to come up with a solution, but the Hong Kong government didn't. They just left police there on the street." It was, therefore, no surprise that protesters vented their frustration on officers, as the force was "the only government department they were in touch with."

Human rights advocate Wong said: "For police to regain the people's trust, the government has to stop using the force as a shield." The current system of lodging complaints against police also needed to be improved, he said, as many had lost faith in going to the Complaints Against Police Office, an investigative arm headed by police officers, and the IPCC, a review body which lacked investigative powers.

Deputy commissioner Siu maintained that politics did not figure in the force's considerations. "Even when we see rioters being attacked, it is our duty to ensure they are safe. We don't selectively protect people," he said. He conceded that the force needed to find a way to put its messages across effectively and rebuild trust with citizens. It had realized that it was up against opponents who were organized and sophisticated in their use of violence and propaganda. "They talk about human rights, but they brutally assault innocent members of the public. Do you call this human rights? When somebody holds different views from them, they attack and vandalize shops. Do you call this freedom of expression? When you talk about freedom, you need to do it in an orderly way," Siu said.

As of March 2020, police had arrested 7,549 people in connection with the protests, more than 40 per cent of them students. Siu said he had spoken to many of the youngest people arrested and was saddened by what they told him. Many did not know what the movement's demands were, but went on the streets after seeing online messages. Some of the posts had told them the courts would be lenient toward them if they were caught and anyway, there would be glory in taking a criminal record for the cause. Some detainees told Siu they had been warned that if they were arrested, they would be beaten up brutally by police, sexually assaulted or murdered, with their deaths made to look like suicide.

Siu said that police found many restricted items on some of the youngest protesters who were caught. He recalled speaking with a 13-year-old boy who had been arrested in Causeway Bay for possession of offensive weapons. "I asked him why he was carrying spanners, knives and hammers, and if he was intending to damage anything. He said, 'No.' I asked, 'Then, why?' He said he heeded a message to bring the weapons and hide them in some bushes for others to use. I said, 'Have you thought why these people asked you to bring the weapons, why didn't they bring them themselves?' He was quiet, then suddenly burst into tears." The force was prepared to reach out to citizens, Siu said. "We are starting to engage different community sectors in order to rebuild the trust between us. I have confidence that we can eventually do it."

Tang King-shing, who was police commissioner from 2007 to 2011, said that Hong Kong's highly polarized society made the role of police more challenging because the definition of crime was no longer as straightforward as before. "In a politicized environment, when you have unlawful situations in a lawful procession, many do not consider these unlawful situations as traditional crimes," he said. "It's definitely a crime. For example, planting a fake bomb is a crime, a serious crime. But people have different perceptions these days."

He said the months of unrest were far from ordinary times, and had sometimes overwhelmed the force. During his term as chief, Tang had to apologize for blunders made by some of his officers. But he said the situation in 2019 was completely different. "A bunch of people take to the streets to riot, making all kinds of claims, and you want police to apologize?" He felt public perception made up only a small part of the consideration when the force evaluated situations requiring action. "The law forms the largest basis, then reasoning and compassion," he said.

Ng, who was inspired to become a policeman after co-writing a book on the force more than two decades ago, remains optimistic. After a career that took him from station duties in Mong Kok to the Narcotics Bureau and Criminal Intelligence Bureau, the 48-year-old feels that police just need to continue delivering quality service to citizens who need help, as they have for decades. "I still think the Hong Kong police force is not just Asia's finest, but also among the best in the world," he said.

Frustration and anger on the front lines

Christy Leung

From being figures that people trusted in a crisis, police officers on the ground found themselves the targets of attacks.

The Legislative Council in Hong Kong rarely sits on Saturdays. The pristine grounds of the complex fall silent, except for a sprinkling of cleaners and security people going about their work.

But on May 11, 2019, rival camps of lawmakers showed up in their weekend khakis, T-shirts and windcheaters well before 8am, rushing to hold their own separate meetings to scrutinize the much hated extradition bill. It was the second time in a week that heated discussions were threatening to spill out into the corridors. This time, exchanges escalated rapidly as the two sides confronted each other. But worse, there was pushing, shoving and flinging of curses at one another. One lawmaker fainted amid the clash and had to be sent to hospital.

Both the pro-establishment and the pan-democratic camps later filed reports with police. Such was their faith in the force's ability to mediate, investigate and resolve clashes.

But that was then. A month later, the unraveling of the reputation of a supposedly neutral institution began. From being a symbol of law and order to whom people could report their grievances, police officers found themselves the target of attacks as pressure mounted for the city's government to abandon the unpopular bill. Among those leading the charge against police were the very same democrats who a month earlier had sought the force's help.

June 12, 2019, was a key turning point when protesters tried to storm the Legco building and clashed with police who tried to stop them. That day of mayhem reminded Hongkongers of scenes they had not witnessed since the 2014 Occupy protests, when the force used tear gas on residents, sparking an outcry. June 12 felt painfully familiar for many, but the intensity of the clashes shocked everyone. At least 80 people were injured, including 22 officers, and 11 people were arrested.

Hong Kong Chief Executive Carrie Lam Cheng Yuet-ngor defended the force that day, saying that the protesters had resorted to dangerous acts, using sharpened iron bars as weapons, hurling bricks at police and destroying public facilities. "Clearly, this was no longer a peaceful assembly, but a blatantly organized instigation of a riot," she said.

Then commissioner of police Stephen Lo Wai-chung revealed that frontline officers had fired more than 150 rounds of tear gas, almost double the amount on the first day of the Occupy protests. They had also used batons, pepper spray, pepper jets, pepper balls, beanbag rounds and rubber bullets, but these were all used widely by law enforcement agencies elsewhere to deal with riots, he said. Condemning the protesters' use of violence and insisting that his officers had acted with proportionate force, he said: "I have not seen such scenes for a long time."

Negative narrative sets in as officers mull a strike

The spotlight, however, fell on the police, not the protesters. A narrative that police were guilty of excessive force was fast taking hold. Among those who came out against police were a group of 39 law academics who issued a statement saying: "We are deeply concerned about the excessive and gratuitous use of force by the police against peaceful protesters, journalists and civilians who happened to be there for work or other good reasons." Another group of 30 lawyers, including six senior counsel, condemned the police action, urged restraint and demanded an independent inquiry.

The widespread portrayal of police officers as brutes who were the enemy of the people upset the rank and file. Overnight, officers became vilified figures in society. Morale in the 31,000-member force slid, and, unknown to the public, some frontline officers talked about going on strike, said Lam Chi-wai, chairman of the Junior Police Officers' Association (JPOA).

Several officers on the ground told the *South China Morning Post* then that many were bewildered by how quickly perceptions of their role had changed, and felt abandoned by top brass and the government as they lacked the right gear to protect them from those who "wanted to take police lives by any means." In the end, the strike did not materialize, but violent clashes between radicals and police became a regular feature at protests in the months that followed.

On June 21, a crowd of protesters gathered from morning and swelled outside the police headquarters in Wan Chai, trapping some officers within the premises for the entire day and into the night. They pelted the building with eggs and smeared it with graffiti and slogans. Thousands of mostly young protesters spilled over into nearby streets, demanding punishment for officers whom they accused of using excessive force on June 12.

Five days later, they were back. After a peaceful rally in the business district of Central ended on the evening of June 26, about 1,000 protesters moved to the police headquarters building and blocked all exits, trapping staff inside. "Release the martyrs," they chanted, referring to those arrested on June 12.

At one entrance, protesters used umbrellas to confront officers on guard. Television footage showed a protester throwing an umbrella at those on duty, while others opened their umbrellas to block the officers. They used metal barricades and umbrellas to prevent people from entering or leaving. At one point, a plainclothes officer was chased by a group as he tried to enter the building.

Some vandalized the building's facade, spraying obscene and abusive graffiti across the walls. One group removed the English letters from the police logo and sprayed Chinese characters which read: "Hong Kong police dog headquarters."

Watching events from inside the building, Deputy Commissioner Raymond Siu Chak-yee, the director of operations at the time, found it heartbreaking to see the force humiliated in this way. "I felt sad because I would never have expected it. Before this, we had a lot of supporters and Hong Kong was regarded as one of the safest cities in the world," Siu recalled in February 2020. "A lot of youngsters supported us too, and we maintained a very good relationship with them. How did it suddenly change to this?"

The siege ended after six hours, with the last 100 protesters leaving at 4am, when officers with riot shields emerged from the building. Chief Secretary Matthew Cheung Kin-chung later reminded protesters to act peacefully. "Hong Kong greatly respects expressing different opinions through peaceful rallies, but we will absolutely not tolerate illegal or violent acts," he said. "The police have been highly tolerant faced with current challenges."

Angry showdown with top brass

However, there was no easing of tension, nor any end to violent clashes. As anti-police sentiment deepened, frontline officers grew angry at being criticized despite having to deal with the increased violence at protests.

July 14, 2019, saw especially vicious clashes which left 13 police officers and 15 protesters injured at Sha Tin, in the New Territories. At the New Town Plaza shopping mall, a police sergeant had part of his finger bitten off by a protester, while a constable was kicked off an escalator and brutally assaulted when he fell. Two other officers were critically injured after being hit by hard objects, believed to be bricks.

Furious at being cast as villains by Hongkongers despite these attacks, the four police associations, representing junior officers, inspectors, overseas inspectors and superintendents, met the force's top brass the next day. An insider who was present said officers had never been so angry. It was bad enough that they had to put up with verbal assaults and physical attacks; they now found it intolerable that Hong Kong society appeared to glorify the radicals while blaming the force.

"It seemed as if everything the protesters did could be justified and forgiven, even when they attacked us with rods and bit off part of an officer's finger, but whatever we did was wrong," said the source. "Many Hongkongers were no longer rational. We upheld the rule of law, but now we could not even exercise the power given to us by the law. What else could we do?"

Another senior officer said anti-police sentiment had become so strong that he no longer dared tell people he was in the force. Frustrated by what appeared to be his superiors' tolerant approach toward radicals at recent protests, he said: "They broke the law in front of us, but we were asked to let them go. The protesters must think we are useless. They will become more brazen and more violent."

As a result of that meeting, police management promised to improve the protective gear for frontline plainclothes officers, mostly detectives collecting evidence. Equipped with only a helmet and an extendable baton, they were often attacked by black-clad radicals.

Two detectives who were at New Town Plaza on July 14 said that improving their protective gear would not be enough. As these officers worked in small groups, they were easy targets. What they needed were better tactics and to stick closely to the riot police team.

"When a few of us are surrounded and assaulted by 30 to 40 protesters armed with metal rods, umbrellas and bricks, having better protective gear may only buy us five seconds from injury," said one detective. The mobs were known to grab the officers' helmets before setting on them viciously. "We are not like *wing chun* master Ip Man, who could fight 10 karate black belts simultaneously. What if a protester throws a petrol bomb at us?"

Recalling what happened to him at the mall, the other detective said that the violent mob had dropped filled plastic bottles from a height onto his head, and a cola bottle had hit and cracked his helmet. He had been beaten up as he helped people to leave the mall, and suffered bruises on his legs. "I was like a dartboard. They kept throwing objects at me. Any officer acting alone will certainly be at great risk in such violent clashes, where protesters outnumber us and we are trapped."

After the meeting between the police management and associations, an internal notice was sent out by top brass, assuring officers of support and saying that the force understood that injured officers and their families had suffered emotionally.

Fending off attacks and accusations

But beyond the support of their bosses, police officers on the front lines felt that Hong Kong society itself had changed. Force commanders and operational chiefs confided repeatedly among themselves that they were troubled by the growing acceptance among Hongkongers of violence against police. Radicals now attacked officers not only with umbrellas, as they did during the Occupy protests, but also with bricks, sharpened metal rods, drain cleaner, ball bearings launched from catapults, and petrol bombs.

On August 11, 2019, an officer suffered second-degree burns when he was hit by a petrol bomb tossed into the Tsim Sha Tsui police station compound, which protesters had besieged for hours. The popular shopping area around the station turned into a war zone. When a young woman in the crowd was hit and injured in the eye, she immediately became a symbol of the protests and proof of police brutality. Police, however, wanted her claim to be verified, suggesting that she might have been hit by a ball bearing fired from a protester's catapult.

That day, the officer's injury went largely ignored, whereas the woman became an heroine on social media and in news reports. A photo of her covering her bloodied eye appeared on posters and protest art, along with much repeated allegations of police brutality. For police, this just showed how firmly the dice were loaded against the force.

A senior operational officer said: "Actual physical violence against police officers was escalating, but no one cared." He said that one only had to go to Telegram, a popular encrypted messaging platform, to find numerous suggestions every day on ways to kidnap or even kill officers. "The general sentiment in society was that this was acceptable," he said.

On October 13, a police sergeant had a narrow escape after a protester slashed him in the neck with a box cutter. He suffered a deep cut that severed a vein, paralyzed one of his vocal cords and damaged his voice permanently. He underwent surgery and was in hospital for nine days. Recalling the attack, the officer said that he was aware at the time that he was bleeding profusely, but only realized he was in "deep trouble" from the looks on his colleagues' faces. "I never feared death until I saw my wife in hospital," said the father of two. "Then I realized I could die and leave her behind."

Police also had to fend off accusations that officers inflicted serious sexual attacks against protesters, but were left to deal with victims reluctant or unable to provide details. At a highly charged dialogue in October between Chinese University president Rocky Tuan Sung-chi and students who wanted him to condemn police violence, a young woman removed her mask and said that she and other women arrested during the protests were subjected to "sexual violence."

Sonia Ng claimed that she had been taken to a police station where she was made to undress, and that two women officers had watched while she used the toilet. She had earlier alleged anonymously that a policeman had hit her breasts while she was being arrested. Police said that they took her allegations seriously and appealed to her to "provide concrete evidence." Ng said she would cooperate only if city leader Carrie Lam set up an independent inquiry to probe police abuses. The case remained under investigation in early 2020.

While many in the police force were disheartened to see Hongkongers turn against them, a few officers were sympathetic to the protest movement and crossed secretly to the other side to work with protesters. The *Post* interviewed a police officer and paramedic who showed their official identification and described how they had helped injured and traumatized protesters near Polytechnic University in Hung Hom, during fierce clashes there in November.

"I just want to help people like a real policeman is supposed to, but I can't do that now with my uniform on," said the officer who used the pseudonym Eric. "But when I am a volunteer medic, I can at least go out and tell Hong Kong people, 'Don't worry, I'm here to help. There's no need to panic.'" Both men said they decided to help protesters after the July 21 Yuen Long MTR attacks on protesters by a white-shirted mob and when they saw a viral video of two uniformed officers walking away from the scene instead of rescuing the victims. "After seeing my two colleagues turning their backs on citizens in need, I really couldn't just sit by," said Eric. "It's a police officer's duty to protect the citizens and enforce the law." The pair added that they intended to continue with their volunteer work despite the obvious risk to their jobs.

Becoming hardened steel

JPOA chairman Lam Chi-wai, whose group represents 80 per cent of the force, said June to October 2019 proved a most difficult period as officers were not psychologically prepared for the protest movement's smear campaign. "Their propaganda attack was unparalleled," he said in February 2020. "To be honest, we were overwhelmed." However, he said, police proved their mettle through the rest of 2019 and into 2020. "The force was like the phoenix rising from the ashes," he said. "The months of social unrest toughened us into hardened steel. We became more determined to safeguard the city's law and order."

In March 2020, Hong Kong police made a rare appearance at the UN, to fend off accusations of using excessive force and insist that they had been victims of unrelenting violence. Addressing the UN Human Rights Council, Deputy Commissioner Oscar Kwok Yam-shu said Hong Kong had been held hostage for eight months by rioting mobs that had vandalized shops, banks, restaurants, traffic lights and train stations; set fire to buildings; and attacked police officers with bricks, petrol bombs and firearms.

The protesters kept accusing police of brutality because police were "the only force that physically stood in the way of those who sought to extort their demands from the government through mob violence." He said that police were not there to judge whether the protesters' cause was a just one, or if it even made sense.

"We don't have to," he said. "We are police officers. Our one and only mission is to find out whether anyone has committed a crime. If someone breaks the law, it is our lawful duty to stop him and arrest him."

— *With reporting by Clifford Lo and Mimi Lau*

The doxxing and the duelling

Danny Mok

As protests intensified, police officers found their personal data leaked online and became the target of threats to their life, limb and family.

I van Chan loved his job, and his children were proud of him. A sergeant in the Hong Kong Police Force, he never imagined that a day would come when officers would wear masks in public to conceal their identity. Nor was he prepared to have his most personal information and photographs exposed online, or watch his family members become targets of malicious attacks by hostile citizens. All because he was a policeman.

After months of facing life-threatening situations at the front lines of anti-government protests, he asked himself how officers could have ended up among the victims. "Being a policeman disturbed my whole life, and my children were affected too," said Chan*.

Almost immediately after the first major protest on June 12, 2019, some police officers on duty that day found their names, identity card numbers, phone numbers, home addresses, photographs and details about their family members posted on the internet. They were victims of doxxing, the online exposure of private details and images. Over just two days, more than 50 complaints were filed with the Office of the Privacy Commissioner for Personal Data regarding officers who had been doxxed, bullied or intimidated, and the force set up a hotline for officers with such grievances.

The swift arrest of nine people in early July for leaking data and other offenses did not deter the doxxers, who continued to target police officers, especially those at the protest front lines or involved in controversial confrontations with protesters. As the clashes continued, all members of the 31,000-strong team appeared to be fair game as police were accused of using excessive force against protesters.

The privacy commissioner's office said in August that the data leaks were on a large scale and trending upwards. Journalists and protesters were among victims but police were the biggest targets. By the end of 2019, the office received 4,370 doxxing complaints, a 75-fold increase from 2018 when there were only 57 complaints. Some 1,580 cases involved police officers and families while 873 cases were about protesters.

Wives and children dragged in

Some officers received a large number of nuisance calls or threatening messages warning them their family members would be killed. Among the senior officers affected was Chief Superintendent John Tse Chun-chung. As head of the Police Public Relations Branch during much of 2019, he was in the hot seat, having to explain frontline action by the force and fielding frequently asked questions about excessive use of force. His personal phone number, identity card number and address were posted online, along with about two dozen pictures of him, his wife, three young children, relatives and friends. He moved his children out of the family home to keep them safe.

Senior Superintendent Kelvin Kong Wing-cheung, also a police spokesman, was doxxed in August 2019. His personal details, as well as those of his wife and two children, were posted online. "I was in a bit of a panic at first, then the inconvenience became a bother," said Kong, who began wearing a surgical mask when he went out. He worried most about his family, who had to be on alert to avoid being confronted by protesters. They stopped going to shopping malls on weekends, and dined out less.

In the end, the family decided to move to a new home. "I felt very sad that some people thought they were justified in doing that to us, saying, 'You deserve this because of your job, and your family must pay too.' It is just uncivilized," Kong said. "I have never said police did not make a single mistake, but only that our purpose was to maintain law and order."

A senior officer who spoke on condition of anonymity said he was angry when he and his family became victims of doxxing. He wanted to know who had done it and how they had gotten his family's data. "You can find pictures on social media, but not my wife's HKID number and telephone number. These are things only people you know well might have access to. It made me wonder if my friends betrayed me, but I couldn't find out," he said.

The harassment left his wife full of dread and fear. Their phones sometimes rang 20 times in an hour, and if they answered, the caller just spewed vulgarities. The family was spooked when people wearing black sometimes appeared near their home. As a precaution, the couple moved their children to another location. The officer said the experience left him feeling that Hong Kong was no longer the society he pledged to serve when he joined the force.

Station sergeant Kwan Kar-wing found himself and his family members exposed online after he was identified as the officer who shot protester Chow Pak-kwan, a 21-year-old college student, during a scuffle in Sai Wan Ho on November 11, 2019. The incident sparked an instant debate over whether the officer was under threat at the time, or acted too hastily. Doxxers punished him right away by going online to post his name, occupation, and academic qualifications, as well as the names of his two daughters and their school. There were also death threats targeting his children.

Aside from the harassment online, some police families were attacked at their homes too. The officers' quarters at Wong Tai Sin became a battlefield over three consecutive days in early August with intense clashes between riot police and masked radicals. Protesters threw eggs and bricks at the officers' homes, smashing some windows. Their graffiti said: "Wives and children have to pay too."

Upset and angry, the police families struck back. There were ugly scuffles when some residents grabbed umbrellas and brooms and confronted the protesters. Households on the lower levels of the police quarters bore the brunt of the clashes, suffering damage which forced some families to move out.

The children of police officers were not spared either. Online, they were threatened and insulted. In school, some found their classmates and even teachers turning against them or acting hostile toward them. They were mocked and called "puppies" because they were children of police officers who had been branded "dogs" by protesters for their loyalty to the government.

A constable recalled worrying about his 13-year-old daughter after she began having nightmares and late-night bouts of weeping. The Form Two student had been singled out, bullied and harassed in school because of his job. "She did not go to school for more than two weeks after anonymous callers warned her to watch out, which made us very worried," the 35-year-old officer said. In the end, the girl changed schools. "Her basic right to education was not respected," he said. "I talked to her teachers, but they had done nothing to stop the problem."

That experience left him feeling bitter, but also showed that the anti-police sentiment had swept over some teachers too. In July 2019, Colin Lai Tak-chung, a liberal studies teacher at Sacred Heart Canossian College, replaced his Facebook profile picture with a message that said: "Whole families of corrupt cops die." Later that month, Alvin Tai Kin-fai, then assistant principal of the Hong Kong Chinese Christian Churches Union Logos Academy, said in a Facebook post that he wished "the children of those policemen who have used excessive force die before seven years old, or die an unnatural death before 20 years old should they now already be seven or older."

Tai's remarks sparked an uproar, with an Education Bureau spokesman saying that spreading hate speech, "especially threats targeting children and young people, was absolutely unacceptable." Both Lai and Tai apologized, but there continued to be complaints involving teachers.

From threats to actual attacks

On the streets, frontline officers found themselves in increasingly dangerous situations as the months of protests passed, because hard-core radicals began using an array of weapons capable of inflicting serious injury. On October 13, they planted a home-made bomb in a roadside flower pot along Nathan Road in Mong Kok. The remote-controlled device exploded near some police vehicles while officers were clearing roadblocks set up by protesters. No one was hurt, but that was the first time a bomb was used in the protests.

Earlier the same day, a police sergeant was attacked at Kwun Tong MTR station by a protester using a box cutter. The assailant pounced from behind, slashing the officer in the neck, inflicting a deep cut that severed a vein and damaged a vocal cord. During the siege of Polytechnic University in November, a sergeant was struck by an arrow shot by a radical occupying the Hung Hom campus. The arrow went right through his left calf. "If I had been just 3 meters in front of where I stood, it could have hit my abdomen or chest," said the officer, who asked to be identified as Sam. He recovered, but needed ongoing physiotherapy. He found it dehumanizing that police officers were attacked while doing their job, and that their wives and children were victimized as well. "I'm a Hongkonger too," he said. "Why would they do that to me?"

Lawmaker Priscilla Leung Mei-fun, vice-chairwoman of the pro-Beijing Business and Professionals Alliance for Hong Kong, said police had been victimized and demoralized and that, in turn, would affect Hong Kong society. To the protesters, she had this to say about their attacks on the force: "You scolded them harshly, but you went to the wrong people. You should turn to the government, the decision-makers instead." But she was hopeful that there would be ways to mend the rift between police and the public eventually.

Between June 2019 and late February 2020, 585 police officers were injured. More than 3,200 officers and their family members reported that they were victims of doxxing. The affected officers were from all ranks.

Ivan Chan, 40, a sergeant in the Police Tactical Unit, did not expect his life to change the way it did as the protests played out from the middle of 2019. First, he was a victim of doxxing. Then, in November, he had a close shave when a petrol bomb shattered on his leg during intense clashes at Chinese University. Fortunately, the bomb was not properly ignited and did not explode.

The veteran officer said his job cost him his friends too, including some he had known from secondary school and university. The polarization of Hongkongers into pro-government and anti-government camps ended up ruining long friendships and affecting family ties. "The social circle I built up over my life was all gone suddenly," he said.

After all his years in the force, he was least prepared for the day he began feeling anxious about his own safety, and that of his family. This happened when large numbers of radicals turned up outside his quarters. He said: "Working as a cop will make you afraid of being beaten up? Have you ever heard of this?"

Pessimistic that the broken relationship between the police force and Hong Kong society could be repaired anytime soon, he said: "Maybe we will see recovery only after a whole generation is gone."

Name has been changed to protect his identity.

New police commissioner, new strategy

Christy Leung

With a new man in charge, police discarded their slow responses and switched to battle mode against protests and hostile media.

Hong Kong rang in 2020 with a massive anti-government protest march that ended in chaos, as radicals went on a rampage blocking roads, smashing traffic lights, throwing petrol bombs, trashing bank branches and shops, and even targeting the High Court. Police responded by swooping in on the protest hotspots, firing tear gas and water cannons, and rounding up at least 400 people, the largest number arrested in a single day since the unrest began. There was a clear change in the way police had tackled the mayhem.

The trouble began on New Year's Eve. Police had approved a march in the afternoon from Victoria Park, in the Causeway Bay shopping hub, to proceed to the Central business district. The organizer, the Civil Human Rights Front, claimed a turnout of more than a million people, making it the biggest rally since the record estimated turnouts of June 9 and June 16 in 2019.

The march was meant to be a show of solidarity to push for the protesters' core demands, which included an independent investigation into police conduct over nearly seven months of social unrest, amnesty for all those arrested, and universal suffrage for Hongkongers.

About two hours after it started, however, black-clad protesters vandalized an HSBC bank branch on Hennessy Road in Wan Chai. A police squad, including masked undercover officers, arrived and arrested five people. One of those caught was dragged away, face-down on the ground, angering other protesters. When some protesters began hurling umbrellas and other objects at police, officers responded with pepper spray, pepper balls and tear gas.

Just after 5.30pm, police ordered the organizers to call off the march, citing the violence. Upset with the abrupt end to the event, defiant protesters refused to leave, and they spilled into the streets of Causeway Bay, Wan Chai and Central. The violence only became worse as night fell. The mobs hurled petrol bombs, dug up bricks from pavements, started fires on roads and painted graffiti on the facade of the High Court.

Police swarmed across the trouble spots and by 7pm had fired tear gas and water cannons to disperse protesters. Causeway Bay became a flashpoint, when officers surprised protesters by charging at them from two sides along Hennessy Road. More than 460 people were rounded up near the Sogo department store and some were made to squat with their hands raised or stand, facing the wall, as they were searched and had their details recorded.

Officers worked late into the night, taking control of one occupied area after another, setting up roadblocks along major routes and checking buses. Most of those arrested were nabbed for illegal assembly and possession of offensive weapons. They added to the 6,494 people arrested earlier, over almost seven months of civil unrest. Nearly 2,000 of those as at the end of 2019 were aged between 11 and 19, and more than 2,500 were students.

Hard and soft tactics

Observers noted the change of police tactics right away. Surprised and impressed, security consultant Clement Lai Ka-chi said: "It was spectacular." A former police superintendent who helped set up the force's Counter Terrorism Response Unit in 2009, he said: "The force is now taking a more proactive and determined approach to curbing violence, instead of being passive, reserved and defensive."

The January 1 protest was the first major rally since Commissioner of Police Chris Tang Ping-keung took command of the 31,000-strong force in November 2019, and many saw his hand guiding the apparent change of strategy. Making his first official visit to Beijing in December, Tang assured central government officials that Hong Kong police would handle the ongoing protests with both "hard" and "soft" tactics – being tough on violence but flexible on minor offenses. Senior Chinese public security officials said the central government gave the force its "strongest backing" and hoped Tang would lead with determination to curb the violence in the city as soon as possible, while also maintaining the morale of his officers.

In a Facebook post a day before the New Year's Eve rally, Tang urged Hongkongers not to condone or cover up violence. He warned those attending the rally: "If you use violence, you will not get public support. We, the police, will do all we can to arrest you. We will step up our efforts and citizens should refrain from breaking the law."

On New Year's Day, police put his promise into action. Security consultant Lai approved of the swift, firm police response, saying: "It will discourage radical and non-violent protesters from coming out, because they know they will be either arrested or have their personal details recorded by police, making it easier to identify them in future." Four days later in Sheung Shui, police acted in the same way, detaining about 100 people after a rally ended at 3pm. About half of those detained were arrested.

A senior officer with direct knowledge of the force's operational plans acknowledged the change of strategy, saying: "We used to play a drawn-out defensive game when dealing with radical protesters. We even let protesters continue marching in illegal rallies, dispersing them only when massive violence erupted. Now, once violence occurs, we intervene early to cut short the rally, rounding up and detaining people to prevent the situation from worsening. We treat these as battlegrounds and aim to reclaim peace before bedtime." Acting earlier also meant using fewer rounds of tear gas and other crowd-dispersal weapons, the source added. Police fired 23 rounds of tear gas and 15 rubber bullets on New Year's Eve, and seven rounds of tear gas and nine rubber bullets on January 1. In comparison, they used almost 3,300 rounds of tear gas and 3,200 rubber bullets on November 18, when protesters occupied Polytechnic University in Hung Hom.

Deputy Commissioner Raymond Siu Chak-yee brushed aside talk that Tang, the new chief, had a different approach to that of his predecessor, Stephen Lo Wai-chung. "To deal with different operations, we have different tactics," Siu said. "Our ultimate objective is to ensure public order and public safety. Now, if crimes are committed, we aim to restore public order as soon as possible to prevent the situation from deteriorating. We keep reviewing our tactics."

Observers noted other aspects of what police had begun doing. From the last quarter of 2019, undercover officers were sent to business premises likely to be targeted by violent protesters, to ambush the vandals early. On December 21, for example, protesters roaming malls in the tourist district of Tsim Sha Tsui to scare off shoppers were themselves surprised. About two dozen riot officers entered the massive Harbour City mall and, together with undercover officers already stationed there, pounced as several hundred hard-core protesters appeared. There were chaotic scenes, and police used pepper spray as radicals scuffled with plainclothes officers. "Those who vandalized shops thought they could get away with it, but we were all around them," the source said. "The police presence had a deterrent effect and showed protesters that we were capable of netting them. They would have to pay the price if they broke the law."

Another frontline battle: Negative, fake news

Another change since Tang took over was that the force began to respond more robustly to negative reports in the media, calling out what it considered to be misinformation, or reports that damaged its image. Between November 2019 and February 18, 2020, police wrote 46 letters to the media objecting to fake or biased reports. Only six such letters had been sent between June and November 2019. The senior source said: "As fake information goes viral very quickly and can have damaging consequences, we must respond immediately."

No fewer than 38 letters were sent to the Chinese-language newspaper *Apple Daily*, whose front page was splashed regularly with reports of alleged police brutality. In a letter on January 9, the force rejected an *Apple Daily* report claiming police had continuously violated international guidelines on the use of force. "Your newspaper always accuses the police of brutality. We have reiterated that we use only the minimum level of force when necessary," the letter read. "Over the past seven months, your newspaper has touched on protesters' violence lightly but has kept smearing the force and inciting hatred against the police with an evil intent. We regret your reporting and reserve the right to pursue action."

Not everyone in Hong Kong was impressed by the new police tactics at protests, or the force's efforts to safeguard its credibility. Hong Kong Human Rights Monitor director Law Yuk-kai called police chief Tang "a wolf in sheep's clothing," and more aggressive than his predecessor despite presenting himself as approachable. Accusing police of making "groundless and arbitrary mass detentions" instead of distinguishing between peaceful and violent protesters, he said: "The new police chief has abandoned all guidelines and the tiny bit of prudence the force had. He sugar-coats police brutality and cruel tactics."

Democratic Party lawmaker Ted Hui Chi-fung noted that, while more protesters were being detained, police were using fewer crowd-dispersal weapons. "Yet, I don't appreciate this approach," he said. "Society needs reconciliation. If you are getting tougher, it only makes society more divided, and people will only hate the police even more." Asked if Tang or his predecessor Lo did a better job, Hui replied: "They cannot be compared, because both are bad."

As of December 13, 2019, the force's Complaints Against Police Office was investigating 1,404 complaints against officers. Its findings have to be endorsed by the police watchdog, the Independent Police Complaints Council. The council was separately looking at complaints that police used excessive force on six occasions between June 9 and August 31, and that protesters detained in August were mistreated while being held at the San Uk Ling Holding Center, near the border with mainland China.

Security consultant Lai maintained that the police response to the protests and violence since June 2019 had been far from extreme. "Honestly, the police have been very lenient," he said. "They have a lot of options, in terms of tactics and weapons – way more than you can imagine – but they have only used the tip of the iceberg in terms of what is available to them." Advising radicals not to underestimate the force's ability to handle unrest, he said the response so far demonstrated that police were trying to avoid mass casualties.

Boosting morale

Lam Chi-wai, chairman of the Junior Police Officers' Association, which represents 80 per cent of the force, said that police chief Tang attached great importance to communicating with frontline officers and had done much to boost morale. While Tang was deputy chief in 2019, he commanded Operation Tiderider, which dealt with the protests. He was seen regularly on the front line alongside his officers, dressed in protective gear. Even after becoming chief, he would appear at high-risk protest spots. "Tang keeps our morale high and we are united," Lam said.

In January 2020, Tang was questioned by predominantly pro-democracy district councilors at two sessions that focused on police conduct during the protests. At the meeting with Central and Western District Council members, he conceded that the force could have handled the social unrest better, and admitted that police sometimes made mistakes in handling protesters. "Of course there is room for improvement ... including in terms of our actions and strategies, communication with the media, our gear and my colleagues' attitudes when talking to citizens," he said.

He rejected the councilors' allegations of police brutality, saying that those who claimed to have been mistreated should file a formal complaint. The councilors showed photographs and video clips of protesters' bloodied faces and accused Tang of blindly protecting his men, as no officer had been punished so far for wrongdoing. Lawmaker and district councilor Hui asked Tang to apologize for the "police violence," but the chief replied: "It is the rioters who should apologize for the harm they have done to society."

In February, Tang was upset with public broadcaster Radio Television Hong Kong over two episodes of its long-running satirical show, *Headliners*. The force made an official complaint to the Communications Authority, claiming that the episodes "undermined police work" and would result in an "erosion of law and order." The February 14 show mocked the force for allegedly stockpiling masks for officers amid a citywide shortage as the coronavirus pandemic struck. Tang complained to Director of Broadcasting Leung Ka-wing, rejecting the suggestion that the force had hoarded tens of thousands of surgical masks as supplies ran low for health care workers. Tang also objected to the February 28 episode which referred to recent deaths in Hong Kong that police had ruled were not suspicious. He argued that even satirical shows had to be based on facts, or people might believe that the force did not investigate deaths thoroughly and officers were not professional in going about their work.

RTHK chief Leung defended *Headliners'* status as a satirical work while conceding the network must be open to criticism. "While we appreciate the hard work and difficulties of other government departments unequivocally, we also aspire for cross-departmental understanding and respect such that each performs its own functions, in hopes of better serving the public and the betterment of society," he said.

Police chief Tang's broader point was that the show failed to reflect views from all sides in its coverage of the anti-government protests, and had never condemned radicals who destroyed shops, blocked roads, set fires and injured people. "Many people in society are disgusted with the actions of the rioters, and there are many voices in support of police to stop the violence," he said. While the force respected media freedom, Tang said, he objected to the show's misleading portrayal of police. He argued: "If the public loses confidence in the police, criminals will get a chance to take advantage of it, and Hong Kong's law and order will be difficult to maintain."

Tear gas: Legitimate crowd-control measure, or menace?

Emily Tsang and Victor Ting

Police fired thousands of rounds of the dispersal weapon during the unrest, including in built-up residential areas, leading to claims it had entered people's homes, and caused serious injuries.

On the afternoon of June 12, 2019, riot police officers advanced toward a crowd trying to storm the Legislative Council complex and unfurled a black banner which said: "Warning: Tear smoke." Within minutes, shots were fired and clouds of stinging fumes sent choking protesters screaming and fleeing the scene, hands covering their mouths and noses.

Waiter Ray Wong Cheuk-hei, 20, was among the tens of thousands there. He recalled the pungent smell, the burning sensation hitting his throat, tears streaming down his face, and having trouble breathing. Someone handed him an N95 respirator mask, which he wore as he ran. It seemed a long time before he was able to stop and splash cool water over his face and eyes, now reddened and hurting. "The most terrifying thing was not knowing what was in the chemicals, and whether they would have a lasting impact on your health," he said.

Police were widely accused of using excessive force in Admiralty that day, including firing numerous rounds of tear gas. Then police chief Stephen Lo Wai-chung defended his officers' actions in what he described as a "riot" situation. He told the *South China Morning Post* that the protesters were armed with sharpened metal bars, and officers had to protect themselves. Assistant Commissioner Rupert Dover, who was among the top commanders who ordered the tear gas that day, said the alternative would have been "huge casualties to the police."

To protesters, that marked the start of more violent clashes to come, along with new demands that included a call for an independent inquiry into excessive use of force by police. The use of tear gas, in particular, stirred deep anger and resentment among protesters. Frontliners began to wear helmets and goggles, and came up with new strategies to counter police action, with teams assigned to douse the canisters of tear gas shot at them.

Police had used tear gas in the 2014 Occupy protests that were sparked in opposition to Beijing's restrictive framework for electoral reform. Even then, many regarded its use as disproportionate and unnecessary, said Assistant Professor Lawrence Ho Ka-ki of Education University's (EdU) social sciences department. The use of tear gas that year marked a shift for Hong Kong's police, who had previously preferred a "negotiated management" strategy when dealing with protests. That meant using discussion and persuasion, and granting official approval for demonstrations, rather than using force to disperse crowds.

First used by the French against the Germans in 1915 during the first world war, tear gas was subsequently banned. But after manufacturers modified the gas and promoted it as a harmless, effective means of crowd control, it came into use worldwide, though it remained dogged by controversy. Critics have called for tighter regulation, including full disclosure of the chemical contents, a system to track its use, and studies to investigate its physical and mental impact on people.

Anna Feigenbaum, author of *Tear Gas: From the Battlefields of WWI to the Streets of Today*, said the use of tear gas always signaled the point when the relationship between a government and its people had broken down, when the authorities felt they were losing control. "In some way, it is a marker of the protesters' success, that they have reached the threshold of actually posing a threat," said Feigenbaum, an academic at Bournemouth University in Britain.

Tear gas gets into people's homes

As Hong Kong's anti-government movement progressed through the second half of 2019, with violence and vandalism not only in the downtown areas but also in neighborhoods across the city's 18 districts, police's response included firing no fewer than 16,000 rounds of tear gas over a six-month period, or about an average of 90 rounds a day. It sparked complaints that gas was filling the air on the street, seeping into homes, schools, offices, vehicles and restaurants.

People questioned the manner in which police deployed tear gas, and demanded to know more about its toxic content and harmful effects. Roger Lee King-hang, a lecturer in philosophy at the Caritas Institute of Higher Education, said public sentiment turned against the force because people felt police were indiscriminate in using tear gas against protesters, affecting innocent residents and passers-by as well.

On July 27, hundreds of thousands of people descended on the heavily populated residential area of Yuen Long, defying a police ban. Protesters hurled objects at officers, who used tear gas, sponge grenades, pepper spray and batons to drive them back. Cyrus Wong Ka-ho, who runs an interior design business there, said: "It was not necessary to use tear gas and deploy riot police. Most protesters were peaceful and polite at first, and the area was close to residential areas and homes for the elderly."

Police said they had called 22 old folks' homes in the area and alerted them to close their windows, and none had been affected. But a video widely circulated over social media showed residents in one of the homes choking as tear gas fumes entered through a window.

After Yuen Long, tear gas was used across Hong Kong, in densely populated neighborhoods like Wong Tai Sin, Sham Shui Po, Tseung

Kwan O, Tin Shui Wai and others. In some incidents, tear gas canisters shattered windows and landed inside people's homes, incurring the wrath of citizens.

In the working-class district of Wong Tai Sin on August 11, angry residents disrupted riot police action against protesters who had besieged the police station and vandalized its facade. Shirtless middle-aged men in slippers and women holding plastic shopping bags blocked police. When the force fired tear gas, furious residents shouted at the officers, some using vulgarities. They cried out:

"Do you know we have children at home? Leave now!"

"We don't want you here!"

"Wong Tai Sin does not welcome you, go away!"

Police insisted their actions were justified, as the Wong Tai Sin protesters had destroyed public property and threatened the safety of residents.

On August 12, tear gas was fired into Kwai Fong MTR station before officers went after retreating protesters. More tear gas followed inside, filling the ground-level concourse with fumes. Police said the protesters there had used catapults to launch ball bearings at officers and tossed "smoke cakes" which emitted fumes.

"The situation was urgent," said police spokesman Kelvin Kong Wing-cheung. "Our consideration was to stop the protesters' radical behavior as soon as possible."

Ho of EdU said: "These are supposed to be dispersal operations. But how can you disperse the crowd when you fire from above or into confined spaces, where the fumes spread in all directions and affect everyone indiscriminately, and protesters have nowhere to flee?"

Professor David Hui Shu-cheong, an expert in respiratory medicine from Chinese University (CUHK), felt that more needed to be done to protect the public. "Proper use of tear gas in an open area can be a very effective way of dispersing crowds," he said. "However, improper use can do great damage to people's health and sometimes even be lethal." He was concerned about people being injured by flying tear gas canisters too.

A senior police officer insisted that Hong Kong police had acted no differently than law enforcers in other advanced countries dealing with riots. In an interview in October 2019, he cited the 2011 London riots and 2018 "yellow vest" protests in France and urged people to compare the way police responded there with local officers.

"What standards are these people referring to, when they judge that police used excessive force and abused their power? They cannot compare the way we handle a riot with the way we deal with a normal street crime."

Barrister Ronny Tong Ka-wah, a member of the government's top advisory panel, the Executive Council, said he believed that police had no alternative but to use tear gas, beanbag rounds, rubber bullets and other crowd-dispersal measures when protesters were armed with bricks and were violent. "It is their responsibility to maintain order," he said.

Expired canisters, fears of impact on health

The use of tear gas raised questions about the effects on public health. Dermatologist Kingsley Chan Hau-ngai said there was a rise in patients with eczema and other skin allergies in the second half of 2019. Protester Wong, the waiter, said an old problem with eczema flared up again, after a tear gas canister exploded near him on November 17. "My skin became very dry and cracked. I couldn't stop scratching," he said, insisting he had no choice but to be out on the streets to fight for the city's future. He spent HK$4,000 (US$516) on medicines and needed frequent visits to the doctor. "My eczema only cleared up in January."

Health concerns moved Hong Kong parents to organize several rallies demanding an end to the use of tear gas. Tai Wai resident Wing

Leung was walking her two young daughters home when police fired tear gas at protesters nearby. She said her younger girl, one-year-old Mimi, broke out in rashes all over her back and stomach, but doctors could not tell if they were the effects of tear gas and if the symptoms were long term. In another case, a man said on Facebook that his seven-month-old son had rashes after wearing clothes that had been hanging outside their flat when police fired tear gas in the area.

Respiratory medicine specialist Hui said people with asthma or chronic bronchitis were more likely to develop inflammation in their trachea, or windpipe, after being exposed to tear gas, though not many long-term health problems had been identified. He said that children, in general, could end up inhaling more tear gas than adults because the heavy fumes would sink to their level.

There were also questions about the supply and quality of the tear gas used in Hong Kong. In June 2019, the British suspended exports to the city following the outcry over the use of force by Hong Kong police.

In October, police confirmed that they had bought supplies from mainland China, but refused to reveal the chemical contents, citing operational reasons. There were unverified claims that mainland-made tear gas burned at a higher temperature, a condition for the release of cancer-causing dioxins.

There were also concerns about dioxin poisoning after a journalist who reported regularly from the protest front lines, Chan Yu-hong of the digital news outlet *Stand News*, was diagnosed with chloracne. The rare skin disease, with symptoms including an eruption of blackheads, cysts and nodules, has been linked directly to dioxin exposure. The Public Health Research Collaborative, a citizen-led research group, asked if chloracne was linked to exposure to tear gas.

Police insisted that the tear gas they procured had passed safety tests. Government officials said there was no evidence of dioxin poisoning caused by tear gas. Professor Chan King-ming from CUHK's school of life sciences said there was no evidence that tear gas emitted dioxins as its burning period was too short. He urged the public not to panic, but felt that the government could have done more to address people's concerns.

There were also raised eyebrows when it was found that police had used some tear gas which had expired. However, security expert and former superintendent Clement Lai Kai-chi said the date on the gas canisters was the "best-before" date and the product had a five-year lifespan beyond that. It did not mean the fumes would be stale or cause harm to people, he said.

Hui and Feigenbaum acknowledged the difficulty of proving the harmful effects of chemicals in tear gas. To ease public concerns, both felt it would be best to disclose the contents.

As the anti-government protests continued, the use of tear gas became less effective in dispersing masked radicals at the front lines. Instead, protesters became bolder in dealing with tear gas. Caritas Institute's Lee observed: "Wearing gas masks, many protesters no longer fled from the smog. Rather, their masks enabled them to face the challenge and carry on with their operations."

Initially, protesters would dash toward tear gas canisters to cover them, or even toss them back at police. Their tactics changed, with frontline radicals forming specific "firefighter" teams to neutralize the gas canisters. Wearing hard hats, gas masks, goggles and gloves, and shielding themselves with umbrellas, team members would spring into action when police fired tear gas. They would dash forward, cover the sizzling canisters with helmets, traffic cones, water bottles or damp clothes, and pour water over it all. "It's better than picking up the canister and throwing it back at police," a protester said.

Through it all, police firmly defended their use of tear gas. An officer frequently at the front lines said: "It is fired from a distance, causes few or no long-term health effects, and is used across the world as a crowd-control weapon." He said tear gas was usually used when protesters became unruly and started to throw objects at officers.

Feigenbaum conceded that tear gas remained in wide use around the world because there was a lack of non-lethal alternatives for use in riot situations. Other methods were more dangerous and likely to cause harm, or may put officers at risk. "To beat you with a baton or shoot you with rubber bullets, they have to be close enough," she said. But there are questions that remain unanswered, not only in Hong Kong but worldwide. "How much damage has tear gas caused? How many lives has it harmed? Nobody knows, because nobody counts," she said.

In recent years, anti-tear gas advocates have urged the Chemical Weapons Convention, an international body with 193 member states, to investigate the harm caused by tear gas and issue clear guidelines on the chemicals permitted for use in them, as well as draw up regulations for manufacturers.

Lecturer Lee said that it was hard to ease public sentiments over tear gas while Hongkongers felt there was no credible system to press complaints against police. The protesters have demanded an independent inquiry, but Chief Executive Carrie Lam Cheng Yuet-ngor has rejected that, arguing that internal investigations and a watchdog review are adequate for now.

"No sensible person would object to reasonable use of force to protect the rights of the people and secure public interests, provided it is properly regulated and follows rules and laws strictly," Lee said.

The problem in Hong Kong, he felt, was that the government had left police to bear the brunt of dealing with protesters. "It is the responsibility of the government to resolve political issues in a political way," he said.

"Sadly, when the leader is not handling it competently, the police force has to bear the burden of blame. The use of tear gas has come to be seen as a way to retaliate against public criticism and protect the interests of those in power."

Who's watching over the police?

Chris Lau and Alvin Lum

Calls for a commission of inquiry to look into allegations of excessive force by officers have been rejected in lieu of a watchdog doing the investigations. Will it be enough to bring peace?

T he government's unpopular extradition bill triggered Hong Kong's season of unrest in June 2019, but, very quickly, protesters began demanding an inquiry into alleged police brutality. Among other allegations, they accused officers of using excessive amounts of tear gas and other crowd-dispersal weapons, manhandling protesters by tackling them to the ground, beating them and dragging them away, and abusing detainees.

Photographs and video clips circulated widely on social media, showing bloodied or cowering protesters and menacing officers in violent clashes which played out on the streets, in MTR stations, shopping malls and university campuses. Police argued that video footage circulated by protesters was deliberately one-sided, only showing officers in action, but rarely focusing on violent masked radicals who attacked officers and ordinary Hongkongers, and damaged or vandalized public property and business premises.

Protesters claimed that they had no choice but to arm themselves with bricks, rods and petrol bombs to defend against the excessive force used on them. Police denied the charges vehemently, insisting they had a job to do as protesters rioted and became increasingly violent over the weeks and months.

Over the summer, the call for an independent commission of inquiry (COI) against police grew louder, emerging as a key demand out of the five that the protesters had been campaigning for. The argument went that protesters were getting beaten and arrested for breaking the law but police were acting like they were above the law, escaping scrutiny for their harsh or even negligent conduct. Two incidents of police misconduct kept being cited.

Protesters pointed to how slowly they had responded during the July 21 Yuen Long attack by a white-shirted mob against them and ordinary residents, even though the force said its manpower was stretched to the limit that night and denied allegations of any collusion with triads. Another tense episode was the night of August 31 inside Prince Edward MTR station, where protesters said they were attacked at will by officers but police insisted they were chasing after radicals.

Police top brass stoutly rejected the call for a COI, even as several prominent figures in the city's establishment, including a former chief justice and religious leaders, supported the idea of an independent inquiry led by a judge.

An angry rank-and-file also made plain they were dead set against such an inquiry. Four police associations expressed their strong opposition, warning that appointing such a panel could damage morale through the ranks. Their objections proved a key reason behind Chief Executive Carrie Lam Cheng Yuet-ngor's refusal to set up a COI.

In early September, when she announced that the extradition bill would be formally withdrawn, Lam did not budge on the protesters' other key demands which included convening a COI.

She said the police watchdog, the Independent Police Complaints Council (IPCC), was capable of dealing with all charges against the force. The role of the IPCC, as a statutory body, was to review and support or reject investigation findings from the Complaints Against Police Office, a police division. It had been criticized in the past as toothless because of its limited powers.

To strengthen the IPCC to deal with complaints related to the protests, a five-member team of international experts was appointed to advise it. It was led by Denis O'Connor, former British chief inspector of constabulary, with the other members comprising former or current heads of police watchdogs in Canada, New Zealand and Australia, and a British scholar on crowd behavior.

The watchdog would focus on protests on six key dates – June 9 and 12, July 1 and August 1, as well as July 21 at Yuen Long and August 31 at Prince Edward MTR station. It would also look into the use of San Uk Ling Holding Centre, near the mainland border. After police were accused of mistreating some arrested protesters held there, the government stopped using it as a holding center.

Lam said the 27-strong IPCC would get two new members – former deputy ombudsman Helen Yu Lai Ching-ping and former Bar Association chairman Paul Lam Ting-kwok.

Things did not go well. In December, the foreign experts exited abruptly, after criticizing the council's lack of investigative powers. Academics and activists said their departure exposed the deficiencies of Lam's decision to rely on the IPCC instead of setting up a COI. The IPCC's interim report, scheduled to be out in February 2020, was also delayed.

Lessons from the London riots

The *South China Morning Post* learned that from as early as June 2019, Lam's officials had begun to study various inquiry and reconciliation methods used overseas after protests and conflicts. Lam and her inner circle apparently drew lessons from Britain's handling of the 2011 London riots. After a 29-year-old man was shot dead by police trying to arrest him on suspicion of having a handgun, mayhem broke out, first in London's Tottenham district before spreading to 66 areas. Shops were looted and fires started in the streets, as an estimated 13,000 to 15,000 people went on the rampage. Five people died and hundreds lost their businesses and homes.

Britain had its own force and watchdog look into police tactics and strategy. It also set up a "community and victims panel" and commissioned a study into the underlying causes of the riots, with researchers interviewing protesters. But critics in Britain pointed out that more than half the recommendations made were eventually ignored or not implemented.

IPCC chairman Anthony Neoh, who visited Britain to study how the unrest was handled and briefed Lam, told the *Post* that the experts there spoke of the "urgency to promote reconciliation."

The city leader then decided to let the IPCC carry out a systematic review and fact-finding exercise to check for evidence of police excesses. She tried to strengthen it by hand-picking reliable figures, much like how the British government had dealt with its 2011 riots, and by inviting the international experts who presumably would not go along with any attempt to protect police morale.

Pro-Beijing lawmaker Priscilla Leung Mei-fun, a law academic at City University, noted that the British community and victims panel focused on mediation and reconciliation even as it investigated the riots. "It didn't have the power to summon witnesses. It was not a statutory body. Yet it had credibility," she said.

She noted that the panel was not established under Britain's Inquiries Act, and it was not led by a judge. Instead, the British government dubbed it a "grass-roots review" as it studied the causes and possible prevention strategies and how key public agencies ought to deal with communities. The team collected 340 witness accounts, and sought views via radio, television and online sources.

A similar panel, she felt, could be useful for Hong Kong. Leung said Hong Kong's protesters might be willing to come forward if a similar platform was created. High-profile witnesses whom the panel invited would also feel compelled to attend or face recrimination from others if they refused. Leung later suggested that the panel could be given the power to summon witnesses.

Professor Stephen Chiu Wing-kai, chair professor of sociology at Education University, pointed out that the London incidents were a more serious case of rioting, but Hong Kong could learn from how the aftermath was handled. "It focused on understanding the truth," said Chiu, who has studied and written on the London riots.

Let's talk: Carrie Lam meets ordinary Hongkongers

In early September 2019, when Lam announced that the extradition bill would be formally withdrawn, she said she planned to reach out to the community through direct dialogues. "People from all walks of life, with different stances and backgrounds are invited to share their views and air their grievances," she said. A temporary "Dialogue Office" was set up under a research unit reporting directly to Lam. Its task was to "take charge of coordinating the dialogue platform programs initiated by the government and suggestions made by the non-government sector."

Some speculated that Lam was taking a leaf from French President Emmanuel Macron's townhalls of 2018 to resolve his own "yellow vest" protest crisis sparked by a fuel price hike. But political observers were skeptical that Lam could pull off meaningful heart-to-heart discussions with angry Hongkongers. They were critical of her handling of dialogues over universal retirement coverage in 2015 and with student activists about universal suffrage during the Occupy protests of 2014. Critics pointed out it was Lam who led the city into the extradition bill calamity, blaming her very disregard for public sentiment.

Sources told the *Post* that the government had studied the British handling of the separatist Irish Republican Army (IRA), in case the city's protest movement developed into a long-running saga. The drawn-out Irish conflict involved deep-rooted problems, including religious and cultural differences, and led the IRA to launch terrorist assaults and bomb attacks in Britain for a good part of the 20th century. Dialogue, especially behind closed doors, had been key to the eventual peace, said Hong Kong academics and government officials who studied the issue.

But dialogue had been difficult to initiate, a government source said. "Every time there is aggravation during the protests, police have no choice but to deal with it and it becomes yet another setback," he said.

In the end, Lam held only one public dialogue, on September 26, 2019. The event, convened under tight security at Queen Elizabeth Stadium in Wan Chai, had more than 130 participants picked randomly from more than 20,200 who applied to attend. They grilled Lam on the reasons she refused to give in to protesters' demands, especially the call for a COI into allegations of police brutality. Lam shouldered the blame for the social upheaval and took the verbal onslaught in her stride, including calls for her to resign, but made clear she would resist the rest of the protesters' demands.

Nearly half of the 30 people who asked questions focused on the need for a COI, but Lam insisted that the IPCC was already on the job. She said: "Shouldn't we let the IPCC complete its work in a few months, then make a judgment on whether or not we can accept its conclusion?"

A woman wearing a surgical mask stood up to respond: "Police have become a political tool and there is no mechanism to monitor their operations. The IPCC is only a toothless tiger." Not a single top official had been held accountable since the protests began in June, she said. "Tonight many of us are calling for a commission of inquiry. If you don't heed these calls, what's the point of today's dialogue?"

A Form Six student became emotional as he questioned Lam, saying: "Have you ever been sympathetic toward people who were tear-gassed or beaten by police? You only care about turnstiles in MTR stations which were vandalized. You have taught me, a naive person, that peaceful protests cannot make a difference."

When the dialogue ended, participants rushed to sign up for the next session, which officials said would be more in-depth. As of early 2020, the first event remained Lam's only public dialogue, although the office said she and her officials had taken part in a total of 37 forums and online sessions. Her Dialogue Office, which cost HK$5.45 million (US$703,088) to set up, stopped operating in March 2020.

An independent review committee tasked to study the underlying discontent of the social unrest was also shelved in late January 2020, after the coronavirus crisis hit the city. Lam conceded that the government had found it hard to get experts and prominent figures on board. The *Post* learned that leading legal figures, including former chief justice Andrew Li Kwok-nang and retired senior judge Robert Tang Kwok-ching, had declined to head the committee.

Experts disagree over watchdog's mammoth task

From the start, critics said the IPCC did not have the same status or legitimacy as a COI, and had too many pro-Beijing politicians. Lawmaker and former IPCC member Kenneth Leung also said it was made up of police-friendly figures. "Its composition needs a complete overhaul to regain public trust," he said.

Lam defended the council, saying: "It is a credible and independent statutory body and everyone I have appointed to the IPCC takes their independence seriously. We should not doubt them."

The IPCC got down to investigating complaints that had come in against police, but with each successive week of protests, its work piled up higher. It said it would present its report in phases, dividing the protests into stages.

Council chairman Neoh said he was prepared for reports to include minority positions, allowing members to disagree openly and be transparent. He planned to interview police officers and seek evidence from the force.

Although then police commissioner Stephen Lo Wai-chung promised the force's cooperation, the process proved slow-moving, and the panel eventually complained that police did not hand over video footage it requested.

Then came the hints of trouble with the overseas experts, whose participation was meant to shore up the IPCC's credibility. In November 2019, the experts said the IPCC did not have sufficient powers, capacity and independent investigative capability "to match the scale of events and the standards required of an international police watchdog operating in a city that values freedoms and rights."

They proposed that the watchdog be given investigatory powers to subpoena documents and summon witnesses. Panel chairman O'Connor said: "[The IPCC] lacks the independent investigative capacity as we would expect to find in a body seeking to exercise oversight of police. In the absence of establishing some facts that people can actually relate to, then rumors or innuendos or fake news are likely to continue and proliferate. I can't imagine that is good for Hong Kong."

But Neoh told a mainland Chinese television station of the expert panel: "They do not really understand our situation, so their proposal has overstepped our statutory function. So I've told them, thank you for your suggestions, but we have to follow the law."

The expert team responded by announcing abruptly that it was "standing down" from participation in the ongoing investigation.

The *Post* subsequently learned that one reason for the experts' displeasure was that Neoh had denied them the right to comment on the IPCC's study before publication. Confirming this, Neoh said: "It's a fact-finding report. Nobody comments on a fact-finding report, because facts are facts. Facts should speak for themselves."

Its interim report, for the period up to July 1, was due to be released in February 2020. But in January, it said it would postpone releasing it because of an ongoing judicial review. The legal challenge, initiated by activist Hendrick Lui Chi-hang, centered on the council's authority to carry out such a review. However, in April, the High Court threw out Lui's case, saying the watchdog was empowered to conduct a study on the protests.

The first phase of the council's work looked into clashes between anti-government protesters and police on June 9 and 12, and July 1. The IPCC said in March 2020 that it would release its entire report after the legal proceedings.

The controversy over the international experts' sudden departure and the delay in the IPCC's work were a blow to Carrie Lam's efforts to tackle the complaints of police brutality without a COI. Chinese University political scientist Ivan Choy Chi-keung said that, ultimately, the public would look at the findings to assess if the IPCC was fearless in speaking truth to power. "That would be in the long run, but we are talking about the short term now, and there is not much confidence," he said.

Courts on trial

Chris Lau

Hong Kong's judiciary has come under intense pressure as cases from the protests pile up even as critics attack judges they disagree with.

I t was past midnight when West Kowloon Magistrates' Court finally wrapped up for the day on November 20, 2019. "This may well be a new record," quipped Principal Magistrate Peter Law Tak-chuen. Six magistrates' courts across Hong Kong stayed open past their usual 4.30pm cut-off that day, to hear the cases of 242 people accused of rioting during anti-government protests.

The courts had to decide whether to grant bail to the defendants, most of whom were students. West Kowloon Court was the busiest, handling 80 cases, and Law dealt with half of them himself.

Unending anti-government protests put Hong Kong's justice system to the test as thousands of people were arrested from June 2019. Commissioner of Police Chris Tang Ping-keung said that by January 16, 2020, more than 1,000 had been taken to court for rioting and possessing firearms – the gravest offenses – as well as more minor ones such as possession of laser pointers.

With about 7,000 people arrested so far, the courts could see their workload growing considerably. As protest-related arrests snowballed through the second half of 2019, legal experts were concerned that the justice system's ability to cope was at risk. Even if not everyone arrested ended up in court, prosecutors still had to examine every case and decide whether to proceed.

Along the way, the courts and at least one judge came in for criticism over protest cases, and court buildings were vandalized. Concerned legal experts and judges cautioned that politicization of the courts could end up a bigger issue than the mounting caseload.

The courts and prosecutors also came under fire for not dealing speedily or harshly enough with protesters. Some worried that the failure to mete out timely punishment could fuel further violence, while those facing charges complained that their lives were on hold indefinitely as they awaited their day in court.

So many cases, so few judges

At the opening of the 2020 legal year in January, Chief Justice Geoffrey Ma Tao-li said he had set up a task force to explore ways to avoid delays in dealing with the increase in cases, including extending court hours. A spokesman for the judiciary said that Ma had discussed the issue with leading judges and the courts had already adopted a more flexible approach. The extended hours at the six magistrates' courts on November 20 were an example.

Among those who welcomed the extension of court hours were former Bar Association chairwoman Winnie Tam Wan-chi and legal sector legislator Dennis Kwok. But former University of Hong Kong (HKU) law dean Johannes Chan Man-mun pointed to the shortage of manpower in the judiciary and said: "Merely extending court hours without increasing judicial manpower will not solve the problem, as you can't expect a judge to work continuously for 18 to 20 hours a day."

A judge, who spoke to the *South China Morning Post* on condition of anonymity, agreed that the courts were short-staffed and admitted that he was concerned about their ability to cope with the influx of protest-related cases. As of March 2019, only 156 of the city's 218 judicial posts had been filled.

However, Simon Young Ngai-man, HKU's associate law dean, noted that the courts had appointed temporary judges to deal with previous manpower shortages. Lawyers and retired judges could be drafted in to help, or lower-court judges could sit temporarily in higher courts.

At the end of 2019, there were 35 deputy judges and judicial officers from outside the judiciary, in addition to 34 deputy judges and judicial officers appointed internally. "The system has this inherent mechanism to increase resources when needed," Young said.

Prosecutors working overtime

Over at the Department of Justice, Hong Kong's prosecutors found their workload expanding with each passing month of the protests. Every case submitted by police had to be reviewed, even if it did not end up in court. For cases that proceeded to the courts, prosecutors had to gather all facts against the defendants.

A prosecutor handling protest cases said he and his teammates had to work long hours, sometimes staying past midnight and coming in on weekends. As the protest-related work piled up, more than 10 officers were added to the initial team of about five dealing with public order cases, the prosecutor said.

The prosecutors came in for criticism, with protesters accusing them of bringing politically motivated charges. In September 2019, a prosecutor was verbally abused in court by protesters' supporters after he urged the court to reject bail for a 15-year-old accused of possessing offensive weapons. The Bar Association called for calm, while Secretary for Justice Teresa Cheng Yeuk-wah said that prosecutors were required to follow their codes strictly.

A Department of Justice spokesman downplayed the issue of overworked prosecutors, saying staff could be deployed internally or prosecution work could be outsourced to private barristers, something that had been done in the past.

Protesters attack courts, judge

For several months after the protests began, the judiciary escaped the attention of radical protesters. Then, on November 13, the flowerbeds of Sha Tin Magistrates' Court were set on fire shortly after the High Court refused an application for an order to stop police from entering Chinese University, which had become a battleground between radical protesters and police.

On December 8, during protests to mark six months of the unrest, protesters hurled petrol bombs at the Court of Final Appeal and High Court buildings. On January 1, 2020, Madam Justice Anthea Pang Po-kam's name was spray-painted on a wall outside the High Court, the graffiti branding her "a judge with red backing," meaning she was pro-Beijing.

The vandalism was widely condemned by the legal sector. In a joint statement, the Bar Association and Law Society said: "Abusive comments implying that judicial decisions were made or influenced by political considerations are wholly unjustified. Any attempt to insult, threaten and bring public pressure on a judge because of decisions made in the course of performing judicial duties is to be deplored as an affront to the rule of law and judicial integrity."

Bar Association chairman Philip Dykes said that people might disagree with the court or even think it was biased, but they should not resort to such attacks. "If court buildings are vandalized, then that is a sort of reflection that people have no respect for the law," he said.

As the months went by, the debate over the slow progress of protest-related cases continued. Those in the pro-establishment camp felt that the courts' failure to act swiftly allowed some protesters to roam free and reoffend while out on bail. In September 2019, about 100 pro-Beijing protesters gathered outside the Court of Final Appeal and demanded the chief justice's resignation, saying he was too lenient to protesters.

HKU's Young felt these politically sensitive cases needed to be dealt with quickly, because the longer the delay, the greater the risk of damaging confidence in the system. He suggested that those facing less serious offenses could be spared conviction and made to perform community service. Noting that some public order offenses did not give judges much flexibility in sentencing, he felt the law needed to be reformed to encourage protesters to plead guilty.

Bar Association chairman Dykes urged the secretary for justice not to press charges in trivial cases, a suggestion supported by his predecessor Tam. But Grenville Cross, a former head of prosecutors, rejected the idea, saying: "Political violence is no less reprehensible than other types of violence, and may actually be more reprehensible, where it has terrorist characteristics. Prosecutors must not only select the most serious charges, but also seek to maximize the number of charges they bring, giving the courts the widest scope for imposing severely deterrent sentences."

Almost all those arrested in protest-related cases have been assisted by a group of about 200 barristers, solicitors and legal clerks from three human rights groups – Spark Alliance, the Civil Human Rights Front and Hong Kong Civil Rights Advocates.

Lawyers have gone to police stations to help those arrested, accompanying them to the magistrates' court to be charged the first time. Some provided their services free of charge, but most were paid by the 612 Humanitarian Relief Fund, a trust fund set up by prominent supporters including outspoken Catholic Cardinal Joseph Zen Ze-kiun, former lawmaker Margaret Ng Ngoi-yee and Cantopop singer Denise Ho Wan-sze. By November 30, 2019, the group had raised a total of

HK$97 million (US$12.5 million), HK$4.96 million of which was for legal fees and assistance to protesters.

Spark Alliance ran a separate effort to help protesters, but its HK$70 million fund was frozen in December 2019 by police, who accused the group of money laundering, a charge it denied. The Legal Aid Department also provided assistance to those who cleared a means test. A spokesman said that it had received 46 protest-related applications and had approved 16 of them as of November 30, 2019.

'Fair trials need time'

In January 2020, Chief Justice Ma said that the attacks on the integrity and impartiality of the courts resulted from a distorted view of the law and the legal system. He said fair trials needed time, with prosecutors having to build their case, and defense lawyers preparing to respond. He also explained that in a system like Hong Kong's, which assumed a person was innocent until proven guilty, bail was usually granted unless there was reason to believe an accused person might flee or tamper with witnesses.

Ma rejected the suggestion to set up a special court to deal with protest-related cases, as was done in Britain to clear the large number of cases related to the 2011 London riots. He said that most of the British defendants chose to plead guilty, whereas he expected most of those arrested in Hong Kong to defend their case.

He said judges were sworn to discharge their duties fairly and uphold the law. "Judges do not have the duty to achieve a certain result in accordance with popular wishes, whether they be majority or minority wishes," he said.

Ma also emphasized that while Hong Kong had laws to protect the rights to freedom of speech and assembly, people should not go overboard when exercising their rights. "The enjoyment or insistence on one's rights does not, for example, provide any excuse to harm other people or their property, or to display acts of violence," he said.

In April 2020, a judge fell into the very trap of being swayed by either side that Ma had warned against. District Court judge Kwok Wai-kin was barred from handling protest-related cases after he compared "Cultural Revolution-like" anti-government demonstrators to a terrorist army.

While the judge was sentencing a tourist guide for stabbing two protesters and a news reporter at a Lennon Wall protest noticeboard in August 2019 out of anger over losing his income because of the social unrest, Kwok expressed sympathy for the defendant. He slammed protesters for "ruthlessly trampling on his right to work, live and survive." The court said his ruling had stirred "controversial discussions in the community."

Another challenge for the courts in early 2020 was the unexpected arrival of the Covid-19 pandemic that forced hearings to be suspended for weeks, adding to the delays in protest-related cases. Those awaiting trial found themselves in limbo, with some having to report to a police station regularly and observe a curfew, while others remained barred from leaving Hong Kong.

A 15-year-old music student who was arrested in July 2019 said that he had never been charged in court and, half a year later, still did not know if police would press charges. As he was required to report to a police station regularly, he was unable to go on a student exchange trip to South Korea. He said: "I feel like I am just waiting endlessly."

BEYOND BORDERS

"BECAUSE FREEDOM IN THEIR OWN BACKYARD IS THE PARTY'S BIGGEST FEAR."

Ted Yoho, United States congressman

The pawn in US-China rivalry

Wang Xiangwei

W hat has become of Hong Kong, the once famously freewheeling fragrant harbor? Can the city emerge stronger from its biggest political crisis since Britain returned its sovereignty to China in 1997, or have the protests hastened an irreversible decline into what its critics would deride as "just another Chinese city?"

We are not yet halfway into the 50-year Sino-British agreement that granted Hong Kong a "high degree of autonomy" under a formula known as "one country, two systems," yet with the dust not settled on more than a year's worth of anti-government protests, it is a question increasingly being asked far beyond the city's borders.

What began as a seemingly local issue – an ill-fated bill that would have allowed the Hong Kong government to extradite criminal suspects to mainland China, among other places – has long since snowballed into a matter of international concern.

The protests sparked by that bill have endured long after the offending article was shelved. Rather than dissipate, they have developed into a wider movement demanding greater political freedoms that has laid bare a schism of mistrust between Hongkongers and the mandarins in Beijing, fueled by misunderstanding and paranoia.

Were the repercussions of this schism purely economic, it would be bad enough, the third prong of a triple whammy that has also seen the city hit by the US-China trade war and the coronavirus pandemic.

Unfortunately, the effects reach far beyond the economic realm.

Hong Kong has become a pressure point in the increasingly antagonistic rivalry between China and the United States, demonstrated most clearly by Washington's signing into force of the Hong Kong Human Rights and Democracy Act in November 2019, a move American politicians explicitly linked to the protests.

Washington claimed that its motive in passing the act, which allows it to suspend Hong Kong's special trading status depending on the outcome of an annual inspection into whether the city retains sufficient autonomy, was aimed at protecting the freedoms granted under one country, two systems.

China, however, saw the act as "meddling," a thinly disguised attempt by the US to undermine the rise of its nearest rival and the latest escalation of a tit-for-tat skirmish that has endured ever since the launch of Donald Trump's trade war in 2018.

Nearer to home, the city became a pawn in the increasingly ill-tempered political chess match between Beijing and the administration of Tsai Ing-wen in Taiwan. Beijing, which considers Taiwan a renegade province to be reunited with the mainland by force if necessary, has long considered Hong Kong's one country, two systems formula as a carrot to coax Taiwanese around to the benefits of reunification. That carrot was obviously attractive when Hong Kong was booming, its economy driven ever higher by its links with the mainland and its people enjoying the sort of political privileges unheard of elsewhere in China.

Yet images of black-clad protesters clashing with police in riot gear amid clouds of tear gas served only to strengthen the hand of Tsai and her independence-leaning Democratic Progressive Party when the island's voters headed to the ballot box on January 11, 2020.

Seen from afar and against this backdrop, it is all too tempting to write off Hong Kong as a city whose soul is in danger of being swallowed up by geopolitical currents far beyond its control.

Closer observers, however, caution against rushing to judgment. Hong Kong still has its resilience, entrepreneurial spirit and world-class financial services, not to mention the rule of law and independent judiciary, which have done so much to make it attractive to international investors. These attributes remain robust, however severe the tests they have faced in recent months.

As great a consideration to anyone questioning Hong Kong's future should be that its continued success is in Beijing's best interests. While Hong Kong's relative economic clout has diminished since 1997 – when its economy represented roughly 20 per cent of the Chinese total, as opposed to just around 3 per cent now – the city retains a key role in funneling investment both into and out of the country. In 2018, for instance, of the US$64.2 billion (HK$498 billion) Chinese companies raised through IPOs globally, US$35 billion came from Hong Kong. Another indicator: mainland Chinese hold more assets in Hong Kong – US$1.1 trillion in 2018 – than lenders from any other region, according to the Hong Kong Monetary Authority's data. That figure equates to roughly 9 per cent of China's gross domestic product. Sidelining the city would be neither cheap nor easy for China.

Still, questions for Hong Kong remain. Among the more pertinent ones is this: how, given the city's importance on the international stage, could the sudden scale and intensity of the mass protests – that took just weeks to morph from the peaceful marches of April to the shocking violence of June – have caught so many people by surprise?

The answer is that Hong Kong's summer of discontent was not as sudden as it seems, but the product of a long winter, particularly for

357

the younger generation, in which years of pent-up anger and frustration at the lack of any meaningful progress in politics, economics or social mobility slowly came to an explosive head. Hong Kong Chief Executive Carrie Lam Cheng Yuet-ngor's ill-timed and ill-advised push for the infamous extradition bill merely pulled the trigger.

Hong Kong, an example to the world

To understand how Hong Kong has landed itself in such a big mess, to the extent that the continued viability of one country, two systems is itself now at stake, some historical context is necessary. Back in 1997 when Hong Kong returned to Chinese sovereignty, expectations were high about the city's smooth integration with the rest of the country under the formula pioneered by China's late paramount leader Deng Xiaoping.

Indeed, in the early years following the return, the formula served Hong Kong quite well as both Hongkongers and officials in Beijing wanted to show the rest of the world that this unique political experiment worked. During that period, the emphasis from both sides was on the "two systems," with Beijing hoping its success would provide a model for eventual reunification with Taiwan.

For instance, Hong Kong's first chief executive Tung Chee-hwa dismissed requests to reinstate the colonial-era special branch tasked with national security and intelligence, and Beijing imposed strict restrictions preventing central government departments and local authorities from bothering Hong Kong in any unnecessary way.

During that period, Beijing's hands-off approach to Hong Kong was better illustrated by a Chinese proverb, popularized by the then president Jiang Zemin, that "river water should not interfere with well water" – that is to say, neither side should meddle with the other's systems.

But such proximity and greater integration still heightened the central government's deeply held concerns that Hong Kong, with all its political and legal freedoms, would serve as a base for people wanting to disrupt and subvert the communist system on the mainland, helped by "foreign forces."

So it pushed for Tung's government to enact a national security law, something that backfired spectacularly in 2003. The bill, as required by the city's mini-constitution, the Basic Law, is aimed at prohibiting treason, secession, sedition and subversion. Yet many Hongkongers felt that the bill went too far, representing an incursion into the principle of "two systems." Half a million took to the streets protesting that it would infringe on their civil liberties. Tung was forced to retire before his second term was completed.

In retrospect, the bill was a watershed in the relationship between Beijing officials and the pro-democracy movement in Hong Kong.

Since then, a vicious cycle has taken hold, in which each side thinks the worst of the other on every major political development – helped by miscalculations, missteps, and misunderstanding from both sides. All this has made any meaningful political and electoral reform very difficult.

In Hong Kong, residents fear that Beijing is tightening its grip on the city; in Beijing, officials fear control of the city is slipping through their fingers.

In an echo of the national security law debacle, the Hong Kong government under Leung Chun-ying in 2012 was forced to shelve a plan to introduce a "national education" curriculum into local schools. Critics said the curriculum amounted to brainwashing due to its positive stance on the Communist Party and its criticisms of the US political model. Mass protests prompted Leung to drop the plan, but the idea of the curriculum has not been abandoned entirely.

Two years later, Beijing's sense that it was losing its grip on the city only grew with the advent of the Occupy protests, when protesters seeking universal suffrage shut down major roads for 79 days. Particularly inflammatory to Beijing was when international support emboldened a small group of young activists to advocate independence from China.

While it was clear then, as it is now, that a majority of Hongkongers did not support any form of independence, Beijing's worst fears kicked in and it started to signal its impatience with Hong Kong for dragging its feet over the national security law.

Since 2003, successive chief executives have reaffirmed the city's intention to pass the law. Significantly, however, none has been able to give a time frame.

More 'one country' than 'two systems'

Meanwhile, mainland Chinese officials have heaped on the pressure by suggesting that "one country" should take priority over "two systems," with some advisers to Beijing warning that it could intervene if the delay continues. Such talk has, in turn, heightened the fears of those Hongkongers who warn that Beijing is tightening its grip.

This circle of distrust has been fueled in recent years by incidents that have caught the world's attention. Infamously, in 2015 a group of Hong Kong booksellers who sold titles banned on the mainland were abducted; in 2017, reports emerged that Xiao Jianhua, a Chinese tycoon, had been spirited away from his luxury hotel in Hong Kong and detained on the mainland on allegations of economic crimes.

At least as corrosive as all this political wrangling and deepening distrust was the fact that, at the same time, officials in Hong Kong and their political masters in Beijing were failing miserably to tackle the many "grey rhino" risks long associated with Hong Kong – sky-high property prices, widening inequality, lack of social mobility for youth, and woefully underfunded social security.

By common consent, these issues have underpinned waves of anti-government demonstrations over the past decades. Indeed, in every crisis since 1997 – the crisis of governance in 2003, the national education controversy in 2012, the Occupy movement in 2014 – the authorities in Hong Kong and Beijing have responded with solemn vows to tackle deep-rooted economic problems concerning housing and inequality.

On each occasion, as soon as the immediate crisis has calmed, these vows have been forgotten and it is back to business as normal. Until the next crisis comes along.

In that sense, it is a wonder the summer of discontent did not happen sooner.

Cross-border ambitions

Before triggering Hong Kong's biggest post-handover political crisis, Lam had been on a roll. In 2017, she was elected as Hong Kong's first female chief executive following reports that Chinese President Xi Jinping favored her over her rival John Tsang Chun-wah, a former financial secretary.

She earned more brownie points with Beijing by pushing through a joint checkpoint at the West Kowloon terminal for the high-speed rail link to the mainland. The move effectively leased a quarter of the terminus to the mainland Chinese authorities – further evidence, in critics' eyes, of a blurring of the line between the "two systems."

Like her predecessors, she was also under pressure from Beijing to enact the national security law, though also like her predecessors she remained non-committal about the time frame. Many observers have suggested that she saw the extradition bill as a worthy alternative in helping her to secure Beijing's support for a second term in 2022. Lam has strongly denied this and was adamant Beijing did not initiate the bill and that she had received no instruction from central authorities regarding it. Less skeptical observers say this might have been true, given that Beijing is more concerned with seeing the national security legislation pass.

Either way, Lam appeared to have gained support from Beijing's top representative in Hong Kong then, Wang Zhimin. Wang, who spent most of his career as a specialist on Hong Kong issues, became the director of the central government's liaison office in the city in 2017. He was reported to have vowed to see the national security legislation pass during his tenure. Looking back, it would appear that Wang and other Chinese officials saw the extradition bill as a test run for the much harder passage of the national security law. That the extradition bill would also make it easier to hunt down businessmen and corrupt officials hiding out in Hong Kong was merely an added bonus.

Whatever their true motivations, it soon became clear that Lam, Wang and their advisers had misread the public mood and underestimated the opposition of Hongkongers from all walks of life, particularly the city's usually docile but powerful business community. Fears over the lack of rule of law on the mainland ran deep.

To compound their mistakes, they continued to pressure the pro-government legislators to push for the passage of the bill, ignoring the obvious warning signs and growing protests. At this point, it was clear that Lam – a career civil servant – was lacking the political antennae that should have warned her this seemingly local issue could have massive geopolitical implications. Perhaps more surprising was that the international repercussions appear to have caught Beijing's officials by surprise too. At least initially, their political antennae were also down.

Local issue, international interest

Beijing's support for Lam began to harden when the British and Canadian foreign ministers expressed concerns about the proposed extradition bill in a joint statement, along with the 28-member

European Union (EU), and after Hong Kong activists including Martin Lee Chu-ming and Anson Chan Fang On-sang visited Washington to seek US support in opposing the law.

Given Beijing's long-standing fears of "foreign forces" meddling in Hong Kong, that flurry of statements from Britain, Canada, the US, and the EU only strengthened its suspicions that there was a conspiracy afoot to inflame tensions in the city and therefore hurt China.

Essentially, what started as a local issue for Hong Kong – the bungled introduction of a controversial bill – had now burgeoned into not only a direct challenge to Beijing's control over Hong Kong but also a major international event. The ensuing, and increasingly violent, protests against the city's government and Beijing made headlines for weeks around the world.

Lam was forced to suspend the introduction of the bill in June and declare a total defeat by formally withdrawing it in September. But that was not enough to stop the protests; instead, with the bill sidelined, they morphed into a movement demanding more political freedom.

Ramifications from the debacle have rumbled far beyond the shores of Hong Kong. In November, the local pro-Beijing faction suffered a resounding defeat in Hong Kong's district council elections; Taiwan's Tsai and her independence-leaning party swept to victory in the January's presidential and parliamentary elections, in no small part by cashing in on the fears of Taiwanese who saw Beijing's tightening grip on Hong Kong as a foreshadowing of their own future.

Another yardstick for measuring the international impact of the protests was when the general manager of the US basketball franchise Houston Rockets, Daryl Morey, made what must now count among the most expensive tweets in social media history.

His tweeting in October of the slogan "Fight for freedom, stand with Hong Kong" – one frequently used by protesters in the city – immediately set off an outcry in mainland China, angering tens of millions of Chinese NBA fans and putting billions of dollars in revenue in jeopardy as Chinese sponsors threatened to withdraw support for both the team and the league.

It also ignited a geopolitical firestorm that saw Chinese and US politicians, media commentators, NBA owners, basketball legends and fans all weighing in and slugging it out with their views on freedom of expression, the rise of China and its colonial humiliations, China's perceived bullying of foreign companies, protesters waving American flags in Hong Kong and China's national sovereignty.

To this day, the implications of that tweet are still being debated. It is unclear who the bigger loser is, whether it is the NBA through its loss of sponsorship or whether it is Beijing, which in fanning the flames of the international coverage may have inadvertently magnified the protests in the eyes of millions of NBA fans around the world who would otherwise be apolitical. It may also have played into the foreign media narrative that portrays the Chinese government as quick to bully foreigners and foreign companies who exercise their freedom of speech.

Adding to Beijing's dismay was how the debacle surrounding the extradition bill complicated its negotiations with Washington to ease trade restrictions. It was with this concern at the fore that Hong Kong soon became the first Chinese territory where the two governments were openly battling for political influence.

For years, Chinese officials have held deep suspicions that Washington has used its intertwined political and business influences in Hong Kong to foment trouble and use the city as a base to subvert the rule of the party, pointing to the fact that its consulate in Hong Kong is the largest of its kind in Asia, among other things.

But at the height of the violence in August last year, Chinese officials made the unprecedented step of putting a name to their pain. The foreign ministry spokesperson Hua Chunying publicly said the protests were "the work of the US" and that "the US owes the world an explanation." She cited meetings between senior US officials and prominent supporters of the protests, and the waving of American flags during many of the demonstrations as proof of its involvement.

Hua's words were echoed by the former Hong Kong leader Tung, who accused the US and Taiwan of orchestrating the "well-organized" protests. But her claims were dismissed as "ridiculous" by US Secretary of State Mike Pompeo.

In November, Trump signed a bipartisan bill into law expressing support for the protesters. Under the Hong Kong Human Rights and Democracy Act the city's continued special trading status with the US – that treats it as an entity separate to mainland China – would be reliant on an annual review of its democratic freedoms. According to Republican Senator Marco Rubio, who introduced the bill in June, the act aimed to "hold China to its promise" to respect the autonomy and freedoms afforded to Hong Kong under the Sino-British agreement that led to the handover in 1997.

While many protesters have welcomed the bill, Lam and Beijing have criticized it as an attempt to interfere in the city's internal affairs. Even within Washington the act has critics who say it will do US interests more harm than good.

But if views on the bill vary, what doesn't seem to be in contention is that hawks in the US and some other Western countries appear keen to frame the unrest in Hong Kong as another example of China's repressive reach and to use it as a rallying cry to push back against Beijing.

At a time when Washington is intensifying its all-out campaign to counter the rise of China, Hong Kong has found itself thrust onto center stage.

Under pressure?

With the spotlight of the international media trained on the city, as its protests grew ever more violent, there was increasing speculation from overseas that the unrest posed a major challenge to Xi's leadership.

But such speculation has proved wide of the mark, based as much on wishful thinking by China's opponents than a sober analysis of the facts. True, the unrest has been an international embarrassment for China, but at home, Xi's position has been strengthened by state media reports attacking the black-clad protesters and blaming the trail of destruction on "foreign instigators."

Reports of Mandarin-speaking Chinese students fearing for their lives, images of them being evacuated and the vandalism of businesses linked to the mainland have caused widespread anger among ordinary mainland Chinese, who have urged the central government to get tougher on Hong Kong.

Early on, Xi had adopted a policy of waiting out the unrest while urging Hong Kong to take tougher measures. This remained his stance even in late July, when law and order in the city were on the verge of breaking down and there were concerns that Beijing would be forced to send in the armed forces.

His strategy seems to have worked, as the Lunar New Year holidays in late January 2020 and the spread of the coronavirus helped discourage mass protests.

Lam, too, appears to have ridden out the storm. Her job appears secure despite previous speculation she could be forced to retire before her term expires in 2022.

Even so, there are signs of a change in Beijing's mindset.

Xi has undertaken a significant reshuffle of senior officials responsible for Hong Kong affairs. Xia Baolong, one of Xi's trusted allies, became the new director of the Hong Kong and Macau Affairs Office in February 2020, effectively reducing the authority of the incumbent chief Zhang Xiaoming who became Xia's deputy. This appointment signals that Xi wants firmer control of Hong Kong affairs. It came after the sacking of Wang as liaison office head in January and his replacement by Luo Huining, a former provincial party chief. Both Xia and Luo share one thing in common: neither has experience managing Hong Kong affairs, giving credence to the theory that Beijing is considering a reset of its approach to the city.

While the protests have eased since that long summer of discontent, the underlying economic, political and geopolitical issues that helped to cause them have remained the same.

It appears that Beijing has realized this. If so, the challenge it now faces is that in adopting any new approach or thinking it must act quickly and decisively. Otherwise it will be just a matter of time before a new crisis comes along, and this time the world will be watching.

Hong Kong's division sows unity in Washington

Owen Churchill

Opponents on Capitol Hill found a common cause in the Hong Kong Human Rights and Democracy Act. What the legislation lacked in substance, it made up for in symbolism.

I t was the autumn of 2019, and Washington was ablaze. House Speaker Nancy Pelosi had started an impeachment investigation into US President Donald Trump, and the Democrats and Republicans were brawling. Angry Republican lawmakers stormed congressional chambers where classified hearings were under way. Mud-slinging became the staple of political dialogue. A Democrat likened Republicans to Judas; to Republicans, the inquiry was a "coup" or even a "lynching." It seemed the only consensus on Capitol Hill was that the other side was wrong.

And yet amid the cacophonic, caustic chaos, almost every lawmaker – red and blue, senator and representative – had found unity behind one cause: the fate of a city on the other side of the world. Eight thousand miles away in Hong Kong, hundreds of thousands – perhaps millions – had taken to the streets to demonstrate against a government bill that would have enabled the extradition of suspects to jurisdictions including mainland China. The proposal terrified many Hongkongers. But it also set alarm bells ringing in liberal Western democracies, where concerns over a perceived erosion of the global business hub's autonomy from Beijing were already running high.

And so, as Hong Kong's legislative body became paralyzed by encircling protests, Washington's was kicking into action. On June 13, a day after the second reading of Hong Kong's extradition bill was postponed due to violent clashes between demonstrators and police, lawmakers introduced the Hong Kong Human Rights and Democracy Act of 2019. Among its provisions, the bill directed the administration to hit any individual responsible for human rights abuses in Hong Kong with sanctions; required an annual assessment from the secretary of state to determine whether Hong Kong remained sufficiently autonomous from Beijing to warrant the continuation of special trading privileges; and ordered the president to assess how faithfully Hong Kong authorities were enforcing commercial sanctions imposed by the US on countries such as Iran and North Korea.

To congressman Chris Smith, a Republican of New Jersey who has made human rights in China a mainstay of his four-decade tenure, the Hong Kong government's "outrageous" proposal posed an existential threat to the city's future. And while the city's chief executive, Carrie Lam Cheng Yuet-ngor, insisted early on that she had not introduced the proposal at the behest of leaders in Beijing, Smith said the move was further evidence of Hong Kong's diminishing autonomy. "If Beijing intends to force Hong Kong into becoming just another Chinese city under authoritarian rule, we must re-evaluate whether Hong Kong warrants the special status granted under US law," Smith said, announcing the legislation in June that year.

Swift passage

Increasing violence in Hong Kong over the following months – by both sides but with protesters' supporters decrying the use of live ammunition by police and attacks against critics of the movement – only fueled support for the legislation as it cleared the many hurdles that each bill must negotiate. After its introduction in June, it took just five months before it was passed by Congress, a notable feat considering a mere 5 per cent of bills introduced end up being voted on, let alone approved and sent to the president.

Like many bills, variations of the legislation had been introduced before. The first was in 2014 during the Occupy movement, when protesters demanding the implementation of universal suffrage for the 2017 chief executive election blocked roads in Hong Kong's financial and retail districts for more than two months. Subsequent variations had been introduced in every two-year term of Congress since, but none gained the official support of more than a handful of lawmakers in either chamber. This time was different, however. Not only did the bill's reintroduction coincide with Hongkongers' revolt against the extradition proposal, it also landed in a Washington that was, in all senses, imploring a drastically more hawkish approach to China than during any administration in recent history.

A year prior, Trump had kicked off what would prove to be a bruising trade war with Beijing, having run for the Oval Office on an "America first" promise to reverse trade deficits and bring manufacturing back to the US. Although many disagreed with his methods – notably the barrage of tariffs – Trump's aggressive approach to confronting China on economic matters found broad support in Washington and catalyzed a hardening of attitudes toward Beijing's policies and behavior in other areas, such as human rights, the Belt and Road Initiative, and national security. It proved the perfect atmosphere for a bill like the Hong Kong Human Rights and Democracy Act.

Samuel Chu, the founder of an advocacy organization that spent the autumn of that year drumming up support for the bill in Congress, put it candidly. "This came at a point where, uniquely, we had an opening that we exploited both because of the administration's fight with the trade deal and because of all the rhetoric [about China]," said Chu, managing director of the Washington-based Hong Kong Democracy Council (HKDC).

Such rhetoric was on full display during the bill's steady passage through Congress, highlighted by one lawmaker's reaction to the *South China Morning Post*'s publication of an interview with an Obama-era diplomat who said passage of the legislation would "only punish the wrong people." Susan Thornton, who led East Asia and Pacific policy at the State Department, had argued that the bill could lead to Hong Kong's isolation, and that "Beijing would like nothing more than the US to remove Hong Kong's special status." Marco Rubio, who had introduced the Senate version of the bill, took to Twitter to call Thornton a career apologist for the Chinese government. And for publishing the interview, the *Post* was a "Chinese government mouthpiece" working at the behest of Beijing to shape narratives in the US, he said.

Rubio, a Republican, did not express the same outrage when Trump criticized the bill and stated, following his signing it into law, that it would interfere with his ability to conduct US foreign policy and could complicate trade negotiations. Indeed, as the *Post* reported then, Trump had quietly leaned on his allies in the Senate to stall the legislation's progress, efforts that proved no match for Congress' appetite for a stern policy response to Hong Kong's predicament.

But Thornton was not alone in her warnings. Trump's former envoy to Hong Kong, Kurt Tong, said that de-certifying the city would have a "dramatic" and "damaging" impact not only on its economic standing but also on its prospects for lasting autonomy from Beijing. Writing in the *Foreign Affairs* magazine, following the bill's enactment, the career diplomat, who retired from the foreign service in the early weeks of the protest movement, called on Washington to resist the temptation to treat Hong Kong "primarily as an opportunity to highlight the flaws of China's approach to governance." A better policy, Tong argued, "would emphasize the lasting value that the United States sees in the city's unique system and do what it can to bolster international confidence in Hong Kong."

Predictably, the legislation's loudest detractors came from Beijing. The bill joined a trove of evidence – which included the presence of "American faces" at the protests – of attempts by Washington to stick its "black hands" into China's internal affairs, the government contended. Allegations that the bill constituted an illegal violation of China's internal affairs abounded, despite the legislation only dictating US policy toward Hong Kong and claiming no authority over how either the central or Hong Kong governments should operate. After Trump signed the bill into law – away from the cameras typically welcomed into the White House to record the signing of legislation about which he is more enthusiastic – a Chinese foreign ministry spokesperson said that the act only further exposed "the malicious and hegemonic nature of US intentions to the Chinese people, including our Hong Kong compatriots." Not content with verbal castigation, China suspended port calls for US navy vessels in Hong Kong and imposed sanctions on US NGOs it accused of aiding and abetting violent criminal acts in Hong Kong and advocating the city's independence.

For their part, those within Congress continued to push the bill with the knowledge that Beijing would denounce the legislative effort as a bid to undermine its sovereignty. "President Xi Jinping and the Chinese Communist Party will continue to blame Western nations for standing with the people of Hong Kong," said Representative Ted Yoho in October. "Because freedom in their own backyard is the party's biggest fear."

Symbolism over substance?

But despite the chest-thumping from the two capitals over the bill, the new legislation, on close inspection, did not break much new ground when it came to US policy. For instance, the government already had the authority, such as through executive order or via the Global

Magnitsky Act, to sanction foreign individuals on the grounds of human rights abuses. And while the new bill ordered a much greater focus on human rights and rule of law in its reporting requirements, the State Department already issues an annual report that includes an assessment of Hong Kong's autonomy and a determination of whether the city still warrants favorable trading relations. That report was mandated by the Hong Kong Policy Act of 1992, introduced in Congress as a means to codify US treatment of Hong Kong after the handover from British to Chinese rule in 1997. As Secretary of State Mike Pompeo put it on November 26, 2019, the day before the new bill was signed into law, "our teams already have a lot of the foundational activity in place."

But Hong Kong activists, including former student leader Joshua Wong Chi-fung and musician Denise Ho Wan-sze, who had canvassed for support in Washington, were jubilant when the law was passed, with Wong calling it a "remarkable achievement for all Hongkongers." Supporters of the latest piece of legislation also said it had an important symbolic role in crystallizing US support for the anti-government protest movement in Hong Kong and making the city's fate a talking point for Americans. For one, the Hong Kong Human Rights and Democracy Act brought the issue to the attention of a Congress that had not seen the city as a priority since the 1992 legislation passed. Only 37 of the more than 500 current members of Congress had been in office when that bill was signed into law almost three decades ago. The youngest, Alexandria Ocasio-Cortez, 30, was not even three years old at the time.

The HKDC's Chu acknowledged that nothing in the bill was new, but said politics was more important than policy, especially when Hong Kong had played only a cameo role in the US-China tussle of the past three decades. "Now there's actual momentum and focus, and this idea of clarity around US-Hong Kong policy," said Chu, whose father, Reverend Chu Yiu-ming, was last year given a suspended sentence on public nuisance charges relating to his role as one of the leaders of the Occupy movement.

One feature that distinguished the most recent demonstrations from those of five years earlier was that this time around many protesters took to carrying US flags and singing the American national anthem. Images of demonstrators waving the stars and stripes as they implored the US Congress to pass the Hong Kong Human Rights and Democracy Act were seen by Beijing as further proof of Washington's imperialist ambitions in the city. The younger Chu, himself one of the loudest voices calling for US action, acknowledged that the flags complicated the picture. "I would say most of the folks we [worked] with on the Hill would rather they not raise American flags," he said, reflecting on his time spent lobbying lawmakers. "The power of it really was Hong Kong fighting for Hong Kong," he said. "And the most politically viable position for the US to take was that 'We are supporting the people of Hong Kong, we're not interfering.'"

Courting controversy

A seven-word tweet by an NBA manager took the Hong Kong protests into American living rooms. It also sparked a nationwide debate about whether the US was selling out to China.

At the time it was to most Americans just another news story about social unrest in a distant place. Venezuelans were marching against President Nicolás Maduro; fuel prices were infuriating the French; Chileans were clashing with police over poverty. Now Hongkongers were at it too, taking to the streets in their thousands to protest against something the media was referring to as an "extradition bill." To many, it was just all so much background noise.

Until, that is, the manager of a National Basketball Association team logged on to Twitter and sent the internet into meltdown. "Fight For Freedom. Stand With Hong Kong," read the image shared in October 2019 by Daryl Morey, of the Houston Rockets. In echoing the rallying cry of protesters demanding universal suffrage in the city's elections – along with four other demands (and "not one less") – Morey might have thought he was onto a winner with fans of a franchise that has long made a point of supporting freedom of expression. What he did not appear to have considered was the reaction of the NBA's deep-pocketed Chinese sponsors.

Within what seemed like a heartbeat, China's largely state-controlled media zeroed in. China Central Television stopped broadcasting Rockets games, and sponsors including tech giant Tencent and sportswear brand Li-Ning suspended relations with the team. Suddenly, foreign affairs were not just for the wonks in Washington. Years' worth of rising US-China tensions, from the trade war to accusations of espionage to the treatment of Uygurs in Xinjiang, all spilled into everyday American life.

A living room debate

"Sports media in the US spent considerable time in the days and weeks that followed discussing the Hong Kong protests in ways that they had not beforehand," said Jeremy Lee Wallace, an associate professor at Cornell University who researches authoritarian politics and China. "In the US, the NBA has become associated with various causes, and so how the league itself and its players would react to this situation where their principles and financial interests seemed in conflict made for compelling stories."

At first, it appeared that concerns about money had won the day. Morey swiftly deleted his message, while Rockets owner Tilman Fertitta took to Twitter to say that Morey did not speak for the team and that the NBA was not a political organization. The franchise's star player James Harden apologized to China while Golden State Warriors coach Steve Kerr and San Antonio Spurs coach Gregg Popovich made evasive comments that critics said nevertheless spoke volumes.

But such actions did little to stem the anger of Chinese fans and sponsors and instead only fueled the narrative taking hold within the US that an American institution once known as a champion of freedom of speech was now kowtowing to Chinese censorship. In one tweet, Morey had managed to do what even US President Donald Trump's widely publicized trade war had never quite managed: make the increasingly troubled US-China relationship a genuine topic of living room conversation. Talk shows debated it, satirical cartoon *South Park* poked fun at it, social media was all over it, there was no getting away from it.

Robert Daly, director of the Wilson Center's Kissinger Institute on China and the United States, contrasted the American public's response with that elicited by issues that had troubled the relationship for decades, such as market restrictions and intellectual property violations. He pointed out that months before Morey's tweet the US had put more than 100 Chinese firms and public security bureaus on its entity list, restricting them from doing business with American companies, due to suspicions that they had undermined US national security or repressed the rights of religious minorities in China. That action had barely stirred the wider public consciousness. "Nobody knows what an entity list is," Daly said. "But everybody knows what the NBA is and who the Rockets player James Harden is, and they all know what *South Park* is."

Forcing the issue

With the controversy threatening to end the league's multibillion-dollar business in China – a market it had been cultivating for decades – perhaps it should not have been surprising that the Rockets and the NBA initially tried to play down the issue. But the debate took on a life of its own, one that went far beyond the confines of the basketball court.

Brooklyn Nets owner Joe Tsai tried to explain to Americans why the Chinese were so upset, offering his view as someone who had spent a good part of his professional life in China where he co-founded the e-commerce giant Alibaba Group. "Supporting a separatist movement in a Chinese territory is one of those third-rail issues, not only for the Chinese government, but also for citizens of China," Tsai, who is also chairman of the *South China Morning Post*, wrote in a Facebook post.

Americans, however, did not seem to be in a mood to listen. Riding on their anxieties, President Trump himself stepped in. "I watched the way that [the coaches] Kerr and Popovich and some of the others were pandering to China, and yet to our own country, it's like they don't respect it," he said. Trump's secretary of state, Mike Pompeo, also chimed in, encouraging US companies in China to question Beijing's edicts. "I think American businesses are waking up to the risks [of complying with the Chinese government's rules]," Pompeo told *PBS NewsHour*. "It may seem profitable in the short run, but the reputational costs will prove to be higher and higher [as Beijing destroys their capacity] to speak freely about their political opinions."

Whether it was top-level political intervention that swung the decision or not, after initial dithering the NBA declined to take any action against Morey. "The long-held values of the NBA are to support freedom of expression, and Daryl Morey enjoyed that right as one of our employees," said NBA commissioner Adam Silver. "I also understand that there are consequences from that exercise of his freedom of speech. We will have to live with those consequences," he added. It was the most prominent defiance of Beijing's hard line on political expression by a US business since Google left the Chinese mainland in 2010 after refusing to comply with an order to censor its search results.

'A wider cultural rift'

Quite how deeply the issue penetrated the public's consciousness was underlined when another American cultural institution, the potty-mouthed cartoon *South Park*, dedicated an entire episode – "Band in China" – to mocking Beijing's censorship and American companies that bow to it. In a move the show's creators Matt Stone and Trey Parker could almost have scripted, Beijing responded by banning *South Park* entirely and scrubbing its existence from the Chinese internet. Stone and Parker in turn issued a sarcastic apology to Beijing that included a tongue-in-cheek reference to a supposed resemblance between President Xi Jinping and Winnie the Pooh, a characterization that Chinese censors are programmed to delete.

"What used to be the gap between the hard consensus on China in Washington and the ambivalence or bias toward a positive perspective on the street, that gap is closing," said Jude Blanchette, chair in China studies at the Center for Strategic and International Studies in Washington. "This contretemps over the NBA may well be the issue that brings them together, because packed into it are issues of censorship and a values clash and of the Communist Party using private companies to enforce its political mandates," said Blanchette, author of *China's New Red Guards: The Return of Radicalism and the Rebirth of Mao Zedong.*

Steve Bannon, Trump's former chief strategist who advocates a decoupling of the US and Chinese economies, said the issue had highlighted a wider cultural rift between the US and China. "I cannot emphasize enough how important this NBA moment is," Bannon said. "We're seeing a collision of all of the concerns about China running from censorship to ideological competition to Xinjiang to economic competition to the Communist Party of China's weaponization of the private sector. All of these have come together. It cuts so against the American sense of fairness. Eighty per cent of the American population was probably not focused on Hong Kong as much, but now ... they're getting immersed in it and coming down hard in solidarity with the protesters."

Game changer?

Months on, it remains difficult to assess the depths of the damage caused by Morey's tweet. The news cycle has moved on and the biggest story out of China in the minds of most Americans is more likely to be the coronavirus than the Hong Kong protests. In February 2020, the

Chinese consul general in New York Huang Ping thanked the US, and especially the NBA, for supporting China's efforts to combat the virus. The NBA pledged aid worth US$1.4 million (HK$10.9 million) to Hubei province, the epicenter of the outbreak in China, including a medical device worth US$285,000 for use at a hospital in its capital, Wuhan.

Even so, that figure is just a drop in the ocean compared with the lasting damage faced by the NBA. Days after Huang expressed his appreciation, NBA commissioner Silver said the league stood to lose up to US$400 million as a result of Chinese business partners cutting ties, even though the issue had disappeared from the news.

Then there is the effect on the Hong Kong protests themselves. While that one tweet sparked countless hours of media coverage, there remains a lingering sense among some that the issue that supposedly sparked it all – Hong Kong's freedoms – took a back seat to the subsequent debate about censorship. As Cornell's Lee Wallace put it: "I don't know if Hongkongers saw this media frenzy as helpful by drawing attention to their issues or whether they saw its eventual flame-out as more significant."

Being water flows overseas

Meaghan Tobin

Seemingly leaderless movements emerged in diverse corners of the world in 2019, taking a leaf from the Hong Kong playbook.

Wearing masks, gloves and backpacks, the protesters create makeshift barricades out of burning rubbish bins and street debris as they face down riot police armed with tear gas, rubber bullets and a water cannon. They are a leaderless, seemingly fearless, group that has learned the art of civil disobedience swiftly, skilled in everything from neutralizing tear gas with traffic cones to coordinating actions in traceless social-media groups.

Many are students, with a list of demands they will never give up. But they also know when to retreat; when to "be water," in the words of Bruce Lee, and disappear into the night. They could be in central Hong Kong. But increasingly, they are as likely to be in Surabaya or Santiago, Paris or New Delhi, Barcelona or Beirut. Protesters in each of these cities have taken their cue from counterparts in Hong Kong, copying the methods tried and tested on its troubled streets and echoing the ethos of its defiant young activists.

While they have their own agendas, they have learned the art of the protest from Hong Kong, using mobile technology and social media to coordinate their actions without coalescing around a central figure. This has made them harder to stamp out and able, in the kung fu icon's words, to "find ways through the cracks." Attitudes have inspired them, too. Many hold dear the advice now scrawled across many graffitied walls in Hong Kong: "Never surrender."

"The spirit is the same," said Anindya Restuviani, 29, a protester in Indonesia who is "sympathetic to what our friends are doing in Hong Kong."

"We want to fight oligarchy and oppression [and] demand democracy," she said. "Our demands are clear, they just need to be fulfilled."

This is Jakarta, not Hong Kong

In September 2019, thousands of students from across Indonesia headed onto the streets to protest against proposed changes to the criminal code that would have outlawed homosexuality and cohabitation for unmarried couples, introduced a four-year jail term for unauthorized abortions and expanded the blasphemy law to include insults against the president and vice-president. The students had also been angered by the passage of a bill they said would undermine the autonomy of the Corruption Eradication Commission, a body which had arrested hundreds of officials since 2002, by requiring it to hire only civil servants.

The students openly borrowed from Hong Kong. Social media posts written in Bahasa Indonesia illustrated how they could dress and equip themselves like Hong Kong protesters, with masks, gloves, backpacks and snacks. National newspaper *Kompas* published a story on how to cope with being tear-gassed, while news portal Narasi TV carried a video explaining how Hong Kong protesters neutralized tear gas canisters using traffic cones and water. Twitter users shared photos of the unrest with captions reading: "This is Jakarta, not Hong Kong."

In another nod to Hong Kong, the students in Indonesia produced a widely circulated list of demands including that parliamentarians reject the changes to the criminal code and a series of other bills regarding land rights and the mining industry and revoke the new law on the corruption commission.

As in Hong Kong, where one original demand (the withdrawal of the extradition bill) expanded to "Five demands, not one less" (including an investigation into alleged police misconduct), the list in Indonesia soon expanded to include issues beyond the scope of the original protests. Ending militarism in Papua province, stopping forest fires in Kalimantan and Sumatra, and punishing human rights violators made the list. When an independent inquiry into police conduct made the mix after the deaths of three students, comparisons only grew.

Unfulfilled demands

Like Hong Kong protesters, who have so far realized just their first demand, the Indonesian students have had only limited success. While the proposed revisions to the criminal code were put on hold, President Joko Widodo plowed ahead with clipping the wings of the corruption commission, even at a time when experts were voicing concern over the country's international transparency ratings.

And legislators continue to consider the reforms to mining and other laws that protesters had demanded they reject. Critics say this is evidence of Widodo backing down from his pre-office promises of reforming government and putting an end to the corruption and human rights abuses that have characterized the tenures of former leaders like the dictator Suharto, whose overthrow in 1998 ushered in Indonesia's democratic era.

"On Jokowi's watch, Indonesia may have seen unprecedented infrastructure upgrades but the rule of law and civil liberties have been sidelined," said political analyst Johannes Nugroho.

Despite all this, many protesters in Indonesia feel they are getting somewhere. "#ReformasiDikorupsi [the protesters' hashtag] made the president open the door for discussion in the past," said the activist

Restuviani, though she admitted that "unfortunately, none of our demands have been fulfilled yet."

Indonesia to India

Indonesia is not the only country where protesters have borrowed a leaf or two from the Hong Kong book. While India already has the democracy many of the protesters in Hong Kong crave, its controversial Citizenship Amendment Act provoked some of the worst violence the country has seen in more than three decades, leading to scores of deaths.

The act, passed by parliament in December 2019, offers fast-track citizenship to Hindus and other religious minorities from Pakistan, Afghanistan and Bangladesh, but excludes Muslim immigrants. Prime Minister Narendra Modi's Bharatiya Janata Party claims the bill is intended to protect non-Muslim immigrants from Muslim-majority countries who may be facing persecution. But critics say the act makes it easier to prosecute and deport the country's nearly 200 million Muslims if they cannot produce documentary proof of citizenship, and jeopardizes the country's secular identity.

As in Hong Kong, the protests in India have been largely leaderless, driven by civil society groups, students and women. And like Hong Kong's movement, India's has been sustained through the use of social media.

In New Delhi in December, police stormed the campus of Jamia Millia Islamia University, severely beating students. Even as they were being attacked, the students sent videos and voice notes through the WhatsApp messaging app and Twitter. Within hours, hundreds of people had gathered outside police stations and the university gates to support the students.

In another incident, in Hyderabad, when the authorities denied permission to gather, the protesters coordinated on WhatsApp to organize Hong Kong-style flash-mob protests. And when the government banned the internet in certain areas of the country, the protesters began using offline messaging apps Bridgefy and FireChat. Many have said they took inspiration from Hong Kong, where protesters have used similar tactics to spread their messages of solidarity.

Still, there are significant differences to Hong Kong. In India, the legislation opposed by protesters has already been passed, and the only way for it to be repealed is for it to be struck down by the notoriously slow-moving Supreme Court. But, as in Indonesia, limited success is enough to keep some protesters hopeful and eager to plan further action. For now, they say they have at least shown Modi he cannot execute his agenda unchecked.

Chile winds blow

The ripples go beyond Asia. In France, a year before the Hong Kong unrest began, the "yellow vest" movement – sparked by rising fuel prices before spiraling into a broader anti-government protest – brought major districts of Paris to a halt with stand-offs featuring protesters, police, and a whole lot of tear gas. Smaller yellow vest movements sprang up in several Western countries, including Bulgaria, Australia and Canada.

However, instead of that movement catching on further, over the past year leaderless demonstrators taking cues from the Hong Kong protests have sprung up in regions as diverse as Europe, the Middle East and Latin America. In Spain, Catalan protesters blocked Barcelona's airport, much as had happened earlier in Hong Kong, after the Spanish Supreme Court jailed nine separatist leaders in October.

Blocking airports to cause economic suffering is a common strategy of protesters the world over, said Simon Shen, an international relations academic from Chinese University. "But if the goal is to arouse global awareness, the Hong Kong protest successfully caught global headlines," he said, noting that it sparked copycats elsewhere.

At least one such group also tried the same tactic. The British arm of Extinction Rebellion, an environmental pressure group, attempted a protest at London's Heathrow Airport in December 2019. Zion Lights, a spokeswoman, said the group studied Hong Kong protesters' occupation of the airport in August closely and based their plans on it, adding: "We thought it's a brilliant strategy." They made little headway, however, because of tight security and a low turnout.

But in Lebanon, protesters did make an impact. In October 2019, protests sparked by a proposed WhatsApp tax escalated into a nationwide uprising against the ruling elite. Protesters there, too, learned from video tutorials showing how their Hong Kong counterparts fought police with traffic cones, tennis rackets and laser lights. And just as Hong Kong's protests have endured beyond the death of the extradition bill, so have Lebanon's, long after its government abandoned the WhatsApp tax.

It's almost as if "a new bond is forming," according to security analyst Christel Ghandour, who joined the protests in Lebanon. "I never thought I'd be able to relate to anyone from Hong Kong."

Half a world away, in Santiago, Chile, there are similar thoughts. Damaged storefronts are boarded up, the streets plastered with anti-police graffiti. Squint a little and it could almost be Hong Kong.

Protests erupted there in October 2019, initially over hikes in metro fares, but later snowballed into a wider movement against inequality. By December, almost 4 million of the country's 19 million people had taken part in demonstrations, and more than 20 people had been killed.

Even today, allegations of police brutality ensure the cause is winning new recruits. Among them, many will have an eye on Hong Kong.

As the Lebanese biologist turned activist Gino Raidy put it, the reason is simple: "People learn from each other."

View from Singapore

Dewey Sim

In some ways, Hong Kong and Singapore are like twins separated at birth. But their reactions to protests could not be more different.

T hey are often referred to as "twin cities" for their striking similarities. Former British colonies with majority-Chinese populations; global port cities and financial hubs; icons of rapid industrialization; economies that are prosperous and business-minded. But the anti-government protests that swept Hong Kong in 2019 showed just how different the Chinese special administrative region is to Singapore. The scenes that most of the world now associate with the protests in Hong Kong – whether thousands marching peacefully through downtown streets, or masked youths in pitched battles with police – remain unthinkable in its Southeast Asian competitor. What is more, the vast majority of Singaporeans prefer it that way.

In the Lion City, political protests of any type are rare and governed by strict rules such as the Public Order Act, which requires the organizers of any such gathering to obtain a police permit. There is only one site dedicated to free speech – Speakers' Corner in Hong Lim Park – and even there a permit is required if racial or religious issues are on the agenda. Even when rallies do occur, they tend to be tame and poorly supported, rarely drawing crowds upwards of 500. They are not allowed to march from the park to any other place.

Little wonder that Singaporeans were captivated by the images of

❁

hundreds of thousands – 2 million, according to organizers – filling the streets of Hong Kong in June 2019 to protest the government bill that would have paved the way for extraditions to mainland China. That month, a Blackbox Research survey found that more than three in four Singaporeans supported the protesters. But this was before the confrontation with the authorities escalated into increasingly intense clashes between protesters and riot police. As soon as that happened, observers say, the tide of opinion in Singapore turned. Support for the protesters among ordinary Singaporeans dried up; the government advised citizens to defer non-essential travel to Hong Kong; and the country's six government-funded universities pulled the plug on student exchange programs.

Eugene Tan, a law professor at Singapore Management University, said that while early support had been based on "fraternal feelings," the more chaotic the protests became, the less Singaporeans found themselves able to understand the protesters' actions. "Singaporeans would feel there is a time and place for this protest," said Tan. "But when protesters play a cat-and-mouse game with the police, I think there is a sense that this is going overboard." Tan's assessment is borne out by the shift in online public opinion. As the protests became more unruly and disruptive, many Singapore netizens objected to the inconvenience that Hong Kong residents and businesses were facing. Images of black-clad youths setting fire to shopfronts and railway station exits tempered many netizens' sympathy for the protests. Singaporeans might not be free to protest, but at least families did not fear stepping out of their homes during the weekends, some said. "Freedom is that you are safe to go for a walk [anywhere] and at any time of the day without facing danger," one Singaporean commented online. If you asked Singaporeans at the start why their countrymen did not have similar protests, they would probably explain that they were not allowed to. At the peak of the protests, most would have replied that they did not want to.

Different mindsets

Few Singaporeans were able to view the street protests as a legitimate form of political struggle, or grasp why Hongkongers were fighting this battle, experts said. Singaporeans have been socially conditioned against civil disobedience. "There is, in Singapore, an emphasis by the government on harmony, which I would argue Singaporeans have internalized to a large extent," Tan said. Stephan Ortmann, an assistant professor of comparative politics at City University of Hong Kong, who has written about the history of student activism, said Singaporeans had a more "materialist perspective and could not understand Hong Kong's struggle for freedom and democracy or against growing encroachment from the mainland."

The two peoples' different mindsets grew from very "real differences," said Reuben Wong, an associate professor of political science at the National University of Singapore. Wong pointed out that Singaporeans, as citizens of a sovereign republic, could not fully understand Hongkongers' anxieties about the ambiguous and impermanent "one country, two systems." "These are issues that Singapore never has to contend with," Wong said. "We do not have that situation, so Singaporeans do not know how it feels." Unlike Hongkongers, Singaporeans were what he termed "law-and-order people" who had accepted that economic progress had its trade-offs, even if it meant giving up some rights. Ortmann said Singaporeans had been taught from school that it was "best to follow orders," with the government promoting the idea that "any opposition or challenge could pose a risk to the survival of Singapore, and thus, must be avoided." Many Singaporeans were therefore unsympathetic to Hongkongers, and this in turn gave Hongkongers the impression that some in the Lion City were gloating at their misfortune.

The view from the top

Perhaps the clearest demonstration of a culture clash was found in remarks by Singapore's prime minister at a business conference in October 2019, in which he criticized Hong Kong protesters' hallowed "five demands," which included the withdrawal of the extradition legislation and an inquiry into police conduct. Lee Hsien Loong told the forum that these demands were intended to "humiliate" the Hong Kong government and that acceding to them was unlikely to solve the deep-seated issues linked to one country, two systems. He said the protesters did not know what their endgame was, but were continuing to demonstrate as a way of expressing their unhappiness. At a separate event, he warned that the city state would be "finished" were it to suffer Hong Kong-style protests.

Following the remarks, Lee became a social media hero in mainland China, where Singapore was praised for its hardline approach to governance and low tolerance for dissent. Not unexpectedly, his comments did not go down as well in Hong Kong.

Unhealthy rivalry?

Another dimension to the relationship between the two cities during the protests was the suggestion – mostly from outside Singapore – that the city could capitalize on Hong Kong's predicament. Some reports stated that wealthy businessmen were shifting assets from Hong Kong to Singapore; others that expatriate workers were looking to relocate; and that Singapore's international schools stood to benefit.

The Singapore government took pains to play down such suggestions, maintaining that there was no upside to regional instability for a nation so reliant on trade. Its long-held position has been that, as a trading hub and financial center, it can thrive only when the countries around it are prospering. The island's trade minister, Chan Chun Sing, also warned that prolonged disruption to Hong Kong's stability would have a "negative spillover impact" on Singapore and the region, due to the two cities' close trade and investment ties. Or, as Lee put it: "It's about confidence in the region, so that investors can come and not think they are in a dangerous part of the world."

The talk was backed by action. Singapore's central bank, for example, cautioned its wealth managers against aggressively wooing clients with assets in Hong Kong. Bernard Yeung, the former dean of the National University of Singapore's business school and a Hong Kong-born American economist, applauded that move, saying even if Singapore banks had made money out of the situation, this was at least being kept "low-profile," unlike in Taiwan, which had been explicit about its intention to woo Hong Kong-based investment. "Singapore knows regional stability and cooperation is critically important for long-term prosperity," Yeung said. "It plays a win-win game, in which Singapore emphasizes broad-based regional growth."

Still, whatever message the government sends out, many economists see it as inevitable that worried businesspeople and investors will keep an eye on Singapore as a potential safe haven. In August 2019, Singapore-based wealth management firm Abacus Asia said it had been approached by "a few" Hong Kong family offices since the protests erupted, while a source at an American bank said it too had noticed an increase in queries from Hong Kong. Meanwhile, property agents in Singapore reported increasing interest from mainland Chinese buyers who no longer viewed Hong Kong as a safe option and were looking at destinations further afield to park their wealth. Neighboring Malaysia, especially the resort island of Penang, has also seen a similar spike in interest, including from Hong Kong families, not just mainlanders. International schools in Singapore said they noticed growing interest from Hong Kong-based parents attracted by the city state's safety, bilingual education, and a social environment where they did not have to fear xenophobic attacks if they spoke Mandarin.

A generational divide

One less commonly known factor in the contrast between Singapore and Hong Kong is the generational divide. In Hong Kong, the split between young and old is clear enough. About 40 per cent of the protesters arrested in Hong Kong have been students. The city's former chief executive Tung Chee-hwa had repeatedly blamed the city's "youth problems" on the school curriculum, which he described as a failure.

In Singapore too there are generational differences. It is the "slightly older generation" in Singapore that has recoiled at the sight of the Hong Kong protests, according to Woo Jun Jie, adjunct senior research fellow at the Asia Competitiveness Institute at the Lee Kuan Yew School of Public Policy and a former assistant professor at the Education University of Hong Kong. "The middle-aged generation cannot wrap their heads around the protests, how and why it happened, and have the mentality that we must never let that happen to Singapore," he said. "Then you hear among the younger generation that there is some kind of envy over what's happening in Hong Kong." Younger Singaporeans coveted the ability of their Hong Kong counterparts to speak up against the establishment, even if they did not agree with the methods used, such as vandalism and hurling petrol bombs, Woo said.

The generational factor should not be exaggerated, though. Singapore has mechanisms designed to prevent resentment from building up, such as meet-the-people sessions that give its lawmakers reliable feedback on their policies, and the government's culture of communicating to citizens the rationale behind its policies. The public housing program gives Singapore's millennials a far better shot at social mobility than their peers in Hong Kong. Most importantly, general elections mean Singaporeans can voice their discontent at the polls. "In Hong Kong, they do not have this mechanism so if they are unhappy and it appears that policymakers are not listening to them, they see it as having no choice but to protest," said Woo.

As Hong Kong draws closer to 2047, the expiry date of the one country, two systems agreement, Hongkongers were likely to "get nervous" and "act out more," in turn impacting how Singaporeans perceive them, he said. Watching from afar, Singaporeans may grow increasingly alarmed at events in Hong Kong – and appreciative of Singapore's law and order. "I suspect there will be a shift toward the right and a more conservative stance among Singaporeans then," Woo said.

Mindsets in these twin cities could diverge even more.

REFLECTIONS

Cary Huang

What's to stop Hong Kong's 'well water' mixing with Beijing's 'river water'?

In reaction to massive protests in Hong Kong against Beijing's bloody military crackdown on the student-led pro-democracy movement of 1989, Jiang Zemin – the president at the time – quoted the Chinese idiom that "the well water does not mix with the river water." Jiang's point was that Hong Kong should not interfere in the affairs of mainland China and that, likewise, mainland China should not interfere in Hong Kong's.

But since the handover of Hong Kong's sovereignty from Britain to mainland China in 1997 – under the formula of "one country, two systems" – the two types of water have increasingly mixed together as economic integration between the two communities has grown.

The recent controversy in Hong Kong over a bill that would allow for extradition to the Chinese mainland is just the latest such instance of the mixing of the waters, to use Jiang's metaphor, to have occurred over the past two decades.

Under the concept of "one country," it is fair to expect Hong Kong and the mainland to forge a relationship with each other that is much closer than their relationships with foreign nations. They should, therefore, join hands to fulfil international obligations. Extraditions are one such instance of these. Both Hong Kong and the mainland are part of a global anti-crime effort aimed at upholding justice across borders. So given the rise of cross-border crimes – such as corruption, drug trafficking, counterfeiting and cyber offenses – the need for some kind of extradition process between Hong Kong and the mainland is becoming more apparent.

However, it should be remembered that under the concept of "two systems," Hong Kong is also accorded its own legal and economic systems, which are supposed to offer more robust protection of civil liberties than anywhere on the mainland under one-party communist rule.

It sounds rational for Hong Kong's government to argue that a new extradition bill is needed to plug a legal "loophole" and prevent Asia's "world city" from becoming a haven for criminals from the mainland.

Currently, Hong Kong has signed agreements covering extradition with 20 nations and mutual legal assistance with 32 others, covering all major developed free democracies, including all G7 nations. Mainland China has signed extradition treaties with 23 nations, most of which are less developed countries. But China has also recently signed such treaties with Italy, France and Spain, though its extradition buddies do not yet include Australia, Canada, Britain and the US.

Hongkongers should welcome an extradition treaty with the mainland, as long as a "dual criminality" approach is strictly applied. That is to say, that only crimes punishable in both jurisdictions – such as murder and rape – should be classified as extraditable.

The reason that the extradition bill has provoked such unprecedented opposition from all walks of life – from legal professionals to rights activists to foreign investors (and even among pro-Beijing elements) is that it has insufficient safeguards guaranteeing fair trials and the protection of rights.

Under Hong Kong's current extradition treaties with other countries, the government can only finally approve an extradition after it has gone through due legal procedures, including court hearings and appeals. Under the new bill, local courts would consider only whether there was sufficient prima facie evidence to convict the suspect. The new bill also effectively diminishes the role of the Legislative Council in giving oversight of extradition arrangements with the ad hoc arrangements it is trying to cover.

Some powerful business groups have argued that the bill, if passed, would damage Hong Kong's competitiveness, while foreign investors in the city fear Beijing could use it to retaliate against foreign nationals, who work in or travel to Hong Kong.

Many among the more than estimated 1 million people who took to the streets on June 9 to oppose the bill – and the nearly 2 million who did the same on June 16 – will no doubt be worried that passing the extradition bill could pave the way for the government to revive the stalled national security law that was shelved in 2003. That bill, which prompted half a million people to march, could lead to maximum life prison terms for treason, theft of state secrets, sedition, secession and subversion.

In a city often regarded as a territory of workaholics more concerned with economics than politics, the recent demonstrations suggest not only fear and anger, but distrust of the mainland's judicial system. Distrust, too, of the lack of rule of law on the mainland, where arbitrary detentions and poor prison conditions are commonly alleged.

Many are also worried about the lack of legal protection for human rights on the mainland. Beijing has not yet ratified the International Covenant on Civil and Political Rights, despite signing it in 1998. The covenant applies to Hong Kong under the city's Basic Law.

There have been reports that political dissidents, activists, human rights lawyers, independent journalists, and even liberal academics have been subject to arbitrary detention, unfair trial and torture on the mainland, though Beijing denies all accusations of human rights abuses.

That is why Hong Kong's current law regarding fugitives – passed before Hong Kong's sovereignty was transferred from Britain to China – explicitly states that it does not apply to requests for extradition and legal assistance from the mainland government.

The fear being stoked is that the latest bill in its present form could enable Beijing to ask the Hong Kong government to extradite political dissidents, civil rights activists and critics of the Chinese government, for trial in mainland courts. This misunderstanding, borne out of a lack of trust, has been purveyed even though political crimes are excluded from the 37 listed in the bill.

The saga speaks volumes about how difficult it is to accomplish two contradictory goals: achieving sovereign unity while maintaining a constitutional distance between two different political entities. The crux of the matter is the lack of a filter to prevent the well water and the river water from getting mixed up.

— Published on June 30, 2019

Chow Chung-yan

Where the next revolution may take place in Hong Kong

I have no idea when and how this festering unrest in Hong Kong is going to end, but I do have an ominous inkling of where the next bout might begin.

Two months after unprecedented protests took hold of our city, there is still no light at the end of the tunnel. The popular protests against the government's hare-brained extradition bill are getting increasingly violent and out of control. The city's government under Carrie Lam Cheng Yuet-ngor, whose jaw-droppingly bad judgment and inaction have plunged Hong Kong into the biggest crisis in decades, continues to demonstrate an abject lack of leadership and courage.

All the mess is left to the city's police, who have to bear the brunt of public anger. Once considered the pride of Hong Kong and the finest in Asia, the force is now a public enemy in the eyes of many. Trained and equipped to tackle law and order problems, they are now being used to resolve what is essentially a political crisis. Given growing public criticism of police's handling of the protests, the odds are stacked against them for a job many believe to be a fool's errand.

There is no hope for compromise. Lam, after vanishing from public view for two weeks, called a press conference on Monday. She was not there to make a peace offer. Instead, the Hong Kong chief executive warned that the nature of the protests had changed: it was no longer a popular movement against her government or the now-abandoned bill, but a challenge to the principle of "one country, two systems" and national sovereignty.

A day later, Beijing had its own press conference and backed Lam unequivocally. Once the movement is characterized as an attempt to undermine national unity, the gloves are off. Beijing would prefer Hong Kong to sort the matter out by itself, but has made it crystal-clear it will not hesitate to send in the troops if necessary. With the majority of the mainland's public backing the central government on a harder stance against Hong Kong, protesters stand no chance. The only uncertainty is exactly how this whole ugly affair will end.

Let's assume everything happens according to Beijing's plan: the protesters run out of steam and lose public sympathy. Hong Kong police quickly nip the unrest in its bud without ever troubling the military. Ringleaders and the worst offenders are rounded up and put away.

Even if things go this way, it will be something of a pyrrhic victory for the government. Out of the frying pan, we will head directly into the fire. So far, more than 500 people – mostly youngsters – had been arrested by police. By the time this ends, hundreds more will be locked up.

What follows will be an acrimonious and costly legal battle that further divides a polarized society and stretches our judicial system to a breaking point. Already facing a dire shortage of judges, the courtrooms will be totally overrun. Even now, before the first case has been heard, public views are divided.

Forget the principles of fair trial and respect for the court, relentless pressure will be put on judges and juries from both sides. Judges, taking over the thankless job from police, will be cursed and screamed at for every sentence they pass.

Let's say our judges – among the finest in the world – grind their teeth and ride out the storm. And let's assume government prosecutors have all the luck and win every case. So what? Things are only going to get worse from there.

In the past, Hong Kong's prisons and corrective services have seldom needed to handle inmates who broke the law out of political motivations. Now all of a sudden they will have to take in hundreds of them.

Any student of history will tell you there is no better place than a prison to breed a revolution. One thing that separates a messy rebellion from a real revolution is that the latter tends to be much more organized, with clearly formed strategies and goals, and driven by a radicalized ideology and conviction.

There is no better place to foster that kind of brotherhood than having them in an enclosed environment and with a shared sense of injustice. Radical young leaders and lecturers locked up by the government after the Occupy movement will be there to welcome hundreds of angry youngsters, whose fates will become more intertwined with those sharing the same beliefs.

From Joseph Stalin to Abu Musab al-Zarqawi, some of the world's most infamous revolutionaries and radical thinkers cut their teeth in jail.

Let's pray there won't be another one among our angry youth.

Don't get me wrong: I'm not calling for an amnesty. That idea itself is on a very weak legal footing and will open a new can of worms. For one thing, how can you selectively pardon some but not others? And if it is a blanket amnesty, what do you do with those gangsters who attacked innocent citizens in Yuen Long? Setting them free would be unacceptable to the public.

But I do know that locking up the troublemakers and throwing away the key cannot be the final answer. Justice needs to be served. But we also need to change our system to tackle the fundamental issues.

It is wrong to solve a political problem with the force of law and order, and it will be tragic if we just leave the aftermath to our prisons.

The present crisis requires a political solution. Beijing and the Hong Kong government have talked about deep-rooted social and economic issues as the source of this unrest. That's correct, but it is not the whole problem. Political reform must be part of the remedy.

Facing our young people is an "ownership crisis." They feel they have little ownership in almost every aspect of their lives. From owning a piece of physical space, to opportunities to move up the social ladder, to having a say in how their city is run and governed, they just feel hopeless. Giving them hope and empowering them in a way that they truly see themselves as "the master of the house" can prevent them from radicalization.

Hong Kong needs to have genuine debates, based on well-established facts, on how to move things forward. A credible body – call it whatever you want – that can carry out this fact-finding mission is important. It will refocus people's minds and start the slow process of rebuilding consensus.

Addressing the underlying issues – particularly housing – will require bold steps from the government and support from all segments of society. This will require us to change our current political structure and strengthen the mandate of our government, making it more inclusive, representative and with a fairer distribution of social resources.

Beijing has hinted it will be open to ideas and suggestions once the chaos in Hong Kong ends. We can only hope they have the wisdom and will to tackle these issues once normality returns to our city.

— Published on August 9, 2019

Yonden Lhatoo

No silent majority, only a terrified minority

I was stranded in our Causeway Bay office with my late-shift colleagues after putting the paper to bed on a Friday night, thanks to democracy.

The company had arranged emergency hotel accommodation for us, but we all wanted to go home after a particularly hard day at work. Only, there were no vehicles on the streets, and complete chaos had taken over as the freedom fighters on the front lines of the great "revolution of our times" went about "liberating" Hong Kong in an orgy of unfettered violence, vandalism and anarchy.

For hours after the government invoked a draconian colonial-era law to announce a midnight ban on the wearing of face masks at all protests – and then did absolutely nothing to enforce it – unhinged youngsters in, yes, masks, went on a rampage across the city, trashing and burning MTR stations, shops, bank outlets and other public or private property.

Anyone who got in their way was beaten to a pulp, and in one notably shocking incident, a rioter grabbed a handgun dropped by a lone plainclothes policeman as they attempted to lynch him and burn him with petrol bombs. The officer managed to snatch the gun back and prevent a real tragedy.

Rioters were allowed to run amok with impunity for hours in my own neighborhood of Hung Hom. A colleague on the ground, who watched them exercise to extremes the very freedoms they claim to have been deprived of, said there was not a single police officer in sight the entire time as they yelled, "Where are you? We are breaking the law! Come and arrest us if you dare!"

They left, disappointed, after vandalizing and firebombing shuttered MTR station entrances, declaring, "It's not worth it, nobody's coming."

On Saturday morning, Hongkongers woke up to find the entire MTR network – their most important means of public transport – closed for the first time in the city's history by popular demand. And by that, I mean the vast majority of the population seems fine with what happened the night before.

Clearly, the fact that our already overwhelmed and much-maligned police force stood by and pretty much let the rioters dance around their bonfires had much to do with public sentiment and satisfaction. If the riot squad had been deployed to stop the anarchy, hysterical residents in pyjamas and flip flops would have been out on the streets, screaming obscenities at them and demanding they leave.

That's not quite true, you say? Only a minority supports protest violence in this city of nearly 7.5 million, and the silent majority is against it? It's starting to sound like bovine feces to me, the existence of these mysterious millions who apparently disapprove of all the nonsense going on in the name of fighting for democracy, but are not going to say or do anything about it.

You can literally count on your fingers the number of people with the courage to say anything aloud nowadays against the destruction of our city. The reality is, more like, there are thousands of youngsters on the streets who have tasted blood and become intoxicated by the success of mob rule.

They are supported by a massive demographic that includes lawyers, teachers, doctors and other professionals who constantly gloss over and find excuses for all the outrageous excesses on the front lines of the anti-government movement.

Well, you know what, the people have spoken and the people have got what they want. The MTR has been so badly crippled that it can't get back on track.

Next, it's the turn of the police force, which the people want defeated and disbanded. And that's coming soon, don't worry, because you can already see discipline among frontline officers unraveling as they reach the end of their tether.

What comes after that? Ask the people, they're singing cheerfully in shopping centers – in masks.

— Published on October 5, 2019

Tammy Tam

The furthest distance between 'one country' and 'two systems'

W hat can a slip of the tongue mean? A reasonable guess is that it comes from something weighing deep in someone's mind.

That might have been the case with President Xi Jinping while he was delivering his speech in Macau last week after officiating at the inauguration ceremony of its next administration. At one point, he said the words "Hong Kong" instead of "Macau" as he was summarizing the successful example set by the small city turned booming casino hub in its 20 years' practice of the "one country, two systems" governing principle.

But President Xi surely had an important message for Hong Kong, including the four expectations he put forward to Macau, all applicable to our Chief Executive Carrie Lam Cheng Yuet-ngor as well: to keep abreast of the times to elevate governance; to be innovative for sustainable economic development; to improve people's well-being; and to be inclusive and to promote social harmony and stability.

And it was Xi's emphasis on Beijing's determination to stick to the special governing formula for the two special administrative regions that touched on the crux of the issue in Hong Kong.

Xi's reiteration dismissed earlier doubts and suggestions that Beijing might consider giving up the one country, two systems governing policy if the situation in Hong Kong kept deteriorating – if not soon, then at least by 2047 when its 50 years' duration guaranteed by the Basic Law expires.

With Xi's firm "no" in answer to that line of thinking, it is more a matter of how to narrow the widening gap between Beijing and Hong Kong on what exactly "one country" is and what "two systems" should be.

By default, this unique formula is bound to cause conflict. Also, understandably, when Chinese paramount leader Deng Xiaoping came up with this innovative idea decades ago, neither he nor Beijing could foresee all the future complexities.

The current inconvenient reality speaks volumes: Hong Kong seems to have moved further away from, rather than drawn closer to, mainland China because of different interpretations of the relation between "one country" and "two systems."

The unprecedented political divide stemming from more than six months of protests further amplifies the deep-rooted problem: protesters and their supporters believe they are fighting for democracy, a "revolution of our times" as they put it, but the pro-establishment camp and Beijing in particular see the social unrest as a threat to national security and challenge to "one country."

The US factor in this saga has further complicated the situation. This well explains why Xi warned in Macau that there was "no need for any foreign force to dictate things to us" regarding how to handle the two special administrative regions' internal affairs.

The next day Xi expressed China's deep concerns over Washington's attitude toward Hong Kong, Taiwan, Xinjiang and Tibet to US President Donald Trump when the two leaders discussed trade and other issues over the phone.

Here's the irony: when one country, two systems is hailed by all as the best for Hong Kong, and for the country, the chance of forging a wider consensus on a mutually agreeable definition of this concept is getting slimmer under the political confrontation currently intensifying in this city.

To borrow from a well-cited poem: "The furthest distance in the world is not between life and death, but that between fish and bird, one is in the sky, another is in the sea." But "one country" and "two systems" are not and should not be like fish and bird, unable to meet.

A meeting point between the two sides must be identified through rebuilding mutual trust between Hong Kong and Beijing. Can Lam and her government take up this tough task to get the city back on the right track as we enter a new year fraught with tension and uncertainty?

— Published on December 22, 2019

Cliff Buddle

Mask ban an ineffective stick. Where's the carrot for moderate protesters?

The deepening political divisions in Hong Kong leave little room for a consensus on anything. But one point which both sides can agree on, after four months of anti-government protests and escalating violence, is the need for the government to act. Something has to be done.

Chief Executive Carrie Lam Cheng Yuet-ngor has faced growing pressure from her pro-establishment allies to take a tougher line and to invoke colonial-era emergency laws in a bid to end the violence. Democrats and protesters, meanwhile, have called on her to meet their demands.

The push for a crackdown no doubt intensified during Lam's visit to Beijing to mark the 70th anniversary of the People's Republic of China. As she celebrated, Hong Kong burned. Three days later, the Emergency Regulations Ordinance was invoked for the first time since the 1967 riots. The dusting off of this outdated and draconian legislation, passed in one day in 1922, is a dangerous step.

Despite assurances from the government that it will be used cautiously, there are understandable concerns that further measures will follow now that it has been triggered.

The ordinance, first used by the colonial authorities to crack down on a seamen's strike, empowers the chief executive to make "any regulations whatsoever" which she may consider desirable in the public interest. This can be done on "any occasion" the chief executive considers to be of emergency or public danger. The scope is breathtaking.

It is difficult to see how it can be reconciled with the human rights protection provided by the Basic Law and Bill of Rights.

There were calls in the 1990s for the law to be repealed by the colonial administration. Even more draconian regulations made under it in the 1940s and 1960s were removed. But the ordinance, described by democrat Martin Lee Chu-ming as a landmine, was left in place. One columnist wrote in the *South China Morning Post* at the time that this was done as a "futile conciliatory gesture toward Beijing."

Almost no other law "symbolizes quite so trenchantly as the Emergency Regulations Ordinance the underlying colonial nature of much of Hong Kong's legislation," said a report by the Hong Kong Journalists Association and the human rights organization, Article 19, in 1993. It called for an urgent review of the legislation.

The first regulation to be imposed under the legislation bans the wearing of masks during protests. This law achieves little beyond allowing Lam to show her political allies and Beijing that she is doing something. The wearing of masks to hide a person's identity or to protect them from police's tear gas and pepper spray (or both) has been a feature of the protests. But those taking part in recent demonstrations are breaking the law anyway.

Police have not given permission for these protests to take place. It is not surprising, therefore, that all those charged under the new anti-mask law so far have also been accused of either unlawful assembly or rioting. The idea that people who are prepared to join unlawful protests, carry offensive weapons, vandalize MTR stations or throw petrol bombs would be deterred by a law against wearing a mask is absurd. What will be next? A ban on umbrellas?

A government source told the *Post* that officials knew the mask ban would not stop hard-core protesters. It was hoped, instead, that their more moderate supporters, described as the outer layers of the onion, would be deterred. But this reasoning is flawed. The law is being broken anyway. If the number of protesters in the streets has dropped in recent days, it is more likely to be because of the growing scale of the violence and the risk of becoming a victim of the increasing force used by police.

The mask ban, which can lead to a HK$25,000 (US$3,200) fine or jail for a year, has caused confusion. The government has sought to limit its scope, no doubt aware that legal challenges would swiftly be brought. Secretary for Justice Teresa Cheng Yeuk-wah even mentioned the tests used by the courts to determine whether restrictions on rights are permissible at the press conference announcing the new law.

It is a defense for a person to wear a mask at a protest if they have a "reasonable excuse." Those who need to wear a mask for their safety while working are regarded as having a reasonable excuse. This is of great importance to journalists who need to wear masks to protect themselves while covering the protests.

The problem, as the Hong Kong Journalists Association has pointed out, is that it is only a defense. There is nothing to stop police from sweeping up everyone wearing a mask, including journalists, leaving them to raise their "reasonable excuses" later. Perhaps this is what Senior Superintendent Ng Cheuk-hang meant when he said on Tuesday that journalists are not exempted under the law (despite the secretary for security appearing to say otherwise).

Police must respect the media's right to cover the protests and the need for them to wear masks. One journalist, according to her lawyer, has already lost her sight in one eye after being hit by a rubber bullet. This was despite her having worn goggles. There are reports of others being challenged about wearing a mask or having their mask removed. The new law must not become an excuse for police to obstruct the media's operations in violation of the Basic Law's protection for freedom of the press.

Further use of the emergency law has not been ruled out. There have been calls for a curfew to be imposed. That can already be done under the Public Order Ordinance. It is not clear how this could work in Hong Kong or what it would achieve.

One likely – and worrying – consequence of a curfew is that the only people affected would be the media. Police and protesters would be on the streets anyway. Would there be an exemption for the media? The Public Order Ordinance does not provide one. Or would police and protesters be left to fight it out, without media scrutiny?

The use of the emergency law raises the stakes. It is no surprise that it has sparked further protests, escalating violence and multiple arrests. There is an urgent need to stop the descent into madness and to restore the values for which Hong Kong is well known: peace, order, respect for people with differing opinions and basic human decency. It appears that some of the protesters are reflecting on the events of recent days and urging a more restrained approach.

The government needs to act. But locking everyone up is not the answer. There is a need to de-escalate and defuse. The mask ban is the stick. But where is the carrot? If the government really wants to win over moderate supporters of the protests, it must make concessions, ensure police are the subject of an impartial investigation, and truly engage with the public.

Even the colonial government, after introducing the emergency law in 1922, made concessions to the strikers.

— Published on October 10, 2019

Postscript: The mask ban was deemed unconstitutional by a lower court after it was challenged in a judicial review by 25 pan-democrats.

The government appealed against the ruling, and on April 9, 2020, the Court of Appeal ruled that, while it was constitutional for officials to ban the wearing of masks at unauthorized or illegal assemblies, the same was not true for legal demonstrations. Language in the ban granting police the authority to physically remove masks was also unconstitutional, it said.

Wang Xiangwei

Forget Lam's extradition U-turn, Xi's channeling of Mao shows he's about to get tough on Hong Kong

Too little, too late. That has been the prevailing reaction from both the protesters and pro-government lawmakers after Hong Kong's embattled leader, Chief Executive Carrie Lam Cheng Yuet-ngor, made a sudden about-face on Wednesday, announcing that she would formally withdraw the extradition bill which sparked the city's worst political crisis in decades.

Indeed, her withdrawal offer would have had a much bigger impact had it come immediately after the protests turned violent in mid-June. But after nearly three months of violent demonstrations, protesters appear to have moved beyond the extradition bill and have since vowed to press on with demonstrations until the rest of their demands are met.

Lam seems to suggest that her peace offering, which also includes beefing up the police watchdog with more independent members to look into the force's handling of protests, and engaging experts and academics to study and find solutions to deep-rooted economic and social problems, should be enough as a first step in calming the unrest.

But that will probably prove to be wishful thinking.

Interestingly, Lam's abrupt turn came two days after the leaked audio recording of her remarks in a closed-door meeting became the talk of the town, prompting all sorts of speculation about her intentions and the implications of her speech.

In the recording, Lam can be heard telling a group of businessmen that she blamed herself for igniting Hong Kong's worst political crisis in decades and saying she would quit if she had the choice, explaining that she has to serve two masters at the same time – the people of Hong Kong and Beijing.

She clearly indicates on the tape that her hands are tied and that political room for maneuvering is "very, very, very limited."

So her announcement on Wednesday suggested she must have sought prior permission from the leadership in Beijing, which has repeatedly said the protests were a threat to national sovereignty. Until this point, Chinese state media reports had long suggested that there was little room for compromise.

Apparently, the U-turn is a very sudden – and risky – decision. There had been no sign nor murmurs of the impending announcement even the day before.

On Wednesday, Hong Kong's main Hang Seng share index rose nearly 4 per cent, an indication that the business community and investors shared Lam's hopes that her about-face would weaken support for the protests.

But their optimism may well be short-lived. Lam's concession could embolden protesters to further escalate their actions in an effort to have their remaining demands fulfilled. The other four of their five demands are: a commission of inquiry to investigate police's handling of the protests; amnesty for those arrested; an end to the government's characterization of the protest as "riots"; and restarting the city's electoral reform process.

Lam said on Wednesday her government would not budge on the remaining demands, but, just three months ago, she had said she would not accede to any of the five demands.

Meanwhile, her U-turn has dismayed and angered pro-government lawmakers and supporters who complained they were not consulted in advance and said their credibility had been dented because of their previous open support for Lam to resist all the protesters' demands.

An even more interesting question is: why did Beijing suddenly agree to allow Lam to make the symbolic move of formally withdrawing the bill after officials and the state media had been taking an increasingly hardline view toward the protesters over the past month, condemning them as "rioters" and warning signs of "terrorism"?

Indeed, many Chinese officials and observers involved in Hong Kong affairs were reportedly caught off guard and were not aware of Lam's decision until a few hours before she made the announcement on television.

Even on Tuesday, when the Hong Kong and Macau Affairs Office in Beijing gave a press conference, the two spokespeople did not give any hint of a policy change, continuing to urge all government branches and social institutions to fight violent criminals and take ending the violence as the "most pressing task."

Some observers have speculated that Beijing's last-minute change of mind could have something to do with the elaborate celebrations, including a massive military parade, planned for the National Day on October 1.

As the carefully planned celebrations are aimed at highlighting Chinese President Xi Jinping's leadership, officials are probably amenable to Lam's attempt to dial down the protests.

It can hardly be a coincidence that on Thursday the Chinese state media reported that Chinese Vice-Premier Liu He and other Chinese officials had spoken over the phone with US Trade Representative Robert Lighthizer and Treasury Secretary Steven Mnuchin.

They have agreed to resume trade talks in Washington in early October. The resumption will most likely ensure that there will not be any immediate bad news about the trade talks from Washington to mar the National Day celebrations.

Even so, officials in Beijing could well be disappointed as Hong Kong protesters are most likely to come out in force in the run-up to, and on, National Day to press their remaining demands.

But if a televised speech by Xi on Tuesday is any guide, their struggle to achieve those goals will be much harder. In that speech, Xi listed Hong Kong, along with Macau and Taiwan, as one of the challenges threatening the rule of the Communist Party. Excerpts of the speech dominated China Central Television's nightly prime-time news slots. Xi gave the speech to a group of young and middle-aged senior officials enrolled in a training course at the central party school. He called for "constant struggles" against myriad challenges and risks in the areas of economics, politics, culture, society, ecology, national defense and the armed forces, diplomacy, party building and, notably, Hong Kong, Macau and Taiwan.

In the nine-minute speech, Xi used the word "struggle" nearly 60 times, eerily evoking an era that many had assumed was long gone. "Struggle" was the buzzword used so often in the speeches of Mao Zedong and features in one of his most famous, and often quoted, sayings: "I feel boundless joy in struggling with heaven, earth and people."

If nothing else, Xi's speech signals a toughening stance toward Hong Kong despite the decision to withdraw the extradition bill.

— Published on September 7, 2019

Yonden Lhatoo

Is it safe to be in Hong Kong? Against all odds, the answer is still a strange 'yes'

I must say it hurts to visit Singapore if your heart is in Hong Kong.

I was there for a couple of days to attend an event that was originally supposed to be held in Hong Kong, but the organizer, a major multinational, changed the venue because of all the protest chaos that has pretty much destroyed our city's reputation.

The contrast with Hong Kong was so acute, so in-your-face, that I couldn't help feeling downright envious and borderline resentful about Singapore and its shiny, happy people. All those law-abiding folk skipping along spick and span streets, business booming in every shopping center and street corner, uninterrupted commerce in gleaming office towers.

I found it warm and welcoming there, and, above all, so peaceful.

After an ample dose of that, our battle-scarred city looks more bent and broken than ever. And angry, always angry.

I'm back now in the middle of mass hysteria and scenes of anarchy as unhinged protesters attack the city's railway facilities over wild rumors online that police "executed" half a dozen citizens in an MTR station and got rid of their bodies in secret. Really!

Just take a step back and process that – as utterly insane as it sounds, people actually believe this, encouraged by certain scurrilous activist-journalists spreading the word. It's the twilight zone out here.

"Is it even safe any more in Hong Kong? Have you thought about leaving?" I get asked frequently by friends and family members alarmed by the daily news barrage of rampaging mobs throwing petrol bombs and vandalizing public property, brawls on trains and buses, fires burning on blocked roads and police brutalizing masked youngsters.

Without glossing over the nihilistic violence or playing down the social and economic carnage, I'm contemplating a standardized answer to questions about how safe it is in Hong Kong in the form of a video clip that a colleague came back with after covering a recent riot.

It shows a middle-aged Caucasian man in Elvis impersonator-style clothes casually negotiating a road blockade while anti-government protesters are limbering up for another showdown with riot police. He cuts quite a quixotic figure, in his glittering silver pants and cowboy boots, climbing over barricades and passing unmolested through the mob of black-clad protesters before disappearing toward the direction of some bars and restaurants.

And that, I must say, is how safe Hong Kong is – in its own, curious, unique way – for the average person on the streets. For all the ferocity of their attacks on police, even hard-core protesters will generally leave "civilians" – especially tourists – alone unless you get into a fight with them over finding your way blocked or your peace disturbed. You'll even see some of them hurriedly helping a frail granny to safety before all hell breaks loose.

Similarly, police issue multiple warnings before they fire tear gas or charge at protesters, mostly for the benefit of rubbernecking spectators who can be injured amid the chaos of an anti-riot operation. The number of curious bystanders and passers-by watching these stand-offs and showdowns from pavements and footbridges is, in itself, testament to how seemingly apocalyptic television footage does not necessarily reflect the reality on the ground.

Of course, it can get tricky and dangerous for innocent commuters when police storm into MTR stations to chase after protesters who take off their masks and change out of their signature black clothing to mingle with the crowds.

And yes, there are no guarantees when it comes to traffic and travel disruptions, which can erupt at any moment, anywhere, leaving you stranded.

"But Hong Kong has something else – it has a soul," a Singaporean friend pointed out when I spoke of the painful contrast with the Lion City.

A soul worth saving. And a heart, too. That's why, at the end of the day, despite everything, against all odds, I'll say Hong Kong is still, strangely, safe.

— *Published on September 7, 2019*

Chow Chung-yan

Hong Kong risks being condemned to its own circle of hell

The most unforgettable scene in Dante Alighieri's *Inferno*, which is also its biggest mystery, revolves around the frozen Lucifer.

In the deepest circle of hell, the prince of darkness is perpetually stuck in a lake of ice. The most powerful agent of evil desperately flaps his wings trying to break free, creating a colossal polar vortex around him.

The ironic thing is that the more he struggles, the colder hell becomes, entrapping the three-faced devil in a pillar of ice for eternity.

When I first studied the Italian poet's *Divine Comedy* at the University of Hong Kong some 20 years ago, I was an undernourished bookworm who knew next to nothing about real life outside.

The scene involving the frozen Lucifer is both fascinating and intriguing. Why did Dante, the most learned man of his age, depict the ninth circle of hell as a frozen world, when all his contemporaries painted it as a place of fire and smoke? Why was punishment for Lucifer permanent entombment in a pillar of ice? These were the questions I tried to answer back then.

Only many years later, as I watch our beloved Hong Kong locked in a death spiral from which we cannot break free, when what were once the world's most peaceful streets are regularly filled with fire and tear gas, and family and friends are divided and turning on each other, have I finally come to understand what Dante meant emotionally.

When the Italian poet imagined hell from the fortress walls of Les Baux-de-Provence in France, what occupied his mind was not the deepest bowels of the Earth, but his home city of Florence hundreds of kilometers away.

Dante, who served as one of six priors governing the city, was later sent into exile amid bitter political turmoil. Florence, the world's financial center in the 14th century, was then gripped by social strife and unrest as Hong Kong is today.

In his imagined version of hell, he assigned each of the nine circles to a particular sin and its related special form of punishment. It is partly based on the work of earlier writers such as Eratosthenes and Ptolemy, but to a great extent it reflects Dante's most inner feelings and his reflections on life.

To most learned people in medieval times, the center of the cosmos was the "unmoved mover," which, according to Aristotle, is the primary cause of all motion in the universe.

The unmoved mover – modern scientific-minded readers should think of the Foucault pendulum, and the religious of God – is in itself perfect, indivisible and omnipresent. It moves the world through the force of love, compassion and understanding. Its opposite, Dante argues, is a corrupted version.

The primary cause of Lucifer's fall from grace is his pride – blinded by hubris, the devil cannot see things from the point of view of others. He is so full of himself that he lacks the ability to feel or understand those around him, and is the epitome of apathy and selfishness.

The way he moves the world is through hatred and anger. Owing to his inability to understand others and feel compassion, he is doomed to remain in this form, never able to evolve.

As a result, Dante makes his Lucifer a gigantic, powerful but immobile figure, who sends cold waves throughout the ninth circle of hell that is forever frozen in hatred.

While I cannot condemn a single party for the problems we face today, when I look around I see the work of hatred, narrow-mindedness and a total lack of compassion.

Tragedy often occurs when two sides believe they are pursuing something noble and worthwhile, but refuse to reflect and look at things from the other's perspective.

In the end, we all live in the hell we create for ourselves. And if we cannot break the mold, we are condemned to this deepest circle of hell forever.

— Published on November 2, 2019

Tammy Tam

A new chain of command

A clear chain of command and good personal rapport among the team are key to any efficient management and governance – it is that simple.

The latest earthquake in Beijing's supervisory mechanism for Hong Kong affairs is shocking, yet telling enough – the reshuffle comes amid a national crisis in combating the coronavirus outbreak, a public health emergency that President Xi Jinping now wants addressed as part of national security interests.

Xia Baolong, the equivalent of a state leader as vice-chairman of China's top political advisory body, the Chinese People's Political Consultative Conference, was appointed as head of the Hong Kong and Macau Affairs Office (HKMAO) under the State Council on Thursday.

Xia's predecessor Zhang Xiaoming, who has spent his whole career handling Hong Kong and Macau, became the number two.

This was unavoidably seen as a demotion for Zhang, but his two counterparts with the same ministerial rank, Luo Huining and Fu Ziying – Beijing's top envoys to Hong Kong and Macau, respectively – were also made Xia's deputies under the new line-up. It means the Beijing-based HKMAO is now empowered to lead the two frontline liaison offices, clearing long-time confusion as to who is in charge.

While the hierarchy within Beijing's own system is clearer, things are completely different if the central government wants to hold the local Hong Kong administration more accountable.

Hong Kong has in recent years developed into quite a headache for China's top leadership, especially now with an unpopular government led by Chief Executive Carrie Lam Cheng Yuet-ngor.

After the Occupy movement of 2014 against Beijing's stringent restrictions on the city's electoral arrangements, last year's anti-government protests, triggered by the now-shelved extradition bill, are still going on, although on a smaller scale amid the spread of the coronavirus epidemic.

Lam's much criticized handling of the new health emergency has not gone unnoticed in Beijing. The fight against the disease officially known as Covid-19 has been dubbed a "people's war" and is now at the top of Xi's agenda.

It is also a political battle for Lam for sure, when she is not only under fire from the public, but also faces criticism from the mainland side for failing to ensure Hongkongers adequate prevention and protection supplies, especially masks. She earlier turned to Beijing for help.

And herein lies a long-standing structural issue in Hong Kong-mainland relations.

According to mainland political protocol, the chief executives of Hong Kong and Macau are ranked half a grade higher than their provincial counterparts and all ministers. Such a design allows the two special administrative regions' leaders more leeway in seeking cooperation from other local authorities on the mainland, with the HKMAO used to playing a coordinating role.

Without smooth personal interaction, however, this could lead to a somewhat awkward relationship between the two chief executives and the ministerial-level liaison offices and the HKMAO.

Lam has apparently tried to do some maneuvering in this regard. When the liaison office in recent years was accused of meddling in the city's affairs and manipulating the pro-establishment camp's strategies in local elections, she openly vowed not to enlist the help of the office in canvassing support for herself from the camp. Her relations with Zhang, when he was heading the HKMAO, were known to be businesslike.

Now, with a trusted protégé of President Xi leading an elevated HKMAO, the chemistry between the resolute and more senior Xia and Lam is a test for her in maintaining Beijing's faith.

But it is also a test for Beijing in its future implementation of "one country, two systems," the special governing formula that promises the city a high degree of autonomy. After all, handling Hong Kong, including the embattled Lam and her administration, is not the same as governing any mainland province.

— Published on February 16, 2020

SCANNING THE HORIZON

"HONG KONG WAS HANDED OVER TO CHINA WITH A CRACK THAT RAN THROUGH ITS ENTIRE CRYSTAL."

George Yeo, formerly Hong Kong-based business leader and Singapore foreign minister

A pause for breath

Zuraidah Ibrahim and Jeffie Lam

The cafe is tucked away on the third floor of a spindly building on a quiet side street in Causeway Bay. At the under-lit entrance is a little blackboard indicating that it is a "yellow" establishment. It bears a chalk drawing of an umbrella, the symbol of the protest movement that has been ebbing and flowing through Hong Kong since 2014. You would miss it if you weren't looking for it, but to the cafe's patrons, it is like a big welcome sign of shelter and refuge in a city that has grown more polarized and intolerant.

Inside, "Fullstop" is already seated at a table. She is polite and articulate, and it is difficult to picture her in her other life as a frontline protester.

She was charged for unlawful assembly after being caught setting up roadblocks in Whampoa late one evening in August 2019. Due to the coronavirus pandemic, she cannot go to school these days. But she does go to court each time she finds out a protester is being charged or tried.

"I want democracy for Hong Kong because this is our right. I do not trust the Communists at all," she says. Her parents run businesses in leather and construction materials on the mainland but that does not diminish her hostility toward Beijing. Her family connection to the mainland just gives her a clearer picture of the evil things Communists do, she says.

It can feel disconcerting to hear her gloss over the extreme violence on the front lines of the protest movement. She makes no apology for petrol bomb attacks on police officers, wanton mob mayhem on the streets and the destruction of public property, shrugging it off as a legitimate means to an end, "because they taught us that peaceful protests never work."

But Fullstop – this is her name on Telegram – is not fixated on the idea of independence. She believes if the protesters' demand for universal suffrage is implemented, she would stand down. "But it's not going to happen," she says, shaking her head.

"Cheeseball Roe," another protester who is biding her time, wants Hong Kong to be free from the mainland. She sees the current system as unjust and favoring only the wealthy and powerful. Native-born Hongkongers like her no longer have a place in the city, she says.

Injured by beanbag rounds and teargas canisters smashing into her knees and shins, the 29-year-old poster designer is trying to regain her fitness to ready herself for the next round. She trains three to five times a week.

Standing at barely 1.5 meters tall, she does weights and goes for runs, including up and down five floors of her public housing block in the New Territories. Cheeseball – another Telegram name – avoids the bottom flight of stairs, though, so that observers do not spot her and get suspicious. "One has to be fit for the protests," she says. "It is very hard work."

Then there are the *wo lei fei*, the peaceful protesters. One of them, Florence*, 21, a nursing undergraduate, has been involved in the protests from the start and was at almost all the gatherings, legal and illegal.

She, Cheeseball Roe and Fullstop may differ in the specifics of their demands and their methods, but what binds them is their sense of hopelessness in the face of a system that they are convinced has failed them.

Florence once had her sights on leaving Hong Kong. She says she did not want to have to fight with new mainland arrivals for jobs and living space. "But the anti-bill movement woke me up, and I am very determined to stay here to protect my home city," she says.

Her involvement in the movement, though peaceful, has taken its toll at home. Whenever she is not in their apartment, her mother worries. "Every time I cannot see the helmet at home, I get scared," says Sally*, an executive secretary. Daughter and father now hardly talk about the protests because he does not support the movement. "They seldom discuss this topic now in order to avoid arguments," Sally says.

"I was sad to learn that some young people were not allowed to go home because they had conflicts with their parents. The two generations communicated badly. I pray love is still in everyone's heart."

She wishes the government would relent on some of the protesters' five demands, which are the withdrawal of the extradition bill, not calling the protests a riot, offering amnesty to those arrested, holding an independent probe into police actions and implementing universal suffrage. Sally blames the government for letting things slide to such an extent that police and protesters are at war. "I was most upset to see young people hate police, and officers hate protesters."

Not about a bill

Like Sally, other Hongkongers across the political spectrum have been longing for a political solution to the unrest, whose mounting cost to their city's youth and its economy appears increasingly irrecoverable with each passing month. The government, though, has made the cessation of violence a precondition for any dialogue but even then has stopped talking about this olive branch. In any case, it will not be able to concede to every one of the protesters' demands.

The government's extradition bill, the original trigger for the 2019 protests, was probably the easiest of the concessions to make. The fact that its withdrawal made no difference showed that the tumult was about something much bigger.

"The extradition bill was not the cause of what happened last year," says George Yeo, senior adviser to Hong Kong-based Kerry Logistics and the Kuok Group, and former Singapore foreign minister. "What the bill did was to unleash forces in Hong Kong society which had been building up over many years."

Its return to Chinese rule after being a possession of the British Empire for more than 150 years turned Hong Kong into a Special Administrative Region of the People's Republic of China. It is beyond dispute that the "one country, two systems" formula has not been able to guarantee a trouble-free relationship between the two.

The bitter, and now violent, disagreement is over whom to blame: Beijing for breaching the "two systems" half of the equation, or Hongkongers for betraying their "one country." The Basic Law or mini-constitution was supposed to turn the one country, two systems principle into a clear operating framework, but that too has been the subject of dispute.

It was not always so. In the run-up to the handover, even a democrat like Martin Lee Chu-ming was among the 23 Hongkongers serving on the 59-member Basic Law Drafting Committee. At the time, Lee says there was mutual trust between Hong Kong people and the Chinese government.

"We put all our hopes in the Basic Law and hoped it would safeguard everything over the next 50 years," Lee acknowledged in a media interview in 2020. But those hopes were dashed in 2003, when the Hong Kong government sought to implement a national security law that led to half a million people taking to the streets in protest, says Lee, who has since spent the rest of his political career resisting what he sees as a steady erosion of the "high degree of autonomy" promised to Hong Kong in the Basic Law.

The sense of despondency and betrayal is shared by the democrats. "I have no difficulties in concluding that one country, two systems has actually failed," says former opposition lawmaker Alan Leong Kah-kit. "It failed because the Chinese Communist Party is not prepared to honor and respect the promises they made and enshrined in the Basic Law."

For the system to work, Leong argues, Beijing needs to exercise self-restraint on its omnipotent power. He accuses the central government of being selective in interpreting the Basic Law in its favor, while at the same time ignoring what the mini-constitution says about freedoms and rights.

While the democrats see themselves as defending what is rightfully Hong Kong's, Beijing sees nothing short of an attempted coup. Prominent mainland expert on the Basic Law, Rao Geping summed up this perspective in an April 2020 issue of *Bauhinia Magazine* to mark the 30th anniversary of the promulgation of the mini-constitution: "The crux of all political squabbles since the handover is about the scramble for the governing power. The extremists advocating 'Hong Kong independence' aim to grab the governing power and seek separation from China."

The intractable disputes over the city's laws and education are perhaps inevitable, as part of the arc of development of the strategically ambiguous one country, two systems principle. The SAR, now 22 years old, is a young adult still trying to figure out who it is. Most post-colonial entities are much older; only four states have become independent since 1997 and each is facing its own set of growing pains.

And Hong Kong's postcolonial experience is of course far more complex since it did not and was not meant to transition to independence. There is no tried and tested roadmap for this particular journey. And so life proceeds in a mire of contradictions. On the one hand, Hongkongers still enjoy immense personal and civic freedoms. They have a rambunctious media, a vocal opposition, and a political culture that instinctively and stubbornly resists being hemmed in.

Yet, on another level they have little control over their city's destiny. Their government policies are overseen by an authoritarian communist administration that often seems unable to comprehend, let alone appreciate, Hongkongers' unique character. If anything, it is a wonder that the enterprise has stayed the course, with economic and political power tilting toward the mainland, but with Hong Kong still preserving its distinct way of life.

The one country, two systems experiment has been conducted in laboratory conditions that have not always been favorable. In 1997, the year of the handover, Hong Kong was hit by the Asian financial crisis. In 2003, it was buffeted by the precursor to Covid-19, Sars. Then came the global financial crisis of 2008 and the mainland stock market crash of 2015. Through most of these shocks, China provided the economic elixir. Hong Kong was able to bounce back because of its unique role as a conduit for funds and professional talent for a China transitioning into an upper-middle-income country and the world's second-largest economy.

Hong Kong's culture of protest was the clearest sign that, regardless of its economic integration and its place within China's borders, the SAR and the PRC were not on the same page politically.

In 2003, after the public fury, the proposed national security legislation was abandoned. The episode brought down the security minister who helmed it, Regina Ip Lau Suk-yee, and probably also the city's first chief executive Tung Chee-hwa, who stepped down before completing his second term ostensibly for reasons of ill-health.

In 2012, mass protests over 10 days forced the government to withdraw its proposal for a new national education syllabus meant to instill patriotism in the young but dismissed by opponents as a "brainwashing" program. The students who took part included Joshua Wong Chi-fung, Agnes Chow Ting, and others who would emerge as leaders of the Occupy protests two years later.

In 2014, the 79-day sit-in along major thoroughfares of the city's business districts was in opposition to the government's proposal for a new election system within a restrictive framework set by Beijing. Although the plan would, for the first time, allow direct elections for the chief executive, a vetting process would screen out candidates frowned upon by the central government. The demand for genuine universal suffrage was not going to be acceded to by Beijing. The Occupy protests petered out after the public lost its patience. The political impasse meant that even the promised direct elections were off the table.

Activists disillusioned by the failure of Occupy began pushing for separation from China. From 2015, the movement's radical fringe abandoned its non-violent approach and vented their anger against mainland tourists and cross-border traders. Localism was the new political cool among youngsters. A night of violence at a shopping area in 2016 presaged the regular clashes with police that would erupt three years later.

The 2019 unrest described in this book was thus part of a long line of protest episodes. But this time it was not just more of the same. This latest round of anti-government protests witnessed radical changes in tactics, and especially in the willingness to use violence against property and people.

Stay firm and Carrie on

Protesters' rampant use of petrol bombs and other lethal weapons such as bows and arrows was unprecedented. So were the airport closure, tunnel blockade, rail sabotage, and attacks on the very Hong Kong institutions that make the city distinct from the mainland, such as its independent court and universities, and its legislature.

The 2019 protests were thus bitterly anti-establishment in a way previous rounds were not. To the protesters, it seemed the entire system was moribund. In the absence of a political solution, the government tasked police to hold the line, and they almost immediately became part of the problem. Through it all, it was clear that the only entity with the power to halt Hong Kong's self-destruction was Beijing. Any conflict resolution strategy would require the central government's assent.

At the height of the protests, talk was rife in the city that Beijing was about to do two things. First, it was going to send in the People's Liberation Army to quash the rebellion. Second, it was going to sack Carrie Lam Cheng Yuet-ngor whom it privately held responsible for the chaos. As of the time of this publication, neither has happened. Beijing can play the long game, especially when it holds the cards.

Observers say the central government realized that removing Lam would be read as an admission of defeat and embolden the opposition. In early 2020, Lam herself must have hoped to reclaim some of her lost standing with her management of the coronavirus health crisis. But most Hongkongers do not credit her government for the city emerging with relatively few fatalities. A study commissioned by the *South China Morning Post* in March 2020 found that seven in 10 Hongkongers believed that the government had little to do with the city's success in flattening the rate of infections.

The dislike for Lam runs deep. But while her stern, no-nonsense demeanor has not endeared her to people, it is the impossible nature of her job that makes her a lightning rod, say analysts. None of Lam's three predecessors – Tung Chee-hwa, Donald Tsang Yam-kuen and Leung Chun-ying – served two terms.

Hongkongers need a political leader, whereas the chief executive's Beijing bosses want the person to serve an administrative function: "someone who can press the right button and get things done," in the words of Ip, who ran for the post in 2017 but did not get enough nominations.

Beijing's preference for someone who knows how to run the bureaucracy was shown in its choice of Tsang and then Lam, Ip says. "Their choice showed they need someone with administrative ability but clearly in this highly politicized era, that is not enough."

Executive councilor Ronny Tong Ka-wah agrees that it is naive to personalize the dispute as if changing a leader would break the impasse. The chief executive is targeted as the face of an unpopular system, he says. "People hate the chief executive, as he or she is representing the one country, two systems principle that they abhor."

Foreign hands

Another concern that has obviously irritated Beijing is the suspected foreign support for the unrest.

"A lot of funding is involved," says Ip. "Frontline people have been trained outside Hong Kong. They followed a playbook, a color revolution playbook." The strategy is to use young people to gain the moral high ground, but then up the ante. "Very violent methods were employed. Where did the young people learn these terrorist tactics? Why are they so emboldened? Are some of them paid? Of course, they denied it but there seem to be some highly-skilled leaders."

Cheeseball laughs off such arguments, saying they reflect the gap of understanding people have on how the young operate. She is adamant that it is a homegrown movement, relying only on moral support from the outside world. Everything else is the sweat and effort of the protesters who learn by what they do on the ground and online research, she insists. "Everything can be found on YouTube, if you bother to search," she says.

But demonstrators did little to help dispel such perceptions of foreign hands when they waved American flags and showed up outside the US and British consulates, as well as other consular offices seeking aid. Opposition figures made high-profile visits overseas, including to the US in 2019 during which they called on Americans to help protect Hong Kong's freedoms and to do so by supporting the passage of the Human Rights and Democracy Act.

Martin Lee and former chief secretary Anson Chan Fang On-sang, who led one of the delegations to the US, became the target of attacks in mainland media. The duo, along with media owner Jimmy Lai Chee-ying and veteran democrat Albert Ho Chun-yan, were labeled the "gang of four," alluding to the allies of the late chairman Mao Zedong who were blamed for the excesses of the Cultural Revolution and convicted in show trials. Hong Kong's gang of four were deemed traitors for conspiring with Western powers to fan the unrest and trying to "bring ruin to Hong Kong," according to angry articles in the *People's Daily*.

Chan slammed the "unwarranted smear campaign" against her and other activists. "The efforts to harass and intimidate me and members of my family are a shameless attempt to deflect the blame for the recent social unrest away from those who are principally responsible, namely the chief executive, Mrs Carrie Lam, and her team," she says.

The allegation of foreign interference has not been laid to rest. In the attacks launched by the liaison office and the Hong Kong and Macau Affairs Office (HKMAO) – the two agencies that oversee Beijing's relations with the city – both repeated the claim that Hongkongers seeking foreign intervention were in breach of China's sovereignty over the city.

Beijing's focus on this issue is understandable when Hong Kong's unrest is viewed against the larger geopolitical canvas of a trade and technological war with the US. Hong Kong is seen as a proxy target by China's opponents, say analysts like Lau Siu-kai, vice-chairman of the Chinese Association of Hong Kong and Macau Studies, a semi-official think tank.

"When ties between Beijing and Washington are good, Hong Kong would mean a partner in the eyes of the US in facilitating peaceful transformation in China," he says. "But the US would see Hong Kong as a pawn during the days when the two countries are battling. Wary of that, Beijing, of course, would step up its emphasis on national security."

A harder line

In the first quarter of 2020, Beijing installed a new and more assertive vanguard. It appointed a new director at the liaison office, its top agency in the city. Its new man, Luo Huining, had held the high rank of provincial party secretary. He immediately made plain he had no qualms about raising the public profile of the office, making public visits and pronouncements. (See our earlier essay *The Beijing connection*).

The central government also upgraded the leadership of the HKMAO in Beijing, again with a state-level appointee. Another pugnacious former provincial party secretary was selected, in this case, someone who used to work very closely with President Xi Jinping in Zhejiang province in the 2000s.

With the reshuffle in personnel done, it was not long before they turned to reform in policies. Seemingly out of the blue, both the HKMAO and liaison office issued strongly-worded missives taking on Hong Kong's pan-democrat lawmakers in April 2020. The target of their ire was the filibustering by the opposition lawmakers.

The Legislative Council's House Committee, which helps run

Legco's business, was due to elect its chairman in October 2019. But lawmaker Dennis Kwok from the opposition Civic Party and his fellow pan-democrats held 14 meetings over six months, effectively blocking the election of a new chairman. Some 14 bills and 89 other pieces of subsidiary legislation were piling up as a result of the delay. The two central government agencies warned the opposition that their "malicious filibustering" to paralyze the legislature could be in breach of their oath and they could be guilty of misconduct in public office. They accused Kwok of deploying the "if we burn, you burn with us" philosophy that had influenced the protest movement in 2019.

The pan-democratic lawmakers and the Bar Association countered that the two agencies themselves were overreaching. They argued that under Article 22 of the Basic Law, departments of the central government should not "interfere" in the city's affairs.

Beijing dug in its heels. The HKMAO, liaison office, and the commissioner's office of the Ministry of Foreign Affairs asserted that the departments had every right to comment, in line with their oversight role in the implementation of one country, two systems.

Lam and her government – after issuing three contradictory statements in more than four hours that created confusion – agreed with the two Beijing offices, clarifying that they were not set up by departments of the central government, as spelled out by Article 22, and therefore not bound by it.

The central government's strong reaction to opposition filibustering may be less a warning to the democrats than a signal of mounting impatience with the enfeebled pro-establishment camp, which had tolerated the non-election of a chairman of the House Committee for six months. "Their inaction is incomprehensible," Exco member Tong says.

Among the bills stalled by the deadlock is the national anthem bill, which sets out how people should behave when *March of the Volunteers* is played in Hong Kong. Paul Tse Wai-chun, a pro-establishment lawmaker and chairman of Legco's Committee on Rules of Procedure, told the *Post* earlier that Beijing was particularly riled by this bill's lack of progress, due to its symbolic importance in enforcing respect for China's sovereignty over Hong Kong.

George Yeo, the former Singapore foreign minister, can see where China is coming from. He believes its frustrations stem from the failure of Britain and Hong Kong to build on one country, two systems. "Under it, Hong Kong should be governed by Hongkongers with the precondition that they must love both China and Hong Kong. During British colonial rule, it was deliberate policy not to engender love for China. Hong Kong was therefore handed over to China with a crack that ran through its entire crystal," Yeo says.

"Engendering love for China should have been a key mission after 1997. It was not. Love for China requires that its national security concerns should be addressed, that the education system should instill patriotism in the young, and that glaring inequities in Hong Kong society should be overcome. Stunned by what happened in Hong Kong in 2019, Beijing is now determined to put right what has been neglected for over 20 years."

That work will be a Sisyphean task. Surveys conducted by the Hong Kong Public Opinion Research Institute show that the proportion of people who identify themselves as Chinese in the city in 2019 was at its lowest levels since 1997. Of 1,010 respondents surveyed in December 2019, a record 55.4 per cent saw themselves as Hongkongers. Only 10.9 per cent said they were "Chinese."

The Hong Kong government has poured millions into programs to boost national identity among students. An arts graduate, who was among the first batch of young Hongkongers handpicked by the government to work as interns at the Palace Museum in 2017, was a protester in 2019. She appreciated Chinese history and culture and found contemporary literature fascinating, she told a colleague in one of the stories we published. But she could not find cultural traits in Chinese society she could feel proud of, especially when it had "no place for dissidents and human rights."

An electoral showdown

The opposition lawmakers are in no mood to back down either. Like their establishment opponents, their eyes are fixed on the prize of the Legco elections due to be held on September 6, 2020. The results of the November 2019 district council elections dealt a humiliating blow to the pro-establishment camp. Another landslide victory for the pan-democrats, this time in the much more consequential Legco elections, would upend Beijing's influence in the chamber and possibly beyond.

Currently, the 70-member legislature has 43 lawmakers who are pro-Beijing and 24 in the opposition camp. The council is made up of trade-based functional constituency seats that have long been dominated by pro-establishment forces and geographical constituency seats open to a wider electorate. The set-up favors the pro-establishment camp which uses its functional constituency majority as well as its share of geographical seats to counter opposition parties' influence in Legco. While the electorate's votes are typically split around 60:40 between the democrats and the pro-Beijing camp, the functional constituencies tilt the balance in favor of the latter.

But this advantage could be overwhelmed by sweeping victories by the pro-democracy candidates in the geographical constituencies and some tactical gains in the functional seats, forcing a loss of control of Legco by the pro-establishment camp. Regina Ip is among those who take such a scenario seriously. "The opposition managed to use the protests to mobilize people to register and vote out the establishment. And if this trend continues in September, the pro-government bloc can lose the majority and we would be on a dangerous path to self-destruction," she warns.

She points to the Civic Party's manifesto, which states that if the pan-democratic camp succeeds in securing a 35-plus majority in Legco, it plans to block all bills and even judicial appointments unless the five key demands of protesters are met.

Control of Legco can also be used to influence the selection of the chief executive. The head of the Hong Kong government is chosen by a 1,200-strong election committee comprising representatives from various sectors. If they win big at the Legco elections, the pan-democrats will gain extra leverage over that choice. In short, Beijing has reason to fear losing control of who gets to be the chief executive.

Even that possible chain of events, though, will not resolve the fundamental contradictions in the interpretation of one country, two systems and the Basic Law, which has over 22 years been the subject of constant debate, mass protests, court rulings and unilateral declarations by mainland authorities.

The contentious April 2020 pronouncements by the mainland institutions once again highlighted the absence of agreed-upon detail within the contours of Hong Kong's governing principles. Lawmakers across the political divide appealed for more clarity. But the real issue may be less about the letter of the law than the spirit with which it is implemented. Simon Young Ngai-man, a legal scholar at the University of Hong Kong, agrees with the government that the two agencies in question are not bound by Article 22. "But I would still advise the office to exercise some restraint, as statements made at certain times and with certain emphasis may undermine the Hong Kong government's authority."

Those on the other side, however, continue to point out that the opposition and many of the protesters have failed to acknowledge and uphold the "one country" side of the commitment. Ip fears that the opposition is threatening the long-term viability of Hong Kong's special status. "We can only maintain our existing way of life after 2047 if one country, two systems can be sustained, and that cannot happen if there is no respect for the nation," she says.

Hong Kong's future after 2047 will be determined by whether Beijing sees any point in continuing with the "two systems" approach. Beijing will not do so at the cost of compromising "one country," according to Ip. "If people try to promote separatism or anti-China sentiment every day in Legco or outside Legco – even on small things like insisting on calling Covid-19 the 'Wuhan virus' or politicizing even health issues to stigmatize mainlanders – then one country, two systems will not work," she says.

Mainland expert Rao believes the Basic Law has a lot of ground for agreement, calling it "the biggest legal consensus between Beijing and Hong Kong and among all sectors of Hong Kong's society." "It is the constitutional basis of the city's rule of law and embodies the overall interests of Hong Kong society," he says. As long as it is well understood, the Basic Law could ensure the smooth development of Hong Kong, he adds. And Hong Kong needs to strengthen people's grasp of one country, two systems, and the Basic Law.

"The governance of Hong Kong should not be solely interpreted as 'Hong Kong people ruling Hong Kong' or 'a high degree of autonomy' because that is not the intention of Basic Law. It is, first and foremost, about national sovereignty," says Rao.

"The unprecedented high degree of autonomy which Hong Kong enjoys is obtained under the premise that it follows 'one country' and the national constitutional order."

If there is a comprehension gap, it is going to be a hard one to bridge. Ip acknowledges that there is a communication chasm between the government and especially young people. "Our government has to do a lot more explanation to our young people on what are our options," she says.

She wishes that youngsters would also take a step back to reflect before claiming that Hong Kong is lost. "This, from a 20-year-old. What have you lost?" she says, her pitch rising, her frustration evident.

"They are under the illusion that they have lost something truly invaluable, but what exactly have you lost and how are you going to rebuild Hong Kong? Hong Kong as it is today is the outcome of generations of hardworking people.

"If you destroy all this, how are you going to rebuild it? You cannot just rise like a phoenix from the ashes."

Civic Party's Leong says Beijing has only one way to really resolve the gridlock, that is, to go back to where it all began and start to honor the promises enshrined in the Basic Law. Leong believes there are still not many people who support the idea of breaking away from China and calls on Beijing to race against time to rescue the one country, two systems model. "We are just about halfway through," he says. "It is late but not a case of we would never be able to do it. If there is a will, there is a way."

Stirring for a fight

Cheeseball has heard such arguments and is not persuaded that taking on the Communist Party of China is an exercise in futility. In her travels, she has met other activists, such as the Catalan independence fighters. She says she is inspired by what they tell her: the journey toward independence might seem impossible now but it has to start somehow, or the destination will be even further.

And so the protests continue.

On New Year's Day of 2020, organizers claimed 1 million people were out in the streets to demonstrate that they were ready to keep up with their campaign. Medical workers from a newly formed union stemming from the protest movement organized a five-day strike in

February to demonstrate against the government for not shutting the border with the mainland to control the spread of the contagion.

In another sign of things to come, the month of April saw Hong Kong authorities arrest 15 veterans of the opposition camp in a citywide sweep that began in the morning and lasted well into the evening. Those caught in the net included two of the so-called "gang of four" for their alleged roles in unlawful protests in August and October 2019.

The authorities were at pains to stress that the arrests were not prompted by the Beijing institutions' uncompromising signals just four days earlier. Police commissioner Chris Tang Ping-keung said the timing was dictated instead by the standard procedures of collecting evidence and seeking legal advice from the Department of Justice. "The arrests were based on sufficient evidence," Tang said. "Some friends warned me to stay cautious as the media would keep smearing police and particularly me if I arrested their boss. I do not care about this. I arrest whoever breaks the law."

The media boss he was referring to was probably Jimmy Lai of *Apple Daily*, a populist, anti-Beijing newspaper that casts itself as the protector of Hongkongers against the mainland government. Lai was in the "gang of four." Another arrestee also in the "gang" was Martin Lee, dubbed by some as the "father of democracy" in Hong Kong and founder of the Democratic Party in 1994. He says defiantly that he was proud to be arrested – for the first time in his long political career – and that he could finally stand side by side with the many young protesters who had been rounded up earlier.

Predictably, the arrests agitated the ground. One of the biggest protest convenors, the Civil Human Rights Front, warned it was planning a mammoth rally on July 1. Western governments voiced their concern at the crackdown.

Clearly, the anti-government group's antagonism has not abated, even if many admit to feeling lost and leaderless.

Fatigue has also set in, with injuries slowing some of the frontliners. The arrests appear to have had a restraining effect. As of February 2020, 7,613 people had been arrested and 1,206 charged. More than 17 per cent of them, or 1,335 people, were 18 or younger. Many are wary of being caught a second time, which could result in a life-changing criminal conviction.

Fullstop is one of those who have avoided joining protests for this reason. But her commitment to the cause remains undimmed.

We have been wearing surgical masks during our conversation, as part of the measures against the coronavirus infection. Past midday, we decide to have lunch. When the food arrives, we finally remove our masks. This is when we realize that Fullstop is a child. She has plump, pink cheeks and an unlined, innocent face.

She is 14. "I'll be 15 later this year," she says.

The night she was arrested, she was mostly concerned that she would not be able to take part in a Chinese debating competition the next day. She had prepared long and hard for it. Her team was supposed to argue for the motion that ignorance was more harmful to society than violence.

She shows us her notes, stating that the government preferred to remain ignorant of the people's views and to "bulldoze ahead with the extradition bill." It was also ignorant for not knowing how to soothe its people and instead used "violent oppression," she says.

She realizes there is no way the government will accept all of the five demands of the protesters. If there was one demand that would make her not protest anymore, what would it be?

"Maybe if we can elect our own chief executive, I don't know."

For now, she is on guard and has lost faith in the system. "I don't think one country, two systems will work. It's broken."

The present arrangement expires in 2047. Whatever else people cannot agree on, they surely accept that adults in charge of the city need to give its 14-year-olds something to believe in.

We say our goodbyes after that afternoon in April 2020, but not before making a promise to meet again. If we are still around, we will meet on this street in 2047. Maybe at that juncture we will have a clearer picture of what the events of 2019 meant – whether they were part of a movement that secured Hong Kong's autonomy for future generations, or squandered it and sent the city into decline. The date seems like a distant prospect. Fullstop will be 42.

Names have been changed to protect identities.